Perspectives of Future Learning

AI through the Lens of Educators

Edited by Asha Kumaran, Boey Chee Kin,
Cleta Milagros Acebedo, Gabrielle Lai,
Linda William, Teo Chee Leng,
Vijayan N, and Zhang Huiyu

CRC Press
Taylor & Francis Group
Boca Raton London New York

CRC Press is an imprint of the
Taylor & Francis Group, an informa business

Designed cover image: Shutterstock

First edition published 2026
by CRC Press
2385 NW Executive Center Drive, Suite 320, Boca Raton FL 33431

and by CRC Press
4 Park Square, Milton Park, Abingdon, Oxon, OX14 4RN

CRC Press is an imprint of Taylor & Francis Group, LLC

ISBN: 978-1-032-98569-5 (hbk)
ISBN: 978-1-032-98560-2 (pbk)
ISBN: 978-1-003-59935-7 (ebk)

DOI: 10.1201/9781003599357

Typeset in Palatino
by Apex CoVantage, LLC

Contents

Editors

Asha Kumaran is a senior academic mentor at the School of Humanities and Social Sciences, Temasek Polytechnic. Trained at the National Institute of Education, Singapore, she has been a teacher, a curriculum developer and a publisher. She holds an MEd. She is enthusiastic about personalising learning for students and about technology as a transformative tool in humanising learning while enhancing students' creative potential and nurturing their unique capabilities.

Boey Chee Kin is passionate about enhancing learning through empathy and innovation. Over the last 25 years, he has explored how technologies like AI and digital tools can seamlessly blend with pedagogy to enrich learning experiences and improve student outcomes.

Cleta Milagros Acebedo is an analytics and quality expert with over 30 years of experience in education and manufacturing. Her contributions to organisational development and productivity in Singapore and the Philippines have been transformative. Mel's academic credentials include degrees in industrial engineering, business administration and business analytics.

Gabrielle Lai is a cognitive developmental psychologist. She manages the Centre for Applied Behavioural Sciences at Temasek Polytechnic. As a behavioural scientist, Gabrielle has extensive experience in teaching, conducting research, and providing consultancy in the areas of psychological and behavioural sciences, behavioural insights and the learning sciences.

Linda William is a senior scientist at Temasek Polytechnic, and she has over 15 years of artificial intelligence and machine learning experience across Singapore's top institutions such as the National University of Singapore, Singapore Management University, and SAP. She leads award-winning research in educational AI and teaches diverse learners. Her work integrates intelligent systems, analytics and serious games to enhance teaching, learning and learner performance outcomes.

Teo Chee Leng is the course chair of the Polytechnic Foundation Programme at Temasek Polytechnic, with a background in engineering. She has consistently leveraged technology to explore innovative solutions. In recent years, she has focused on harnessing data and AI to advance educational practices and support student learning outcomes.

Vijayan N is a senior academic mentor at the School of Business, Temasek Polytechnic, with over 25 years of experience in the polytechnic education sector. He holds an EdD and is deeply committed to nurturing learners and fostering meaningful, practice-oriented education in business and applied learning contexts.

Zhang Huiyu was previously a research scientist at A*STAR and is now a senior academic mentor at Temasek Polytechnic. She has trained over 1,000 learners in AI and analytics, and she was a 2024 President's Award for Teachers finalist. Her research explores using AI chatbots to personalise learning and enhance engagement in education.

Contributors

Paul Cheung is an experienced and skilled educational developer at Temasek Polytechnic's Learning Academy. He is well versed in the integration of edtech in classroom and online teaching and has extensive experience with eLearning. Committed to helping others grow, Paul is passionate about developing individuals' skills and knowledge.

Ho Li Chin has a background in electrical engineering and business analytics and has dedicated her career to harnessing data for insight and decision-making. She has overseen analytics programmes and led data-driven projects. Her work reflects a deep passion for bridging education with the real-world application of data and analytics.

Joey Neo is a lecturer at Temasek Polytechnic's Centre for Foundation Studies, where she teaches mathematics and essential life skills. She supports data initiatives by building analytics dashboards. Her interests lie in AI and educational analytics tools that enhance student learning experiences.

Caron Ong is a senior academic mentor at Temasek Polytechnic's School of Humanities and Social Sciences, specialising in educational innovation through generative AI. A passionate mathematics educator with experience from mainstream to prison school settings, he pioneers AI integration in teaching, assessment redesign and personalised learning solutions.

Tan Wah Pheow is a cognitive psychologist with a PhD from Iowa State University, specialising in judgement, decision-making and human factors. He lectures at Temasek Polytechnic and serves as a consultant on behavioural insights projects. He was instrumental in establishing the Centre for Applied Psychology and the Behavioural Insights Collaboratory.

Thong Wei Qi is a manager at Temasek Polytechnic with a background in applied mathematics and data analytics. She is actively engaged in advancing education and passionate about enhancing learning experiences. Wei Qi is particularly interested in leveraging analytics and AI to improve educational outcomes. She is also dedicated to integrating technology with teaching for more effective learning.

Chan Hui Ying is a manager at Temasek Polytechnic. With a background as a senior course developer in the aviation industry and a former level head for mathematics at a secondary school, she has a keen interest in educational technologies and personalised learning. Her efforts focus on inspiring students and advancing educational practices through innovative approaches.

Preface

This book, *Perspectives of Future Learning: AI through the Lens of Educators,* was conceived out of my intention to bring together the collective experiences and insights of the talented educators at Temasek Polytechnic (TP) who have been pioneering the integration of AI into teaching and learning. These practitioners, with their unique perspectives, have explored innovative approaches to using AI, and I felt it was important to share their work with a wider audience, particularly as we look towards shaping the future of learning.

The idea for this book came from my ongoing involvement in various AI-related projects with colleagues, where I saw first hand the potential of AI to enhance education. I wanted to create a platform where their valuable contributions could be showcased, and where their stories of success, challenges, and learning could inspire others. From using data to drive early interventions to supporting the diverse needs of learners, the contributors to this book have demonstrated a commitment to improving education through AI.

One key initiative highlighted in this book is a joint polytechnic project focused on empowering lecturers to use data more effectively to provide timely support to students. Many of the authors in this book were instrumental in driving this initiative forward, continually refining their practices and adopting new methods as they explored how AI can enhance educational outcomes.

In my role, I have had the privilege of piloting AI tools and have seen first hand the complexities of selecting the right solutions for different educational contexts. My colleagues have done the same, exploring not only the acquisition of these tools but also how to scale their use and implement them effectively within educational institutions. Each has brought their own unique insights to the table. Their willingness to experiment with new EdTech solutions and their openness to share what they've learned are at the core of this book.

I have also been inspired by the innovative EdTech tools developed by my colleagues, which have enriched our teaching landscape. Their readiness to share these innovations was one of the key reasons for creating this book. Additionally, I've invited experts in assessment and behavioural science to contribute their insights, as their knowledge is crucial in shaping the future of AI in education.

This book is a celebration of the work of these dedicated practitioners and a reflection of my initiative to bring their insights to a broader community. I hope that the experiences shared here will guide and inspire other organisations to explore and implement AI in ways that are both effective and efficient.

Zhang Huiyu
Temasek Polytechnic
31 March 2025

Introduction

As AI continues to reshape many industries, innovations in education will not only adapt to these changes but also set the path for future advancements in the workforce. This book provides practical guidance for educators and educational leaders navigating the evolving landscape of AI in education. Understanding and applying AI models in teaching and learning can be challenging, and this book aims to support educators in evaluating the qualities of AI models and aligning them with their instructional goals.

The topics in the book are wide-ranging but carefully curated to form a cohesive guide. It begins by addressing the importance of data in AI development, followed by discussions on AI's potential for personalised learning, specific applications like chatbots, and how AI can be used to gamify learning. The book also explores the changing role of teachers in an AI-driven world, the risks students may face when using AI, the ways behavioural sciences can enhance AI tools, and how student assessments need to evolve in light of these new technologies.

Each chapter draws on the experiences and insights of educators and practitioners who have implemented AI in different educational settings. These contributors provide a range of perspectives on how AI can be effectively applied in various contexts, from K-12 to higher education and workplace learning. The book is written primarily for educators, educational leaders, and policymakers who are looking to understand how AI can be integrated into their educational frameworks. While the specifics of each implementation may differ, the lessons and examples shared in this book are intended to be adaptable and useful for educators in diverse environments.

The book does not seek to offer definitive solutions but instead presents valuable insights that may serve as a starting point for others. By sharing these practical examples, the hope is that educators can explore AI's potential and apply it meaningfully within their own unique settings. As you read, consider how the ideas and approaches presented here might inform your own teaching practices and how AI can support the evolving needs of learners.

DOI: 10.1201/9781003599357-1

1

Cultivating a Data-Driven Enterprise: From Vision to Value

Cleta Milagros Acebedo and Ho Li Chin

1.1 Strategic Framework for a Data-Driven Transformation

1.1.1 Digital Transformation in Education

Digital transformation in education refers to the integration of digital technologies into all aspects of an educational institution, from administration and curriculum delivery to student engagement and assessment. This transformation is reshaping the way knowledge is imparted, consumed, and assessed, making learning more accessible, personalised, and efficient. The shift towards digital learning has accelerated due to advancements in technology and the increasing reliance on data-driven decision-making.

With the adoption of digital tools such as learning management systems (LMS), artificial intelligence (AI)-powered personalised learning, and predictive analytics, educational institutions can optimise teaching methodologies, enhance student engagement, and improve institutional effectiveness. The education sector has been increasingly leveraging technology and data to better engage students, parents, and educators, making digitalisation a core focus.

1.1.1.1 Critical Role of Data in Driving Transformation

Data plays a crucial role in digital transformation by providing actionable insights that help educators and administrators make informed decisions. With the increasing availability of student performance data, learning analytics, and institutional metrics, education stakeholders can better understand learning patterns, identify challenges, and implement interventions proactively. The data platform should emphasise the need for structured data collection, integration, and analytics to support decision-making, ensuring that data governance and accessibility are streamlined.

According to the book *"Competing on Analytics: Updated with a New Introduction—The New Science of Winning"* (Davenport & Harris, 2017), extracting value from information is not primarily a matter of how much one has

DOI: 10.1201/9781003599357-2

or what technologies one uses to analyse it. Instead, it's how aggressively one exploits these resources and how to use them to create new or better approaches for an enterprise. The science of winning for organisations did not always use the latest tools, but they were very good at building strategies and frameworks around their analytical capabilities.

It became clear that the evolution of industry has played a significant role in shaping the way we use data (Technical Laboratory Systems, Inc., 2023). During the Industrial Revolution 3.0 (20th–21st century), the digital revolution ushered in transformative advancements with the emergence of computers, relational databases, and early analytics. These innovations laid the foundation for automated data processing, structured information management, and the initial adoption of digital decision-making across industries.

Now, in the Industrial Revolution 4.0 (21st century–present), we are witnessing an era dominated by big data, AI, machine learning, and automation. Data has become the cornerstone of innovation, driving intelligent decision-making, real-time analytics, and predictive modelling across every sector—including education. Institutions are no longer just collecting and storing data; they are leveraging advanced analytics, AI-driven insights, and automation to enhance strategic planning, operational efficiency, and personalised learning experiences in a rapidly evolving digital landscape.

Business intelligence (BI) and AI are distinct yet complementary technologies that organisations leverage to derive insights from data and enhance decision-making processes (Domo, Inc., 2025). The evolution from BI to AI has been characterised by an escalating dependency on data as a strategic asset to drive decision-making. BI primarily revolves around descriptive and diagnostic analytics, enabling organisations to analyse historical data to understand what happened and why. However, the advent of AI has transformed data analytics into a more proactive and intelligent framework, incorporating predictive analytics to forecast future trends and prescriptive analytics to recommend optimal actions.

AI is viewed as one of the most disruptive technological forces that the world is facing today. There are a variety of different technologies under the cognitive technologies; machine learning is one of the most common ones. The rise of machine learning and AI is a response to the rapid growth of data, along with the availability of software and the power of today's computing architecture.

As data volumes continue to expand and computational power advances, AI-driven decision-making has become indispensable, enabling institutions to transition from reactive insights to proactive, automated, and intelligent strategies. This shift compels educational institutions to leverage AI-powered analytics not only to enhance student success strategies through early intervention and personalised learning but also to optimise operational efficiencies, streamline resource allocation, and drive continuous institutional improvement.

Of course, all these rapid changes in how analytics and AI are done have important consequences for organisations. That means new skills, new mindsets, new behaviours from staff, and new ways of managing capability development.

1.1.2 Transforming into a Data-Driven Institution

In today's digital landscape, data has become the foundation of modern educational transformation, driving strategic decision-making and optimising learning outcomes, particularly in the institute that the authors are in—Temasek Polytechnic (TP). The vast amount of data collected in education includes student demographics, admission records, attendance tracking, academic performance, financial assistance, extracurricular involvement, engagement metrics, and institutional operations. The ability to collect, analyse, and interpret data is crucial for shaping educational policies, optimising teaching strategies, and enhancing student learning experiences.

The institute is rapidly evolving into a data-driven enterprise, embedding AI, advanced analytics, and data intelligence into its institutional framework to drive strategic decision-making, optimise teaching methodologies, and improve student outcomes. This transformation is guided by the vision of becoming "digital to the core", where data is not only collected but actively harnessed to enhance operational efficiency, predictive insights, and real-time interventions.

Building a data-driven enterprise in education requires a strategic approach that integrates data analytics, AI, and machine learning into institutional decision-making. By harnessing data insights, educational institutions can enhance student learning experiences, optimise educator's performance, streamline operations, and drive continuous improvement. As education continues to evolve in the age of AI and big data, institutions that embrace data-driven strategies will be better positioned to adapt, innovate, and lead in the future of learning.

By leveraging data as a strategic asset, an ecosystem is fostered where leaders, educators, and other staff engage in evidence-based decision-making, personalised learning experiences, and ensuring continuous innovation and institutional excellence in a rapidly evolving digital landscape.

> *"If you want to go fast, go alone; but if you want to go far, go together."*
>
> *—Origins unknown*

For example, leaders, educators, and staff have leveraged data analytics to:

- Identify learning gaps and adjust instructional methods to meet student needs.
- Make informed decisions on course design and curriculum development, ensuring content remains relevant and effective.

- Optimise admissions and enrolment strategies by using predictive models to forecast application trends and seat availability.

1.1.2.1 Leader's Perspective

Educational administrators and policymakers rely on data to make strategic decisions regarding curriculum development and policy formulation. Data analytics help institutions measure programme effectiveness, assess educator's performance, and forecast future trends in education. The data-driven transformation should further underscore the importance of building Data and AI competencies at all levels of the organisation to drive transformation effectively. Singapore's journey towards a skills-first, data-driven human capital development emphasises leveraging technology and data to create a more responsive and effective skills workforce (World Economic Forum, 2025).

1.1.2.2 Educator's Perspective

For educators, data-driven transformation offers insights into student learning behaviours, helping them tailor instructional methods to individual students' needs.

Singapore's education sector has been actively integrating data-driven strategies to enhance teaching and learning experiences. The Ministry of Education (MOE), in collaboration with the Government Technology Agency (GovTech) of Singapore, launched the Student Learning Space (SLS)—a platform that enriches students' learning through technology (Government Technology Agency of Singapore, 2025).

At TP, by leveraging assessment data, educators can identify students at risk and provide timely interventions to enhance academic success. Data-driven insights enable educators to identify at-risk students early and implement targeted interventions.

1.1.2.3 Administration Staff's Perspective

Staff benefit from data-driven transformation by streamlining operations, automating administrative tasks, and improving student services. The educational communities, including parents and support groups, can leverage data insights to monitor student progress, foster engagement, and support holistic development.

Non-academic staff in Singapore's higher educational institutions are experiencing significant benefits from data-driven transformations, which streamline operations, automate administrative tasks, and enhance student services. For instance, the National University of Singapore (NUS) has implemented an AI-driven learning management system that adapts coursework and learning materials based on students' performance and learning styles, thereby enhancing operational efficiency and educational outcomes (Kadence International, 2025).

1.1.3 Framework for Data-Driven Transformation

In today's rapidly evolving educational landscape, data- and AI-driven transformation has become essential for enhancing educational outcomes and student learning experiences. Recognising this, the institution has committed to championing its data-driven transformation through the LEAD-AI Framework (Figure 1.1), a structured approach that ensures strategic implementation and sustained impact.

The LEAD-AI Framework stands for:

- **L**eading by Example
- **E**mpowering through Data Democratisation
- **A**ccelerating Proficiency in Data and AI
- **D**riving Innovation with Data and AI

The following section provides an overview of the first three pillars of the LEAD-AI Framework, which serve as the foundational pillars driving this transformation: "Leading by Example", "Empowering through Data Democratisation", and "Accelerating Proficiency in Data and AI". These three pillars form the core strategy for embedding data-centric practices and equipping the community with the necessary skills to leverage Data and AI effectively, enabling the fourth pillar—"Driving Innovation with Data and AI".

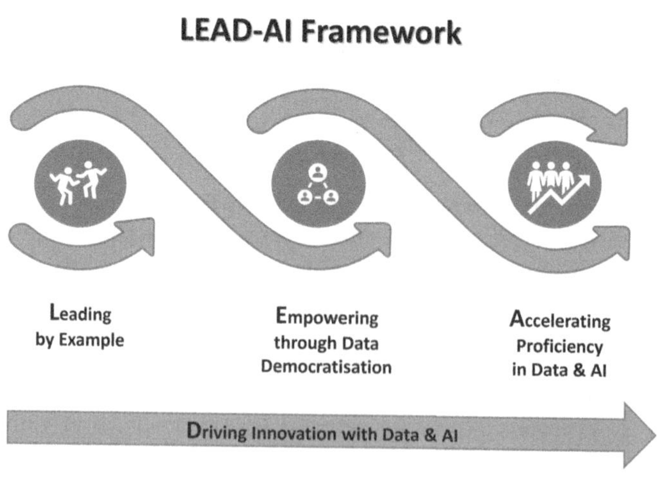

FIGURE 1.1
LEAD-AI Framework

1.1.3.1 First Pillar—Leading by Example

Section 1.2 of this chapter lays out the discussion on the first pillar—Leading by Example.

To cultivate a truly data-driven enterprise, educational leaders must set the standard for data-informed decision-making, demonstrating a commitment to leveraging analytics for continuous improvement. Their leadership is crucial in fostering a culture of data literacy, accountability, and innovation across all levels of the institution.

The institute is at the forefront of data-driven transformation, leveraging AI and analytics to enhance education and institutional effectiveness. This shift is not just about adopting technology but also about building a culture of data-driven decision-making. Leadership plays a crucial role in this transition by fostering data literacy, innovation, and collaboration. By leading by example, educators, administrators, and staff are actively engaged with data to drive meaningful improvements.

A successful data-driven transformation requires structured implementation across all levels. The institution focuses on accelerating data adoption, building a data-rich culture, strengthening data competencies, enhancing data architecture, and ensuring governance and security. Educators are not just passive recipients but key drivers of change. By integrating AI-powered learning analytics and predictive modelling, educators are enabled to personalise learning experiences, detect at-risk students early, and refine instructional strategies dynamically.

Beyond student outcomes, AI and analytics drive institutional efficiency. An institution could utilise AI-powered scheduling, workforce planning, and operational analytics to optimise resources and decision-making. By shifting from passive data collection to proactive data utilisation, the impact of data insights is maximised through various projects.

Looking ahead, the institute continues to pioneer AI-driven innovation, reinforcing the importance of continuous learning and sustainable data practices. By championing data literacy, fostering collaboration, and leveraging AI, a new benchmark is set for education transformation, ensuring that future learning remains adaptive, intelligent, and impactful.

1.1.3.2 Second Pillar—Empowering Through Data Democratisation

Section 1.3 of this chapter describes the second pillar—Empowering the Community Through Data Democratisation.

In a truly data-driven enterprise, ensuring that data is accessible, understandable, and actionable for all stakeholders is essential for fostering transparency, accountability, and informed decision-making. At TP, data democratisation aims to eliminate silos and empower educators, administrators, and researchers by providing them with the tools, training, and structured frameworks necessary to leverage data for teaching, learning, and decision-making. By dismantling data silos, ensuring data quality, and providing self-service analytics, the institute fosters a data-driven culture that enhances institutional effectiveness.

Educational data includes a wide range of information, such as student performance, attendance, engagement metrics, faculty effectiveness, and resource utilisation. By leveraging data insights, institutions can improve curriculum design, personalise learning pathways, and support strategic planning. The Singapore government also plays a role in data democratisation by maintaining publicly accessible datasets (e.g. student demographics, school performance, and funding reports) through data.gov.sg (Open Government Products, 2025).

Within the institute, core institutional data such as student records, research outcomes, and educator's performance metrics have been made available for internal analysis and innovation. The institute adopts the principle of *"Data of the People, by the People, and for the People,"* ensuring data is relevant, inclusive, and beneficial to all stakeholders.

1.1.3.3 Third Pillar—Accelerating Proficiency in Data and AI

Section 1.4 of this chapter describes how the institute builds the capacity of its educators, administrators, and staff to effectively leverage analytics to fully harness the power of data. The institute recognises the critical role of data proficiency and has developed structured frameworks to equip its workforce with the necessary skills. By integrating Data and AI capabilities, educators, administrators, and other staff can leverage analytics for innovation, operational efficiency, and continuous improvement.

To advance Data and AI competency, the institute introduced the DATA+ Framework, which aligns with Singapore's national digital transformation initiatives. This framework aims to transform staff from data enthusiasts to proficient data practitioners through curated learning programmes, real-world applications, and a collaborative ecosystem. The framework categorises data expertise into three tiers:

- Basic (Data-Ready Officers)—Focuses on data collection, cleaning, and visualisation using tools like Excel.
- Intermediate (Data Power Users)—Enhances skills in business intelligence tools (Power BI, Tableau), statistical analysis, and pattern and trend identification.
- Advanced (Citizen Data Scientists)—Upskills staff in machine learning, predictive analytics, and AI model deployment using Python, KNIME, and GenAI.

Through DATA+, continuous learning is fostered through stackable skills training, project-based mentorship, and targeted workshops.

The institute embarked on its data-driven transformation journey in 2021, focusing on integrating data analytics into decision-making, operations, and education. Over the years, it has championed data literacy, democratised data access, and empowered staff with analytical tools, reinforcing a culture where data-driven insights guide institutional strategies. The institute has led by example in adopting data-driven practices, provided the necessary tools for data democratisation, and positioned data proficiency as a core skill across all levels. As AI redefines the data landscape, it is evolving its data-driven approach to embrace AI-powered automation, predictive analytics, and intelligent decision-making. AI is no longer just an enhancement but a fundamental shift in how data is leveraged for efficiency, innovation, and personalised learning. Moving forward, the institute will integrate AI into its future strategies, ensuring that AI and data analytics work in tandem to drive excellence, operational agility, and a future-ready workforce.

1.2 First Pillar—Leading by Example

The future of education is increasingly shaped by Data and AI, requiring educators, administrators, and policymakers to adopt a data-driven approach to improve learning outcomes and institutional effectiveness. However, fostering a culture of data-driven decision-making is not just about introducing new technologies—it demands leadership commitment, strategic planning, and cultural change.

A key determinant of success in establishing a data-driven education system is obtaining buy-in from leadership. A broad shift towards data analytics and AI-driven decision-making requires changes in organisational culture, processes, behaviours, and skills proficiency. Such changes do not happen by accident; they must be championed by leaders who advocate for analytics, fact-based decision-making, and the responsible use of AI. Leadership support is essential for resource allocation, policy development, and fostering an institution-wide culture that values data insights. Without this commitment, data-driven initiatives will lack traction and long-term sustainability.

At TP, its data-driven transformation journey requires a structured approach to ensure effective implementation across multiple layers of the education system. To drive this change, it is important to establish the following five foundations:

1. **Accelerating Data Use Cases**

   Promoting both top-down and bottom-up data-driven initiatives is key to cultivating a strong analytics culture. Institutional leaders play a vital role in laying the groundwork for staff to engage confidently with data in their daily work. This leadership commitment is clearly reflected in the "Accelerating Proficiency in Data and AI" pillar of the LEAD-AI Framework. With support from management, staff are encouraged to identify real workplace data challenges or use cases and are provided with access to data, resources, and dedicated time to take part in a project-based mentorship programme. This hands-on experience allows them to design and implement Data and AI solutions, building both their technical skills and practical problem-solving capabilities.

2 **Building a Data-Rich Culture**

A central component of this effort is the LEAD-AI Framework; this involves embedding data-centric thinking and practices across the entire institution. Rather than isolating data initiatives within a specific department, the institute fosters a campus-wide mindset shift—ensuring that educators, administrators, and staff all see data as a shared and valuable asset. Importantly, the leadership champions this culture by leading data initiatives, encouraging data-driven decision-making, and enabling access to data resources.

At TP, educators play a pivotal role in this transformation. As frontline implementers, educators are at the heart of its data journey—regularly interacting with students and applying real-time analytics to enhance teaching and learning. By using AI-powered tools, they can monitor student progress, identify learning gaps, and dynamically adjust instructional strategies to meet diverse learning needs.

More than end users, educators are key drivers of cultural change, helping to embed data use into everyday educational practices. Their active engagement with data fosters a culture that values evidence-based decision-making, where insights are used to inform curriculum design, refine teaching methods, and guide targeted student interventions.

3 **Enhancing Data Architecture**

The institute has established a centralised corporate data analytics platform since 2017 to support data integration, warehousing, governance, dashboarding, and analytics. It functions as a central hub where data from various sources is extracted, cleaned, transformed, and loaded into the system, enabling consistent and reliable access to institutional data. By consolidating multiple data streams into a unified platform, it supports the institute-wide data analysis and generates insights through dashboards and visualisations, ultimately supporting more informed and strategic decision-making across the institution.

The institute has migrated its Data Analytics Platform to a secure cloud-based ecosystem, significantly enhancing institutional efficiency. This platform improves data accessibility, allowing for seamless discovery and usage; supports self-service analytics, enabling users to independently explore data insights; and facilitates interoperability between academic departments, administrative functions, and data sources to promote holistic decision-making. In addition, the platform supports data visualisation and dashboarding through tools like Power BI, allowing users to present transformed data in an intuitive and accessible format.

Leading by example also means shifting mindsets from passive data collection to proactive data utilisation. Moving beyond simply storing information, the institute leverages advanced analytics to extract meaningful insights that drive strategic improvements. This shift is exemplified through key data projects, including the Student Analytics Dashboard, Admission Analytics Dashboard, and Subject Evaluation Analytics Dashboard, which provide actionable insights to optimise student performance tracking, admissions management, and curriculum evaluation.

Finally, the system includes machine learning models and operations, offering a full suite of tools, frameworks, libraries, and services to develop, deploy, and manage machine learning applications. Together, these components create an integrated, scalable platform that enhances the institution's ability to perform advanced analytics, support decision-making, and drive innovation.

4 Ensuring Data Governance and Security

Beyond investing in robust infrastructure, the institute has placed strong emphasis on establishing clear data governance policies and processes to support its data-driven transformation. These policies form a structured framework that governs how data is collected, accessed, shared, and utilised across the institution. This not only ensures the reliability and quality of data used in decision-making but also fosters transparency, accountability, and consistency in its application across various departments.

Data security and compliance are central to its governance approach. Access to data is managed through defined roles and permissions, ensuring that users only interact with data relevant to their functions. At the same time, policies are aligned with national data protection regulations and internal standards to protect against misuse and ensure ethical handling of sensitive information. Regular audits, access reviews, and data quality checks are part of the governance mechanism to safeguard institutional data assets.

To operationalise governance practices, the institute has embedded these policies into its enterprise data systems, such as the cloud-based data analytics platform. Through this system, metadata management and user activity monitoring are enabled, providing clarity on how data flows through the institution and who is responsible for its use. This level of transparency supports trust in the system and helps mitigate risks associated with data misuse or misinterpretation.

By integrating data governance frameworks with analytics and AI initiatives, the institute reinforces a culture of data-driven decision-making that is both innovative and responsible. Governance is not treated as a barrier but as an enabler—ensuring that, as the institution continues to adopt advanced technologies like AI and machine learning, it does so with ethical considerations, compliance assurance, and institutional excellence at its core. This alignment ensures that data remains a strategic asset, supporting its mission to drive continuous improvement in both operations and learning outcomes.

5 **Strengthening Data Competencies**

The institute acknowledges that educators and administrators play a crucial role in driving data-driven transformation and must be actively involved in this shift. Recognising that a small, centralised group of data experts was insufficient, the institute developed the DATA+ Framework, which categorises skills based on different data user roles, ensuring that educators, administrators, and staff acquire the necessary expertise to leverage data effectively. More details on the DATA+ Framework, including its structured approach to data literacy, will be discussed in Section 1.4.

Additionally, a community of practice was also established to foster collaborative learning, knowledge-sharing, and experimentation with Data and AI applications. Recognising that building a data-driven culture requires collective effort, a diverse team of stakeholders are actively engaged, promoting cross-functional collaboration to embed data literacy and analytical thinking across the institution.

The earlier foundations of transformation ensure that the institute is not only adopting Data and AI but also leading by example in its implementation. A successful Data and AI-driven education ecosystem require collaboration among various stakeholders. Educators, administrators, IT professionals, and staff from all levels must be involved in decision-making processes. Each group brings unique insights that contribute to a holistic understanding of data applications.

The institute has incorporated adaptive learning technologies that utilise student data to enhance personalised education and improve learning outcomes. Through learning analytics, student learning patterns are identified, enabling the customisation of the curriculum to better suit individual needs. Additionally, predictive analytics helps detect at-risk students early, allowing for timely interventions to support their academic success. To further enhance teaching effectiveness, AI-driven recommendations assist educators in dynamically adjusting lesson plans, ensuring that instructional strategies remain responsive to student progress and engagement.

Additionally, AI-driven insights foster innovation by enabling institutions to experiment with new teaching methodologies. For example, flipped classrooms—where students engage with content before class and apply knowledge during in-person sessions—can be optimised using engagement data to determine which approaches yield the best results.

The institute is committed to scaling its Data and AI across the institution by emphasising data literacy at all levels and providing structured training opportunities for educators, administrators, and staff. Recognising the power of data-driven decision-making, several key initiatives have been implemented that promote the development and application of data analytics and AI to enhance institutional efficiency and educational outcomes.

1.2.1 Future Directions: Cultivating a Data-Driven Culture Powered by AI for Sustainable Innovation

TP's transformation into a data-driven enterprise is not just about integrating technology—it is about fostering a culture of continuous learning and data-driven decision-making. By leading by example, the development of a sustainable data culture has been prioritised, ensuring that leaders, educators, and administrators understand the importance of data literacy and AI-driven insights. This commitment empowers individuals at all levels to embrace innovation, utilise data effectively, and drive institutional excellence.

The philosophy of *"It's both people learning and machine learning"* reflects the institute's belief that data transformation is a shared journey between technology and human expertise. The data literacy initiatives are continually refined and actively build communities of data practitioners, embedding data-driven thinking into daily operations.

The institute's journey towards becoming a data-driven enterprise highlights the power of AI and analytics in reshaping education. Through strategic leadership, infrastructure development, and educator engagement, a model was created that leverages data to drive student success, operational efficiency, and policy innovation.

The transition to a data-driven education system is not just about adopting new technologies—it is about people, culture, and leadership. Educators and institutional leaders play a crucial role in ensuring that data-driven insights translate into meaningful improvements.

By championing data literacy, fostering collaboration, and leveraging AI, the institute is setting a new benchmark for sustainable, data-driven innovation in education, ensuring that the future of learning remains adaptive, intelligent, and impactful.

1.3 The Second Pillar—Empowering Through Data Democratisation

1.3.1 Data Democratisation Defined

Data democratisation refers to the process of making data accessible to all stakeholders within an organisation, regardless of their technical expertise (Marr, 2017). However, it is crucial to avoid the misconception that this means unrestricted access to data without control (Lefebvre et al., 2023).

At TP, the goal of data democratisation is to empower data enthusiasts at all levels to access, understand, and utilise data for their Data and AI projects and to be able to make data-driven decisions. This strategy involves dismantling data silos, ensuring data quality, and providing the necessary tools and training to enable effective data usage, while adhering to data governance policies and protocols.

In an educational institution, data encompasses a wide range of information that can be used to enhance teaching, learning, and administrative processes. The institute leverages data to inform curriculum and learning-teaching practices, promote effective use of data for research, and support decision-making in work innovation and improvements.

From a broader perspective, data in education primarily refers to information on students, such as statistics on student performance, attendance, and engagement. This data is used to identify trends, measure progress, and tailor educational interventions. The Singapore government (Open Government Products, 2025), for example, oversees over 300 datasets and statistical resources that collect and analyse data to help policymakers and researchers make strategic decisions.

1.3.1.1 Sample Democratised Data

In the realm of education, the democratisation of data plays a pivotal role in fostering transparency, enhancing decision-making, and driving innovation. For instance, government data is available from Singapore's open data portal (Open Government Products, 2025), Singapore Department of Statistics (2025b), and the Ministry of Education (2025a). Democratised data in educational institutions that is publicly available include:

- Programmes under the Ministry of Education
- General information of schools
- Educator-student ratios
- Funding and expenditure reports
- School performance metrics
- Yearly intake, enrolment, and graduates
- Subjects offered
- Co-curricular activities
- Graduate employment rate
- National examination results

Within educational institutions, democratised data extends to detailed records on programmes, courses, and subjects offered, student demographics, academic and co-curricular information, among others. The institute exemplifies this approach by initiating a data whitelisting initiative, starting with essential core data for Data and AI projects, and making these datasets accessible for self-service analytics across departments. Democratised data within educational institutions includes:

- Programs, courses, and subjects offered
- Student demographics
- Student prep-poly information
- Student academic information
- Student co-curricular activities
- Student financial records
- Student internship and placement records
- Alumni tracking and engagement data
- Graduate employment survey
- Library usage statistics
- Educators' demographics
- Educators' teaching effectiveness
- Educators' learning records
- Educators' employment records
- School sensor data
- School facilities procurement and maintenance records
- Financial records
- Industry partners
- Applied research information
- IT infrastructure and usage data

As part of creating a data-driven framework, the institute started with the core data essential for conducting Data and AI initiatives and made these datasets available for sharing across departments.

1.3.1.2 Strategies for Democratising Data

The article "5 Pillars for Democratizing Data at Your Organization" (Lefebvre et al., 2023) outlines key strategies for making data accessible and usable across an organisation. This discussion highlights these pillars and shares experiences from TP on their necessity in democratising data.

1 **Broaden Data Access**

Implement data catalogues and marketplaces to make data easily accessible to all staff. Initially, data was siloed within various functional departments, requiring researchers to approach data owners separately for metadata elements. Inspired by the Singapore government's approach (Open Government Products, 2025), metadata for available data tables related to admission and enrolment, assessment, course delivery, course management, student services, graduate services, human resource management, IT application and infrastructure, and property and facilities management, and more was provided. Making staff aware of existing data through a data catalogue, while adhering to data governance policies and providing secure access, is a vital first step in data democratisation.

2 **Stimulate Data-Driven Insights**

Encourage self-service analytics to empower educators to generate insights independently. Basic IT software like Excel has limitations in data processing and business intelligence analysis. To enable self-service analytics, enterprise tools were needed to encourage staff to take ownership of data analysis and report generation. Following a low-code, no-code strategy, out-of-the-box tools like SAS, Tableau, Power BI, and KNIME were provided, along with corresponding training opportunities to upskill staff. Institutions must develop intuitive, interactive, and role-specific dashboards that allow stakeholders—whether educators, administrators, or policymakers—to visualise and interpret key metrics effortlessly. Dashboards should provide real-time insights on student performance, resource utilisation, educators' effectiveness, and institutional operations, enabling data-driven decision-making at every level.

3 **Level Up Data Literacy**

Develop specific curricula to enhance data literacy tailored to different roles within the organisation. Data alone is not enough—stakeholders need the skills to analyse and apply insights effectively. Institutions should invest in data literacy programmes, workshops, and hands-on training that equip users with the ability to extract meaningful insights, interpret trends, and make informed decisions. By fostering data confidence, institutions empower educators to use data as a strategic asset rather than just raw information. As will be shown in Section 1.4, the institute established the DATA+ Framework, which was built on the premise that data literacy should be viewed in the context of staff members' roles, their need for data analysis, and how their data proficiency can be expanded while providing opportunities to keep their Data and AI skills relevant and current.

4 **Advance Data Practices**

Create communities of practice to share knowledge and improve data management techniques. A community of practice creates a safe environment for data enthusiasts and practitioners to share knowledge, experiences, and challenges and seek solutions together. Collaboration and networking foster a data-driven culture of continuous learning and improvement organically. The community offers support by providing access to tools, resources, and expertise, making it easier for individuals to engage with data and apply it to their work. It also encourages experimentation and innovation by providing a safe space to test new ideas and approaches without fear of failure.

5 **Promote Data Culture**

Use corporate communication channels to highlight the importance of data and celebrate data-driven successes. To encourage more data projects, successes with low-hanging fruit were shared with the larger community, and Data and AI prototypes were celebrated. For instance, a Data and AI portal was created to consolidate all data-related information and showcase staff projects that can be scaled to other departments. An annual celebration acknowledges staff who have completed their projects, with ongoing management commitment and support. Participants have become ambassadors and data champions who continue to advocate for data within their departments.

A data-driven culture thrives on collaboration, where educators, administrators, and policymakers collectively leverage insights to drive innovation and improve institutional performance. Encouraging cross-functional teams to use data in strategic planning, curriculum design, student support initiatives, and resource allocation ensures that decisions are made with a holistic and evidence-based approach.

These strategies aim to integrate data into a data-driven culture, making it a fundamental part of decision-making and innovation.

1.3.2 Governing Data of the People, by the People, and for the People

The article "Science and Data Science" (Blei & Smyth, 2020) addresses the challenges and opportunities in *"democratising data of the people, by the people, and for the people"*. The phrase draws inspiration from the famous democratic principle *"government of the people, by the people, for the people"*.

In the context of data democratisation, it emphasises the following:

- *Of the People:* Data should be relevant and beneficial to those who generate and use it. This means that the data collected and analysed should reflect the needs, interests, and behaviours of the staff within the organisation.
- *By the People:* Data democratisation should involve the active participation of individuals at all levels. This includes not only data practitioners but also educators, administrators, and community members who contribute to data collection, analysis, and decision-making processes. It promotes a collaborative approach where everyone has a role in managing and utilising data.

- *For the People:* The goal of data democratisation is to serve the people by making data-driven insights accessible and actionable. This means that the benefits of Data and AI analysis, such as improved decision-making, innovation, and efficiency, should be shared widely and equitably among all members of the organisation or community.

1.3.2.1 Emphasising the Principles of Data Democratisation

At TP, educators are dedicated to preparing students for a future of dynamic change by equipping them with relevant knowledge, life-long skills, and strong character. They are committed to enhancing the learning experience through innovative teaching methods and a student-centred approach, ensuring that every student is empowered to achieve their full potential. Examples of democratised data include:

1. *Student Academic Performance:* Data on grades, attendance, and progress reports to help educators identify trends, address learning gaps, and tailor teaching strategies to better support student success.
2. *Satisfaction Survey Responses:* Feedback from students, educators, and industry partners to inform decisions on programme effectiveness, services, and overall campus experience. Analysing this data helps in making informed decisions to improve satisfaction and engagement.
3. *Course Enrolment and Graduation:* Insights into which courses have high enrolment and completion rates to aid in curriculum planning and resource allocation. This data also highlights areas where students may need additional support.
4. *Student Services Utilisation:* Data on the usage of counselling, career guidance, and co-curricular activities to develop programmes that better meet student needs.
5. *Graduate Outcomes:* Tracking employment rates, further education pursuits, and career progression to align programmes with industry demands.
6. *Resource Management:* Information on the utilisation of facilities, IT infrastructure, and other resources to ensure efficient management and planning, ultimately enhancing the learning environment.

By democratising these types of data, the institute has created a data-driven culture that empowers educators to make informed decisions, enhances the student learning experience, and drives continuous improvement across the institution.

1.3.2.2 Data for All: Strategies for Empowerment

In essence, democratising data *"of the people, by the people, and for the people"* ensures that data is a shared resource that empowers everyone, fosters collaboration, and drives collective success. In the data democratisation journey of the institute, here are three key considerations:

1. **Involve All Levels of the Institution**

   Effective data democratisation requires the involvement of stakeholders at all levels, from management to educators and other staff.

   - *Providing Training on Data Literacy:* The institute offers comprehensive training programmes, like the DATA+ programme, to enhance data literacy and upskill staff in data analysis and AI competencies.
   - *Creating Collaborative Data Teams:* Collaborative data teams are formed to bring together diverse perspectives and expertise. These teams work on data projects that address institutional goals and improve student outcomes.
   - *Encouraging a Culture of Data-Driven Decision-Making:* By promoting the use of data in everyday decision-making, the institute fosters a culture where data-driven insights are valued and utilised. Regular workshops and community sharing are held to highlight the importance of data in planning and operational efficiency.

2. **Address Challenges Related to Data Integration, Quality, and Governance**

   Data integration, quality, and governance are critical challenges that must be addressed to ensure successful data democratisation.

   - *Establishing Clear Data Standards:* The institute has implemented standardised data formats and protocols to ensure consistency and accuracy across all data sources.
   - *Implementing Quality Control Measures:* Regular audits and validation processes are in place to maintain high data quality. For instance, data from student surveys and academic records are routinely checked for accuracy and completeness.
   - *Creating Governance Frameworks:* Governance frameworks are established to ensure data is used ethically and responsibly. This includes policies on data privacy, security, and compliance with regulations such as the Personal Data Protection Act (PDPA).

3. **Democratise with Control**

   While democratising data, it is important to maintain control over sensitive information.

- *Setting Up Access Controls:* The institute uses multi-factor authentication and role-based access controls to ensure that only authorised personnel can access classified and sensitive data. This helps protect students' and staff's information from unauthorised use.
- *Ensuring Compliance with Data Protection Regulations:* Compliance with data protection regulations is a top priority. Regular review sessions are conducted to keep staff informed about legal requirements and best practices in data protection.
- *Regularly Monitoring Data Usage:* Continuous monitoring of data usage helps prevent misuse and ensures that data is used appropriately. Automated systems are in place to track data access and flag any suspicious activities.

By following these strategies, the institute ensures that data democratisation is achieved in a way that empowers all stakeholders, maintains high standards of data quality and governance, and protects sensitive information.

1.3.3 Future Directions: Ensuring Data Accessibility for AI-Driven Projects

Data accessibility is a fundamental aspect of data democratisation. Here are strategies that TP has found useful in its continued efforts to democratise data:

1. **Breaking Down Barriers to Data Access**

   To democratise data effectively, it is essential to identify and eliminate barriers that hinder stakeholders from accessing the necessary information. This involves addressing challenges such as data silos, lack of system interoperability, and restrictive data policies. The institute has implemented an enterprise-wide data analytics platform to integrate data from various departments, ensuring seamless information flow across the institution. Serving as a central data repository and a single source of truth, this platform makes data accessible and usable for all stakeholders, including leaders, educators, and staff for use in Data and AI projects.
2. **Modernising Tools and Technologies for Democratising Data**

   Leveraging modern tools and technologies can significantly enhance data accessibility. The institute uses data visualisation tools like Tableau and Power BI, cloud-based data storage solutions, user-friendly data management platforms, and AI tools like ChatGPT and Copilot. These tools allow stakeholders to access and interpret data easily, making it more actionable.

3 **Providing a Secure and User-Friendly Data Platform**

Choosing the right platform is essential for effective data democratisation. The institute has implemented a robust data platform that supports data integration, provides strong security features, and offers intuitive interfaces for users at all levels of technical expertise. This platform ensures that data is accessible, secure, and easy to use. Key features may include (a) a user-friendly data catalogue that allows data to be easily discovered, understood, and accessed when needed, (b) pre-built data models and dashboard templates to enable users to do self-service business intelligence reports, (c) automated machine learning capabilities that allow users to build and deploy machine learning models with minimal effort, and (d) a large language model-powered AI bot that assists users in navigating the platform, answering queries, and providing insights.

4 **Maximise Automation**

Automation plays a key role in data democratisation by streamlining data collection, processing, and reporting. At TP, automated systems are used to reduce the manual effort required to manage data, ensuring that information is readily available and up to date. This includes automated data pipelines and up-to-date dashboards.

5 **Establish Feedback Loop and Conduct Regular Reviews**

Creating a feedback loop allows stakeholders to provide input on data processes and accessibility. The institute conducts regular reviews of data practices to ensure that the system remains effective and responsive to the needs. Feedback from educators, students, and administrative staff is used to continuously improve data accessibility and usability.

By implementing these strategies, data democratisation empowers all stakeholders, enhances collaboration, and drives collective success.

1.4 The Third Pillar—Accelerating Proficiency in Data and AI

1.4.1 Data and AI as a Core Competency

In today's data-driven landscape, data competency transcends being merely advantageous; it is indispensable. This foundational skill enables individuals to leverage data for analytics, AI, and strategic decision-making. Mastery in data analysis and interpretation is pivotal for problem-solving and informed decision-making, rendering data proficiency a critical asset in the contemporary workforce. As data evolves into a strategic asset, it is imperative for institutions of higher learning to proactively enhance their capabilities. By equipping the workforce with relevant data skills, these institutions can adeptly meet the ever-changing demands of the industry.

According to the UN Global Working Group on Big Data for Official Statistics (2020), data competency is defined as the ability to effectively manage, analyse, and discern trends and patterns within data. This competency involves a deep understanding of data sources, collection methodologies, and the factors that influence data quality. Furthermore, it encompasses proficiency in data governance, stewardship, and adherence to standards. Crucially, data competency also includes the capability to communicate findings clearly and make evidence-based decisions, thereby driving innovation and enhancing productivity.

In addition to data skills, AI competency is becoming increasingly essential. Proficiency in AI techniques and tools enables individuals to develop predictive models, automate processes, and derive deeper insights from data. Integrating AI competency into the workforce ensures that institutions can harness the full potential of Data and AI, driving innovation and maintaining a competitive edge in the rapidly evolving digital landscape.

1.4.1.1 Data and AI Competency Framework

To advance digital literacy, the Government Technology Agency (GovTech) of Singapore (2024) established the Data Science and AI Competency Framework and its corresponding training roadmap to leverage Data and AI to enhance operational efficiency across the whole of government. Additionally, a Digital Capability Framework was introduced by the Polytechnics and Institutes of Technical Education to address the digital competencies required by staff, thereby bolstering digital efforts within the higher education sector.

Building on these foundational frameworks, the institute developed the DATA+ Framework (Figure 1.2). This strategic initiative aims to elevate capabilities by transforming staff from data enthusiasts into proficient data users and practitioners. This transformation is facilitated through curated learning programmes, active engagement in data projects, and the creation of an inclusive ecosystem for networking and collaboration. The DATA+ Framework is a dynamic guide that requires continuous updates to incorporate relevant knowledge and emerging skills, enabling staff to better exploit data opportunities and apply analytics and AI directly in their work.

The DATA+ Framework strategically organises the workforce based on their data expertise and skill application. At the foundational level, Data-Ready Officers, who form the backbone of the workforce, regularly analyse small datasets to ensure smooth operations. At the intermediate level, Data Power Users delve deeper into data using business intelligence tools to uncover valuable insights, aiding tactical discussions. At the advanced level, a select group of Citizen Data Scientists tackles complex Data and AI projects, generating actionable insights to drive innovation and strategic

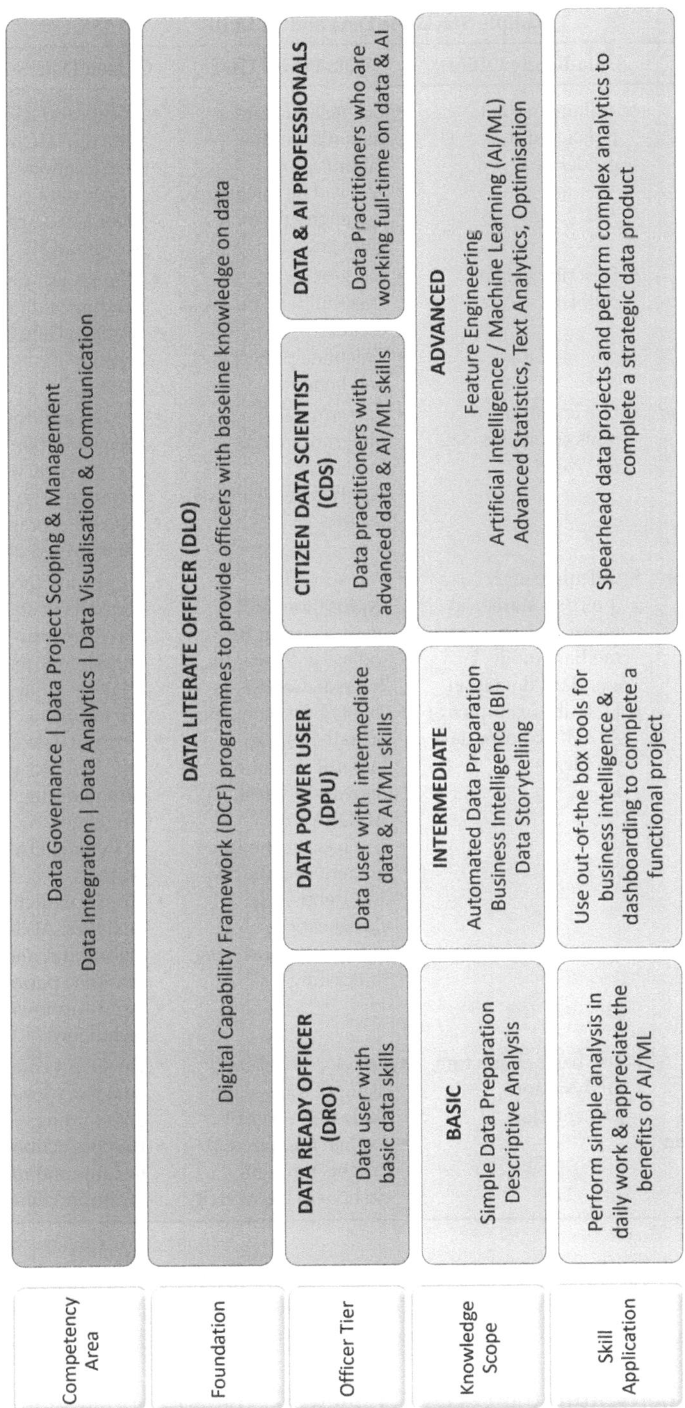

FIGURE 1.2
DATA+ Framework: Enhancing Data and AI Capabilities at TP

Sample Stackable Data and AI Skills

Competency	Data-Ready Officer	Data Power User	Citizen Data Scientist
Data Governance	• Adhere to data policies and guidelines	• Locate and source data within the organisation • Apply data safeguards, e.g. anonymisation, aggregation	• Locate and source data outside the organisation • Apply data safeguards, e.g. scrambling
Data Project Scoping and Management	• Describe a data problem	• Understand stakeholders' business context • Calculate project cost and benefits	• Plan project resources, funding and timeline • Manage Data and AI project
Data Integration	• Use common office tools to process data, e.g. Excel	• Perform data integration and modelling • Apply data cleansing techniques	• Design and conduct data collection plans, e.g. surveys, web scraping • Plan the storage of transformed data
Data Analytics	• Calculate and interpret statistical measures, e.g. mean, median, mode, standard deviation • Describe examples of AI/ML to solve data problems	• Perform data exploration and analysis using BI tools, e.g. Power BI, Tableau, GenAI • Apply basic concepts of statistics, e.g. hypothesis testing, regression, t-test, ANOVA • Use basic techniques to identify patterns and trends, e.g. classification, regression, clustering, forecasting	• Apply advanced concepts of statistics, e.g. K-nearest neighbours, survival analysis, time series, AB testing • Perform data cleaning and analytics using programming languages, e.g. R, Python, DAX, AI tools • Apply predictive analytics, AI/ML algorithms, and fine-tune performance • Apply optimisation techniques
Data Visualisation and Communication	• Use basic charts for analysis and presentation	• Develop dashboard using BI tools, e.g. Tableau, Power BI • Explain findings and insights through dashboard interactivity	• Develop a coherent data story leveraging data findings • Propose actionable insights and monitor for improvement

growth. Leading the deployment of this framework are Data and AI professionals who strategically oversee front-end and back-end operations, ensuring robust and effective data management, enterprise dashboards, and AI/ML operations.

For each tier within the DATA+ Framework, the appropriate data skills have been meticulously identified, encompassing an end-to-end data lifecycle approach from problem identification to analytics and ultimately deriving insights to propose actionable steps. These skills are intuitively grouped and designed to be stackable, enabling staff to logically progress from data enthusiasts to data practitioners, while acquiring advanced skills and tackling more complex Data and AI projects.

1. **Basic Tier.** At the basic tier, Data-Ready Officers are equipped with essential skills such as data collection, basic data cleaning, and simple data visualisation using tools like Excel. These competencies ensure they can efficiently handle small datasets and perform routine data tasks.
2. **Intermediate Tier.** At the intermediate tier, Data Power Users are trained in more advanced skills, including data manipulation, statistical analysis, and business intelligence, using out-of-the-box tools like Power BI, Tableau, or GenAI. These abilities allow them to develop dashboards, uncover trends and patterns, and support informed decision-making within their departments.
3. **Advanced Tier.** At the advanced tier, Citizen Data Scientists receive comprehensive training in data science and AI techniques. They learn to manage complex datasets, build predictive models, and apply AI/machine learning algorithms. Their expertise is crucial for tackling sophisticated data projects and making strategic recommendations to management.

By adhering to this structured approach, the workforce is well prepared to navigate the complexities of the digital age, fostering a culture of continuous learning and innovation in the evolving field of Data and AI.

1.4.1.2 Data and AI Skills Assessment

Data proficiency is as fundamental as literacy and numeracy, with everyone striving to attain the core competency needed to navigate the complexities of the digital age. However, the required level of data literacy varies based on one's role within the organisation and the extent to which data is utilised in both personal and professional contexts. Given the plethora of learning opportunities and platforms available to the workforce, it becomes nearly impossible to maintain a comprehensive record of the training and data-related projects undertaken by staff.

Adhering to the ancient maxim "know thyself", the DATA+ Skills Inventory Survey empowers staff to self-assess their proficiency in relation to the stackable Data and AI skills outlined in the DATA+ Framework and share their experiences with Data and AI projects. Designed as a developmental tool, the survey encourages honest self-evaluation. The collected information serves as an excellent starting point to identify knowledge and skill gaps. This enables the curation of targeted training programmes to upskill staff with diverse competencies, provide opportunities for hands-on application through real-case projects, and foster a culture of continuous learning in the evolving field of Data and AI.

Conducting a data needs assessment involves several key steps to identify and address gaps between current and desired outcomes. Here's a structured approach that guided the institute:

1. **Define the Scope and Purpose**
   - *Clearly outline the objectives of the assessment.* For instance, the DATA+ survey aims to identify the current data proficiency levels of staff, understanding the skills they can perform and mentor, and those they lack, especially regarding data governance policies.
   - *Determine the specific areas to focus on.* Understanding staff's data proficiency allows categorisation according to the DATA+ Framework, providing targeted capability development opportunities.
2. **Identify Stakeholders**
   - *Engage key stakeholders who have vested interest in the data and its outcomes.* Capability development is driven by the capability unit and people developers across departments. Consulting these units is crucial for feedback and buy-in.
   - *Form a needs assessment group to oversee the process.* For DATA+, a survey was employed using an internal platform. Key collaborators are needed to increase response rates, and a needs assessment group to oversee planning, administration, and analysis. This role was taken by the Data and AI unit, which has the resources and oversight of the DATA+ Framework.
3. **Collect Data**
   - *Gather quantitative and qualitative data from various sources.* Learning records of staff provide valuable input for planning the data needs assessment. Prior information on training courses and activities is necessary to ensure the survey is understandable.
   - *Use surveys, interviews, focus groups, and existing data to get a comprehensive view.* The choice of method depends on workforce size, target audience, resources, depth of information needed, time constraints, and data confidentiality. A combination of methods can be employed at different planning stages to ensure a thorough and nuanced understanding of the data needs. For instance, initial surveys can provide a broad overview, while follow-up interviews and focus groups can delve deeper into specific areas of interest. Existing information can be analysed to identify trends and patterns, complementing the insights gathered from direct interactions. This multifaceted approach ensures that the

assessment is comprehensive, capturing both quantitative and qualitative dimensions, and ultimately leading to more informed data upskilling.

4 **Analyse and Interpret Data**
   - *Examine the collected data to identify patterns, trends, and gaps.* Running a user acceptance testing (UAT) is key before conducting the assessment. People developers and a small group of staff from different departments can help refine the survey.
   - *Use statistical tools and qualitative analysis methods to interpret the findings.* For example, survey responses can be analysed using Power BI or Tableau to showcase business intelligence capabilities.

5 **Identify and Prioritise Needs**
   - *Determine the most critical needs based on data analysis.* The survey findings can help curate learning programmes targeting gaps in staff's data competency.
   - *Prioritise these needs to focus on the most impactful areas.* For instance, the DATA+ programme created more opportunities for staff to apply their skills on real business use cases, addressing a key survey finding.

6 **Develop Action Plans**
   - *Create actionable plans to address the identified needs.* One possible action is to curate learning programmes on digital platforms that staff can pursue at their own pace.
   - *Assign responsibilities and set timelines for implementation.* Engage people developers and relevant stakeholders as part of the DATA+ planning so that staff are targeted based on their data needs and anticipated data engagement.

7 **Implement and Monitor**
   - *Execute the action plans and monitor progress.* Record staff learning in corporate systems to track progress and adjust plans accordingly.
   - *Adjust strategies based on ongoing evaluation.* Feedback from participants is sought after each learning programme to continuously improve the programme. The DATA+ programme is reviewed and updated regularly.

8 **Evaluate and Revise**
   - *Assess the effectiveness of the implemented solutions.* A data needs assessment is not a one-time activity. As staff learn and apply their skills, and as data competency grows, re-assess data gaps to ensure programmes remain relevant.
   - *Revise action plans based on feedback and new data.* Update and enhance the programme to consider updated data assessment results, project needs, and new technologies.

By following these steps, organisations can ensure a comprehensive and effective data needs assessment process.

1.4.2 Curating and Customising Data and AI Programmes

Building on the insights from the DATA+ Skills Inventory exercise, the institute launched the DATA+ initiative—a transformative programme designed to upskill staff in Data and AI/ML through personalised learning and mentoring in real-world applications. This initiative offers two distinct pathways:

- **Project Mentoring.** A six-month programme that pairs staff with mentors to tackle real business use cases. Participants can choose between the Data Power User (DPU) Track, which focuses on creating dashboard prototypes, and the Citizen Data Scientist (CDS) Track, which involves completing a dashboard and developing predictive data solutions for deployment.
- **Workshops.** Standalone sessions on tools such as Power Excel, Power BI, Tableau, KNIME, Python, and GenAI. These workshops cater to staff looking to refresh or acquire new data skills and to work on their projects independently.

1.4.2.1 Project Mentoring Programme

The Project Mentoring Programme is offered biannually, aligning with the academic calendar to help educators and administrators plan their schedules effectively. The programme begins with staff identifying a data problem statement and seeking management support to secure access to data, resources, and time commitment. The project proposal is then submitted to a committee of potential mentors, who evaluate the feasibility of the project based on its impact, data availability, alignment with programme objectives, and the officer's readiness. Qualified staff are then matched with mentors who possess the relevant experience and skills needed for the project.

The weekly sessions consist of a learning clinic and project mentoring to equip staff with the necessary knowledge and skills for end-to-end data solutioning, from project scoping to dashboarding and data product deployment. The programme is designed to provide easily accessible data tools to accelerate the staff's data journey. Drawing from past experiences, potential challenges and resistance to certain programming tools were recognised. To address this, a low-code-no-code strategy is utilised, employing intuitive, user-friendly, and affordable tools. These include Tableau and Power BI for business intelligence, Alteryx, KNIME, and GenAI for predictive modelling and text analytics, and Python for the most complex and advanced data analytics tasks. As part of the evolving needs of recent Data and AI projects, the basket of tools has been expanded to include ChatGPT, Microsoft Power Automate, and Copilot for data preparation and analytics.

Unlike conventional training, this programme emphasises hands-on learning through real-case projects and mentorship, effectively bridging skill gaps and delivering tangible outcomes for the institute. In addition to fostering future-ready skills, the programme offers personalised learning pathways tailored to diverse project needs, empowers staff at different levels to make data-driven decisions, and ensures scalability and sustainability through continuous training. The curriculum is regularly reviewed to ensure that mentees acquire relevant, current, and in-demand skills. It also highlights the value of an interdisciplinary approach, integrating data analytics with fields like social media, the Internet of Things, and sustainability, fostering a holistic understanding of how data can be leveraged across various domains and applications.

1.4.2.2 Workshops

While the project mentoring programme is designed specifically to upskill Data-Ready Officers to Data Power Users and Citizen Data Scientists, the workshops are tool-based and aimed at targeted skills acquisition or refreshing. These one-day sessions offer test drives and masterclasses, depending on the participants' prior experience with the tool.

To reach the right audience and maximise learning, the workshop invitation should clearly outline the skills to be covered, the targeted tier, and any preparation needed prior to attending. In line with the low-code-no-code strategy, consider offering workshops that utilise easily accessible data tools while also teaching participants how to conduct Data and AI projects independently.

Some examples include:

- Data Preparation and Visual Analytics using Power Excel
- Data Ingestion and Preparation using Power Query or Tableau Prep
- Data Modelling and Exploration using Power BI or Tableau Desktop
- Dashboarding and Analytics using Power BI or Tableau Desktop
- Feature Engineering and Predictive Modelling using KNIME or Python
- Automating Data Ingestion and Preparation using Power Automate or GenAI

1.4.2.3 Holistic Learning Through the DATA+ Initiative

Continuous learning is essential for maintaining and enhancing Data and AI proficiency. Programmes like DATA+ offer structured learning paths that help individuals stay updated with the latest tools and techniques in Data and AI. These programmes provide opportunities for staff to deepen their knowledge and skills through learning clinics, community sharing, and online courses.

The DATA+ initiative provides a comprehensive learning experience through three main approaches: experiential learning, social learning, and formal learning.

1. **Experiential Learning**
   - *Project-Based Work.* Staff engage in a six-month project experience, working on real-world Data and AI projects. This hands-on approach allows them to apply theoretical knowledge to practical challenges, enhancing their data and problem-solving skills.
   - *Community Learning and Interdisciplinary Collaboration.* Staff collaborate with peers from different disciplines, gaining exposure to various perspectives and methodologies.
2. **Social Learning**
   - *Team Environment.* Staff interact with co-mentees on a weekly basis, fostering a collaborative environment where they can learn from each other.
   - *Networking Opportunities.* The programme includes interactions with mentors, management, stakeholders, and other colleagues, providing valuable networking opportunities and the chance to learn from experienced professionals. These connections facilitate ongoing collaboration beyond the DATA+ engagement.
3. **Formal Learning**
   - *Structured Curriculum.* While primarily project-based, the programme includes structured learning components such as face-to-face learning clinics and digital learning on data science techniques and tools.
   - *Mentorship.* Staff receive guidance and feedback from mentors, ensuring they gain a deep understanding of their Data and AI work and develop their skills systematically.

These elements combine to create a rich learning environment that supports staff growth and prepares them for a data-driven future.

1.4.3 Future Directions: Expanding Reach Through a Data and AI Community of Practice

While learning programmes are essential for upskilling staff, they often have limited slots and cannot accommodate everyone. With the rapid rise of AI, a broader approach is needed to reach as many staff as possible within a short time and with available resources. This is where a community of practice comes in, comprising data users and practitioners eager to learn and engage with each other.

At TP, this community enables inclusivity, continuous learning and active engagement.

1. **Inclusivity**
   - *Diverse Representation.* The community actively promotes diversity by ensuring representation from various backgrounds, skill levels, and perspectives. Data-driven success depends on cross-functional collaboration between institutional leadership, educators, and administrators, from data enthusiasts to data scientists.
   - *Safe and Welcoming Environment.* Community meet-ups create a space where all members feel valued and respected, encouraging open dialogue and collaboration. Encouraging interdisciplinary teams to work together allows for a more holistic interpretation of data, leading to innovative solutions for curriculum enhancement, student engagement, and operational efficiency.
2. **Continuous Learning**
   - *Hands-on Experience.* The community schedules hands-on sessions to help members stay updated with the latest tools, techniques, and trends in Data and AI. Institutions must embed data literacy training into their capability development programmes, ensuring that educators and administrators can confidently analyse, interpret, and apply data insights. Workshops, certification programmes, and hands-on analytics exercises can empower AI-enabled staff to make evidence-based decisions that enhance student success and institutional performance.
   - *Mentorship Programmes.* Experienced members mentor newcomers, fostering a culture of continuous learning and professional growth.
3. **Active Engagement**
   - *Community Gathering.* The community plans to host events, such as hackathons, project sharing, and industry talks, to initiate conversations and facilitate networking, knowledge sharing, and continuous improvement.
   - *Online Platforms.* The community utilises online forums and collaborative tools, like Microsoft Teams and SharePoint, to keep members engaged, connected, and abreast of the new tools and the latest technology. To sustain a data-driven enterprise, institutions must continue to refine their approaches, provide data practitioners with the tools and resources they need, and create an environment that encourages experimentation and innovation.

These efforts collectively create a vibrant and supportive environment where members can continuously learn, feel included, and actively participate in the community's growth and success. Moreover, fostering a culture of continuous learning among staff is crucial. Encouraging staff to engage in ongoing professional development and stay updated with the latest advancements in industry and professional organisations can enhance Data and AI proficiency and contribute to the overall improvement of educational outcomes.

1.5 Unlocking the Full Potential of the LEAD-AI Framework—Driving Innovation with Data and AI

1.5.1 Navigating the LEAD-AI Framework

1.5.1.1 Overcoming Common Challenges in Deploying a Data-Driven Framework

Deploying a data-driven framework presents several challenges that organisations must navigate to achieve success. These challenges include data silos, data quality issues, change management, resource constraints, and scalability concerns. Addressing these obstacles requires strategic planning and proactive measures. Here are some common challenges and how the institute has effectively addressed them:

1. **Data Silos**

   Data stored in disparate systems can hinder accessibility and integration. The institute addressed this by creating an enterprise data platform almost ten years ago, integrating data from various in-house and outsourced systems for strategic analysis across departments. The platform is regularly updated to accommodate new data systems and operations, including on-premises and cloud technologies.

2. **Data Quality**

   Inconsistent or inaccurate data can undermine decision-making. In addition to establishing robust data governance practices, the institute created a data catalogue and data pipeline to ensure data is interpreted and processed consistently before analysis.

3. **Change Management**

   Shifting to a data-driven culture can face resistance from staff. Change management involves introducing the benefits of a data-driven approach, providing training, and allowing staff to experience the benefits first hand. Engaging stakeholders early and communicating the advantages of data-driven decision-making is crucial. The institute's Chief Executive Officer led the initiative to incorporate both quantitative and qualitative analytics into planning, updating, and strategising curriculum, educational outcomes, and administrative processes.

4 **Resource Constraints**

Organisations often have limited budgets, time, and personnel that can impede implementation. The Data and AI unit comprises a small group of passionate staff with diverse competencies, including database administration, data engineering, dashboarding, AI/ML ops, teaching and learning, and strategic planning. Securing key stakeholders' buy-in to prioritise Data and AI initiatives, leveraging existing resources, and seeking external expertise when needed are essential.

8 **Scalability**

Ensuring the data strategy can scale with growing data volumes and complexity is crucial. The institute has seen an exponential increase in data collection, especially from Internet of Things devices, sensors, and digital resources. Using scalable data management solutions and planning for future growth are baseline considerations for the data-driven framework. Another challenge could be the integration with upstream data sources; as more application systems are also migrated to the cloud, change becomes a constant, hence the data architecture needs to be scalable and able to integrate.

By addressing these challenges proactively, organisations can successfully deploy a data-driven framework that enhances their data capabilities and drives strategic success.

1.5.1.2 Assessing the Effectiveness of the Data-Driven Initiatives

Assessing the effectiveness of data-driven initiatives involves evaluating various metrics and outcomes to ensure they align with organisational goals and the intended outcomes of the data-driven framework. Here are some key steps and metrics to consider:

1 **Define Clear Objectives**

Establish specific, measurable goals for Data and AI initiatives using S.M.A.R.T. (Specific, Measurable, Achievable, Relevant, and Time-bound) goals (Forbes Media LLC, 2025). This approach helps align efforts with the overall data-driven strategy. At TP, the strategy is framed by enablers with specific deliverables, such as the DATA+ initiative, which allows for monitoring progress and achieving desired outcomes.

2 **Identify Key Performance Indicators**

Select relevant key performance indicators (KPIs) that reflect the success of initiatives. To extract actionable insights, educational institutions must define KPIs that align with their strategic goals. These KPIs provide a quantifiable measure of success and help institutions track progress in key areas. These could include metrics related to data quality, accessibility, governance, and analytics. KPIs are analysed and monitored using business intelligence tools to identify trends, patterns, and areas for improvement.

Examples of KPIs used to assess the effectiveness of data-driven initiatives at the institute include:

- *Data Quality KPIs:* Percentage of data entries uploaded using data pipelines that are correct and error-free.
- *Data Accessibility KPIs:* Average time taken to fulfil data requests, number of times enterprise data is accessed and used by staff, percentage of data access requests that do not comply with established policies.
- *Data Analytics KPIs:* Percentage of data-driven decisions that result in positive outcomes.
- *Strategy Alignment KPIs:* Percentage of Data and AI projects completed on time and within budget.
- *Operational Efficiency KPIs:* Percentage of processes automated using AI solutions, increase in productivity due to AI tools and data-driven insights.
- *Continuous Improvement KPIs:* Percentage of staff indicating satisfaction with data projects, number of areas for improvement addressed.
- *Training and Development KPIs:* Number of staff who have completed the DATA+ project mentoring and workshops.

These KPIs help organisations measure the success of their Data and AI initiatives and identify areas for improvement.

3 **Analyse Data and AI Impact**

Assess the return on investment (ROI) and benefits of Data and AI projects to determine their value. As shown in the following examples, the DATA+ projects have contributed to both organisational and educational outcomes.

By following these steps and tracking relevant metrics, organisations can effectively assess and enhance the impact of their Data and AI initiatives.

1.5.2 Data and AI Case Studies

The completed projects at TP have significantly enhanced student learning experiences, academic effectiveness, and operational efficiency. These initiatives demonstrate the transformative potential of Data and AI projects within educational institutions. While not exhaustive, the following projects can inspire other opportunities for Data and AI exploration:

1.5.2.1 Enhancing Student Learning Experience

- Identifying High-Performing Students, to predict students likely to graduate with merit or distinction, with results visualised in a dashboard for easy access.
- Analysis of Student and Organisation Feedback to Enhance Student Internship Experience, to conduct descriptive and text analytics to student and supervisor feedback surveys, identifying areas for improvement.
- Enhancement of the Teaching Evaluation and Subject Satisfaction Dashboard, to provide a consolidated dashboard, highlighting comparisons of KPIs across subjects and educators to improve course and teaching quality.
- Interdisciplinary Learning Survey Analyses, to analyse student feedback on their experience to deliver actionable insights to improve the programme.
- Analysing Transition from Common Science Programme to Diploma Courses, to predict students at risk during transition, enabling timely support.

1.5.2.2 Enabling Academic Effectiveness

- Graduate Employment Survey Deep-Dive Analysis, to provide a consolidated dashboard for detailed course analysis and comparative employment data.
- Analysis of Teaching—Research Effectiveness, to assess educator's effectiveness in research and teaching.
- Adult Learners' Dashboards to Support Growth and Productivity, to enhance Continuing Education and Training programme effectiveness using data visualisation and machine learning tools.

1.5.2.3 Optimising Operational Efficiencies

- Fault Reporting Analysis, to improve operational efficiency using Pareto analysis and text analytics.
- Human Resource Dashboard, to visualise headcount trends and other metrics for better decision-making.
- Wi-Fi Performance Analysis, to automate Wi-Fi data reporting and analysis to improve IT efficiency.

The DATA+ Programme has markedly improved the data proficiency of staff, elevating their confidence and deepening their data comprehension. These initiatives have collectively advanced the institution's data-driven strategic objectives, promoting continuous improvement and nurturing a data-centric culture. This strategic framework can serve as an exemplary model for other Data and AI initiatives.

1.5.3 Future Directions: Ensuring the Sustainability of the LEAD-AI Framework

The successful deployment of data initiatives represents a significant milestone. To ensure sustainability and scalability, consider the following strategic actions:

1. **Foster a Data-Driven Culture**
   - *Engage Stakeholders.* Involve key stakeholders early to gain buy-in and support. Regular communication and feedback loops are essential. At TP, internal training providers, people developers, management, and relevant stakeholders are engaged from the planning stage and continuously consulted to improve various data initiatives.
   - *Promote Continuous Learning.* Provide ongoing training and development opportunities to ensure staff are equipped with the necessary skills to leverage Data and AI effectively. The DATA+ Competency Framework guides the upskilling of staff, keeping pace with changes in the Data and AI domain.
2. **Implement Robust Data Governance**
   - *Ensure Data Quality.* Establish data governance practices to maintain data accuracy, consistency, and reliability. This includes creating a data catalogue and data pipeline to standardise data processing. Continual efforts are made at the institute to refresh the data platform, catalogue, and pipelines in response to rapid technological changes.
   - *Harden Data Security.* Implement security measures to protect sensitive data and ensure compliance with regulations. At the institute, standard operating procedures are reviewed regularly to harden data platforms and business intelligence facilities, addressing cybersecurity concerns.
3. **Leverage Scalable Technology**
   - *Adopt Scalable Solutions.* Use scalable data management and analytics platforms to handle growing data volumes and complexity. The institute is migrating its data and platforms to the cloud, aligning with Singapore's cloud-first direction.

- *Automate Processes.* Implement automation tools to streamline data collection, processing, and analysis, improving efficiency and reducing manual effort. Staff are being trained in automated data collection and processing, and AI tools are adopted for analysis.
- *Scale Data and AI Projects.* Encourage more staff to join the DATA+ mentoring programme by starting with projects within their functional purview. An agile approach is adopted to expand these innovative projects to other departments, leveraging the proven benefits of the DATA+ programme to foster a culture of data-driven decision-making and enhance overall institutional efficiency.

4 **Encourage Collaboration and Sharing**

- *Create a Community of Practice (CoP).* Develop a CoP to foster collaboration among data practitioners, sharing best practices, insights, and innovations across the organisation. The Data Community of Practice brings data enthusiasts and practitioners together to upskill and learn from each other.
- *Showcase Success Stories.* Highlight successful Data and AI projects to inspire and motivate others. Completed projects are showcased in the DATA+ Poster Book, available within the intranet, fostering community sharing and collaboration, and highlighting the transformative power of data analytics.

5 **Monitor and Evaluate Progress**

- *Regularly Review KPIs.* Continuously monitor and evaluate KPIs to track progress and identify areas for improvement. The DATA+ programme and workshops invite participants to rate the programme and provide areas for improvement. Exceptional feedback and a high Net Promoter Score affirm the programme's success and relevance.
- *Conduct Audits.* Perform regular audits to ensure data governance practices are followed and to identify any gaps or issues. At the institute, audits are conducted at regular intervals, varying according to data and system classification.

6 **Plan for Continuous Improvement**

- *Maintain Feedback Loops.* Collect feedback from stakeholders and participants to identify areas for improvement. Insights gained through Data and AI projects and interactions among data practitioners lead to continuous improvements. Engagement with other institutions and industries helps stay updated on changes in the Data and AI domain. A data-driven feedback loop enables institutions to continuously assess and refine teaching strategies, student interventions, and administrative processes. By using real-time analytics and AI-driven insights, educators and administrators can proactively identify areas for improvement, test new approaches, and measure their impact over time.

- *Enhance Iterative Process.* Continuously refine and adjust the data-driven strategy based on insights and feedback to ensure it remains relevant and effective. Emphasise collaboration with data teams in other institutions and explore to share developments and initiatives.

By adopting these strategies, organisations can ensure the sustainability of their Data and AI initiatives, driving continuous improvement and fostering a data-driven culture.

1.6 Conclusion

1.6.1 Navigating the Future with Data and AI

As education continues to evolve in a rapidly digitalising world, the convergence of Data and AI is redefining how institutions deliver value, enhance learning outcomes, and optimise operations. From its data-driven transformation that began in 2017, the institute has made significant strides by embedding data literacy, analytics, and AI competencies throughout its ecosystem. Through the strategic LEAD-AI Framework, it has not only cultivated an environment that values evidence-based decision-making but also laid the groundwork for long-term innovation and impact.

The future of education is set to be shaped by increasingly intelligent, adaptive, and predictive technologies. AI-powered tools, such as personalised learning platforms, real-time performance dashboards, and automated curriculum adjustments, are already transforming how students engage with content and how educators tailor instruction. Predictive analytics and natural language processing (NLP) will soon play larger roles in early intervention strategies, allowing institutions to support at-risk students with greater precision and timeliness. As machine learning and generative AI mature, their applications in educational content creation, intelligent tutoring systems, and workforce planning will accelerate.

These innovations, however, require more than just the adoption of new tools—they demand a mindset shift. Institutions must evolve from seeing data as a by-product of operations to treating it as a strategic asset. AI, when paired with clean, well-governed data, becomes not just a tool for automation but a catalyst for human-centred innovation in teaching, learning, and administration.

Sustaining its data-driven momentum requires institutional commitment, continuous learning, and cross-functional collaboration. Central to this is the DATA+ Framework, which scaffolds data proficiency across multiple roles and skill levels and fosters a growing community of data practitioners and champions. As AI capabilities expand, upskilling must be matched by effective data governance, ethical AI practices, and clear leadership direction.

TP's approach offers a sustainable blueprint: (1) Empower all stakeholders through democratised data access and intuitive analytics tools; (2) Embed a culture of continuous improvement, supported by feedback loops and measurable KPIs; and (3) Drive innovation through interdisciplinary collaboration, shared best practices, and project-based learning. By doing so, institutions can avoid stagnation and continuously respond to emerging opportunities and challenges.

The LEAD-AI Framework has provided a robust foundation for its transformation. Its pillars—Leading by Example, Empowering Through Data Democratisation, and Accelerating Proficiency in Data and AI—serve not just as strategies, but as cultural anchors and are valued as a core driver in driving innovation sustainably.

The journey is not without challenges—ranging from data silos and integration issues to change resistance and ethical considerations. However, as experience shows, with visionary leadership, structured frameworks, and a strong data culture, institutions can overcome these barriers. The time to act is now.

References

Blei, D. M., & Smyth, P. (2020). Science and data science. *Harvard Data Science Review*. https://hdsr.mitpress.mit.edu/pub/o3qm160v/release/6?readingCollection=a6db7dff

Davenport, T., & Harris, J. (2017). *Competing on analytics: Updated with a new introduction – The new science of winning*. https://www.tomdavenport.com/book/competing-on-analytics-updated-with-a-new-introduction/?utm_source=chatgpt.com

Domo, Inc. (2025). AI vs BI explained: Differences and how they work. *Domo*. https://www.domo.com/glossary/ai-vs-bi

Forbes Media LLC. (2025). The ultimate guide to S.M.A.R.T. goals. *Forbes*. https://www.forbes.com/advisor/business/smart-goals/

Government of Singapore. (2025a). Ministry of education. *Ministry of Education*. https://www.moe.gov.sg/coursefinder

Government of Singapore. (2025b). Singapore department of statistics. *Singapore Department of Statistics*. https://www.singstat.gov.sg/find-data

Government Technology Agency of Singapore. (2024). Data science & AI programmes overview. *GovTech Digital Academy*. https://www.thedigitalacademy.tech.gov.sg/category-data-science-and-AI

Government Technology Agency of Singapore. (2025). AI in education: Transforming Singapore's education system with student learning space. *GovTech*. https://www.tech.gov.sg/media/technews/ai-in-education-transforming-singapore-education-system-with-student-learning-space/

Kadence International. (2025). How AI is reshaping higher education in Singapore. *Kadence International*. https://kadence.com/en-us/how-ai-is-reshaping-higher-education-in-singapore/

Lefebvre, H., Legner, C., & Teracino, E. (2023, November 24). 5 Pillars for democratizing data at your organization. *Harvard Business Review*. https://hbr.org/2023/11/5-pillars-for-democratizing-data-at-your-organization

Marr, B. (2017). What is data democratization? A super simple explanation and the key pros and con. *Enterprise Tech*. https://www.forbes.com/sites/bernardmarr/2017/07/24/what-is-data-democratization-a-super-simple-explanation-and-the-key-pros-and-cons/

Open Government Products. (2025). Singapore's open data portal: Education. *Open Government Products*. https://data.gov.sg/

Technical Laboratory Systems, Inc. (2023). The evolution of Industry 1.0 to 4.0 and beyond. *Tech-Labs*. https://tech-labs.com/blog/evolution-industry-10-40-and-beyond

UN Global Working Group on Big Data for Official Statistics. (2020). Competency framework for big data acquisition and processing (C. a. Task Team on Training, Ed.). *UNBigData*. https://unstats.un.org/bigdata/task-teams/training/UNGWG_Competency_Framework.pdf

World Economic Forum. (2025). How Singapore's data-driven approach is building a skills-first economy. *Education and Skills*. https://www.weforum.org/stories/2025/01/singapore-data-driven-approach-build-skills-first-economy/

2

Embracing and Sustaining the Journey of AI in Education: Possibilities and Challenges

Boey Chee Kin and Paul Cheung

2.1 Preamble

Have you ever come across phrases that go with the analogy of *"Data is to AI what . . . is to . . ."*? For instance, "Data is to AI what water is to humans". Indeed, data is the lifeblood that fuels AI algorithms, allowing them to learn, adapt, and make decisions (Sehgal, 2023). However, the reverse is not true, as data does not need to depend on AI. By itself, data can offer meaningful insights. In the context of education, data can inform educators of possible learning gaps that a student might have and thereby enable educators to intervene not just timely but effectively. In other words, data is the enabler that brings about responsive teaching in the classroom.

2.2 Believing in the Value of Data-Driven Insights in Education

As covered in Chapter 1, the institution values the use of data to support educators in making informed decisions, not just in enhancing teaching and learning but in running the administration more effectively. From the perspective of teaching and learning, the culture of democratising data in the institution was an important shift to provide educators with data-informed insights that complement their professional judgement to make decisions for effective student learning support. For instance, the educators in the Polytechnic Foundation Programme use AI-enabled analytics dashboards to gain insights into the profile of the students under their care. Within the dashboard, there is an element of predictive analytics that provides the educators with projected needs of individual students. Based on the projected needs and the rest of the students' data presented by the dashboards, the

DOI: 10.1201/9781003599357-3

educators from the Polytechnic Foundation Programme make sense of the support that students might require, such as weakness in specific subject areas or requiring financial aid. As the Polytechnic Foundation Programme is a one-year high-stake programme, such insights enable educators to intervene timely and effectively so that students can progress to their full-time diploma courses. This initiative was made possible as the institution believes in an evidence-informed approach of teaching and learning, where data is made available for educators on a needs basis to support them in performing their role effectively, and students would be adequately supported in their learning journey. More about this initiative will be covered in Chapter 5.

2.3 Considering Pedagogy Before Technology

The institution started its journey on digital learning way before COVID. When the pandemic struck, the institution was able to pivot over to home-based learning quickly and ensure that learning continued to take place effectively. It was also during this period that the institution established its vision to enable every student to learn in a highly personalised and flexible manner, not least enabled by digital technology. Recognising that educational technology has its place in teaching and learning, the institution started to ramp up its exploration of educational technology tools and solutions to support the pedagogical needs of its educators across various disciplines. In recent years, there have been many more educational technology tools and solutions enabled by AI and analytics being rolled out in the market. The use of such tools and solutions has enabled educators in the higher education to be more responsive in identifying students' learning gaps and providing support to them to close those gaps. At the same time, learning can also be tailored for students according to their needs such as pace, content, and feedback.

In the journey of exploration, the institution was clear that the use of educational technology was not about novelty. According to Vaz (2021), technology is about being able to create real differentiation and value for the customer. Therefore, the fundamental question that should be asked in any digitalisation initiative is for what purpose the educational technology tool or solution serves the educators. At the heart of any exploration, pedagogical considerations have always been placed at the forefront, while technology is the enabler to support the pedagogy used by our educators. In other words, the learning outcomes, students, and student engagement should always be the main considerations for the choice of technology. According to Howland et al. (2011), technology facilitates meaningful learning when students are learning with technology in contrast to learning from technology.

2.4 Delivering Value to the Users Is What Digitalisation Is About

For instance, an educator who was teaching language and communication in a Continuous Education and Training (CET) subject was keen to explore AI tools to help students improve oral presentation delivery. Bear in mind, this was in early 2020, just before the COVID lockdown. When the lockdown came and the institution had to pivot to home-based learning, the educator raised concerns that it was nearly impossible for students to practise oral presentation with tutors providing feedback face to face since students were only connected via the virtual platform. This gave rise to an opportunity to source an educational technology solution to support the pedagogical needs for the CET subject. Thankfully, an AI-enabled tool called Speaker Coach was chanced upon. This tool allows the user to practise or rehearse their presentations on PowerPoint, and feedback in the form of an analytics-driven report would be provided by the Coach in real-time or immediately after the presentation. Being the subject matter expert, the educator tried using the tool and found the AI-generated feedback to be reasonable, and the scope of the feedback covered was adequate. This AI-enabled tool has helped the educator to address the challenges of teaching oral presentation delivery in a home-based learning environment that had never been done before. Given the circumstances, the face-to-face feedback given by the tutors that had been the case all along had now been turned over to the AI to augment the tutors in giving feedback to students on their oral presentations. Looking back, the benefit of harnessing the AI tool has enabled educators to be more responsive in their teaching, as they could now glean insights from the analytics report to find out the gaps that individual students might have and provide personalised support to improve their oral presentation skills. Should there be common skill gaps, educators could consider addressing them as part of their lesson delivery. For the students, they could practise anytime and anywhere to sharpen their oral presentation skills.

What was the lesson learnt from this initiative? This initiative has driven home the importance of finding the intersection between the user needs and technology. Always go back to the problem statement to be addressed. The basis should always be about the pedagogical needs. To put simply, it is first and foremost about the user needs before looking for the right technological solution that addresses those user needs meaningfully and effectively. When all these are aligned, it can be sure that the technological tools and solutions will bring value to the educators. More importantly, students will find the technological tools useful in supporting them to attain the learning outcomes rather than a distraction to their learning. More about the initiative on Speaker Coach will be covered in Chapter 6.

2.5 Taking an Agile Approach to Scale Digital Learning

Considering the rapidly evolving digital landscape, the institution took on an Agile approach when exploring technological tools and solutions to scale digital learning. Such an Agile way of working has enabled the institution to be responsive to emerging trends and explore new tools and solutions to bring about innovative ways of teaching and learning. As Agile emphasises a user-centred perspective based on regular feedback through iterations, this also ensures that the final product meets the needs of the users and delivers meaningful value to them.

When COVID struck in 2020, home-based learning was implemented, and the institution needed to adapt quickly to the use of technologies to provide support to students who were engaged in various modes of learning, be it lecture, tutorial, or practical. As the pandemic started to ease and some face-to-face lessons had resumed, the institution recognised that blended learning—in the form of blending synchronous with asynchronous, or the blending of onsite with online—would be the new normal of lesson delivery moving forward. This was when the institution took an interest in exploring the feasibility of HyFlex Learning.

HyFlex Learning can be defined as a way of learning whereby students have the flexibility in the modes of participation, enabling them to choose either face-to-face class sessions in person or via online without physically attending class (Beatty, 2019). It is worth noting that HyFlex Learning started as a ground-up initiative in late 2020 when one of the academic schools piloted it using a combination of the video conferencing platform that the institution is primarily using, alongside a web camera and a wireless earpiece that enabled the educator to rove among onsite students while remaining audible to the remote students (Tan & Loh, 2023). This initiative was found to be beneficial as some students were placed on "Stay Home Notice" during that time. The affordance of HyFlex Learning meant that these students, who were feeling well but had to stay home due to COVID restrictions, could continue to attend lessons without disrupting their learning. Moreover, the need to observe safe distancing measures back then meant that we could control the number of students joining lessons onsite through the implementation of HyFlex Learning with proper planning and scheduling of students joining onsite or online.

Recognising the relevance and need for HyFlex Learning, the institution started its first Digital Factory in mid-2021 with the vision to set up a future-proof learning space that provides an engaging and interactive learning experience, is easy for the educators to use, is adaptive to sudden changes, and is scalable. Taking on an Agile approach, a multi-disciplinary team that consisted of the product owner from the School of Applied Science and colleagues from IT Services, Estates and Facilities Management, and the Learning Academy was formed. The Digital Factory team was entrusted

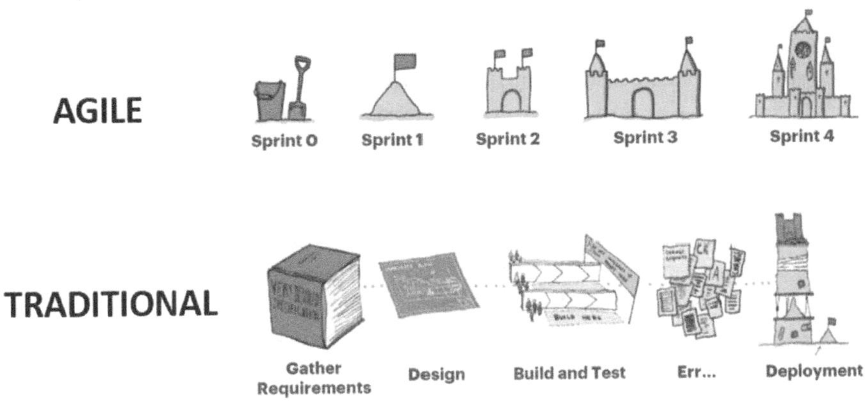

FIGURE 2.1
Source: https://poyankarbor.com/designing-for-uncertainty-two-perspectives-on-agile-design/

with the mission to deliver a minimum viable product in the form of a HyFlex Learning Space within 16 weeks.

It was indeed challenging for the author to lead a multi-disciplinary team in this project due to the unfamiliarity with the Agile way of managing projects, and so too for most members in the team. Unlike the traditional waterfall approach, the Agile way of managing projects (Karbor, n.d.) (Figure 2.1) required much more collaboration within the team, listening to the viewpoints of team members who brought with them different expertise, and learning to see things in perspective. The user-centric approach in Agile meant that the design of the HyFlex Learning Space was subject to constant changes, especially during the initial sprints of the project. In the end, the team underwent seven iterations of the design within 10 days! It might not sound like a lot, but it was certainly not something common to the team at that point in time. However, the team appreciated going through the process, as the eventual design was something that the team co-created with the users, that is, educators and students from the school who would be using the learning space.

While the learning curve was steep initially, the team managed to overcome the hurdles by putting into action what had been learnt about Design Thinking and the Lean Management and Agile methodologies. Looking back, the need to work in short cycles in the Agile approach kept the team focused on working towards the outcomes for each sprint. The team worked cohesively to put together the different parts of the HyFlex Learning Space: namely the audio-visual system, integration with the institution's IT network, and the pedagogical toolkit to support the educators in managing the HyFlex learning environment and delivering the lesson effectively, within a short span of six weeks! It was something the team could not have imagined at the start of the project.

Nonetheless, the team experienced first hand how the Agile approach has enabled the delivery of prototypes early enough and allowed stakeholders to see value sooner rather than waiting for the entire project to be completed. By the end of the fourth sprint, the product owner managed to conduct some trial lessons and collated more user feedback for the team to refine the solution further. By the end of the sixteen weeks, the minimum viable product was delivered! Subsequently, the team went on to replicate and adapt the minimum viable product for several schools in the institution that found it suitable for their pedagogies. Beyond the typical tutorial rooms, the team also expanded the use of the HyFlex Learning Spaces in a couple of laboratories, and it has proven to be effective (Loh et al., 2025).

The HyFlex Learning was the institution's response to not only ensure learning continuity but also enhance learning experiences during the pandemic. Beyond the pandemic, HyFlex Learning continues to remain relevant as it affords students with the flexibility in deciding how they wish to learn and engage with content. Think about it: providing the flexibility and choice of attending class in HyFlex Learning is somewhat similar to the flexibility given to working professionals to work from home where possible. A potential use case of HyFlex Learning could be in the CET arena for the adult learners. Thinking in the light of Singapore's push for lifelong learning and the need for working professionals to upskill and reskill in order to remain relevant at the workplace, the flexibility given to the CET learners in deciding how they might wish to join lessons could be well received, given the other commitments they might have.

Looking back, the adoption of the Agile approach in this project reflects the realities of digital projects in the current times where speed, user centricity, and adaptability are critical for success. On the other hand, the traditional waterfall approach might be better suited for projects with well-defined and stable requirements and minimal need for flexibility. Think about it again—these conditions are getting increasingly rare in digital learning and digitalisation projects of the current times.

2.6 Experimenting and Tinkering as the Basis to Embrace the Journey of AI in Education

While the institution has started to explore what AI could bring to education much earlier, the launch of ChatGPT in late 2022 has brought the use of AI to the masses. The access to ChatGPT has given students potentially a personal tutor on hand. Among the educators in the institution, there was initially much apprehension rather than excitement towards the emergence of generative AI technology. "How would ChatGPT impact our role as educators?",

"How would this impact student learning and assessment?" These were the questions lingering in the mind of the educators.

According to Wen (2023), it is important to experiment when it comes to AI in education. Wen posited that people will not understand the tools unless they are "played" with. And that was how the institution started using ChatGPT. Based on the exploration during the early days of ChatGPT, the institution gained a better understanding of its capabilities and limitations and established its posture of "**E**ncouraging the **E**ffective and **E**thical use of Generative AI tools for teaching and learning". While the institution embraced the use of AI, there were genuine concerns about the responsible use of AI by students and students who might plagiarise their assignments. In the same article, Wen wrote:

> None of us learnt to swim or ride a bicycle simply by watching tutorial videos or having people demonstrate it to us. The value of practice, through real-life practice or simulation, cannot be understated. I believe the same goes for working with training students to use AI responsibly. To do that, we will need authentic situations for students to practice using AI in their work.

As polytechnic educators, the mission is to prepare students for the future of work, one in which they need to work alongside AI in the workplace. From the developments observed so far in this space, AI is unlikely to be a passing fad. Therefore, there is a need to understand what AI can do in a hands-on and experiential manner. Everyone should actively engage with the AI tools and platforms, learn to manipulate them, and exploit their potential to support the pedagogical needs. In the words of Lim (2023),

> Tinkering is the key to understanding the potential, limitations and biases of generative AI.

She urged educators to create opportunities to experiment with generative AI and redesign teaching and assessment that encourage students to use generative AI as a co-pilot, critically evaluate generative AI output, and weave in their personal experience into the generative AI output to enhance their learning.

2.7 Overcoming Mindset Shift Is the Key, Not the Technology

What was the key to getting the educators on board with the journey of AI in Education?

When COVID struck in 2020, all lessons had to be moved online. The educators in the institution had to acquire digital skills to deliver lessons effectively, such as creating interactive video lectures, using digital tools to engage students during online tutorials, and so on. The pandemic had disrupted the education sector, but so too had many other sectors. The educators understood the need to adapt to new practices, given this was a necessity due to the circumstances. As mentioned earlier, the institution had started on digital learning way before the pandemic. Hence, the adjustment to the new norms was not too steep for the institution, with some support and encouragement given to the educators. Looking back, the pandemic could have been a blessing in disguise, as it has helped to accelerate digital learning in the institution and enabled educators to be more responsive in their teaching based on insights derived from data.

Just as the effects of the pandemic were ebbing and things were getting back to normal, the education sector faced another disruption with the emergence of generative AI technology. There was genuine concern over how ChatGPT could help students complete their assignments without being cognitively engaged much. Based on the experiences gained from the previous disruptions, the belief was that it was only a matter of time before the institution figured out how to overcome the impact, in particular the threats posed by generative AI to assessments. Moreover, AI is an evolving space, and therefore, there should be no surprise with even more disruptions coming in the near future, regardless of the forms and shapes they might take. No matter what happens, just keep in mind that no technology can replace the human in education. Therefore, one of the areas that the institution had embarked on was to shift the mindset of the educators towards AI. Of course, shifting mindset was easier said than done. However, when one clearly understands the roles that humans and AI play in education, then it might not be as complex as it seems. Perhaps, it could be understood from the following perspectives:

2.7.1 AI to Augment Human Capabilities, Not Replace

Much has been heard and read about how AI could replace the jobs performed by humans. While there is value in harnessing AI for automating the mundane and repetitive tasks for efficiency gain, the use of AI in education should remain largely as an augmentation of the work performed by educators. For instance, ChatGPT could assist educators in drafting lesson plans with suggested activities for student engagement. However, human oversight would still be required to validate and enhance the AI-generated output since ChatGPT lacks the contextual understanding. Would ChatGPT understand the profile of the students in the class better than the educators?

2.7.2 Synergy, Not Supremacy

This is closely related to the previous point. Referencing the earlier example, is ChatGPT viewed as a versatile partner in the work of the educators or as a threat, as some parts of the work could potentially be taken over by the AI?

Demirdag (2023) once remarked that if machines are seen as superior to humans, then AI is placed on a pedestal, and if humans are seen as incapable, fragile beings, the AI is again being placed on a pedestal, but this time with the power of an authority. Going back to the example of the Speaker Coach that was brought up earlier in this chapter, the educators appreciated the value of leveraging AI to augment their work of giving feedback to students to improve their oral presentation delivery. Even as face-to-face lessons have resumed after the pandemic, this AI-enabled tool continues to be used by the educators, as they can now focus on the insights drawn from the AI feedback to provide personalised support for students based on the gaps identified. Likewise, they can curate materials and tweak the lesson delivery to address the gaps commonly faced by students in the class. Beyond the AI, the significant impact of the educators' support and encouragement in helping students become more confident and effective in their oral presentations must not be overlooked. Thus, it is important to find the synergistic connection between human and AI, and not about one being superior to the other. And this nicely leads to the next point.

2.7.3 Evolving Role of Educators in the Age of AI

In recognising the synergy between human and AI, it is important to be cognisant of how the role of educators would evolve in this AI era. As described in the earlier example on the Speaker Coach, the educators recognised how their role has evolved from that of a lecturer to one of a facilitator. It is no longer about creating content but curating it for personalised learning and support. With the AI alleviating some of the educators' workload from the mundane and repetitive tasks, this should free up time and space for them to focus on problem-solving, critical thinking, and the creative aspects of their work. All these require human judgment. Finally, human empathy is one thing that AI can never replace, and this leads to the final point.

2.7.4 The Human Touch That AI Can Never Replace in Education

The ability to empathise and connect with the students is fundamentally human. While one might not have remembered everything learnt in school, surely one would have remembered the teachers who have made an impact and shaped the person they are today. The author recalled how two teachers in his secondary school days made a deep impact on him. One was his physics teacher, while another taught him additional mathematics during his upper secondary days. They were very patient and able to make difficult concepts crystal clear in a grounded manner. Bear in mind, there were no educational technology tools for engagement during those days. All they had were chalk and a duster.

When the author started his professional journey as an educator in the institution, he had this guiding principle close to his heart: to always put himself in the shoes of the students, whether it was preparing the learning materials or delivering a lesson, just like the two teachers who had made a difference in him. He realised that he was not so good at delivering lessons using PowerPoint slides, so he started to make handwritten notes because, as he started writing, he reflected on how his students might be able to understand and draw connections from the content covered better. He was most comfortable when he stepped into the class with just the transparency and markers on the overhead projector (yes, that was the era!) and later on with recycled papers and markers on the visualiser when the overhead projector was phased out. He could relate to how students might struggle to understand, and the scribbling together with his explanation could help them to learn better. Guess what? His students told him that they loved his handwritten notes as though these were the notes that they would have made for their exam revision.

The author shared this experience to remind us that we are in the business that thrives on human connections, empathy, communication, and being able to adapt to the needs of individual students. It was not just about the use of educational technology tools. Having said that, he opined that educational technology has its place and value in the modern era of education and will continue to play an important role in supporting student learning.

2.8 Tackling Assessment Challenges in the AI Era

Another area that the institution had prioritised was supporting the educators in overcoming the challenges faced in assessments, given the prevalence of generative AI tools. In particular, the use of open-ended assessments, such as take-home assignments in some of the courses, experienced varying degrees of vulnerabilities where students could potentially use generative AI tools to complete their assignment work. This also raised concerns about plagiarism and threats to academic integrity. All the while, educators have been using anti-plagiarism software to detect if students have plagiarised their work. However, detecting if students have plagiarised their work by using AI tools works differently compared to traditional anti-plagiarism tools.

A few of the educators who felt the impact of generative AI on their assessments took on the challenge to research and explore the capabilities of several AI detection software available in the market, with the hope of finding a perfect solution. However, the attempt proved futile, as the team came to the conclusion that AI detection was probably not effective. Despite that, the effort had not gone to waste, as the exploration led to the realisation that it was perhaps more important to address the human factor by educating students on the responsible and ethical use of AI, and educators on the mindset shift to not solely rely on the use of the detection software to identify students who had plagiarised using AI tools.

Just as Furze (2024) has articulated, trying to catch students using generative AI creates mistrust and opens up potential ethical issues for equitable assessment. Look for opportunities to move beyond the "cheating" narrative. Moreover, there are other hurdles to overcome. There are also generative AI tools that could not only produce seemingly well-written and compelling text, but now "write like a human" by rewriting AI text into human-like text to help bypass AI detection. It was also observed how some of the students were savvy enough to work around a few generative AI tools to make AI detection even more challenging.

It was with that the team came to the conclusion that the focus should instead be on reviewing the existing assessment design and evaluating how it could be adapted to make assessments AI-resilient. Hence, the team came up with the following guidelines to support fellow educators in addressing concerns about plagiarism:

- **Educating the Students:** Place ownership on students to check for AI plagiarism. Be honest about and declare the use of generative AI in assignments.
- **Educating the Educators:** Trust the professional discretion. Check reports from the detection software and other tools if the use of generative AI is suspected. Check the student's draft. Arrange an interview with the student.
- **Redesigning the Assessments:** Where possible, include draft submission as part of the assessment. Strengthen the rubrics design. Tweak the questions to include informed opinions and personal experiences rather than facts.

Indeed, there is a need to adapt assessment practices amid the generative AI influences. Referencing the point made earlier in the chapter on the human and AI synergy, it is important to encourage students to use AI effectively and let the AI handle the heavy-lifting tasks, while they can focus on developing human-centred skills such as critical thinking and problem-solving. More about rethinking and redesigning assessments in the AI era will be covered in Chapter 8.

2.9 Piloting and Scaling the Use of AI in Education

Thus far, the fundamental principles and strategies that have guided the institution in driving digital transformation for teaching and learning were covered. In a nutshell, the institution leverages on technology to enhance teaching and learning, that is, technology plays an enabling role while pedagogy is always at the forefront of any initiatives. The institution takes on an evidence-based approach to teaching. By digitalising teaching and learning, data is collected, and the insights from the data enable educators to provide timely learning interventions for students. For any new digitalisation initiatives, the institution adopts an agile approach towards implementation by starting with a small-scale pilot before making decisions based on user findings to decide the extent of scaling so that more students can benefit from those initiatives. At the end of the day, the institution believes that digitalisation is about delivering value to the users. The use of digital tools should enhance student learning and engagement, rather than for the reason of novelty. Hence, the identification of the tools and solutions still falls back based on the pedagogical needs of the academic schools.

The institution has also embarked on the journey of AI in education just before the outset of the COVID pandemic. Based on the experience gained in the journey, the institution learnt that overcoming mindset shift was key to making progress in implementing AI in education. The appearance of ChatGPT and the advancement of generative AI technology have certainly challenged the norms that have been entrenched in the higher education sector for a long time. It is fair to say that generative AI has obliged many stakeholders in the education ecosystem to react. While some institutions of higher learning have started writing policies on the use of generative AI, the institution recognised that AI technology is evolving rapidly. While the institution continues to keep a close watch on the development of AI technology, it has responded by providing the guiding principle of encouraging the effective and ethical use of generative AI for teaching and learning. With this posture, the institution encouraged educators to experiment and tinker with AI and decide how it could be used effectively in their respective disciplines. The next section will provide a detailed account of how various AI initiatives were piloted and scaled to support the pedagogical needs of the academic schools.

2.9.1 Chatbots: A Practical First Step in AI Integration

2.9.1.1 Motivation

The integration of chatbots into the online learning environment stemmed from a need to provide timely and consistent student support. During the COVID-19 pandemic, students experienced social isolation and a lack of engagement in home-based learning. (Wai-Cook, 2020). As online learning continued beyond the pandemic, tutors faced an increasing workload responding to repetitive student queries, many of which could be addressed by an automated system.

Chatbots are conversational agents for supporting questions asked by users instantaneously (Okonkwo & Ade-Ibijola, 2021). In this 4th Industrial Revolution (4IR) era, educators are increasingly using chatbots to improve student interaction and engagement, as teaching is now distributed through online platforms where communication and interactive learning activities are becoming easier. Chatbots provide instant course contents to students, such as FAQs and short responses, and have the capability to personalise certain aspects of learning (Cunningham-Nelson et al., 2019). Not only can they improve learner support and engagement, but they can also reduce tutors' repetitive administrative chores for better channelling of time to areas like curriculum or assessment design.

Earlier research studies have made limited coverage on how students use chatbots for collaborative learning and describe how chatbots can be beneficial for students' social learning. In the early years of chatbot emergence, Bii (2013) suggested integrating chatbot technology into existing teaching and learning environments to promote collaborative learning from a social constructivist perspective. The institution started its exploration for a chatbot with a pedagogical focus, such as collaborative learning. There were several vendors who were eager to share their chatbot solutions for education. However, most of them turned out to be generic solutions except for QBot. QBot was a Q&A chatbot built by an Australia-based EdTech company, and it could involve human agents in the questioning-answering loop, potentially promoting a collaborative learning experience. The project team who worked on this initiative liked how QBot was designed to involve peers by tagging them randomly in a virtual classroom chat group to answer a question whenever the knowledge base (KB) did not have the answer. The classroom conversation is monitored by the tutor who can help or intervene when he or she deems it necessary.

There were two use cases with needs that a chatbot seemed to be able to serve well when the project team was identifying pilot users:

2.9.1.2 Use Case #1: Supporting Students With Just-in-Time Assistance For APA-Style Referencing

In persuasive communications, a core subject read by all students in the institution, they are expected to prepare their reports using APA-style referencing, and this assignment is their first using formal referencing. Over the years, the subject leader has received emails from students for help with different referencing needs. She felt that the torrents of questions can be answered more efficiently and timely using a chatbot. She could see how repetitive those questions were and felt that her time could be ploughed into areas that are more meaningful. The idea of how students can help one another to build a shared understanding of the APA-style elements with a social tagging feature appealed to her, as this is something that replying to her students by email would not achieve.

2.9.1.3 Use Case #2: Developing Students' Critical Thinking in a Flipped Learning Environment

Marketing fundamentals is a core subject read by students in all business diploma courses. To engage a large cohort of students to think critically, the subject team designed flipped learning lessons that encouraged students to pose questions in the virtual classroom of Teams after watching the online videos. This would promote a culture of asking questions and greater involvement of students in taking part in answering questions that the chatbot was not capable of answering.

The chatbot aimed to serve three primary objectives for both use cases:

- **Provide instant student support** by answering content-related and administrative queries 24/7.
- **Enhance student engagement** in an online environment through collaborative activities.
- **Improve staff productivity** by reducing the repetitive workload of responding to frequently asked questions.

2.9.1.4 Implementation and Findings

To test the chatbot's effectiveness, a mixed-method pilot study was conducted with the two subjects mentioned. All students in the pilot study were enrolled on their various tutorial classes in Teams. The chatbot was embedded within Microsoft Teams, where students could ask questions, and responses were generated based on a KB. If the chatbot could not provide an answer, it tagged up to three peers for assistance before the tutor intervenes. The subject leaders of the two piloted subjects designed activities based on the subject content to get students acquainted with the chatbot system in Teams, as well as role-modelled the use of the bot. During a classroom lesson, they demonstrated how QBot works in the Teams virtual classroom by asking it a few questions followed by encouraging students to join in.

For persuasive communications, 130 Year 1 students from three diploma courses were involved in the pilot study. To start them off learning about APA-style referencing, she crafted an introductory task to nudge students to ask questions regarding different parts of a paper that uses the APA style of referencing. She knew that not all the questions would have answers; hence, some students were tagged in Teams to suggest answers, and some of them did.

For marketing fundamentals, all 597 Year 2 students from four business diploma courses were involved in the pilot study. The subject leader designed two activities: (1) probing questions were included in summary notes served to nudge students to think about the topic and to chat with QBot to deepen their understanding. (2) Tutors encouraged students to use QBot to help them with learning tasks planned for online tutorials. Whenever tutors were approached with questions that will help students deepen their learning, they will invite students to post them to QBot so that these questions were visible to the other students.

Over four months, 395 student queries were recorded in Microsoft Teams for marketing fundamentals:

- 45% were answered by the chatbot,
- 46% were resolved by peers and tutors, and
- 9% were left unanswered due to irrelevance.

As the chatbot accumulated more interactions, its KB expanded, improving its ability to respond effectively.

Survey responses indicated that 90% of students found the chatbot useful, appreciating the immediacy of responses. Moreover, 89% of students were willing to respond to peers' queries, fostering a collaborative learning environment. A notable 68% of students reported improved understanding by reviewing chatbot-facilitated discussions (Cheung et al., 2024).

The tutors who piloted initially found the chatbot time-intensive due to the need to build and refine the KB. However, in the long run, they recognised its potential to reduce the burden of answering repetitive queries and instead focus on higher-value teaching activities.

2.9.1.5 Procurement Experience

- **Pedagogy Before Technology**

  In both use cases, the tutors considered pedagogy before technology. Their intention was to engage their students using a critical thinking approach by encouraging them to ask questions based on subject content. They hoped to see collaborative learning made possible even on digital platforms, knowing that home-based learning during the pandemic had robbed students of such opportunities in the classroom. A pilot user described her students' needs at one of the exploratory discussions:

  > My interest to explore QBot stems from a commitment to foster student engagement, collaborative and self-directed learning, particularly in an ever-evolving digital landscape. When we pivoted to an online learning environment during COVID-19, it highlighted challenges for educators in maintaining student participation and ensuring timely feedback for learners. So QBot which is integrated within Microsoft Teams, emerged as a potentially effective solution by providing students with immediate feedback, facilitating peer-to-peer knowledge sharing and encouraging active learning through social tagging.

- **Delivering Value to the Users**

  Gathering user requirements was an important part of the procurement and would not be complete without consulting early adopters who had some experience tinkering with early-day chatbots. Discussions were mostly informal chats and often a two-way conversation to understand their needs and prior experience using chatbots while informing them what the chatbot technology is currently capable of. On hindsight, having those conversations helped manage the pilot users' expectations, and they knew what they had to do in terms of student support and learning intervention during the implementation. An ideal chatbot to them should have a real-time adaptive KB that was easy to update as question-answer data builds up over the weeks. To encourage peer learning and co-construction of knowledge, a social tagging feature was essential to rope in classmates to participate.

  A chatbot for teaching should have dashboards that support tutors in making observations about student learning and equip them with insights to design interventions for achieving better learning outcomes. Dashboard analytics were put up as one of the chatbot critical requirement specifications, for example, the frequency of questions asked by students on a particular concept, the success rate of the chatbot replying to students with the correct answers, and the frequency of peers and tutors replying to the questions. Having these user metrics support our understanding of student satisfaction in conjunction with the survey instrument.

  In a reflection shared by the subject leader of marketing fundamentals, it was noted:

  > By nudging students to engage with QBot across various learning activities, we have observed enhanced knowledge co-construction and a stronger culture of collaborative problem-solving. The real-time learning analytics also enabled us to respond more effectively to student needs, reinforcing a more adaptive and student-centred learning experience. While some students remained hesitant about peer interactions in QBot, the majority indicated that it has been effective in shaping a more engaged and resilient learning community.

  Procuring a digital solution into an institution has several considerations. For example, the institution has a cloud-first policy that supports cloud-based services such as Software-as-a-Service (SaaS) as the digital solution. There are benefits to favouring SaaS, such as flexibility in scaling up or down as needed and being cost efficient when the institution moves away from expenditures related to hardware purchase, operation, and maintenance. To comply with this policy, it was a priority to look at SaaS solutions to support our pedagogical needs.

One of our key concerns was the alignment of the chatbot system with one of the key instructional systems, namely the Microsoft Teams app. The chatbot needs to work seamlessly when integrated with the virtual classrooms in Teams. Failing to do so will affect user experience, hence leading to poor usage and subsequent adoption by other subject teams. To reflect how pivotal the integration of the chatbot with MS Teams is, this was highlighted as one of the critical criteria to be assessed in vendors' solutions. Other key aspects of the evaluation criteria included a collaborative feature like social tagging, dashboard analytics, and compliance with government policies related to Info-Communication Technology and Smart Systems.

The scale-up phase of this project was a classic example of learning from others who had walked the journey. While conducting a procurement exercise to scale up the chatbot solution, another institution had just piloted a chatbot system called Noodle Factory, and the institution tapped into their pilot experience and use cases to better assess the chatbot capabilities.

- **Taking an Agile Approach**

  The procured bot solution was not perfect. It met the institution's key requirements, but pilot users felt that there could be additional features that would add value for teaching and learning, such as a built-in feature for generating discussion within the chat environment. The project team gave feedback to the vendor based on the experience of the pilot users and worked out a reasonable timeline for them to build the new feature. Another "upgrade" on the users' wish list was to provide more insights on student questions in the dashboard. In response, the vendor clustered similar questions to help tutors understand the learning gaps, and the frequency of the concept or topic being asked was provided to inform on the learning needs.

2.9.1.6 Lessons Learned and Moving Forward

The chatbot proved to be a scalable and sustainable support tool, but its effectiveness was contingent on accurate KB development and ongoing refinements. Some students still preferred direct tutor interactions, highlighting the need for a hybrid approach that blends automation with human in the loop. This finding did not come as a surprise, as it is known that education is all about human connections.

Students were hesitant to post answers or make suggestions when they were tagged to help answer questions. From the study findings, it was understood that they were mainly worried about providing incorrect answers; some were too shy as they were aware that their replies were visible to everyone in the class. This is often observed in classrooms too and partly attributed to Asian culture.

What about students who did not post any questions or answers? Were they learning? Most students read the posts, and the findings revealed that this helped them to learn even when they were not contributing. This is further supported by the Lurker Theory, which refers to the phenomenon where a significant proportion of participants in online communities or digital learning environments engage passively—they observed discussions, read content, and consume resources without actively contributing, but they may still learn and benefit from the community (Sun et al., 2014).

Although data and Power BI dashboards were provided, some piloting tutors struggled to draw meaningful insights from the analytics. This coincided with the institution's ongoing journey into learning analytics, which began in 2020 as part of building data competency among staff. The chatbot project, therefore, provided lecturers with a valuable opportunity to strengthen their ability to leverage data for responsive teaching.

Looking back, the initiative began against a backdrop of widespread scepticism towards chatbots during the COVID era. Had the team not started experimenting with a chatbot, supported by a group of tutors who were willing to dedicate time beyond their teaching duties to enhance the student experience, they would have missed out on valuable early lessons in chatbot implementation.

Moving forward, efforts should focus on designing opportunities for students to exercise their questioning skills. Designing collaborative activities that involve the chatbot to facilitate the discussion based on a topic or a piece of learning material in the chat group is more challenging but not impossible.

At the time of scaling up chatbot usage, generative AI was maturing, and with generative AI, the initial construction of the KB and improvement of chatbot usability were painlessly enhanced through natural language processing (NLP) capabilities. Although tutors still need to check the question-answer pairs that were generated, they were relieved that so much time was saved compared to manual efforts to achieve the same. This project demonstrated that chatbots can transform digital learning by facilitating knowledge sharing and engagement while lightening tutors' workload.

2.9.2 Nudges in Education—Is IA (Rule-Based Automation) Still Relevant Now That There Is AI?

Shaping student behaviour has long been a key goal of education. The educators in the institution have continually adapted to changing classroom environments—from teaching in virtual classrooms on Microsoft Teams to supporting students returning post-COVID. During COVID, getting students to submit assignments online posed a challenge, and tutors posted announcements in both Microsoft Teams and the learning management system (LMS) to remind students. The transition from online lessons to flipped learning required students to complete their learning tasks before attending the face-to-face class so that their learning can be reinforced through in-class activities. A small team comprising staff from the Learning Academy and Centre for Applied Behavioural Sciences came together to explore leveraging behavioural science to shape student behaviour, particularly in improving online task completion and assignment submission. Behavioural science, through mechanisms such as nudging and positive reinforcement, can be potentially powerful tools to encourage desirable learner habits. Nudges are subtle interventions that steer people towards desired behaviours while not taking away the freedom of choice (Thaler & Sunstein, 2008). In educational contexts, nudges can help students overcome procrastination, improve time management, and increase task engagement. Damgaard and Nielsen (2018) analysed over 120 studies in a comprehensive review and found that:

- Nudges tend to be most effective on students facing the largest behavioural barriers, such as disengaged learners.
- Simple interventions, such as email reminders or progress feedback that are timely and personalised, can significantly improve student participation.

Positive reinforcement has its roots in behavioural psychology, and it involves recognising and rewarding desired behaviours to encourage habituation. Teachers use praise, leaderboards, and rewards to motivate students to participate and make contributions in classrooms.

Weijers et al. (2020) proposed that nudges in education should go beyond short-term compliance if the intention is to foster long-lasting behavioural change. For nudges to be truly effective, they should be aligned with learners' intrinsic motivation and support cognitive engagement, such as reflecting on past behaviours and setting future goals. This aligns closely with Daniel Kahneman's (2011) dual-process theory in thinking, fast and slow, where:

- System 1 thinking is fast, automatic, and intuitive, often triggered by environmental cues or habits. For example, clicking on a video link in an email reminder to learn about the topic is intuitive and made convenient for the learner.
- System 2 thinking is slow, deliberate, and effortful. For example, this is applied in problem-solving, analysing options, or making decisions to override initial impulses. Weijers et al. suggest that nudges should be designed to eventually hand over control to the learner, encouraging self-regulation.

2.9.2.1 Project Genesis

This project started with the discussion of the MINDSPACE framework for behavioural change. Subsequently, there were engagements with an EdTech vendor that specialises in the use of persona-based nudges infused with elements of behavioural science that drive users to act. Based on the insights shared by the vendor, the project team decided to carry out a proof-of-concept using an automation tool found in Brightspace LMS. Intelligent agent (IA) is an automation tool embedded in the LMS which can help tutors to nudge students by sending them reminders and encouragement messages.

2.9.2.2 Use Case #1 in the School of Applied Science: Students' Completion of Flipped Learning Activities

The transition to a flipped learning model post-pandemic introduced a new challenge: many students failed to watch lecture videos or complete preparatory activities before face-to-face sessions. This lack of preparation has led the tutors to invest more time than planned to help students who were not prepared to keep up with in-class activities.

2.9.2.3 Use Case #2 in the School of Humanities and Social Sciences: Timely Submission of Assignments

In coursework-based subjects, students often have high-stakes assignments, making timely submission essential to avoid penalties. However, tutors have observed a troubling pattern of students submitting these critical assignments late or not at all. This raises concerns about their self-regulation skills, particularly time management, which is crucial in a coursework-based subject. Late or missed submissions can significantly affect students' grades, heighten stress levels, and impact their motivation. To address both problems, tutors had to closely monitor the completion of tasks and assignments. Then, they followed up with reminder emails to students, many of which were left unread. This process is time-consuming and diverts tutors' attention from more meaningful tasks. Hence, both student success and teaching efficiency are affected.

The primary objectives of the IA-nudge solution were to:

- encourage timely completion of learning activities or submission of assignments by sending automated reminders to students before due dates.
- promote self-regulated learning by developing students' time management skills.
- increase student engagement in flipped classroom activities such as discussing tutorial questions.

2.9.2.4 Pedagogy Before Technology

The project team approached the School of Applied Science (ASC) and the School of Humanities and Social Sciences (HSS) to assess the suitability of their use cases for the pilots. The mapping of their pedagogical needs to the solution was discussed over a few sessions. In each discussion, it was clear that student outcomes and pedagogical practices were the top priorities, and the methodology was designed accordingly to achieve those goals. Technology was the flexible piece of the puzzle, and the team remained open to exploring tools that could better serve the pedagogical objectives.

2.9.2.5 Taking an Agile Approach Towards Designing the Solution

Both teams in the earlier use cases leveraged a built-in feature in Brightspace LMS called IAs to send automated reminders to students based on conditions such as student inactivity or non-submission of assignments. With inputs from ASC and HSS, the team fine-tuned the methodology over a few semesters of iterations. The reminder messages were designed to incorporate elements of behavioural science, termed "nudges". More about the principles of behavioural sciences and how they can be applied to enhance the use of AI in education will be covered in Chapter 7.

Some of the principles that were applied to the reminder message are as follows:

- **Crafting a clear message,** for example, "We've noticed you have not watched the videos on Topic 5."
- **Call-to-action**: making the content or task more accessible for students to act, for example, "With a quick click, you can access the videos right from here."
- **Providing support,** for example, "If you have questions regarding the tasks, be sure to reach out to me."
- **Providing resources on time management**. Encouraging students to explore reading up on managing time by rousing their curiosity to develop themselves in self-discipline, for example, "Suspect you procrastinate because you're lazy? Well, it's not your laziness . . . read on."

To encourage students who were timely in completing the tasks or submissions, encouragement messages were included in the solution to help them sustain such positive learner behaviour.

The methodology was modified in the second iteration to improve the reach to students. This enhancement stemmed from the survey findings that three out of four students preferred to receive reminders via MS Teams compared to email. Many students revealed that they "rarely check emails". Brightspace IA was designed to send messages to email inboxes; hence, a workaround was required to forward the nudges to the Teams app as notifications. The team learned to use Power Automate workflows to enable the forwarding of emails to Teams as chat messages. In this learning journey, they also reached out to colleagues who are experienced users of Power

Automate. Based on students' feedback, the nudge frequency was reduced to once instead of twice from the second iteration onwards.

Besides some of the limitations of the IA tool described earlier, the experiences from some tutors were not ideal. One of the obstacles faced was getting the buy-in from all subject tutors. There was a tutor who objected to receiving "extra" messages arising from the student reminders, as all tutors were copied (cc-ed). However, this feedback pushed the project team to modify the automated workflow to avoid cluttering the tutors' mailboxes, affecting their work productivity.

In the third iteration, the team enhanced personalisation by incorporating animated images (GIFs) into chat messages, catering to students' preference for engaging and visually appealing content. The light-hearted nature of these GIFs made the nudges more attention-grabbing and encouraging, effectively leveraging behavioural science principles to increase student receptivity and motivation to act. Taking an Agile approach, the focus was on user experience, and, based on that, four iterations of the methodology were made before scaling up.

To scale up, the propagation of the methodology to more tutors will be a lot more challenging as adoption required a series of steps and technological know-how in Power Automate. The team does not have sufficient manpower to support a campus-wide implementation for all academic staff. More efforts had to be made to simplify the Power Automate workflow specifically. The team consulted colleagues in the IT Services (ITS) department to get ideas and tips to do so. In the process, the team realised their solution was not able to be mass-propagated in the Power Automate environment. Coincidentally, the co-pilot was introduced at a time when the team was about to give up. The colleagues from ITS suggested using a generative AI prompt to generate the workflow for staff, as it is much less technical. The idea is that the prompt will work like a fairy spell, weaving the workflow for tutors effortlessly. As generative AI outputs are often random, the team spent time on engineering and testing the prompts to achieve one that gave consistent output. The efforts taken to simplify for adoption were necessary for a scalable and sustainable solution.

2.9.2.6 Implementation and Findings

The subject basic microbiology was taken by close to 500 freshmen from ASC, and the IA intervention was piloted over three tutorial sessions. The IA tool sent two levels of reminders:

- **First reminder (two days before class):** sent to students who had not watched the lecture video.
- **Second reminder (one day before class):** sent to students who still had not engaged with the content.

Additionally, encouragement emails were sent to students who completed the tasks early, reinforcing positive behaviour. The emails included direct links to lecture videos, tutorial worksheets, and time-management resources to lower barriers to action.

The LMS analytics revealed a steady decline in the number of students who needed reminders, suggesting an improvement in time-management behaviours (Cheung et al., 2024; Lee et al., 2023):

- The percentage of students receiving IA reminders dropped from 48% to 42% over three tutorial sessions.
- Video analytics showed a spike in views corresponding to the weeks with IA intervention, confirming its effectiveness in prompting students to engage with course materials before face-to-face tutorials.
- 95% of students logged in to watch the videos, with an average 85% video completion rate.

2.9.2.7 Lessons Learned and Moving Forward

The IA nudging strategy proved effective in shifting student behaviour, and the implementation revealed key insights which were adopted in the following semester:

- **The timing of nudges is crucial**—reminders sent too early or too late might not be as effective.
- **Two reminders were too many**—one reminder is enough!
- **Personalised, supportive messaging** works better than generic reminders.
- **Students preferred receiving Teams notifications** on their mobile phones, as they do not check emails regularly.

Survey and focus group discussions further validated the intervention's effectiveness:

- Students **appreciated the just-in-time reminders**, particularly those who struggled with **time management.**
- The **personalised and encouraging tone** of the emails made a difference, as many students felt supported rather than pressured.
- **One tutor remarked,**

  > This tool enabled us to send targeted nudge messages that encouraged students to view the lectures and enhance their self-regulation skills. We continuously optimised this strategy to maximise its effectiveness and ease of use, aiming to enrich both the teaching and learning experience.

- For the HSS pilot, the set of nudges used proved effective, as the rates of late and non-submissions were very low. The assignment non-submission rate was low: 0.63% (17 out of 2,679 students) for the subject effective communication, and 0.32% (4 out of 1,233 students) for another subject, professional communication.
- Furthermore, students shared that when they received the personalised messages sent from the subject leader, it increased their sense of urgency to submit their work.

Beyond its positive impact on students, this automated solution also provides substantial benefits to tutors. Since the nudges are sent automatically, tutors no longer need to monitor and remind students manually, freeing up valuable time. For example, in just one semester of teaching effective communication, over 9,000 personalised nudges were delivered to more than 2,600 students, a scale that would be impossible to achieve through manual efforts. The resulting time savings for educators are both significant and invaluable.

So, in the AI era, does automation still have a place in education technology? Though IA has no AI powers, it alone can be a relevant tool by giving it a new life through redesigning the messages and the way the messages reach students more effectively, potentially leading to positive behavioural changes. The team has brought together a blend of technology and behavioural science to design and develop an innovative solution to help students develop self-regulation. Institutions of higher learning can support self-regulated learning and improve student preparedness in flipped classrooms, ultimately enhancing learning effectiveness and student success.

Nilson (2013), in her book *Creating Self-Regulated Learners*, mentioned:

> Study skills really aren't the point. Learning is about one's relationship with oneself and one's ability to exert the effort, self-control, and critical self-assessment necessary to achieve the best possible results, and about overcoming risk aversion, failure, distractions, and sheer laziness in pursuit of real achievement. This is self-regulated learning.
>
> *(p. xxvii)*

2.9.3 Personalised Learning: The Key to Unlock Subject Mastery?

2.9.3.1 Motivation

When it comes to practice-intensive subjects, traditional methods of instruction and feedback were often time-consuming and inefficient, leading to learning gaps, disengagement, and low participation in voluntary practice activities.

The implementation of the KiteSense adaptive learning platform was driven by the teaching team's desire to provide personalised support in practice-intensive subjects and support concept mastery in subjects with "killer topics" (topics with high casualties, usually due to difficult concepts that are not straightforward).

2.9.3.2 Use Case #1: To Support Personalised Learning for Large Cohort of Students in Practice-Intensive Subjects

The teaching team of business accountancy (BA) in the institution faced the challenge of guiding a cohort of 500 Year 1 business students with diverse learning needs and proficiency levels. The teaching team envisioned how an adaptive learning platform with AI capabilities can meet students' diverse learning needs. As the subject leader puts it:

> BA students come in with little to no experience in accounting. Accounting concepts can be daunting and sometimes confusing, and it is only through constant and consistent practice that mastery of the subject and its concepts can be achieved. The use of KiteSense to generate practice questions for the first two topics of the subject was borne out of a practical thought process as students, in preparation for their tests, had voiced out the need for more similar questions to work on. It was envisioned that with the help of the AI generated feedback in KiteSense, students would be able to plot their own learning journeys and set their pace to achieve mastery.

2.9.3.3 Use Case #2: To Bridge Learning Gaps in Students Struggling With Difficult Concepts

Diploma students of the engineering disciplines find certain concepts in subjects like thermodynamics and fluid mechanics hard to grasp. From past years' performances, students scored badly when it comes to these topics and this is also the main reason for the higher failure rates seen when compared to other subjects the same students studied. In the subject leader's own words:

> Fluid Mechanics is often seen as challenging because it requires both a strong grasp of concepts and proficiency in mathematics. To excel, students need structured practice that builds from basic to advanced levels, like the classical approach in math education. By integrating KiteSense, I aimed to provide an adaptive learning experience that meets students at their individual levels, encouraging a more engaged, personalised approach to mastering Fluid Mechanics.

The primary objectives of this pilot project were to:

- Enhance personalised learning experiences by using AI-driven recommendations for practice questions of varying difficulty levels.
- Provide real-time, automated feedback to address individual learning gaps and foster self-regulated learning.
- Investigate student perceptions of AI-generated feedback and its impact on their learning engagement.

2.9.3.4 Implementation and Findings

The study adopted a mixed-method research approach, incorporating both quantitative data (student survey responses, platform analytics) and qualitative insights (focus group discussions). The subject leaders worked with the following features afforded by the KiteSense adaptive learning system:

- **AI-driven question pool expansion:** To create sufficient practice questions with variations, generative AI was used to generate two to three times the number of existing questions the subjects had. Given the lack of accuracy in the AI output, subject leaders curated the question-answer-feedback sets comprising at least 10% of the new question bank.
- **AI-driven adaptive questioning:** Students received personalised practice questions tailored to their proficiency levels. At the start of the session, students had to complete a diagnostic test to measure their proficiency level for a particular topic or concept.
- **Automated AI feedback:** AI provided instant feedback, helping students correct mistakes and refine understanding. For instance, when a student gets an MCQ answer wrong, the AI feedback will attempt to explain why the selected option is incorrect, though it may not always be able to explain clearly. Tutors had to remind students to be critical of the AI feedback as it will not always be correct, and triangulating the facts and theories with their subject materials is recommended whenever they are in doubt.
- **Tracking**: Platform analytics help tutors to monitor student participation rates and performance improvements. By studying the performance of students for individual questions, tutors can reassess the difficulty of the questions as well as spot any errors in the answers that may have slipped during the curation stage.

Findings from student surveys and focus groups provided several key insights:

- Students appreciated the interactive and intuitive interface, finding it easier to use compared with the typical LMS.
- The majority of students agreed that KiteSense provided adequate and relevant practice questions.
- AI-generated feedback was seen as effective for learning, particularly for clarifying mistakes and reinforcing understanding.
- AI feedback was considered useful, particularly step-by-step worked solutions, though most students were unaware that the feedback was AI-generated despite efforts made to inform them.

The on-screen display of the disclaimer for AI inaccuracy was not obvious either.

- The difficulty level of practice questions was generally well balanced, though students reported some repetition issues. One student exclaimed that she had two questions that were the same appearing one after the other. Her case was more of an exception.
- While participation rates in voluntary practice activities improved, further motivational strategies were needed to sustain engagement. The intuitive interface and rewards system offered by KiteSense were not enough to keep students wanting to come back for more practices.

2.9.3.5 Lessons Learned and Moving Forward

The KiteSense pilot demonstrated the potential of AI-driven adaptive learning but also highlighted key areas for improvement:

- **Feedback enhancements:** While worked solutions were valued, some students felt the explanations could be more detailed and contextualised.
- **Sustaining motivation:** Participation in voluntary practice tasks requires additional motivational strategies, including gamification and nudges.

Moving forward, personalised learning approach can be refined by:

- **Enhancing feedback quality** with more detailed explanations and contextual hints. Subject leaders could curate larger sets of questions to achieve greater accuracy in the question stem, answers, worked solutions, and feedback.
- **Implementing structured nudges** (e.g. reminders, encouragement emails) like the IA used to enhance self-regulated learning in students.
- **Reducing question redundancy** to maintain engagement.

This study reinforces the importance of human-centred AI design in education, emphasising that AI alone cannot drive engagement—pedagogical strategies must complement the technology.

2.9.4 Final Thoughts on the Institution's Use Cases of AI in Education

Both the chatbot and personalised learning interventions showcase the power of AI-driven digital tools in improving student learning experiences. While the chatbot enhanced peer interactions and knowledge accessibility, the IA tool cultivated self-regulated learning habits. KiteSense enabled personalised learning at scale by using AI to generate practice questions for learners with varied proficiency levels and providing instant feedback to students. As project coordinators facilitating such implementations, the key takeaway is that successful EdTech adoption requires continuous refinement, teachers' buy-in, and student-centred design.

2.10 Sustaining the Journey of AI in Education: Enabling a Culture of Innovative Teaching Practices

The key success factor from the various initiatives in which the institution had piloted and scaled the use of AI in education was a shift in the mindset of the educators who were willing to embrace technology to enhance teaching and improve student learning experiences. The institution recognised that digitalisation in teaching and learning takes time. Therefore, through agile methods of working, it typically started off with a pilot by working with educators who are early adopters of education technology. They are typically the ones who are willing to take risks and explore new and innovative ways to enhance the way they teach. Together with the teaching and learning advocates from the schools, they serve as agents of change to support scaling up when the pilot works in order to roll out to the wider community.

The institution also believes that digitalisation in teaching and learning should not just be a top-down effort but also a bottom-up initiative as the educators are full of energy and filled with creative ideas. Therefore, the institution has created platforms for educators to harness their creativity in digital learning. One such initiatives was a peer-to peer digital mentoring programme that encourages educators to learn new digital tools from their peers to support them in enhancing their teaching and making lessons more engaging. Another was setting aside an innovation fund, which has made it easier for educators to gain access to the tools and resources they need in order to experiment with innovative ways of delivering their courses.

2.11 Sustaining the Journey of AI in Education: Nurturing a Culture of Learning and Sharing of Good Practices

Having provided an account of the various AI-driven initiatives that had been piloted and scaled over the past few years, one of the contributing factors that have enabled the institution to sustain the journey of AI in Education is due to the effort put into cultivating a culture of learning and sharing of good pedagogical and educational technology practices. It is certainly more than just implementing the technology enabled by the infrastructure because the educators are at the heart of sustaining any meaningful teaching and learning initiatives.

Within the institution, there is a community of practice that comprises advocates and practitioners from the academic schools and departments who share common interests in improving teaching and learning. The advocates have been playing a significant role in the community as they not only explore and implement innovative pedagogies and AI-driven educational technology solutions but also inspire and support their peers to adopt the use of educational technology for better student engagement and outcomes. Such sharing and support not only accelerate the diffusion of innovative practices but also minimise duplication of efforts, as educators can build on each other's successes and lessons learned, thereby creating a KB that benefits the entire institution. Through the community of practice, the aim is to foster an environment of trust, support, and continuous learning.

The community of practice takes several forms:

- **Quarterly in-person meet-ups** to learn and share good teaching and learning practices and to discuss common and trending issues in education.
- **Monthly newsletter** to share about pertinent topics on AI in education for the community to tinker with and experiment with AI.
- **Ongoing curated webinars** to showcase initiatives explored by fellow educators to highlight possibilities and challenges of integrating AI into education.

As mentioned earlier, the emergence of generative AI technology and ChatGPT had created some anxieties among the educators initially. Having a strong culture of learning and sharing helped to mitigate those concerns through a supportive community where educators feel empowered rather than threatened by AI. Within the institution, educators are strongly encouraged to openly discuss and seek guidance from peers who have overcome similar challenges. By learning from peers who have tried and succeeded, this has helped to build confidence. On top of that, training and resources provided by the community of practice have helped to level up the competency of educators to ensure that they are able to use AI effectively in the classroom to support their pedagogical practices.

2.12 Conclusion: A Future of Human and AI Collaboration in Education

Although the institution encourages the effective and ethical use of AI for teaching and learning, the journey of embedding AI into education is not without its challenges. Adopting a mindset shift to learn to collaborate with AI for improved learning outcomes was a major challenge. On top of that, educators must adapt their teaching and assessment methods to harness the value of AI while fostering and developing students' skills that are uniquely human. Finally, having a strong culture of learning and sharing through a community of practice ensures a conducive and supportive environment where educators feel empowered to embrace AI technologies. On this note, the teaching and learning advocates from the academic schools play an important role to provide training and resource support to build confidence and capabilities to leverage AI for better student outcomes.

Looking back at the journey that the institution had navigated over the past few years, one could perhaps consider the following questions to gauge how far progress has been made as far as AI in education is concerned:

- Have we **A**cknowledged the existence of generative AI technology?
- Have we **A**ccepted the technology?
- How **A**ware are we of the capabilities and limitations of the technology for teaching and learning?
- How have we **A**pplied the use of the technology to aid teaching and learning?
- What have we **A**ssessed from the outcomes on the use of the technology to inform the way forward?

As Lakhani (2023) aptly articulated, AI won't replace humans, but humans with AI will replace humans without AI. The authors believe that the future of education is one where humans must collaborate effectively with AI, while the skills that are uniquely human should be elevated through the augmentation of AI.

Acknowledgement

The author gratefully acknowledges Dr Loh Gin Hin, Dr Shirley Ong-Tan, Rowena Zheng, Dr Matthew Kong, Goh Miah Kiat, Michael Yap, Kenneth

Goh, M Fadlin Mohamed Saffri, Dr Chao Jang Yuan, Irene Chan, Dr Lee Koon Guan, Guo Ren, Nurzahiah Jumat, Joanna Tan and Caitlin Chee Feng Ping for their valuable insights and contributions to the addition of use cases in this chapter.

References

Beatty, B. J. (2019). Designing a hybrid-flexible course: Creating an effective learning environment for all students. In B. J. Beatty (Ed.), *Hybrid-flexible course design: Implementing student-directed hybrid classes*. EdTech Books. https://edtechbooks.org/hyflex/hyflex_design

Bii, P. (2013). Chatbot technology: A possible means of unlocking student potential to learn how to learn. *Educational Research*, 4(2), 218–221.

Cheung, P., Chan, I., Guo, R., & Woo, B. S. (2024, March). Educational bots: How Chatbots and intelligent agents can improve student experience. In *Proceedings of the 18th International Technology, Education and Development Conference*. https://doi.org/10.21125/inted.2024

Cunningham-Nelson, S., Boles, W., Trouton, L., & Margerison, E. (2019). A review of Chatbots in education: Practical steps forward. In *30th Annual Conference for the Australasian Association for Engineering Education (AAEE 2019): Educators Becoming Agents of Change: Innovate, Integrate, Motivate* (pp. 299–306). Engineers Australia.

Damgaard, M. T., & Nielsen, H. S. (2018). Nudging in education. *Economics of Education Review*, 64, 313–342.

Demirdag, P. S. (2023). What is Generative AI: Caution when working with Gen AI [Video]. *LinkedIn Learning*. https://www.linkedin.com/learning/what-is-generative-ai/caution-when-working-with-gen-ai?resume=false

Furze, L. (2024). Rethinking assessment for generative artificial intelligence. *Citizen Digital Foundation*. https://citizendigitalfoundation.org/wp-content/uploads/2024/08/Rethinking_Assessment_for_Generative_AI_1723797596-1.pdf

Howland, J. L., Jonassen, D., & Marra, R. M. (2011). *Meaningful learning with technology* (4th ed.). Boston, MA: Pearson Education, Inc.

Kahneman, D. (2011). *Thinking, fast and slow*. Farrar, Straus and Giroux.

Karbor, P. (n.d.). *Designing for uncertainty: Two perspectives on Agile design*. Poyan Karbor. Retrieved August 17, 2025, from https://poyankarbor.com/designing-for-uncertainty-two-perspectives-on-agile-design/

Lakhani, K. (2023, August 4). AI won't replace humans—but humans with AI will replace humans without AI. *Harvard Business Review*. https://hbr.org/2023/08/ai-wont-replace-humans-but-humans-with-ai-will-replace-humans-without-ai

Lee, K. G., Guo, R., Cheung, P., & Lau, P. N. (2023, December). A proof-of-concept study on the efficacy of agent-enabled nudge messages on learners' online learning behaviours (Conference presentation). *eLearning Forum 2023*.

Lim, S. S. (2023, December 1). Happy birthday, ChatGPT: The family's grown and we should get to know it better. *The Straits Times*. https://www.straitstimes.com/opinion/happy-birthday-chatgpt-the-family-s-grown-and-we-should-get-to-know-it-better

Loh, G. H., Boey, C. K., Guo, R., & Goh, M. K. (2025). Piloting HyFlex Learning Space (laboratory) at Temasek Polytechnic. *Cyber-Physical Learning Journal*. Singapore: Singapore University of Technology and Design. https://www.sutd.edu.sg/innovation/campusx/cpl-journal/publication/piloting-hyflex-learning-space-at-TP

Nilson, L. B. (2013). *Creating self-regulated learners: Strategies to strengthen students' self-awareness and learning skills*. Stylus Publishing. https://doi.org/10.4324/9781003443803

Okonkwo, C. W., & Ade-Ibijola, A. (2021). Chatbots applications in education: A systematic review. *Computers and Education: Artificial Intelligence*, 2, 100033.

Sehgal, R. (2023, October 5). AI needs data more than data needs AI. *Forbes*. https://www.forbes.com/councils/forbestechcouncil/2023/10/05/ai-needs-data-more-than-data-needs-ai/

Sun, N., Rau, P. P. L., & Ma, L. (2014). Understanding lurkers in online communities: A literature review. *Computers in Human Behavior*, 38, 110–117.

Tan, S., & Loh, G. H. (2023). HyFlex Learning: Starting from where you are: Temasek Polytechnic, Singapore. In B. J. Beatty (Ed.), *Hybrid-Flexible course design*. EdTech Books. https://edtechbooks.org/hyflex/hyflex_starting

Thaler, R. H., & Sunstein, C. R. (2008). *Nudge: Improving decisions about health, wealth, and happiness*. Yale University Press.

Vaz, N. (2021). *Digital business transformation: How established companies sustain competitive advantage from now to next*. John Wiley & Sons, Incorporated.

Wai-Cook, M. S. S. (2020). The reality of home-based learning during COVID-19: Roles of parents, teachers, and school administration in promoting self-directed learning. *Journal of School Administration Research and Development*, 5, 86–92.

Weijers, D., de Koning, B. B., & Paas, F. (2020). Nudging in education: From theory towards guidelines for successful implementation. *European Journal of Psychology of Education*, 36(3), 715–736.

Wen, K. (2023, December 12). Towards responsible use of AI in the classroom. *The Ensemble*. https://theensemble.substack.com/p/towards-a-framework-of-responsible

3

Unleash the Power of Conversational AI Into the Classroom with the ADDIE Model

Zhang Huiyu

3.1 Introduction

Classrooms have shifted toward a blended learning mode in today's educational landscape, combining both in-person and online experiences. Despite this shift, the desire for human connection through conversation remains strong. As highlighted by Deci and Ryan's self-determination theory (1985), constructive student-teacher relationships fulfil psychological needs through relatedness—a sense of connection to others. Students value social interaction and personal connections, finding two-way communication between students and teachers essential in the online component of blended learning settings (Ausburn, 2004; Graham, 2006). Capon-Sieber et al. (2022) found that video chats facilitate relatedness support, while Alonso et al. (2005) noted that the chat function helps build community by supporting social talk.

Learning, at its core, thrives through interactions and discussions—questioning, exchanging ideas, and collaborative thinking, as suggested by Vygotsky's social constructivism (1978). Conversations clarify concepts, deepen understanding, and build relationships, all essential for effective learning. The community of inquiry framework (Garrison et al., 1999) emphasizes that conversation enhances cognitive presence, enabling learners to explore, understand, and refine ideas. Techniques like Socratic questioning guide students in reflecting on their knowledge, identifying gaps, and developing higher-order thinking skills, boosting analytical capacity (Paul & Elder, 2006). Research by Chin and Osborne (2008) reveals that student-generated questions hold significant educational potential, especially in science, underscoring their importance in learning. In virtual or asynchronous settings, however, these valuable conversations can become fragmented if not thoughtfully integrated. This raises the question: how can we carry these meaningful discussions into our blended classrooms? AI maintains the depth and spontaneity of conversational interactions by

DOI: 10.1201/9781003599357-4

enabling on-demand discussions, allowing students to engage in thoughtful, self-paced dialogues while receiving personalized feedback. This approach allows for flexible learning, ensuring that the rich, discussion-based nature of education is not sacrificed in the shift toward digital and blended learning environments.

3.1.1 Defining Chatbots

Chatbots are conversational interfaces enhanced by artificial intelligence (AI), allowing them to engage with users in a way that mimics human interaction (DeeAnn, 2012). These chatbots can communicate via text, much like how we interact in instant messaging apps (Smutny & Schreiberova, 2020). Additionally, advanced chatbots, such as Alexa, Siri, and Google Assistant, can process spoken language and respond audibly (Garcia Brustenga et al., 2018). The aim is to replicate the experience of interacting with a human agent, whether the task is requesting information, making a reservation, or receiving personalized recommendations. With the rise of generative AI (GenAI) chatbots, the capability to generate dynamic, context-aware responses has further elevated user interactions, providing even more personalized and flexible experiences.

For a programme to qualify as a chatbot, several essential elements must be present. As defined by Zhang and Fang (2024), it needs a user interface (UI) and a platform where the chatbot is hosted, such as on websites, mobile apps, or messaging services like WhatsApp, Facebook, or Telegram. The user experience (UX) should also ensure that conversations are natural, intelligent, and coherent. Central to this is conversational AI, which uses machine learning, particularly natural language processing, to understand user intent and deliver appropriate responses. The recent advancements in large language models fuelling the GenAI chatbots take these abilities a step further to create responses that are not pre-programmed but dynamically generated, adapting to the user's context and needs in real time. This allows for richer, more flexible conversations, often indistinguishable from human-like interactions. Additionally, the chatbot's conversational flow determines how the interaction starts, progresses, and concludes, typically structured to guide the user towards a goal. To enhance the overall experience, many chatbots also include a human-agent fallback, transferring conversations to a human when the AI reaches its limitations. Having the human agent is an example of human in the loop (HITL). Having the HITL approach helps ensure accuracy, accountability, and better handling of complex or ambiguous tasks that machines may struggle with alone. Finally, analytics are crucial, enabling chatbots to capture real-time data and logs from interactions, which can be used to track key performance indicators (KPIs) like usage rates, unresolved queries, or misunderstood inputs, ensuring the continuous improvement of the chatbot's effectiveness.

3.1.2 Types of Educational Chatbots

Before GenAI chatbots such as ChatGPT took the educational sector by storm at the end of 2022, raising questions about academic integrity, potential misuse in assessments and yet offering benefits like opportunities for enhancing personalized learning support, educational chatbots had already seeped into classrooms and learning environments. Educational chatbots have been applied across several key functions: teaching and learning, administration, assessment, advising, and research and development (Okonkwo & Ade-Ibijola, 2021). They have also been applied across many domains. Hwang and Chang (2021) identified studies from 1999 to 2020 focusing on areas such as languages, engineering, science, health, social sciences, business, arts, and mathematics. In this chapter, these roles of AI chatbot are classified into the categories "smart classmate", "teaching assistant", "learning companion", and "coach or advisor".

Chatbots are employed as smart classmates or practice buddies for skills such as language proficiency and counseling, that guide students through self-regulated learning (SRL) and problem-solving (Huang et al., 2019; Mckie & Narayan, 2019). These chatbots prompt students with questions that encourage planning, reflection, and critical thinking. For example, CLIVE, an AI chatbot, supports beginner learners in foreign languages by enabling students to converse in English and respond in another language like Greek (Zakos & Capper, 2008). Another AI chatbot had been used to help learners use MS Planner features for planning and self-monitoring an assignment (Glick et al., 2024). Habitica gamifies task management to provide a low-pressure environment to help students develop productive study habits with a game-like experience (de Sales & Antunes, 2021). Replika, deemed the "AI friend", can offer personalized advice based on user's preferences, supporting them to navigate both academic and personal challenges (Pentina et al., 2023).

Most commonly, chatbots are deployed as teaching assistants. They administer quizzes (Durall & Kapros, 2020), evaluate student performance, and provide feedback, making them invaluable in both in-person and online education. These tools can handle many students, providing timely feedback and supporting learning continuity, especially during disruptions such as the COVID-19 pandemic (Hannan & Liu, 2021). A notable example is "Jill Watson", the AI-powered teaching assistant at Georgia Tech, which successfully supported students in an online master's programme. Jill's adaptive learning capabilities enabled it to guide students through coursework much like a human assistant (GVU Center, n.d.). Jill has since been integrated with VERA, a virtual research assistant that helps students with science experiments (Design Intelligence Lab, n.d.). AI chatbots made strides in developing students' writing skills. For example, Pengel et al. (2021) developed a chatbot that supports students by offering writing assignments, providing automated feedback, and facilitating self-study activities. Schmitt and Buschek

(2021) introduced CharacterChat, a chatbot that helps writers shape fictional characters through conversation, a process they describe as progressive manifestation. Furthermore, Lin and Chang (2020) designed a chatbot to assist post-secondary writers in refining their thesis statements based on peer feedback.

AI chatbots also act as personalized learning assistants, delivering tailored content and real-time feedback to enhance learning experiences. These chatbots provide on-demand support, answering students' questions, clarifying concepts, and offering individualized help. For instance, "Ada" offers personalized tutoring by responding to specific student queries and facilitating independent learning (Kabiljo et al., 2020). Lin and Tsai (2019) reported their chatbot anchoring upon IBM Watson Assistant and Facebook Messenger to help non-technical students, primitive to computer programming, gain interest and competency in this area. Socratic, an educational platform, while goes beyond being just a chatbot, assists students in learning new concepts through its chatbot-like interface (Alsanousi et al., 2023). Furthermore, chatbots serve as coaches, offering guidance on career paths, educational advice, and job market trends to help students make informed decisions. These roles are exemplified by various platforms providing personalized career guidance (D'Silva et al., 2020) and delivering information related to academic processes, scholarships, tuition fees, and even facilitating the personal productivity of the user, such as reminder of tasks and deliveries or collection of evaluations (Hien et al., 2018).

As educational chatbots gain global traction, it is important to highlight developments in Singapore, where innovations are shaped by the region's unique diversity in languages, educational systems, and varying levels of access to technology, distinguishing it from other parts of the world. In 2018, chatbots became popular in institutes of higher learning (IHL) in Singapore. Singapore Management University (SMU) was the first IHL to launch an AI chatbot to address more than 1,000 frequently asked questions across student areas like academic, admissions, student life, internships, exchanges, and career tips (SMU Corporate Communications, 2018). The IT department of the National University of Singapore began onboarding chatbots for service requests and subsequently propagated them to other service-centric units such as the Registrar's Office, Student Services Centre in 2019 (Conversations with chatbots, n.d.). Thilarajah and Divaharan (2019) designed a chatbot, "Tessa" using the Quriobot to support trainee teachers from the National Institute of Education (NIE) in the understanding of learning theories, pedagogies, instructional strategies, the affordances of technology tools, and the ability to design technology-mediated learning activities. In the same year, an "AskPoly" chatbot, to help teenagers receive relevant information across all five polytechnics, was launched (5 Things to Know about the AskPoly Chatbot, 2019). A "Chem Quest" chatbot was deployed by the Singapore Institute of Technology to revise concepts and formulas in a fully online, self-directed, three-month Chemistry bridging course designed for pre-university students starting in 2021 (Jasin et al., 2023). A larger-scale use of educational chatbots was implemented by Temasek Polytechnic (TP) starting in 2020, deploying chatbots across 13 subjects for both pre-employment training (PET) and continuing education and training (CET) learners (Zhang & Fang, 2024; Fang et al., 2023), including one that was developed collaboratively across three polytechnics (Kannurao et al., 2023).

Since 2023, the era of GenAI has emerged, where ChatGPT has become a household name. Alongside ChatGPT, advanced chatbots like Gemini, Claude, Microsoft Copilot, and Meta AI are being used in similar educational settings but with enhanced capabilities. These large language models offer more personalized support by understanding user intents with greater accuracy. Particularly for ChatGPT, OpenAI (the company behind ChatGPT) make available Application Programming Interfaces (APIs) for developers to easily integrate ChatGPT into their existing educational platforms or services. Non-coders can also customize their own versions of GPT frills-free using OpenAI's Explore GPTs interface. This nature makes ChatGPT scalable and accessible to higher educational users globally. In a systematic review conducted by Baig and Yadegaridehkordi (2024), 209 published research papers pertained to the keywords "ChatGPT" and "higher education" or related terms from renowned academic databases. This only represents a fraction of the ongoing work, as there would be numerous other initiatives currently under review or being implemented by practitioners in educational settings that have yet to be formally documented or reported in scholarly literature.

Emerging trends indicate that ChatGPT is being employed in a variety of ways to enhance both teaching and learning. Prominent uses by academic staff span the full spectrum of education, from curriculum development to lesson planning and assessments. At the curriculum level, educators are utilizing ChatGPT to assist with syllabus design and overall curriculum development (Ali et al., 2024; Meron & Araci, 2023). At the lesson planning stage, ChatGPT is being used to create detailed lesson plans and topic-specific activities that cater to diverse learning needs (Tajik & Tajik, 2023; Rahman et al., 2023). In assessments, academic staff are leveraging ChatGPT for a range of tasks, including grading these assessments (Sallam & Al-Salahat, 2023; Cheung et al., 2023), providing formative feedback (Rawas, 2023; Mogavi et al., 2024), and designing and creating assessment questions (Cheung et al., 2023; Onal & Kulavuz-Onal, 2024; Jafari & Keykha, 2023).

Students, on the other hand, are using ChatGPT in ways that traditional AI chatbots have been supporting. They use it for content acquisition in various disciplines, from language learning (Rawas, 2023; Baskara, 2023), writing support (Currie et al., 2023; Keiper et al., 2023), coding and debugging assistance (Rahman et al., 2023; Von Garrel & Mayer, 2023; Singh et al., 2023), to communication and problem-solving skills (Fauzi et al., 2023). Non-academic staff in the educational organizations are using ChatGPT for content creation for internal and external communications, including emails, administrative documents, social media, marketing, customer support, training, and school updates (Adeshola & Adepoju, 2023; Tajik & Tajik, 2023), as well as documentation, reports, or summary generation (Dwivedi et al., 2023). Akin to academic staff who generate questions for assessing students, non-academic staff responsible for managing systems use ChatGPT to generate test cases (Adeshola & Adepoju, 2023).

In Singapore, ChatGPT has also become a versatile tool for enhancing learning in several innovative ways. Students use ChatGPT in literature subjects to refine their writing skills, develop clearer and more vivid character analyses, and refine their narratives, adjusting them to better fit the Singaporean context. Beyond content-specific support, ChatGPT is also used to foster AI literacy among students. With teacher-developed guides, the students engage with the chatbot to understand GenAI's limitations, potential biases, and responsible AI. ChatGPT's ability to provide personalized academic support is continually harnessed to offer tailored feedback, with educators utilizing it to promote independent learning, critical thinking, and a more equitable experience for students in Singapore (Ang, 2024).

3.1.3 Benefits and Challenges of Educational Chatbots

The review by Okonkwo and Ade-Ibijola (2021) identifies five key benefits of using an educational chatbot: (1) easy integration of subject content into the chatbot; (2) quick access to information, enabling students to maximize their learning potential and achievement; (3) increased motivation and engagement due to the interactive and supportive learning environment; (4) support for multiple users, allowing simultaneous access for large cohorts; and (5) immediate responses to queries. Apart from these benefits, additional studies have highlighted how AI chatbots support goal-setting, SRL behaviors, and foster affective relatedness (Hew et al., 2023; Huang et al., 2019; Glick et al., 2024). These findings align with those from Labadze et al. (2023), who similarly reported that chatbots not only enhance motivation and engagement and provide timely assistance but also contribute to improved pedagogy.

While AI chatbots bring significant advantages, technology remains a double-edged sword if not used responsibly. The same review reveals challenges in the use of chatbots in education, including ethical concerns, user attitudes, supervision needs, evaluation practices, and maintenance issues. For instance, the chatbot technology stack can heavily influence the adoption and effectiveness of chatbot systems, potentially skewing users' perceptions and limiting educational applications (Deng & Yu, 2023; Wollny et al., 2021). User attitudes, shaped by familiarity with and trust in technology, may also determine the extent to which chatbots are effectively integrated into learning environments (Al-Abdullatif, 2023; Wollny et al., 2021). Ethical concerns arise around data privacy and security, with possible bias through data-driven insights provided by AI seeping through as the teachers assess the students (Williams, 2024; Kooli, 2023). As chatbots gather conversational data, establishing stringent guidelines for data handling and confidentiality is crucial, where care must be taken when sensitive information such as patient details is at play (Miao & Ahn, 2023).

Apart from the stated concerns, GenAI chatbots present specific challenges, particularly in terms of response reliability and accuracy. Williams (2024) highlights that algorithmic bias within these chatbots can lead to misjudgements, affecting both teachers' assessments and students' learning. Adeshola and Adepoju (2023) similarly note the risk of reinforcing existing prejudices, which could skew learning outcomes if not carefully managed. Dwivedi et al. (2023) emphasize the need for ongoing monitoring and ethical oversight to prevent these biases from compromising academic reliability, especially in contexts that require accurate, unbiased outputs. Concerns about fair assessment are valid, as GenAI tools may oversimplify complex learning (Mogavi et al., 2024) and influence student responses, reducing the authenticity of their work (Cheung et al., 2023). Excessive reliance on AI for learning could also undermine critical thinking and problem-solving skills, as students may become dependent on automated answers rather than engaging deeply with the material (Ali et al., 2024).

3.2 Self-Regulated Learning

Generative AI (GenAI) has demonstrated both positive and negative applications. With its potential to replace tasks traditionally performed by knowledge workers, educators share the responsibility for ensuring its appropriate use. They play a crucial role in equipping learners with effective learning strategies and self-regulatory skills, which research highlights as essential for improving outcomes (Glick et al., 2023; Zimmerman, 2011). By fostering these skills, educators prepare learners for lifelong learning and empower them to adapt to evolving technologies with critical thinking, enabling responsible and strategic use of AI.

Zimmerman (1990) characterized self-regulated learners as individuals who approach academic tasks with confidence, persistence, and creativity and who are aware of their own knowledge and skill levels. These learners actively seek strategies to achieve success, even in the face of challenges. To foster self-regulation, Azevedo et al.'s (2019) intelligent tutoring system (ITS) provides students with targeted support. This ITS uses four pedagogical agents, each agent offering adaptive prompts and feedback: one guides navigation, another aids in setting goals and planning, a third monitors progress toward goals, and the fourth connects students with learning tools to implement strategies they choose. Aleven et al. (2006) and Roll et al. (2011) implemented "Help Tutor" and "Self-Assessment Tutor" to enable students to refine help-seeking skills and assess their progress through active practice and feedback. More recently, AI chatbots specifically designed for SRL have demonstrated effectiveness in supporting academic tasks such as mastering APA (7th edition) style in writing (Fang et al., 2023). These chatbots offer real-time feedback, helping students apply rules accurately while fostering skills that align with the lifelong learning strategies educators aim to instil.

SRL provides an essential foundation for effectively integrating AI in education, as it empowers learners to take an active role in their own learning process. Bringing SRL into the design process through the ADDIE model allows educators to ensure that AI tools like chatbots are structured to support skills such as goal-setting, progress monitoring, and strategic adjustment. This integration is crucial for developing tools that not only assist with academic tasks but also promote autonomy and resilience. The following section explores how SRL principles can be applied within the ADDIE model to shape chatbot design and implementation for a self-directed learning experience.

3.3 ADDIE Model

Instructional design is critical for integrating chatbots into classrooms because it ensures the chatbot is aligned with specific learning goals and effectively supports both teachers and students. Several models are available for educational designers and training programmers to structure and deliver effective learning experiences. Among these, ADDIE is one of the most widely recognized frameworks due to its clear, systematic process. The ADDIE instructional design model originated in the 1970s, developed by Florida State University's Center for Educational Technology for the U.S. military (Branson et al., 1975). The model's name is an acronym representing its five phases: analysis, design, development, implementation, and evaluation. Critics highlight this model's prolonged development cycles, rigid step-by-step process, limited focus on teacher-student interaction, and potential for high costs with minimal returns. Some advocate for agile alternatives like Allen's successive approximation model (SAM) (Allen & Sites, 2012; Bates, 2015; Rosenberg, 2014; Ali et al., 2021).

3.3.1 Validity of ADDIE

Indeed, ADDIE has received some criticisms for being less applicable in today's modern learning environment, where the rapid evolution of technology demands more flexibility and adaptability in instructional design models. However, many distance education providers still find that applying the ADDIE model can meet their different teaching requirements in their online educational environments, with good practices to consider such as multimedia presentations, feedback, a variety of interactive exercises or activities, and learning strategies to address the concern of lack of teacher-student interactions (Spatioti et al., 2022). Furthermore, ADDIE remains applicable across various domains, including nurse training, virtual reality-based training, computer-assisted language learning, actuarial mathematics, and even adaptations for flipped learning environments (Kim et al., 2020; Li & Sun, 2024; Yeh & Tseng, 2019; Vijayakumar et al., 2023; Widyastuti & Susiana, 2019). This versatility speaks to ADDIE's foundational structure, allowing it to be customized to meet the unique demands of different educational and training contexts.

The ADDIE model remains widely used in Singapore across educational institutions and corporate training settings. At SMU, it was employed to design a library orientation and information literacy program for students (Munoo & Abdullah, 2018). It was also utilized to redesign staff development programs for Singapore's largest group of healthcare institutions (Lee & Tan, 2016). Additionally, professional development courses offered by NIE and Republic Polytechnic include training on implementing the ADDIE model.

3.3.2 ADDIE for Conversational AI Experience

In TP, the professional development program for new polytechnic lecturers includes teaching Gagné's Nine Events of Instruction (Joint Polytechnic Academy for Educators, n.d.) as part of their curriculum and lesson design. While Gagné's model also offers a systematic approach, it can be less straightforward compared to ADDIE due to its multiple steps, and harder to remember without a simple acronym. On the other hand, ADDIE's structured nature and easy-to-remember acronym make it a practical choice, particularly because it emphasizes the importance of the evaluation phase, allowing for processes that produce measurable and specific outcomes.

Even Allen and Sites (2012), who proposed the SAM model, acknowledged that ADDIE effectively ensures outcomes are achieved. Adapting ADDIE to fit specific educational systems would always be a sensible approach. No instructional design model developed today is likely to remain unchanged for the next 50 years, as technology continues to evolve at an even more rapid pace. ADDIE's adaptability makes it an enduring choice, evolving with technological changes and diverse learning environments. In terms of making ADDIE more iterative, variations have been developed to emphasize continuous feedback and adjustment throughout the entire process (Dick et al., 2009; Kurt, 2022; van Vulpen, n.d.). Rather than following a strictly linear path, instructional designers can revisit earlier stages, regularly seeking feedback, testing outcomes, and iterating through stages of their learning products to ensure they deliver the best possible outcomes.

The successive approximation model (SAM) is a three-step process focused on rapid prototyping and iterative development, ideal for small-scale projects where quick adjustments and feedback enhance learning.

However, scaling SAM increases complexity, requiring strong management and leadership to handle uncertainty and ambiguity. In contrast, ADDIE remains a versatile framework adaptable to diverse learning environments, from traditional classrooms to virtual settings, addressing both simple and complex needs. In designing chatbot-based learning experiences, phases may not be fully iterated, but student feedback is gathered during implementation to refine prototypes. This feedback-driven approach keeps content relevant, supports adaptive classrooms, and strengthens teacher-student interactions.

3.4 Strategy

Each phase of the ADDIE model will be elaborated by addressing some guiding questions using practical examples from Temasek Polytechnic (TP). Through these examples, how educational chatbots were effectively integrated to enhance learning in our various subjects, supporting diverse needs, is showcased. This chapter focuses on the AI chatbots developed by the School of Informatics and IT (IIT) for collaborator schools, namely the School of Applied Science (ASC), School of Engineering (ENG), and School of Humanities and Social Sciences (HSS). Additionally, the TP team has developed chatbots specifically tailored for use within the IIT school itself. The following is an overview of these AI chatbots and their functions:

- EXCELBot for optional independent learning of Microsoft Excel for PET students in the ASC.
- APABot for self-correction of errors in the application of APA citation style for PET students in HSS
- AiLin to assist CET students in ENG in acquiring theoretical know-how to run an airline and technical competencies to use a software AIRLINE Online (Simulate, n.d.) to simulate and forecast the operations of an airport.
- AskCherBot to assist PET students in ENG with understanding conceptual knowledge in bipolar junction transistor direct current biasing and solving related tutorial questions.
- D'Ava to support PET students in IIT in understanding the fundamentals of data visualization with a particular focus on statistical concepts and applications.
- SOMABot to provide supplementary theoretical support for software usage in performing social media and text analytics for CET students in IIT.

3.4.1 A: Analyse

3.4.1.1 "Whom Can I Work With to Launch the AI Chatbot?"

The **Analyse** phase in ADDIE focuses on identifying the learning needs, goals, and audience characteristics to ensure the instructional design aligns with desired outcomes. A guiding question, *"Whom can I work with to launch the AI chatbot?"* underscores the collaborative and consultative nature of this phase. In the AI-driven digital age, instructional design evolves from a technical problem with straightforward solutions to an adaptive challenge, requiring behavioral and mindset changes. Tackling such challenges involves diverse perspectives, experimentation, and ongoing feedback to find effective, sustainable solutions.

To confirm these learning needs, the TP team drew on internal and external sources, including subject review reports, subject evaluation surveys, teaching effectiveness evaluation reports, student performance data, ongoing feedback from students during their learning, as well as insights from external examiners, industry feedback, and professional development opportunities. Beyond the course leaders, module leaders, and tutors, it is important to involve others, such as the IT department and funding agencies. The IT department can provide critical guidance, endorsing or rejecting implementations based on data privacy, security, and other IT concerns, while funding agencies can support the project or programme's strategic roadmap, offering resources and direction for long-term development and sustainability.

In Singapore, the Instruction Manual for Information and Communications Technology & Smart Systems (ICT&SS) Management (also known as IM8) (Singapore Government Developer Portal, 2024) supports government and public service agencies in adopting ICT&SS to drive digital transformation. It outlines best practices on "what" and "how" to manage ICT, focusing on areas such as system criticality, security, and sensitivity classification. Within this framework, the Data Domain Group addresses data governance, architecture, protection, sharing, and storage, ensuring effective data management practices across the data lifecycle. A potential concern for AI chatbots is compliance with these standards, as the capture and handling of student data may risk infringing established privacy and security protocols. Where a public cloud solution is chosen, data classification typically falls under Official-Sensitive (Normal), requiring measures such as data masking to protect sensitive information. Engaging the IT department at the start phase of the ADDIE model ensures that these security requirements, whether using Government Commercial Cloud (GCC) or public cloud, are thoroughly assessed and addressed from the outset. This collaboration helps identify potential compliance issues early and supports proactive planning in design (the next phase), establishing a solid foundation for the ethical and secure use of AI in educational settings.

Building on this foundation, the TP team's funding journey has played a pivotal role in advancing the strategic roadmap for AI chatbot implementation.

Beginning with an initial grant from the TP Research Fund (TPRF) in June 2020, the School of Informatics and IT (IIT) developed a technological package to build and deploy AI chatbots in a no-code way, enabling collaborator schools to create chatbots that support engagement and learning outcomes in a polytechnic setting. Subsequent funding from the national Workforce Development Applied Research Fund (WDARF) enabled us to examine the effectiveness of these chatbots for adult learners, focusing on how chatbot interactions can deepen content or skills mastery differently from traditional PET approaches. Further funding supported platform customization, expanding usability and adding features such as gamification and customizable UI/UX assets to enhance engagement. This approach enabled us to build a robust platform that adapts to varied and evolving learning needs across different environments.

3.4.2 D: Design

3.4.2.1 "What Technology Should I Use?"

In the **Design** phase, several key considerations emerge based on the earlier analysis to guide decision-making for chatbot development:

a) **Chatbot development platform**: Selecting a suitable platform is critical. This decision may depend on factors such as the availability of IT specialists adept in cloud platforms, AI algorithms, programming languages, and data visualization. For teams with limited technical resources, low-code or no-code platforms might be preferred, while coding-intensive platforms offer more customization options for teams with strong expertise.

   In the earlier section, some of the reported educational chatbots were developed on cloud services or calling APIs such as Dialogflow (Hew et al., 2023; Hien et al., 2018; Wan Hamzah et al., 2021), Amazon Lex (Gowtham et al., 2021; Sreeja & Chithra, 2022), or commercial platforms offering a drag-drop no-code interface such as IBM Watson (GVU Center, n.d.; Design Intelligence Lab, n.d.), Chatlayer (Jasin et al., 2023), Rasa (Lin & Chang, 2020), or coding from scratch (Ng et al., 2024; Mckie & Narayan, 2019).

   For the large-scale implementation of educational chatbots in TP, the Google Cloud Platform (GCP) was chosen as the all-in-one platform to develop and deploy the chatbots. Dialogflow allows conversational flow into mobile or web applications. Logs can be retrieved with Python scripts. The ES agent was used for greater flexibility in programming features or automation with codes. Firebase, the database service under GCP, was also used to enable the storage and retrieval of data such as learner credentials and rich media (e.g. images) for chatbot responses.

b) **Chatbot features for data tracking and intelligence**: Determining which features to incorporate to track user interactions and other relevant data is essential, as these will enable the continuous improvement of the chatbot's intelligence and support data-driven enhancements over time.

Hew's group (Huang et al., 2019; Tang & Hew, 2022; Hew et al., 2023) tracked chatbot data on engagement patterns, frequently asked questions, and time spent on tasks. The chatbots also incorporated quick polls, quizzes, and instant feedback mechanisms—thumbs-up or thumbs-down emojis to gauge understanding or satisfaction. Fei and Petrina (2013) used logs of verbal interaction to predict and advise on the design of their chatbots, whereas Wan Hamzah et al. (2021) tracked the frequency of conversations and queries for each session by day, and their successful response rate (i.e. able to match the intent of query) to inform the content students wanted.

For TP, users are required to log in so that chatbot interactions can be triangulated with other data for learning analytics. Before the main curated menu of topics, subtopics, and specific intents, there is a "Hot Topics" section to ensure learners without questions can still view them, keeping their knowledge on par with the cohort. It also provides easier access to FAQs. The hot topics were regularly refreshed to maintain relevance for immediate help required by the cohort. Upon accessing a specific intent, users can upvote or down-vote a response based on its usefulness or succinctness. This data is made available to module leaders to update the training knowledge base for improved chatbot intelligence.

The chatbot can also recognize user free text inputs and provide the responses. Apart from the main menu, a personalized recommended menu is activated upon an assessment of the competencies. The learner can focus on the specific items to work on identified gaps. A recommender system in the form of "You may also like" prompts was developed, too, to provide related questions to the current one that the user has just asked. This is to further support learners' agency by introducing possibilities and supporting access to (more) resources at the right moment, in the right format, at the right level, in sync with the recommended strategies for designers of learning environments who aim to support the development of learner agency.

Last but not least, a fall-back mechanism is developed to handle the scenario when the chatbot could not understand the intent of the user and/or provide a satisfactory response. This complex task would then be handed over to the human agent (aka module leader). The user would be guided to send an email to the module leader via the chatbot interface. The types of insights that chatbot data can provide will be described in the **Evaluation** phase.

c) **Learning analytics dashboard**: Defining which graphs and charts to generate is crucial for creating actionable insights. This includes considering the types of data required and identifying the sources to pull from, ensuring that the dashboard offers meaningful analytics for decision-making.

   Fei and Petrina (2013) utilized text analytics to evaluate chatbot-user interactions, focusing on metrics like the chatbot's ability to repeat responses and accurately identify intents. Their approach centered on assessing chatbot performance; however, by using AI markup language (AIML) log files, they also opened opportunities for more comprehensive quantitative and qualitative analyses of student learning behaviors. Similarly, recent studies on the challenges of using ChatGPT (Cheung et al., 2023; Onal & Kulavuz-Onal, 2024; Goodings et al., 2024) have primarily leveraged data generated by the chatbot to evaluate performance factors such as response accuracy, relevance, and adaptability. This approach often emphasizes functionality over insights into how students engage, process information, or personalize their learning. Subsequent researchers have expanded the scope to gain deeper insights into student learning and metacognition. For instance, Chang and his team (2023) utilized the chatbot to deliver learning analytics, tracking students' real-time chatbot usage in relation to various language metrics. Likewise, Lin and Husni (2021) analyzed and codified student text responses to understand their inquiry behaviors more deeply.

   None of these studies, however, have implemented a dashboard to visualize and integrate these insights in real time, which could provide educators with a more comprehensive view of student learning behaviors and engagement patterns.

   TP has taken this further by developing a real-time learning analytics dashboard (see Figure 3.1), providing the subject team with KPI cards and graphs to monitor student engagement and learning behaviors. For instance, the dashboard includes time series charts to reveal usage seasonality, average time spent per visit, total unique users, and visualizations of the most accessed or frequently asked topics, displayed as bar charts and word clouds. These analytics can be drilled down to the class level, allowing tutors to gain behavioral insights into students' motivation and self-regulation. Tutors can then use this information to intervene as needed, such as nudging students to complete tasks on time, thereby supporting timely and personalized learning interventions.

d) **Conversational flow and user interface design**: Designing an effective conversational flow to initiate, sustain, and conclude learner-chatbot interactions is key to promoting engagement. This design should support a seamless UX that enhances learning outcomes.

FIGURE 3.1
Typical dashboard showing different learning signals to educator.

Creating an intuitive user interface is also important to ensure that the chatbot is easy to navigate and visually appealing, contributing to a positive UX.

The review by Kuhail et al. (2023) revealed a common approach of anchoring chatbot design to specific pedagogical principles. For example, experiential learning was used where the chatbot asks reflective questions to help students construct knowledge, like a tutor guiding explanations. Chatbots also engaged students through small talk, telling jokes, or sharing fun facts to build rapport and trust. Affective learning involved providing empathetic feedback to increase motivation in challenging situations. Additionally, chatbots sometimes reversed roles, prompting students to explain concepts, thus making learning interactive. Scaffolding was also employed, with chatbots breaking down complex ideas during online lectures.

Researchers have emphasized the importance of a structured conversation flow in chatbot design, as well-planned interactions can prevent user frustration and early termination of conversations. This includes incorporating options to escalate to a human if the conversation stagnates, a critical success factor in chatbot development, deployment, and usage (Janssen et al., 2021). Such strategies act as "damage control", aligning with Liu et al. (2023), who found that humorous emojis mediated the positive impact on users' intentions to reuse the chatbot after a service failure. Students terminated conversations prematurely with Lucy—the chatbot developed by Fei and Petrina (2013)—when it repeatedly failed to respond meaningfully, despite students attempting to restart the interaction with the same opening sentence in the hope of triggering the correct conversational flow. In contrast, the chatbot created by the University of Hong Kong (Hew et al., 2023) utilized a structured flowchart to minimize off-topic interactions and ensure conversations concluded appropriately.

When a chatbot takes on a persona or is infused with verbal anthropomorphic design, UX or compliance with the chatbot's recommendations also seems to improve (Adamopoulou & Moussiades, 2020; Martin et al., 2021). Studies by Weber and Ludwig (2020) and Janssen et al. (2021) further emphasize that the interface should be intuitive, with initial guidance provided for inexperienced users to prevent confusion during interactions.

From our implementation experience and data analysis of chatbot logs, surveys, interviews, and learning task performances across six deployed chatbots, the TP team observed that, beyond selecting a stable and private chatbot builder platform for reliability, a well-designed conversational flow with logical progressions, as well as affective and gamification elements, is crucial to enhance

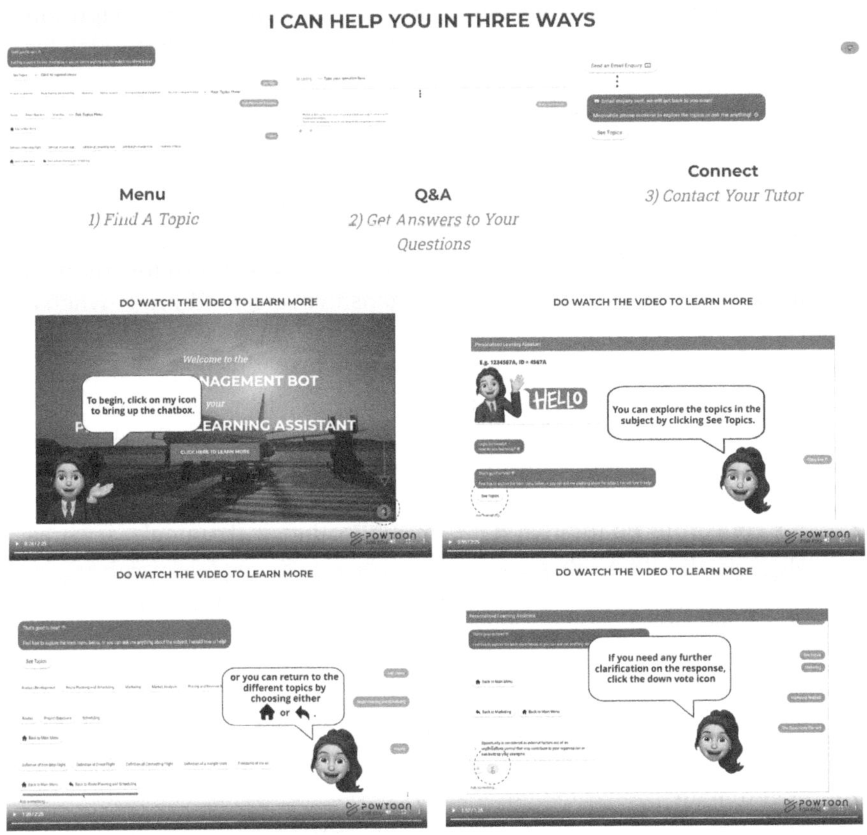

FIGURE 3.2
How to provide guidance to chatbot users.

engagement. Furthermore, our learnings indicate that chatbot design should incorporate clear entry points to orient learners. This was achieved by clearly indicating the chatbot's purpose and providing instructions on the hosting webpage, detailing three different ways to interact with the chatbot, available as either static content or video (see Figure 3.2).

e) **Personalized and Self-Regulated Learning (SRL) features:** Identifying features that support personalized, SRL, as well as collaborative or social learning opportunities, will be crucial for maximizing the chatbot's educational impact.

Students were required to use the goal-setting chatbot (Hew et al., 2023) to set personal learning goals related to the course they would attend before their first class. They answered five questions based on the SMART (specific, measurable, attainable, relevant, and time-bound) goal framework. Students found the chatbot helpful in clarifying their learning goals, developing a goal-setting strategy for future learning, and understanding how goal-setting supports SRL. Similarly, the TP team (Fang et al., 2023; Zhang & Fang, 2024) also reported how their AI chatbots features were able to support the three stages of SRL behaviours: from using the curated menu to set SMART goals, using the recommended menu and follow-up intents to focus on and work on areas for improvement or further exploration in terms of the performance stage, and a report card for students to be aware of remaining learning gaps to bridge and know when a task is adequately performed.

f) **Research instruments**: Understanding how students learn and respond to these AI educational chatbots is essential for both reflective practitioners and chatbot developers. While the data and insights from chatbot logs will be covered in the evaluation phase of the chapter, it is crucial during the design phase to integrate plans for collecting qualitative data through other instruments, such as surveys and interviews.

Many researchers have used various experimental designs, that is, pre-experimental, quasi-experimental, and controlled experimental with either posttest or pre/posttest (Fryer et al., 2017; Tang & Hew, 2022; Hobert, 2019), to prove the effectiveness of the AI chatbots. These include running surveys to understand the acceptability and usability of the AI chatbot, as well as learning success and motivation that are brought about.

For TP, the use of a pre-survey would highlight the prior experiences, learning disposition of the users, and their expectations of the AI chatbot technology. This would help in gathering insights into what motivates the students in using an AI educational chatbot. The post-survey would capture the UX in terms of accessibility, ease of use, system intelligence, and whether the affordances (features) of the chatbot supported them in their learning. There was also the use of a semi-structured group interview with selected users to elaborate on their responses in the pre- and post-survey while sharing their experience with the chatbot, for example expectations, joys and frustrations, preferences, and further needs. Task performances, such as marks from the midpoint (process) and the final deliverable (output) marks, were used to differentiate different users. Along with the data described in the learning analytics dashboard segment, these instruments provided a comprehensive view of student interaction and engagement with our AI chatbots. This multilayered approach not only allowed the tutors to understand their students better but also informed iterative improvements to the chatbot design, ensuring that it better aligns with the needs and preferences of diverse learners.

As a reminder, for applications where safety and reliability are paramount, it may be more secure to use rule-based chatbots, like "Wysa" (Wysa, n.d.)—an emotionally intelligent chatbot that supports individuals experiencing low mood, stress, or anxiety, and helps those interested in building emotional resilience, promoting mental well-being in a self-help context. This approach reduces the likelihood of AI generating uncontrolled responses, a consideration especially relevant in educational settings where consistent and predictable interactions are critical.

3.4.2.2 "Which Subject Would I Use It for and for What Purpose?"

Educators have been using chatbots to support specific learning objectives and enhance student engagement. Another critical success factor for chatbot that Janssen et al. (2021) proposed was the presence of user-centric use cases. There should be a logical use case suitable for the use of chatbot technology. In a review by Kuhail et al. (2023), two reasons cited for some chatbots failing to meet their objectives were users losing interest over time and the chatbot's potential to distract from the essential. This is why it is essential to determine the specific subject area and purpose for which we want the chatbot to support our learners. As discussed in the literature review section earlier in this chapter, educators worldwide have successfully implemented AI chatbots to address various educational goals. Readers are encouraged to refer to that section for specific examples and insights on how chatbots have been used, and which type of agent the chatbot should play (teaching, peer, motivational, administrative, and so on). In TP, the team implemented AI chatbots with very focused objectives, from subject-specific to generic learning strategies ones, as outlined in this section's introduction.

As with all teaching and learning activities, whether or not they involve technology, it is crucial to apply the principle of constructive alignment (Biggs, 1996). This framework emphasizes aligning learning objectives, teaching methods, and assessments so that they work cohesively toward desired learning outcomes. In a constructively aligned approach, educators first clarify the intended learning outcomes, then design activities and assessments that directly support and measure those outcomes. When using technology, such as AI chatbots, this means ensuring that the chatbot's functions and interactions genuinely facilitate the knowledge or skills students need to develop, rather than being an add-on.

Consider how educational AI chatbots are intended to be used—whether on demand to support learning, as a complementary tool for enhancing online learning in a blended environment, or as a must-use resource for in-class activities. For instance, the goal-setting chatbot required students to interact with it before coming to class (Hew et al., 2023), and the "Chem Quest" chatbot was deployed for pre-university students in a fully online bridging course (Jasin et al., 2023). Chatbots such as "Jill Watson" (GVU Center, n.d.), "Tessa" (Thilarajah & Divaharan, 2019), and TP's Excelbot provided support on a needs-basis, offering conceptual clarifications whenever needed. Meanwhile, TP's D'Ava served as a resource for completing flipped learning activities, and in Roll et al.'s study (2011), a self-assessment chatbot was used in physical lessons to assist with metacognition.

3.4.2.3 "What Resources Would I Like to Provide for My Learners?"

When designing the resources that educational chatbots should deliver, it is essential to consider the types of content and interactions that best support learners' cognitive and learning needs. Sweller's cognitive load theory (1988) suggests that instructional methods should avoid overloading learners with information. Using concise text and complementary visual aids is one way to manage this. Mayer's multimedia learning principles (2001) emphasize that combining verbal and visual formats enhances understanding by engaging dual processing channels. Drawing on Bloom's Taxonomy for guidance, the verbs used in learning outcomes can inform the selection of content modes that the chatbot should deliver. For example, tasks at the knowledge and comprehension levels are well suited to text and visual aids for recall and recognition, while apply and analyze tasks may be better supported through interactive simulations or step-by-step video tutorials. Applying these principles in deciding what type of resources to get the chatbot to deliver can help create a learner-centric experience.

For TP's APABot, formatted text is a key resource being considered, as the chatbot is intended to support students in applying the correct referencing style in their writing tasks. For AiLin, images depicting calculations and formula applications within the simulator are essential, as they guide students in using formulas correctly and help them understand the mechanics of calculations for accurate application in simulated environments, whereas EXCELBot provides instructional videos on using Excel for chemical analysis, guiding students through essential functions and techniques for accurate data analysis in this field.

As a cautionary note, consider reviewing the points in the earlier section on "What technology should I use". For example, even when building a custom GPT with a ChatGPT plus account, free-tier users interacting with the chatbot may face limitations, with responses restricted to text-only, lacking multimedia capabilities like images or videos. Under the same section, it was also described that TP's chatbots feature a main menu with curated intents to support learners who may not have specific questions or who face language barriers, ensuring they can still use the chatbot as intended. OpenAI likewise provides quick prompts to guide users in interacting with the chatbot effectively, helping them explore its capabilities with some ideas for engaging interactions.

To enhance the reliability of the resources delivered, particularly for GenAI-powered chatbots, retrieval-augmented generation (RAG) (Heitzman, 2024; Burgan et al., 2024; Kaif et al., 2024; Mustafa & Madhi, 2024) should be employed. By setting boundaries that limit the chatbot to draw only from trusted sources, such as teaching and reference materials developed by the team, responses become accurate and relevant, aligning with students' learning objectives. When a query falls outside the subject's scope or context, the chatbot can provide a polite refusal, preventing it from generating inaccurate or misleading information and maintaining the integrity of the learning experience. Implementing RAG thus creates a "safety net" that enhances students' engagement with trustworthy information.

At the time of publication, TP's IT department has piloted seven RAG-based "TP AI Assistants" for both staff and student use. The assistants for staff cover areas such as organizational policies, advisory and assistance for IT system support, and finding information and answering questions related to CET. For students, the assistants provide support for independent study and offer guidance on administrative matters. These RAG-based assistants use MS Azure services, such as Azure OpenAI Service with Azure AI Search, to retrieve and generate accurate responses from indexed, trusted content sources.

3.4.3 D: Develop

3.4.3.1 "In House or External?"

Among the 12 critical success factors identified by Janssen et al. (2021), project resources stand out as a key consideration, forcing organizations to deliberate on issues such as human resources—whether to allocate full-time staff to oversee the development and maintenance of the chatbot or to forgo developing core competencies and outsource these tasks to contract-for-service developers or chatbot solution providers such as Noodle Factory and Mizou. As with all other AI development, the main struggle between building an in-house team or outsourcing lies with budget concerns. A report by Gartner (Thyagarajan et al., 2023) predicts that by 2026, 80% of organizations will achieve a 30% improvement in team productivity if they effectively combine insourced and outsourced software engineering teams through clear roles and responsibilities. One key principle highlighted is maintaining a culture of continuous improvement, enabling blended teams to iterate more effectively. The same principle emphasizes that continuous improvement also entails the ability to produce new innovations. Investing in in-house development fosters talent growth, equipping staff with valuable competencies that can further drive innovative AI products. For academic institutions, developing AI capabilities in-house provides them with the ability to conduct both longitudinal and latitudinal studies on, for example, student outcomes, learning behaviors, and the effects across different disciplines and learning environments. This approach not only enables institutions to gather valuable insights but also fosters innovation and adaptability, allowing them to tailor AI solutions to address the unique needs and findings of these studies effectively.

The ability of an in-house team or outsourced team to safeguard data privacy and security is another critical consideration. Maintaining stricter control over data and ethical practices ensures compliance with regulatory standards and aligns with institutional values. The growing adoption of AI in education has prompted some universities to develop their own custom AI tools (Paykamian, 2023). This allows them to maintain full control over data security, ensuring that no data is shared with third parties. Additionally, these tools often include a core large language model (LLM), which serves as a foundation for developing applications like chatbots and data analysis tools, enhancing functionality and accessibility.

For TP's case, three grants from both internal and external funding agencies were obtained to hire one research executive—an IT specialist adept in cloud platforms, AI algorithms, computer programming languages such as HTML, CSS, JavaScript, MySQL, and Python, as well as data visualization techniques using commercial tools like Tableau and Power BI—to program and implement the chatbot design. Additionally, seven final-year diploma students on internship programs were engaged as assistants to the research team, contributing to the development and deployment of the chatbots. Having educators on the research team played a pivotal role in shaping the design of how AI chatbots should be developed and deployed in educational contexts. This strategic combination of in-house expertise and resources resulted in three invention disclosures, one successful licensing to an EdTech company, and paved the way for several academic publications.

3.4.4 I: Implement

3.4.4.1 "What Would I Have to Do to Encourage Usage?"

The TP team took on an Agile approach—drawing on lessons from what the team learnt from an earlier AI chatbot, they made iterative improvements for the next one to enable those features previously lacking or to address areas of concern. There were common teething problems. Getting students to use the AI chatbot was the biggest challenge. Some students tended to prefer consulting their tutors over using a chatbot, while some were unaware that the chatbot could connect them to a tutor, leading to its underutilization. Even those who did engage with the AI chatbots faced challenges with sustained usage. CET students in particular encountered difficulties in accessing and navigating the chatbots. Additionally, they were unsure how to proceed or what to expect when the chatbot reached a conversational dead end, such as responding with "We will get back to you on this question," which left them confused. According to Davis' technology adoption model (1989), students exhibit varying profiles in their adoption of technology, ranging from innovators to laggards. To reduce the likelihood of students falling into the laggard category, targeted interventions such as personalized training, hands-on support, and clear demonstrations of the technology's value in their learning can be implemented.

The team studied the students' reactions to them, their motivation to use them, as well as the efficacy of the AI chatbot features to support specific purposes and found that to engage and motivate students, there is a need for a structured developmental process (Zhang & Fang, 2024). A delivery model for practitioners to use was thus developed.

a) **Initiate the Access**

   There is a need to boost awareness and lower the barrier among students to use the AI chatbot. They must know that an educational AI chatbot exists as one of the online learning resources and what can be achieved in precision using the chatbot. Announcements made in the learning management system, and in both physical and virtual classroom (e.g., Zoom or MS Teams) spaces, are not sufficient. Static welcome greetings, words of encouragement, and guide (e.g., in the form of written user manual) alone do not suffice to assist the students use the high-tech solution, the chatbot, effectively. Video clips can be a great tool in this aspect.

b) **Springboard the Learning**

   Getting students to learn how to use the AI chatbot effectively with active learning strategies such as working on the completion of an activity in class with the help of the chatbot is recommended. It is required to help the students kick-start the use of the AI chatbot, whether it is designed to obtain quick responses to questions of lower cognitive order or to identify and correct learning task errors.

c) **Differentiate for Autonomy**

   We emphasize again here the importance of choosing the appropriate chatbot development platforms or technology to enable feature(s) for learners to perform SRL. Students should be supported by the chatbot in a student-centric, autonomous environment to set SMART goals, self-instruct in learning the subject, monitor what aspects they are lacking, be aware of remaining learning gaps to bridge, and know when a learning task is adequately performed.

In this implementation phase of the ADDIE model, alpha and beta tests should be conducted by module leaders (or chatbot owners) in collaboration with tutors to ensure the functionality and usability of the chatbots before their official launch. These tests will not only identify potential technical issues but also provide an opportunity for the module team to familiarize themselves with the chatbot's features and capabilities, in the event they are not the developers themselves. By involving the module team in the testing process, their confidence in the tool increases, which plays a crucial role in encouraging adoption and usage. Shi et al. (2024) reported that tutors who had utilized the AI tool's functions and had experience with it would be able to bring in pedagogical benefits of the tool into their classrooms. In the research by Kim (2024), one of the emergent themes coming out from the study participants on how teachers and AI collaborate in education is to have teachers gain greater familiarity with the AI tools so that they will be able to incorporate AI tools as an integral part of instruction more effectively. Additionally, feedback from these tests can be used as the final refinement for the chatbot, ensuring an effective and engaging experience for the students when it is "live".

Finally, first impressions of AI chatbots matter significantly. Research have found that they could lead to perception bias, where users' reliance on the AI tool was dictated by their first impressions of it (Rey et al., 2020; Nourani et al., 2020; Deng & Yu, 2023; Wollny et al., 2021). TP encountered this challenge earlier in 2024 when piloting a RAG-based chatbot, which at the time was still in its nascent stage of development. The chatbot faced issues such as conversational dead ends, laggy responses, and an overall lack of fluid interaction. Despite refinements in the subsequent semester, the same group of students, carrying their initial biases into the new subject, were reluctant to try the improved chatbot. To rebuild confidence, the module team introduced more teaching and learning activities such as getting students to find curated answers more quickly to diagnostic assessments to highlight the chatbot's enhancements. These efforts gradually helped students recognize its value and overcome their skepticism.

3.4.5 E: Evaluate

3.4.5.1 "What Would I Want to Evaluate?" "Why Would I Want to Evaluate?" "When Would I Want to Evaluate?"

There is a subtle difference between monitoring and evaluating. Monitoring is about process and progress—are we doing it right; whereas evaluating is about results and impact—did we do the right thing. Building on Hobert's (2019) analysis of evaluation approaches to AI chatbots—focusing on technology acceptance and adoption, tool usability, and algorithmic or technical correctness—earlier literature reviews on educational chatbots in Section 3.2 also highlight similar areas of emphasis. Several studies report findings on how chatbots are received by learners, evaluating their acceptance and effectiveness in enhancing engagement and learning outcomes. Additionally, research often examines usability aspects, such as ease of use, alongside the chatbot's technical performance, including its accuracy in providing contextually relevant responses. These shared focus areas underscore the importance of aligning chatbot development with both user-centric and technical evaluation criteria and also resonate with the fundamental principles of AI ethics or responsible AI frameworks: agency, fairness, inclusivity, and safety (MOE, 2024). However, it is important to consider whether such criteria can be effectively evaluated by individuals other than chatbot developers. Atkins et al. (2021) proposed that the evaluation framework should focus more on creating measurable standards and less on stating high-level principles.

Drawing reference from the Singapore Ministry of Education's AI in Education Ethics Framework (MOE, 2024) and contextualizing it to AI chatbots, agency can be assessed by examining whether the chatbot empowers learners to take charge of their learning experiences. Fairness can be evaluated by ensuring equitable access and unbiased responses, regardless of students' backgrounds or abilities. It is important to evaluate if the chatbot promotes inclusivity by accommodating diverse needs, such as varying learning styles, languages, and accessibility requirements. Lastly, safety can be assessed by verifying that data privacy and security are upheld and by considering the potential social and psychological effects on both tutors and students.

Apart from waiting for post-deployment evaluations, another angle is to actively monitor chatbot interactions from the beginning. As highlighted in the section on "Design", a real-time learning analytics dashboard can inform insights regarding learning behaviours and gaps. The tutor should be monitoring such data from the day access to the chatbot is initiated and, wherever possible, provide interventions based on the insights gleaned. An AI chatbot is a natural receptacle of data collection. The logs from chatbots built on TP's TPEBot platform provide valuable insights, as shown in Table 3.1. These logs enable descriptive analytics, summarizing statistics such as counts, ranges, averages, and usage seasonality, as well as deeper

TABLE 3.1

Data Collected via User's Chatbot Interactions

Mechanism	Data Type	Data	Insights
Log in	qualitative	timestamp (date, time)	Accessibility, adoption rate, seasonality of utilization
Close chatbot window	quantitative	usage duration (in minutes)	
Click the top hierarchical full learning menu or recommended menu	quantitative qualitative	frequency of topics accessed goal-setting, reflection	Learning preference, learning itinerary, knowledge gaps, SRL behaviors
Click second hierarchical menu/ last hierarchical menu item	quantitative	frequency of subtopics/ specific intents accessed	
Click item in "Current Hot Topics"	quantitative	frequency of intents accessed	

(Continued)

TABLE 3.1 (*Continued*)

Mechanism	Data Type	Data	Insights
	qualitative	self-regulated learning behaviours	
Click "You may also like" intents	quantitative	frequency of intents accessed	
	qualitative	self-regulated learning behaviours	
Click thumbs-up/thumbs-down	quantitative	frequency of approval/disapproval	Sentiments
	qualitative	sentiments to indicate insufficiency of response	
Click send email enquiry	qualitative	text to indicate complexity of user intents and/or sentiments	Engagement level
Enter free text	quantitative	frequency of interaction type	Learning preference, learning itinerary, knowledge gaps, SRL behaviors
	qualitative	action verbs to indicate depth of thinking	

analyses like identifying learning behaviors, SRL, higher-order thinking skills, and students' learning itineraries. Following students' navigation through the chatbot allows tutors to understand and refine learning itineraries, ensuring content and activities are well sequenced. Representing navigation as a directed graph reveals students' flexible paths but also highlights potential incomplete or incorrect itineraries, enabling tutors to address disorientation (Martín-SanJosé et al., 2014). SRL behaviors like goal-setting can be inferred when students repeatedly traverse nodes, indicating unclear goals as shown in Figure 3.3.

Logs capture the nature and quality of students' free-text questions, including the types of questions they ask (e.g., "What . . .?", "Why . . .?", "How . . .?"), the articulation level (e.g., fully structured questions like "How are . . . different from . . .?" or less elaborated ones like "What is . . .?"), and the presence of interconnected or combination questions. Research by Lim et al. (2021) highlights the educational value of fostering high-quality questions, such as "causal antecedent" (Why . . .?), "causal consequence" (What happens if . . .?), "goal orientation" (What is the purpose of . . .?), and "instrumental/procedural enablement" (How . . .?). By analyzing this data, tutors can identify gaps in students' questioning strategies and provide targeted support to help students formulate more effective questions.

When triangulated with performance data and demographics such as background, technology adoption profile, prior knowledge, and work experience collected through surveys or during matriculation, a comprehensive view of students' engagement, comprehension, and learning patterns

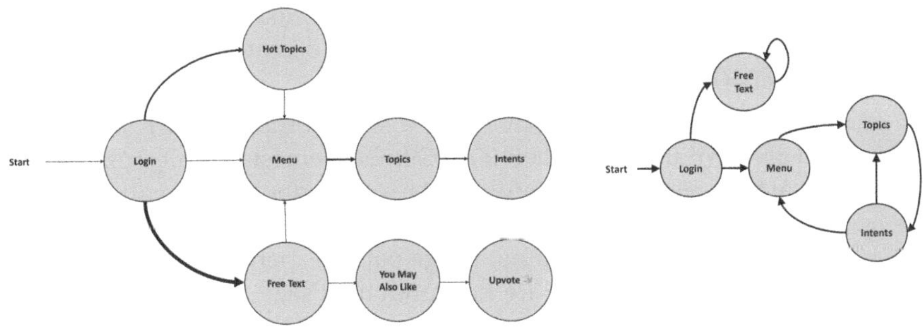

FIGURE 3.3
Learning itineraries sampled from users of AiLin. (Left) Self-regulated. (Right) Disorientated.

emerges. The TP team proposes a triad model: "Preference Insights" using chatbot logs to understand user preferences, "Performance Impact" linking interactions to learning outcomes, and "Inclusive Learning" incorporating demographics for personalization and inclusivity. Statistical tests further validate these insights based on the type of data involved. For instance, Welch's right-tailed t-tests are used to analyze quantitative, continuous data to determine if differences in task performance are linked to varying chatbot usage patterns or demographics. Chi-square tests are applied to categorical data, such as assessing associations between demographic groups and chatbot usage behaviors. Spearman's correlation explores the relationship between two quantitative variables, like the frequency of chatbot visits and task performance scores. These methods provide a robust, data-driven foundation for leveraging chatbot logs to evaluate the effectiveness of the tool and/or the integration of educational strategies.

a) User preferences: From the logs of the very first chatbot that was built using the TPEBot platform—Excelbot, the team discovered three distinct groups determined by the number of sessions, the number of interactions, and time spent (Zhang et al., 2022). The team described them as Explorers, Focused Learners, and Window Shoppers. Explorers used the chatbot multiple times and, each time, interacted with more than ten intents. They had an open agenda, looking at various chatbot features before deciding what they wanted to view. Focused Learners only used the chatbot once and during that only session zoomed into specific intents to view specific content. Window Shoppers logged in to the system but did not venture further into the content.
b) Learning outcomes: For 24 APABot users, 91.7% reduced 6 to 34 errors, 4.2% had more errors in the final draft, and another 4.2% showed no change in errors but corrected some while introducing

new ones under different concepts. Among user types, Explorers reduced the most errors, followed by Focused Learners and Window Shoppers (Fang et al., 2023).

c) Personalization and inclusivity: In a study of 22 TP CET students who used AiLin during their 2023 October semester, while some statistical tests resulted in insignificant p-values due to the small sample size, the medium effect sizes (calculated using Cohen's d) suggested that the differences in chatbot usage patterns between performance groups or demographics are not random. Usage patterns based on industry experience demographics indicated that less experienced users tended to engage with the chatbot more frequently and for longer durations.

Evaluation of the chatbot does not necessarily require data to come directly from chatbot logs. In the research by Glick et al. (2024), they traced evidence of SRL activities by examining student activity on another tool—MS Planner. This approach investigates whether student interactions with the AI chatbot influence their engagement with SRL processes, that is, planning, self-monitoring, and reflection, as evidenced by their utilization of MS Planner.

3.4.5.2 "Who Can I Share My Findings With?"

Drawing from Brookfield's (1995) four lenses of critical reflection, sharing findings with a broader community can provide valuable perspectives beyond an individual module leader's view. Brookfield highlights the importance of examining practice through multiple lenses: the teacher's own perspective, the student's viewpoint, peer reviews, and theoretical literature. In the evaluation phase, the reflection is done through the developer or teaching team's autobiographical lens and the theoretical literature lens to help us make sense of data and observations. This is enriched through the student's eyes upon their feedback of their learning experience with the AI chatbots, but seeing through the lens of colleagues who are not part of the team requires deliberate effort. Sharing findings and insights from this phase with a broader community allows for diverse interpretations, fostering deeper understanding and promoting collaborative growth.

The journey of the TP team exemplifies the power of such sharing. It began with internal discussions among project investigation team members to refine ideas, followed by the establishment of a community of practice (CoP) to engage with peers and share experiences. This CoP became a platform to exchange insights, tweaks, and implementation strategies. Building on this foundation, the team conducted workshops for colleagues at institutional professional development events, equipping them with practical knowledge on how to implement chatbots effectively. These workshops covered a range of topics, from tips for successful deployment to identifying and resolving common challenges. Over time, these efforts expanded beyond the institution, leading to participation in conferences and the publication of findings. This progression—from internal collaboration to external dissemination—illustrates the importance of organizational support, which now becomes more evident, explaining why the first strategy shared was to answer the guiding question, "Who can I work with?".

3.5 Conclusion

The integration of AI chatbots into education, as discussed in this chapter, is a continuation of established learning theories and principles, rather than a departure from them. Vygotsky's (1978) social constructivism emphasizes the centrality of interaction and collaboration in learning, while Deci and Ryan's (1985) self-determination theory highlights the importance of relatedness, autonomy, and competence. Zimmerman's (1990) concept of SRL further underscores the role of learner agency and strategic effort in achieving success. These foundational principles continue to provide the theoretical underpinning for effective teaching and learning with AI. The advent of conversational AI does not change these principles; instead, it offers new tools to implement them. Instructional design processes for AI integration using the ADDIE model remain valid in ensuring that the teaching and learning activities are pedagogically sound and aligned with these evergreen theories, enabling meaningful, learner-centred outcomes. Unpacking the phases to share the key considerations (guiding questions), it is hoped that practitioners keen to adopt integrate AI chatbots into their classroom can effectively support learner engagement, autonomy, and outcomes while adhering to ethical principles such as agency, fairness, inclusivity, and safety.

Future directions for conversational AI in education are expanding rapidly. Researchers are focusing on multimodal interactions that combine text, voice, and visual elements for more immersive experiences and enhance anthropomorphism (Glick et al., 2023; Pentina et al., 2023; Garcia Brustenga et al., 2018). Ethical considerations, including addressing algorithmic bias, safeguarding data privacy, and ensuring inclusivity, remain at the forefront (Williams, 2024; Dwivedi et al., 2023; Kooli, 2023). Additionally, advancements in emotional intelligence within AI are paving the way for chatbots to provide empathetic, contextually appropriate responses (Liu et al., 2023; Janssen et al., 2021; Alsanousi et al., 2023). These developments demonstrate the growing potential of conversational AI to enhance engagement, support diverse learners, and address complex educational needs.

At our institute, significant strides have been taken in applying conversational AI to meet the educational needs. Initiatives like a playbook for using ChatGPT respectively for staff and student and in-house development of retrieval-augmented generation (RAG)-based AI assistants showcase the commitment to leveraging AI chatbot responsibly and effectively. A comprehensive learning roadmap is also designed to support staff in developing the knowledge and skills necessary for the effective and ethical use of AI in teaching and learning. The roadmap includes undergoing modules that provide a practical foundation in AI, techniques for crafting effective AI prompts, strategies for leveraging AI to enhance teaching and learning, and approaches to designing assessments in an AI-augmented landscape. With AI chatbot potential in providing personalized learning, resources site, and mentorship programs for interested tutors to be guided by an experienced colleague in using the AI chatbot effectively, it ensures that learners and educators alike can benefit from these technological advancements. Notably, our recent research into using conversational AI for intangible cultural preservation highlights its versatility beyond academic learning. By developing an AI chatbot to revive Baba Malay, an endangered Singaporean ethnic language, the team is demonstrating the potential of AI to contribute to cultural sustainability.

In conclusion, while the technologies surrounding conversational AI continue to evolve, the principles guiding their integration into education remain constant. By grounding AI applications in established learning theories and robust instructional design frameworks, educators can harness their potential to create engaging, inclusive, and meaningful learning environments.

References

5 Things to Know about the AskPoly Chatbot. (2019, June 20). *Schoolbag*. https://www.schoolbag.edu.sg/story/5-things-to-know-about-the-askpoly-chatbot/

Adamopoulou, E., & Moussiades, L. (2020). Chatbots: History, technology, and applications. *Machine Learning with Applications*, 2, 100006. https://doi.org/10.1016/j.mlwa.2020.100006

Adeshola, I., & Adepoju, A. P. (2023). The opportunities and challenges of ChatGPT in education. *Interactive Learning Environments*, 1–14. https://doi.org/10.1080/10494820.2023.2253858

Al-Abdullatif, A.-M. (2023). Modeling students' perceptions of chatbots in learning: Integrating technology acceptance with the value-based adoption model. *Education Sciences*, 13(11), 1151. https://doi.org/10.3390/educsci13111151

Aleven, V., Mclaren, B., Roll, I., & Koedinger, K. (2006). Toward meta-cognitive tutoring: A model of help seeking with a cognitive tutor. *International Journal of Artificial Intelligence in Education*, 16(2), 101–128.

Ali, C. A., Acquah, S., & Esia-Donkoh, K. (2021). A comparative study of SAM and ADDIE models in simulating STEM instruction. *African Educational Research Journal*, 9(4), 852–859.

Ali, K., Barhom, N., Tamimi, F., & Duggal, M. (2024). ChatGPT—a double-edged sword for healthcare education? Implications for assessments of dental students. *European Journal of Dental Education*, 28(1), 206–211. https://doi.org/10.1111/eje.12937

Allen, M. W., & Sites, R. (2012). *Leaving ADDIE for SAM: An agile model for developing the best learning experiences*. American Society for Training and Development.

Alonso, F., López, G., Manrique, D., & Viñes, J. M. (2005). An instructional model for web-based eLearning education with a blended learning process approach. *British Journal of Educational Technology*, 36, 217–235. http://doi.org/10.1111/j.1467-8535.2005.00454.x

Alsanousi, B., Albesher, A. S., Do, H., & Ludi, S. (2023). Investigating the user experience and evaluating usability issues in AI-enabled learning mobile apps: An analysis of user reviews. *International Journal of Advanced Computer Science and Applications*, 14(6). https://doi.org/10.14569/IJACSA.2023.0140602

Ang, H. M. (2024, February 12). ChatGPT is making its presence felt in classrooms: Here's how schools in Singapore are harnessing it. *Channel News Asia*. https://www.channelnewsasia.com/singapore/chatgpt-schools-singapore-teachers-students-4109836

Atkins, S., Badrie, I., & van Otterloo, S. (2021). Applying ethical AI frameworks in practice: Evaluating conversational AI chatbot solutions. *Computers and Society Research Journal*, 1. https://doi.org/10.54822/QXOM4114

Ausburn, L. J. (2004). Course design elements most valued by adult learners in blended online education environments: An American perspective. *Educational Media International*, 41(4), 327–337. http://doi.org/10.1080/09523980420003148 20

Azevedo, R., Mudrick, N. V., Taub, M., & Bradbury, A. E. (2019). Self-regulation in computer-assisted learning systems. In J. Dunlosky, & K. A. Rawson (Eds.), *The Cambridge handbook of cognition and education* (pp. 587–618). Cambridge University Press. https://doi.org/10.1017/9781108235631.024

Baig, M. I., & Yadegaridehkordi, E. (2024). ChatGPT in higher education: A systematic literature review and research challenges. *International Journal of Educational Research*, 127, 102411. https://doi.org/10.1016/j.ijer.2024.102411

Baskara, R. (2023). Exploring the implications of ChatGPT for language learning in higher education. *Indonesian Journal of English Language Teaching and Applied Linguistics*, 7(2), 343–358. http://doi.org/10.21093/ijeltal.v7i2.1387

Bates, A. W. (2015). *Teaching in a digital age* (1st ed.). Tony Bates Associates Ltd.

Biggs, J. B. (1996). Enhancing teaching through constructive alignment. *Higher Education*, 32(3), 347–364. https://doi.org/10.1007/BF00138871

Branson, R. K., Rayner, G. T., Cox, J. L., Furman, J. P., King, F. J., & Hannum, W. H. (1975). *Interservice procedures for instructional systems development (Phases I, II, III, IV, V, and executive summary)*. US Army Training and Doctrine Command Pamphlet 350. https://apps.dtic.mil/dtic/tr/fulltext/u2/a019486.pdf

Brookfield, S. (1995). *Becoming a critically reflective teacher*. Jossey-Bass.

Burgan, C., Kowalski, J., & Liao, W. (2024). Developing a Retrieval Augmented Generation (RAG) chatbot app using adaptive Large Language Models (LLM) and LangChain framework. *Proceedings of the West Virginia Academy of Science*, 96(1). https://doi.org/10.55632/pwvas.v96i1.1068

Capon-Sieber, V., Köhler, C., Christ, A. A., Helbling, J., & Praetorius, A.-K. (2022). The role of relatedness in the motivation and vitality of university students in online classes during social distancing. *Frontiers in Psychology*, 12, 702323. https://doi.org/10.3389/fpsyg.2021.702323

Chang, D. H., Lin, M. P.-C., Hajian, S., & Wang, Q. Q. (2023). Educational design principles of using AI chatbot that supports self-regulated learning in education: Goal setting, feedback, and personalization. *Sustainability*, 15, 12921. https://doi.org/10.3390/su151712921

Cheung, B. H. H., Lau, G. K. K., Wong, G. T. C., Lee, E. Y. P., Kulkarni, D., Seow, C. S., & Co, M. T. H. (2023). ChatGPT versus human in generating medical graduate exam multiple choice questions—a multinational prospective study (Hong Kong SAR, Singapore, Ireland, and the United Kingdom). *PLoS One*, 18(8), e0290691. https://doi.org/10.1371/journal.pone.0290691

Chin, C., & Osborne, J. (2008). Students' questions: A potential resource for teaching and learning science. *Studies in Science Education*, 44(1), 1–39. https://doi.org/10.1080/03057260701828101

Conversations with Chatbots. (n.d.). *Inside NUS*. https://www.nus.edu.sg/inside-nus/stories/conversations-with-chatbots

Currie, G., Singh, C., Nelson, T., Nabasenja, C., Al-Hayek, Y., & Spuur, K. (2023). ChatGPT in medical imaging higher education. *Radiography*, 29(4), 792–799. https://doi.org/10.1016/j.radi.2023.05.011

Davis, F. D. (1989). Perceived usefulness, perceived ease of use, and user acceptance of information technology. *MIS Quarterly*, 13(3), 319–340. https://doi.org/10.2307/249008

de Sales, A. B., & Antunes, J. G. (2021). Evaluation of educational games usage satisfaction. In *2021 16th Iberian Conference on Information Systems and Technologies (CISTI)* (pp. 1–6). Chaves, Portugal. https://doi.org/10.23919/CISTI52073.2021.9476400

Deci, E. L., & Ryan, R. M. (1985). *Intrinsic motivation and self-determination in human behavior*. Springer. https://doi.org/10.1007/978-1-4899-2271-7

DeeAnn, A. (2012). Chatbots in the library: Is it time? *Library Hi Tech*, 30(1), 95–107.

Deng, X., & Yu, Z. (2023). A meta-analysis and systematic review of the effect of chatbot technology use in sustainable education. *Sustainability*, 15(4), 2940. https://doi.org/10.3390/su15042940

Design Intelligence Lab. (n.d.). VERA. *Georgia Institute of Technology*. https://dilab.gatech.edu/vera/

Dick, W., Carey, L., & Carey, J. (2009). *The systematic design of instruction* (7th ed.). Pearson Higher Education Inc.

D'Silva, G., Jani, M., Jadhav, V., Bhoir, A., & Amin, P. (2020). Career counselling chatbot using cognitive science and artificial intelligence. In H. Vasudevan, A. Michalas, N. Shekokar, & M. Narvekar (Eds.), *Advanced computing technologies and applications: Algorithms for intelligent systems* (pp. 1–9). Springer. https://doi.org/10.1007/978-981-15-3242-9_1

Durall, E., & Kapros, E. (2020). Co-design for a competency self-assessment chatbot and survey in science education. In P. Zaphiris, & A. Ioannou (Eds.), *Learning and collaboration technologies: Human and technology ecosystems: HCII 2020: Lecture notes in computer science* (Vol. 12206). Cham: Springer. https://doi.org/10.1007/978-3-030-50506-6_2

Dwivedi, Y. K., Kshetri, N., Hughes, L., Slade, E. L., Jeyaraj, A., Kar, A. K., Baabdullah, A. M., Koohang, A., Raghavan, V., Ahuja, M., Albanna, H., Albashrawi, M. A.,

Al-Busaidi, A. S., Balakrishnan, J., Barlette, Y., Basu, S., Bose, I., Brooks, L., Buhalis, D., . . . Wirtz, J. (2023). So what if ChatGPT wrote it? Multidisciplinary perspectives on opportunities, challenges and implications of generative conversational AI for research, practice and policy. *International Journal of Information Management*, 71, 102642. https://doi.org/10.1016/j.ijinfomgt.2023.102642

Fang, L., Zhang, H., Chao, J. Y., & Goh, E. (2023). AI chatbot to assist students applying APA (7th edition) style in their academic writing in a polytechnic in Singapore. In D. Glick, J. Bergin, & C. Chang (Eds.), *Supporting self-regulated learning and student success in online courses* (pp. 209–236). IGI Global. https://doi.org/10.4018/978-1-6684-6500-4.ch010

Fauzi, F., Tuhuteru, L., Sampe, F., Ausat, A. M. A., & Hatta, H. R. (2023). Analysing the role of ChatGPT in improving student productivity in higher education. *Journal on Education*, 5(4), 14886–14891. https://doi.org/10.31004/joe.v5i4.2563

Fei, Y., & Petrina, S. (2013). Using learning analytics to understand the design of an intelligent language tutor—chatbot Lucy. *International Journal of Advanced Computer Science and Applications*, 4. https://doi.org/10.14569/IJACSA.2013.041117

Fryer, L. K., Ainley, M., Thompson, A., Gibson, A., & Sherlock, Z. (2017). Stimulating and sustaining interest in a language course: An experimental comparison of chatbot and human task partners. *Computers in Human Behavior*, 75(17), 461–468. https://doi.org/10.1016/j.chb.2017.05.045

Garcia Brustenga, G., Fuertes-Alpiste, M., & Molas-Castells, N. (2018). *Briefing paper: Chatbots in education*. eLearn Center, Universitat Obertade Catalunya. https://doi.org/10.7238/elc.chatbots.2018

Garrison, D. R., Anderson, T., & Archer, W. (1999). Critical inquiry in a text-based environment: Computer conferencing in higher education. *The Internet and Higher Education*, 2(2–3), 87–105. https://doi.org/10.1016/S1096-7516(00)00016-6

Glick, D., Bergin, J., & Chang, C. (2023). *Supporting self-regulated learning and student success in online courses*. IGI-Global. https://doi.org/10.4018/978-1-6684-6500-4

Glick, D., Miedijensky, S., & Zhang, H.-Y. (2024). Examining the effect of AI-powered virtual-human training on STEM majors' self-regulated learning behavior. *Frontiers in Education*, 9, 1465207. https://doi.org/10.3389/feduc.2024.1465207

Goodings, A. J., Kajitani, S., Chhor, A., Albakri, A., Pastrak, M., Kodancha, M., Ives, R., Lee, Y. B., & Kajitani, K. (2024). Assessment of ChatGPT-4 in family medicine board examinations using advanced AI learning and analytical methods: Observational study. *Journal of Medical Internet Research Medical Education*, 10, e56128. https://doi.org/10.2196/56128

Gowtham, S., Harish, R., Bharathi, I., & Rose, B. (2021). Chat bot using AWS. *Iconic Research and Engineering Journals*, 5(1).

Graham, C. R. (2006). Blended learning systems: Definition, current trends, and future directions. In C. J. Bonk, & C. R. Graham (Eds.), *The handbook of blended learning: Global perspectives, local designs* (pp. 3–21). Pfeiffer. http://doi.org/10.2307/4022859

GVU Center. (n.d.). Virtual teaching assistant: Jill Watson. *Georgia Institute of Technology*. https://gvu.gatech.edu/research/projects/virtual-teaching-assistant-jill-watson

Hannan, E., & Liu, S. (2021). AI: New source of competitiveness in higher education. *Competitiveness Review*. Advance online publication. https://doi.org/10.1108/CR-03-2021-0045

Heitzman, N. (2024, July 16). Understanding the evolution: From classic chatbots to RAG chatbots to AI-powered assistants. *Security Industry Association*. https://www.securityindustry.org/2024/07/16/understanding-the-evolution-from-classic-chatbots-to-rag-chatbots-to-ai-powered-assistants/

Hew, K. F., Huang, W., Du, J., & Jia, C. (2023). Using chatbots to support student goal setting and social presence in fully online activities: Learner engagement and perceptions. *Journal of Computing in Higher Education*, 35, 40–68. https://doi.org/10.1007/s12528-022-09338-x

Hien, H., Pham-Nguyen, C., Hoai, N. L. N., Nhung, H. L. T. K., & Thang, L. D. (2018). Intelligent assistants in higher-education environments: The FIT-EBot, a chatbot for administrative and learning support. In *9th International Symposium on Information and Communication Technology Proceedings* (pp. 69–76). Association for Computing Machinery. https://doi.org/10.1145/3287921.3287937

Hobert, S. (2019). How are you, chatbot? Evaluating chatbots in educational settings—results of a literature review. In *Proceedings of Interaktives Lernen* (pp. 259–270). Berlin, Germany. https://doi.org/10.18420/delfi2019_289

Huang, W., Hew, K. F., & Gonda, D. E. (2019). Designing and evaluating three chatbot-enhanced activities for a flipped graduate course. *International Journal of Mechanical Engineering and Robotics Research*, 8(5), 813–818.

Hwang, G. J., & Chang, C. Y. (2021). A review of opportunities and challenges of chatbots in education. *Interactive Learning Environments*, 1–14. Advance online publication. https://doi.org/10.1080/10494820.2021.1952615

Jafari, F., & Keykha, A. (2023). Identifying the opportunities and challenges of artificial intelligence in higher education: A qualitative study. *Journal of Applied Research in Higher Education*, 16(4), 1228–1245. https://doi.org/10.1108/JARHE-09-2023-0426

Janssen, A., Grützner, L., & Breitne, M. (2021). Why do chatbots fail? A critical success factors analysis. In *Proceedings of the International Conference on Information Systems* (pp. 1–6). AIS Electronic Library.

Jasin, J., Ng, H. T., Atmosukarto, I., Prasad, I., Iyer, Faiezin, O., Wong, P. Y. K., Pua, C. Y., & Cheow, W. S. (2023). The implementation of chatbot-mediated immediacy for synchronous communication in an online chemistry course. *Educational Information Technology*, 28, 10665–10690. https://doi.org/10.1007/s10639-023-11602-1

Joint Polytechnic Academy for Educators. (n.d.). *Certificate in Teaching and Learning for Polytechnic Educators (CTLPE)*. https://jpace.polytechnic.edu.sg/ctlpe/

Kabiljo, M., Vidas-Bubanja, M., Matic, R., & Zivkovic, M. (2020). Education system in the republic of Serbia under COVID-19 conditions: Chatbot-acadimic digital assistant of the Belgrade business and arts academy of applied studies. *Knowledge-International Journal*, 43(1), 25–30.

Kaif, M., Sharma, S., & Rana, Dr. S. (2024). Gemini MultiPDF chatbot: Multiple document RAG chatbot using gemini large language model. *International Journal for Research in Applied Science and Engineering Technology*, 12(5), 24–30. https://doi.org/10.22214/ijraset.2024.61195

Kannurao, S., Kwan, E. E., Calaiselvy, Soon, H. W., Zhang, H.-Y., Narayan, S., & Udayakumar, T. (2023). AI for personalised learning support for students in engineering: A joint-polytechnic collaboration project. In *Presentation at SITE Interactive Online Conference 2023*.

Keiper, M. C., Fried, G., Lupinek, J., & Nordstrom, H. (2023). Artificial intelligence in sport management education: Playing the AI game with ChatGPT. *Journal of Hospitality, Leisure, Sport & Tourism Education*, 33, 100456. https://doi.org/10.1016/j.jhlste.2023.100456

Kim, J. (2024). Leading teachers' perspective on teacher-AI collaboration in education. *Education and Information Technologies*, 29(7), 8693–8724. https://doi.org/10.1007/s10639-023-12109-5

Kim, S., Choi, S., Seo, M., Kim, D. R., & Lee, K. (2020). Designing a clinical ethics education program for nurses based on the ADDIE model. *Research and Theory for Nursing Practice*, 34(3), 205–222. https://doi.org/10.1891/RTNP-D-19-00135

Kooli, C. (2023). Chatbots in education and research: A critical examination of ethical implications and solutions. *Sustainability*, 15(7), 5614. https://doi.org/10.3390/su15075614

Kuhail, M. A., Alturki, N., Alramlawi, S., & Alhejori, K. (2023). Interacting with educational chatbots: A systematic review. *Education and Information Technologies*, 28, 973–1018. https://doi.org/10.1007/s10639-022-11177-3

Kurt, S. (2022, August 29). ADDIE model: Instructional design. *Educational Technology*. https://educationaltechnology.net/the-addie-model-instructional-design/

Labadze, L., Grigolia, M., & Machaidze, L. (2023). Role of AI chatbots in education: Systematic literature review. *International Journal of Educational Technology in Higher Education*, 20, 56. https://doi.org/10.1186/s41239-023-00426-1

Lee, S. M., & Tan, H. L. (2016). Instructional design – a new tool in human resource development [Poster]. *Singapore Healthcare Management*. https://www.singaporehealthcaremanagement.sg/Documents/Posters%20Competition%202016/Human%20Resource/HR014%20-%20Lee%20Sook%20May_SHS%20-%20Instructional%20Design%20%E2%80%93%20A%20New%20Tool%20in%20Human%20Resource%20Development.pdf

Li, R.-Y., & Sun, J. C.-Y. (2024). Identifying key factors of dynamic ADDIE model for instructional virtual reality design: An exploratory study. *Interactive Learning Environments*, 1–13. https://doi.org/10.1080/10494820.2023.2296519

Lim, L., & Bannert, M., van de Graaf, J., Molennar, I., Fan, Y., Kilgour, J., Moore, J., & Gašević, D. (2021). Temporal assessment of self-regulated learning by mining students' think-aloud protocols. *Frontiers in Psychology*, 12. https://doi.org/10.3389/fpsyg.2021.749749

Lin, C.-J., & Husni, M. (2021). Learning analytics for investigating the mind map-guided AI chatbot approach in an EFL flipped speaking classroom. *Educational Technology & Society*, 24(4), 16–35. https://doi.org/10.30191/ETS.202110_24(4).0002

Lin, M. P.-C., & Chang, D. (2020). Enhancing post-secondary writers' writing skills with a chatbot: A mixed-method classroom study. *Journal of Educational Technology & Society*, 23(1), 78–92. https://www.jstor.org/stable/26915408

Lin, Y. H., & Tsai, T. (2019). A conversational assistant on mobile devices for primitive learners of computer programming. In *2019 IEEE International Conference on Engineering, Technology and Education Proceedings* (pp. 1–4). IEEE Press. https://doi.org/10.1109/TALE48000.2019.9226015

Liu, D., Lv, Y., & Huang, W. (2023). How do consumers react to chatbots' humorous emojis in service failures. *Technology in Society*, 73, 102244. https://doi.org/10.1016/j.techsoc.2023.102244

Martin, A., Wessel, M., & Alexander, B. (2021). AI-based chatbots in customer service and their effects on user compliance. *Electronic Markets*, 31(2), 427–445. https://doi.org/10.1007/s12525-020-00414-7

Martín-SanJosé, J.-F., Juan, M. C., Gil-Gomez, J.-A., & Rando, N. (2014). Flexible learning itinerary vs. linear learning itinerary. *Science of Computer Programming*, 88. https://doi.org/10.1016/j.scico.2013.12.009

Mayer, R. E. (2001). *Multimedia learning*. Cambridge University Press. https://doi.org/10.1017/CBO9781139164603

Mckie, I., & Narayan, B. (2019). Enhancing the academic library experience with chatbots: An exploration of research and implications for practice. *Journal of the Australian Library and Information Association*, 68, 268–277. https://doi.org/10.1080/24750158.2019.1611694

Meron, Y., & Araci, Y. T. (2023). Artificial intelligence in design education: Evaluating ChatGPT as a virtual colleague for post-graduate course development. *Design Science*, 9, e30. https://doi.org/10.1017/dsj.2023.28

Miao, H., & Ahn, H. (2023). Impact of ChatGPT on interdisciplinary nursing education and research. *Asian/Pacific Island Nursing Journal*, 7, e48136. https://doi.org/10.2196/48136

Ministry of Education. (2024). AI in education ethics framework. *Student Learning Space*. https://www.learning.moe.edu.sg/ai-in-sls/responsible-ai/ai-in-education-ethics-framework/

Mogavi, R. H., Deng, C., Kim, J. J., Zhou, P., Kwon, Y. D., Metwally, A. H. S., & Hui, P. (2024). ChatGPT in education: A blessing or a curse? A qualitative study exploring early adopters' utilization and perceptions. *Computers in Human Behavior: Artificial Humans*, 2(1), 100027. https://doi.org/10.1016/j.chbah.2023.100027

Munoo, R., & Abdullah, R. (2018). Adding ADDIE to the library orientation program at Singapore Management University libraries. In K. Bailin, B. Jahre, & S. Morris (Eds.), *Planning academic library orientations: Case studies from around the world* (pp. 263–271). Chandos Publishing.

Mustafa, B. S., & Madhi, Y. E. (2024). LLM and RAG powered chatbot for the college of computer science and mathematics at the University of Mosul. *International Research Journal of Innovations in Engineering and Technology*, 8(10), 59–61. https://doi.org/10.47001/IRJIET/2024.810010

Ng, T.-J., Ng, K.-W., & Haw, S.-C. (2024). Lib-bot: A smart librarian-chatbot assistant. *International Journal of Computing and Digital Systems*, 16(1). http://dx.doi.org/10.12785/ijcds/160101

Nourani, M., Honeycutt, D. R., Block, J. E., Roy, C., Rahman, T., Ragan, E., & Gogate, V. (2020). Investigating the importance of first impressions and explainable AI with interactive video analysis. In *CHI Conference on Human Factors in Computing Systems Extended Abstracts*. ACM. https://doi.org/10.1145/3334480.3382967

Okonkwo, C. W., & Ade-Ibijola, A. (2021). Chatbots applications in education: A systematic review. *Computers and Education: Artificial Intelligence*, 2, 1–10. https://doi.org/10.1016/j.caeai.2021.100033

Onal, S., & Kulavuz-Onal, D. (2024). A cross-disciplinary examination of the instructional uses of ChatGPT in higher education. *Journal of Educational Technology Systems*, 52(3), 301–324. https://doi.org/10.1177/00472395231196532

Paul, R., & Elder, L. (2006). The thinker's guide to the art of Socratic questioning. *Foundation for Critical Thinking*. https://www.criticalthinking.org/files/SocraticQuestioning2006.pdf

Paykamian, B. (2023, November 16). Should universities build their own custom AI tools in house? *Government Technology*. https://www.govtech.com/education/higher-ed/should-universities-build-their-own-custom-ai-tools-in-house

Pengel, N., Martin, A., Meissner, R., Arndt, T., Neumann, A. T., de Lange, P., & Wollersheim, H. W. (2021). TecCoBot: Technology-aided support for self-regulated learning. In *CEUR-WS Proceedings* (Vol. 3046). https://do.org/10.48550/arXiv.2111.11881

Pentina, I., Hancock, T., & Xie, T. (2023). Exploring relationship development with social chatbots: A mixed-method study of Replika. *Computers in Human Behavior*, 140, 107600. https://doi.org/10.1016/j.chb.2022.107600

Rahman, M. S., Sabbir, M. M., Zhang, J., Moral, I. H., & Hossain, G. M. S. (2023). Examining students' intention to use ChatGPT: Does trust matter? *Australasian Journal of Educational Technology*, 39(6), 51–71. https://doi.org/10.14742/ajet.8956

Rawas, S. (2023). ChatGPT: Empowering lifelong learning in the digital age of higher education. *Education and Information Technologies*, 29, 6895–6908. https://doi.org/10.1007/s10639-023-12114-8

Rey, A., Le Goff, K., Abadie, M., & Courrieu, P. (2020). The primacy order effect in complex decision making. *Psychological Research*, 84, 1739–1748. https://doi.org/10.1007/s00426-019-01178-2

Roll, I., Aleven, V., McLaren, B. M., & Koedinger, K. R. (2011). Metacognitive practice makes perfect: Improving students' self-assessment skills with an intelligent tutoring system. *Artificial Intelligence in Education*, 6738, 288–295. https://doi.org/10.1007/978-3-642-21869-9_38

Rosenberg, M. (2014, March 11). Marc my words: Why I hate ADDIE. *Learning Guild*. https://www.learningguild.com/articles/1365/marc-my-words-why-i-hate-addie/

Sallam, M., & Al-Salahat, K. (2023). Below average ChatGPT performance in medical microbiology exam compared to university students. *Frontiers in Education*, 8, 1333415. https://doi.org/10.3389/feduc.2023.1333415

Schmitt, O., & Buschek, D. (2021). CharacterChat: Supporting the creation of fictional characters through conversation and progressive manifestation with a chatbot. In *Proceedings of the 13th Conference on Creativity and Cognition (C&C '21)* (Article 10, pp. 1–10). Association for Computing Machinery. https://doi.org/10.1145/3450741.3465253

Shi, L., Ding, A.-C., & Choi, I. (2024). Investigating teachers' use of an AI-enabled system and their perceptions of AI integration in science classrooms: A case study. *Education Sciences*, 14(11), 1187. https://doi.org/10.3390/educsci14111187

Simulate. (n.d.). *Aviation management simulations*. https://simulate.aero/

Singapore Government Developer Portal. (2024, May 13). *Developer instruction manual for Infocomm Technology and Smart Systems (ICT&SS) management*. https://www.developer.tech.gov.sg/guidelines/standards-and-best-practices/instruction-manual-for-ict-ss-management.html

Singh, H., Tayarani-Najaran, M. H., & Yaqoob, M. (2023). Exploring computer science students' perception of ChatGPT in higher education: A descriptive and correlation study. *Education Sciences*, 13(9), 924. https://doi.org/10.3390/educsci13090924

SMU Corporate Communications Team. (2018, February 28). SMU is first IHL to launch AI-Chatbot to better serve its students. *SMU Newsroom*. https://news.smu.edu.sg/news/2018/02/28/smu-first-ihl-launch-ai-chatbot-better-serve-its-students

Smutny, P., & Schreiberova, P. (2020). Chatbots for learning: A review of educational chatbots for the Facebook Messenger. *Computers & Education*, 151(103862), 1–11. https://doi.org/10.1016/j.compedu.2020.103862

Spatioti, A. G., Kazanidis, I., & Pange, J. A. (2022). Comparative study of the ADDIE instructional design model in distance education. *Information*, 13(9), 402. https://doi.org/10.3390/info13090402

Sreeja, M. K., & Chithra, R. N. (2022). An intelligent chatbot for college enquiry with Amazon Lex. *International Research Journal of Engineering and Technology*, 9(12).

Sweller, J. (1988). Cognitive load during problem solving: Effects on learning. *Cognitive Science*, 12(2), 257–285. https://doi.org/10.1016/0364-0213(88)90023-7

Tajik, E., & Tajik, F. (2023). A comprehensive examination of the potential application of ChatGPT in higher education institutions. *TechRxiv*, 1–10. https://doi.org/10.36227/techrxiv.22589497.v1

Tang, Y., & Hew, K. T. (2022). Effects of using mobile instant messaging on student behavioral, emotional, and cognitive engagement: A quasi-experimental study. *International Journal of Educational Technology in Higher Education*, 19(3). https://doi.org/10.1186/s41239-021-00306-6

Thilarajah, S., & Divaharan, S. (2019). Conversational bots as electronic performance support system for the professional development of teacher educators. In S. Chew, Y. Wei, C. Kah Mun, & A. Alphonso (Eds.), *Australasian Society for Computers in Learning in Tertiary Education (ASCILITE) 2019 Conference Proceedings* (Vol. 36, pp. 577–581).

Thyagarajan, J., Gupta, G., & Matvitskyy, O. (2023). *How to manage blended teams of in-house and outsourced software engineering personnel*. Gartner Research.

van Vulpen, E. (n.d.). ADDIE model explained: All you need to know. *Academy to Innovate HR*. https://www.aihr.com/blog/addie-model/

Vijayakumar, S., Tamil Arasan, P., & Venkateswara, U. (2023). Efficacy of ADDIE-integrated flipped learning model: An intervention study. *International Journal of E-Adoption*, 15(2), 1–10. https://doi.org/10.4018/IJEA.316536

Von Garrel, J., & Mayer, J. (2023). Artificial Intelligence in studies—use of ChatGPT and AI-based tools among students in Germany. *Humanities and Social Sciences Communications*, 10(1), 1–9. https://doi.org/10.1057/s41599-023-02304-7

Vygotsky, L. (1978). *Mind in society*. Harvard University Press. https://doi.org/10.2307/j.ctvjf9vz4

Wan Hamzah, W. M. A. F., Ismail, I., Yusof, M. K., Mohd Saany, S. I., & Yacob, A. (2021). Using learning analytics to explore responses from student conversations with chatbot for education. *International Journal of Engineering Pedagogy (IJEP)*, 11(6), 70–84. https://doi.org/10.3991/ijep.v11i6.23475

Weber, P., & Ludwig, T. (2020). (Non-)interacting with conversational agents: Perceptions and motivations of using chatbots and voice assistants. In *Proceedings of Mensch und Computer 2020* (pp. 321–331). New York, NY: Association for Computing Machinery.

Widyastuti, E., & Susiana. (2019). Using the ADDIE model to develop learning material for actuarial mathematics. *Journal of Physics: Conference Series*, 1188(1). https://doi.org/10.1088/1742-6596/1188/1/012052

Williams, R. T. (2024). The ethical implications of using generative chatbots in higher education. *Frontiers in Education*, 8, 1331607. https://doi.org/10.3389/feduc.2023.1331607

Wollny, S., Schneider, J., Di Mitri, D., Weidlich, J., Rittberger, M., & Drachsler, H. (2021). Are we there yet?—a systematic literature review on chatbots in education. *Frontiers in Artificial Intelligence*, 4, 654924. https://doi.org/10.3389/frai.2021.654924

Wysa. (n.d.). FAQ. *Wysa*. https://www.wysa.com/faq

Yeh, H.-C., & Tseng, S.-S. (2019). Using the ADDIE model to nurture the development of teachers' CALL professional knowledge. *Journal of Educational Technology & Society*, 22(3), 88–100. https://doi.org/10.30191/ETS.201907_22(3).0008

Zakos, J., & Capper, L. (2008). CLIVE—an artificially intelligent chat robot for conversational language practice. In J. Darzentas, G. A. Vouros, S. Vosinakis, & A. Arnellos (Eds.), *Lecture Notes in Computer Science: Vol. 5138. Artificial Intelligence: Theories, Models and Applications, SETN 2008*. Springer. https://doi.org/10.1007/978-3-540-87881-0_46

Zhang, H.-Y., & Fang, L. (2024). Successful chatbot design for polytechnic students in Singapore. *Educational Media International*, 60(3–4), 224–241. https://doi.org/10.1080/09523987.2023.2324585

Zhang, H.-Y., Fang, L., Miao, H., & Goh, E. (2022). AI chatbot to teach Microsoft Excel [Poster presentation]. In *Applied Learning Conference*. Singapore: Singapore Institute of Technology. https://doi.org/10.25447/sit.19210686.v1

Zimmerman, B. J. (1990). Self-regulated learning and academic achievement: An overview. *Educational Psychologist*, 25(1), 3–17. https://doi.org/10.120715326985ep2501_2

Zimmerman, B. J. (2011). Motivational sources and outcomes of self-regulated learning and performance. In B. J. Zimmerman, & D. H. Schunk (Eds.), *Handbook of self-regulation of learning and performance* (pp. 49–64). Routledge.

4

Reimagining Teaching and Learning for Computer Science Education: Implementation of Serious Game With Learning Analytics

Linda William

4.1 Introduction

The evolution of digital learning tools has transformed the landscape of education, particularly in fields requiring complex problem-solving skills such as computer science education. Serious games have emerged as an innovative pedagogical approach designed to enhance engagement, motivation, and skill acquisition by integrating interactive elements with targeted learning objectives (Becker, 2021; Ifenthaler et al., 2015). Unlike traditional instructional methods, which often rely on passive learning, serious games create an immersive environment that promotes active problem-solving, logical reasoning, and strategic thinking—skills that are fundamental to mastering computer science courses (Muratet et al., 2009). Serious games address these challenges by offering dynamic, real-time feedback and interactive problem-solving tasks that align with core programming principles.

However, despite their potential benefits, implementing serious games in programming education presents significant challenges. Two primary concerns are: (1) understanding students' skill development and performance improvement and (2) effectively capturing and analyzing relevant data to optimize learning outcomes (William et al., 2021). Addressing these challenges requires integrating Artificial Intelligence (AI)-based learning analytics, which can provide deeper insights into student progress and offer personalized recommendations tailored to individual learning needs (Garcia-Ruiz et al., 2011). By leveraging learning analytics, educators can track students' engagement levels, problem-solving approaches, and overall comprehension, enabling them to refine instructional strategies and support students more effectively (Loh et al., 2015).

The integration of serious games with learning analytics serves a dual purpose. First, it enhances students' learning experiences by providing

DOI: 10.1201/9781003599357-5

continuous feedback, helping them identify strengths and areas for improvement while reinforcing programming concepts through interactive problem-solving (Coelho et al., 2011). Second, it empowers educators by offering real-time data-driven insights into student challenges, facilitating timely interventions and personalized guidance (William et al., 2019). This adaptive feedback mechanism aligns with modern pedagogical frameworks that emphasize student-centered learning and self-paced mastery of complex subjects (de Freitas & Jarvis, 2008).

This chapter shares the experience and insights gained from the design, development, and implementation of a serious game analytics engine integrated with AI-driven learning analytics, developed to support and personalize computer science education. The initiative was guided by strong alignment with stakeholder needs and learning theories—ensuring the engine serves both students and educators effectively. For students, the game offers an engaging, adaptive learning environment that fosters active participation and supports self-paced mastery of computer science concepts. For educators, the learning analytics engine provides real-time, actionable insights into student progress through intuitive analytics dashboards. Key aspects of the engine design and development include the selection of appropriate AI and machine learning (ML) models and seamless integration with a structured database to capture and analyze student interactions. These elements collectively enable a data-driven, personalized learning pathway tailored to each student's understanding and performance. The chapter also details the engine's deployment at Temasek Polytechnic (TP), focusing on feedback from students' and educators' experiences. Findings show that the integration of learning analytics and personalized recommendations not only supports student learning outcomes but also empowers educators to make timely interventions. Finally, the chapter discusses practical insights and challenges encountered during development, including issues related to data privacy and scalability. These are intended to serve as a guide for educators aiming to implement similar serious games in computer science courses or other domains, highlighting key considerations for successful adoption and sustainability.

4.1.1 Serious Game Definition

There are numerous definitions of serious games, also known as educational games, reflecting their diverse applications and evolving role in education and training (Doerner et al., 2016). De Freitas (2006) defines a serious game as a system designed to create engaging and immersive learning experiences by leveraging the characteristics of video and computer games to achieve specific learning goals and outcomes. Similarly, Michael and Chen (2005) describe a serious game as one that extends beyond simply teaching facts and rote memorization, encompassing all aspects of education, including teaching, training, and informing. Sawyer (2011) emphasizes serious games as games that are specially designed for purposes other than or in addition to pure entertainment. These definitions highlight the fundamental role of serious games in promoting active learning through interactivity and engagement (Alvarez & Damien, 2011; Laamarti et al., 2014; Djaouti et al., 2011; Loh et al., 2015). While some scholars define serious games broadly, applying the term to both digital and non-digital formats (such as board and card games), others emphasize that serious games must be digital (Doerner et al., 2016). Historically, Abt (1987) first coined the term "serious game" with a focus on board and card games, showing that the concept predates digital technology. However, with the rise of video games, the definition has evolved to predominantly refer to digital games used for educational or training purposes. In essence, a serious game is any game designed with a primary purpose beyond entertainment, integrating learning objectives within an engaging and interactive experience. Through engagement and interaction with information, tools, materials, and other students in the serious game, students would voluntarily learn and master their knowledge and skills (Kim et al., 2009).

4.1.2 Serious Game Versus Gamification

Serious games should also be distinguished from gamification, as they serve different purposes. Gamification refers to the application of game elements and methodologies to non-game contexts (Deterding et al., 2011), enhancing processes through game-related features that increase engagement, usability, and user satisfaction (Huotari & Hamari, 2017). It is often used to drive behaviors, improve productivity, and create enjoyable experiences in various domains, including business and education (Morschheuser et al., 2018; Rajanen & Rajanen, 2017; Liu et al., 2017). Unlike serious games, gamification does not inherently involve learning and can be implemented in any context without requiring a fully developed game structure (Becker, 2021). For example, companies use gamification techniques such as points, reward systems, and badges to enhance brand loyalty and customer engagement. In education, gamification may introduce game-like elements, such as narratives, multiple learning paths, and choice-based assessments, to create a more engaging and student-centered experience. However, while gamification applies game mechanics to enhance non-game activities, serious games are structured as full-fledged games designed with a primary educational or training purpose. Thus, gamification is not necessarily a game, whereas a serious game integrates both gameplay and learning objectives.

4.1.3 Benefits and Limitations of Serious Games

Serious games have been widely recognized for their ability to enhance learning engagement, motivation, and cognitive development, making them valuable educational tools across various disciplines (Ma et al., 2011). One of the key benefits of serious games is their capacity to encourage active participation by immersing students in interactive and dynamic learning environments (Pacheco-Velazquez et al., 2024). Unlike traditional learning methods, serious games stimulate curiosity and motivation, which increases intrinsic engagement and promote sustained learning efforts (Ma et al., 2011; Rieber, 1996; Knight et al., 2010; Kumar, 2000). Through problem-solving tasks and challenges, these games help students develop critical thinking, analytical reasoning, and strategic decision-making skills that are transferable to real-world situations. Furthermore, serious games provide immediate feedback, allowing students to self-monitor their progress, identify areas for improvement, and adapt their strategies accordingly (Hou, 2015). This aspect is particularly beneficial in skill-based learning, where students refine their abilities through iterative practice, reinforcement, and real-time corrections. In addition, serious games cater to different learning styles and paces, offering adaptive difficulty levels that ensure students remain challenged without feeling overwhelmed (Dyulicheva & Glazieva, 2021). This personalized approach fosters a sense of achievement and mastery (Bontchev et al., 2021), which further reinforces engagement and retention of knowledge.

While serious games offer numerous educational benefits, they also present significant limitations, particularly in evaluating students' skill development and performance improvement, as well as in effectively capturing and analyzing relevant gameplay data (William et al., 2021). One of the key challenges in serious games is understanding how well students acquire and apply skills throughout their interactions within the game. Mayo (2007) examined the learning effectiveness of three serious games—Geography Explorer, Virtual Cell, and Dimenxian—and found that students who engaged with these games showed higher learning outcomes compared to those in control groups who learned through interactive lectures. In contrast, Wong et al. (2007) evaluated Metalloman, a serious game designed to teach physiology concepts, by comparing its effectiveness with hypertext and text-based instruction (Wong et al., 2007). Their findings revealed comparable knowledge gains across all enriched media formats (game, replay, and hypertext), suggesting that media richness alone may not be a determining factor in learning effectiveness. This contrasts with Mayo's (2007) results, indicating that while some serious games significantly enhance learning outcomes (Mayo, 2007), others may not necessarily outperform alternative media-based learning approaches. These contrasting findings highlight the need for further investigation into the specific conditions and design elements that make serious games effective learning tools.

In addition to the findings mentioned earlier, unlike traditional assessments such as exams or structured assignments, where progress is measured in a standardized manner, serious games often involve non-linear learning paths that allow students to explore concepts at their own pace. This flexibility makes it difficult to track learning gains and compare student progress accurately (Wouters et al., 2013). Additionally, students may develop problem-solving strategies or acquire knowledge in unintended ways, making it harder to evaluate whether a game is effectively teaching the intended concepts. If the game does not provide detailed learning analytics or structured evaluations, educators may struggle to determine whether students are truly progressing or simply engaging with the game without meaningful learning outcomes (Loh et al., 2015).

Another major limitation is the complexity of capturing and analyzing in-game data to assess learning outcomes. Serious games generate vast amounts of student data, including decision-making patterns, task completion times, interaction sequences, and problem-solving approaches. However, translating this data into meaningful insights about student learning behaviors and cognitive processes remains a challenge. Unlike traditional learning environments, where structured assessments offer direct performance metrics, serious games require advanced data analytics and AI-driven learning assessment tools to extract meaningful learning indicators (Serrano-Laguna et al., 2018). Furthermore, while some serious games incorporate learning analytics, they may not always align with educational standards, making it difficult for educators to interpret results in an actionable way. Privacy and ethical concerns also arise in storing, processing, and sharing in-game data, as educational institutions must ensure compliance with data protection regulations while leveraging these insights for curriculum improvement (Ifenthaler et al., 2016).

4.1.4 Challenges in Computer Science Education

The rapid advancement of digital technology has significantly increased the demand for skilled computer science professionals, with projections indicating that this demand will continue to outpace the average growth of other occupations (Kerk, 2024). As a result, computer science courses have been incorporated into curricula at various educational levels, from secondary schools to universities, to equip students with essential computational skills (Singapore Ministry of Education, 2018; Infocomm Media Development Authority, 2024). However, these courses are often regarded as some of the most challenging subjects, leading to high failure and dropout rates worldwide (e.g., (Bornat & Dehnadi, 2008; Jenkins, 2002; Mendes et al., 2012)).

The difficulties encountered by students in learning computer science are multifaceted. Researchers have categorized these challenges into ten key areas, including understanding syntax and semantics, problem decomposition, algorithmic thinking, debugging skills, and managing cognitive load when writing complex code (Butler & Morgan, 2007; Ismail et al., 2010; Sarpong et al., 2013). One of the primary challenges is the abstract nature of computer science and programming, which requires students to think in a structured and logical manner, often different from how they approach problem-solving in other disciplines (Jenkins, 2002). Additionally, many students struggle with applying theoretical knowledge to practical coding tasks, as they often learn computer science or programming concepts in isolation without sufficient hands-on experience (Hou et al., 2023). Computer science courses also demand precision and attention to detail, and even minor errors such as a missing semicolon can lead to code failures, causing frustration and discouragement among beginners. Furthermore, introductory computer science courses tend to adopt a one-size-fits-all approach, failing to accommodate the diverse backgrounds, learning paces, and cognitive abilities of students, which exacerbates learning difficulties (Lahtinen et al., 2005). The cognitive load imposed by learning multiple aspects of programming simultaneously—such as syntax, logic, debugging, and problem-solving—can overwhelm students, making it difficult to retain information and apply concepts effectively.

Addressing these challenges requires a holistic approach that combines pedagogical innovations, adaptive learning technologies, and personalized teaching methods. Educators focus on scaffolding learning experiences, providing incremental challenges, and incorporating game-based learning, visual programming tools, and real-world problem-solving tasks to make programming more accessible and engaging (Guzdial, 2015). Additionally, integrating AI-driven learning analytics into programming courses can offer personalized insights, detect learning difficulties early, and adapt instructional methods to suit individual students' needs (Ihantola et al., 2015). Given the increasing demand for computer science skills, refining teaching methodologies, assessment strategies, and support systems is crucial to ensuring that students not only learn to code but also develop the problem-solving mindset necessary for success in the evolving digital landscape.

4.1.5 Serious Games in Computer Science Education

Serious games have been increasingly implemented in computer science courses to address the shortcomings of traditional teaching methods by transforming abstract theories into practical, hands-on experiences (Coelho et al., 2011; Muratet et al., 2009; Miljanovic & Bradbury, 2018; Kazimoglu et al., 2012). These games provide an engaging, interactive learning environment where students actively participate in coding-related challenges, rather than passively absorbing theoretical concepts (Robins et al., 2003). By simulating real-world programming tasks such as debugging, algorithm design, and logical reasoning, serious games enable students to apply and refine their coding skills in a risk-free setting, where they can experiment with different solutions without the pressure of real-world consequences or abilities (Wouters et al., 2013).

One of the key advantages of serious games in computer science education is their ability to enhance problem-solving and critical-thinking skills (Wouters et al., 2013; Kazimoglu et al., 2012). Computer science courses require a structured and logical approach, and serious games encourage students to develop these skills through iterative learning and adaptive challenges. Unlike traditional instructional methods, which often focus on syntax and memorization, serious games place students in complex, real-world problem-solving scenarios, helping them build a deeper understanding of algorithms, data structures, and computational thinking. This active learning approach improves students' engagement and motivation, making programming more accessible and enjoyable, especially for beginners who may feel intimidated by the subject. Another benefit of serious games is the personalized feedback and adaptive learning experience they provide (Bellotti et al., 2013; Wouters et al., 2013). Many serious games include built-in analytics and tracking systems that monitor students' progress, identify their strengths and weaknesses, and adapt the difficulty level accordingly (Miljanovic & Bradbury, 2018). This ensures that students receive immediate, tailored feedback based on their actions, allowing them to correct mistakes and reinforce their understanding of computer science concepts in real time. Unlike traditional assessments, which often provide delayed feedback, serious games help students learn from their mistakes on the spot, accelerating their learning curve. Additionally, these games can accommodate varied learning styles, offering visual, hands-on, and experimental learning experiences that cater to different student needs (Muratet et al., 2009).

The majority of serious games designed for computer science education utilize block-based environments to facilitate learning among novices (Vahldick et al., 2021). These environments employ visual blocks that represent code segments, enabling students to construct programs by assembling these blocks. This approach effectively reduces syntax-related challenges, especially for younger students. It allows students to focus on understanding fundamental computer science concepts without the frustration of debugging errors (Eguiluz et al., 2017; Perin et al., 2023). In contrast, text-based and quiz-based serious games are less commonly employed in computer science education. The effectiveness of these approaches has not been extensively examined, resulting in a gap in understanding their impact compared to block-based methods.

4.2 Weighing the Pros and Cons of Commercial Serious Games

Commercial serious games for computer science education offer ready-made, interactive platforms designed to engage students in learning programming concepts, problem-solving, and logical thinking through gameplay. These games often feature user-friendly interfaces, gamified challenges, and structured progression systems that make learning more accessible and enjoyable.

To explore the potential and challenges associated with commercial serious games, CodeCombat (Code Combat, 2013) was implemented as an additional tool for teaching the Python programming language at the School of Informatics and IT, TP (William, 2021). CodeCombat is an educational game launched in 2013 that introduces programming concepts through an interactive, text-based game environment. Unlike block-based programming games, CodeCombat requires students to write actual script-based code, supporting languages such as JavaScript and Python as inputs to navigate the game world and complete levels. The game is an online web game that is structured as a medieval adventure, where students control a hero character who embarks on a journey through multiple levels. Each level presents a unique programming challenge that must be solved using real coding commands to collect gems and defeat multiple enemies by inputting the real code lines from a specific programming language (Yücel & Rızvanoğlu, 2019). The students would not need to use a specific programming interpreter tool. However, it would create a similar experience from which the students can go on to learn programming more easily (Wood et al., 2015).

4.2.1 Implementation in Computer Science Courses

The free and paid version of CodeCombat was incorporated into a Python programming subject for a class of students in October 2019 as a supplementary learning tool to reinforce their understanding of Python programming concepts (William, 2021). The decision to adopt CodeCombat was driven by several key factors. One of the primary reasons for choosing this game was its open-access model, allowing educators to integrate it into introductory programming courses without financial constraints. The first subject in CodeCombat, Introduction to Programming Science, particularly benefited from this, as it enabled students to access foundational programming lessons freely, reducing barriers to entry for those new to coding. Additionally, CodeCombat provides flexibility in classroom management, which was another major reason for its selection.

The students were given one week to explore and play the game independently. During this period, they were expected to complete a designated number of levels that covered fundamental programming concepts such as sequential execution, loops, conditionals, and functions. The purpose of this activity was to allow students to engage with programming in a self-paced manner, fostering problem-solving skills and logical thinking through progressively challenging game scenarios. To ensure accountability and track their progress, students were required to submit proof of completion at the end of the week. This proof consisted of screenshots or exported progress reports from CodeCombat, demonstrating that they had completed the assigned levels. This submission served as a graded component of the course, allowing students to earn participation marks based on their engagement with the game.

4.2.2 Learning Impact and Positive Experience

The effectiveness of CodeCombat in enhancing students' programming skills was evident through a marked improvement in post-test scores following the game's implementation. A comparison between pretest and posttest results revealed a significant increase in the number of correct responses, indicating measurable gains in students' understanding of computer science concepts. This positive learning progression suggests that the game-based approach not only engaged students but also effectively facilitated the acquisition and application of coding skills. The results reinforce the value of serious games like CodeCombat in supporting the development of computer science proficiency through interactive and experiential learning.

Feedback from students also highlighted a highly positive learning experience with CodeCombat, particularly noting the value of the real-time feedback provided during gameplay. Students found the instant responses to their code submissions both effective and supportive, as the guidance and error messages helped them troubleshoot, refine their logic, and reinforce key programming concepts. This immediate feedback was perceived as instrumental in building coding confidence and fostering a deeper understanding. Moreover, students consistently described the game environment as enjoyable and engaging, with its interactive challenges and game-like progression contributing to a motivating and rewarding learning journey. These reflections underscore the potential of serious games like CodeCombat not only to teach computer science but also to create a positive and immersive learning experience that encourages persistence and active participation.

4.2.3 Limitations of the Commercial Serious Games

While the positive feedback from the commercial game implementation highlights its potential to enhance computer science education, several limitations were identified that constrain its effectiveness as a structured instructional tool. As a commercially developed platform, these games offer limited flexibility in aligning with specific curriculum goals. Designed with a predefined structure and general-purpose content, the game does not allow educators to modify or supplement learning materials, introduce additional concepts, or adapt the game flow to match institutional syllabi. This rigidity forces educators to work within the constraints of the existing framework, reducing the game's applicability across diverse teaching contexts and student needs.

Another notable limitation is the lack of robust progress monitoring. Educators are only provided with basic indicators, such as level completion, without access to deeper insights into student performance. Key metrics—such as coding efficiency, common error patterns, and time spent on tasks—are not available, making it difficult to identify learning gaps or intervene effectively. As a result, students who struggle with specific programming concepts may not receive timely support, which can hinder their overall learning progression.

Furthermore, the absence of personalized learning features restricts the game's ability to accommodate individual learning differences. The standardized approach means that all students receive the same tasks and feedback, regardless of their proficiency levels. Those who face difficulties are limited to retrying the same challenges without receiving adaptive guidance or tailored feedback. In contrast, personalized learning systems dynamically adjust the difficulty, provide context-specific hints, and adapt to student performance in real time—features that are critical for supporting differentiated learning pathways.

Together, these limitations reveal important areas for future enhancement. Improving content customization, integrating detailed learning analytics, and incorporating adaptive learning mechanisms would significantly increase the game's educational value. Addressing these gaps presents an opportunity to evolve platforms into more powerful tools that support both effective teaching and individualized student learning in computer science education.

4.3 From Design to Delivery: Smart Serious Game Analytics Engine

Recognizing the limitations of commercial serious games—such as limited customization, basic progress tracking, and lack of personalized learning—there is a clear need for a more adaptable and pedagogically grounded solution. To bridge this gap, a serious game analytics engine was conceptualized to support diverse learning contexts while aligning with specific curriculum outcomes. From design to delivery, several key aspects must be addressed to ensure the serious game effectively supports learning objectives and functions smoothly in real-world educational settings. These key aspects are summarized in Figure 4.1.

4.3.1 Design: Stakeholder-Driven Requirements Gathering

To ensure that the serious game analytics engine effectively meets the needs of both students and educators, it is essential to gather comprehensive requirements through direct engagement with stakeholders (Whitehead, 2007). The requirement-gathering processes were conducted from October 2019 to July 2020. It was a multistep, stakeholder-driven approach to ensure the engine aligned with both pedagogical goals and practical classroom needs. Initial discussions and interviews were held with educators to understand the challenges in assessing student performance, identifying learning

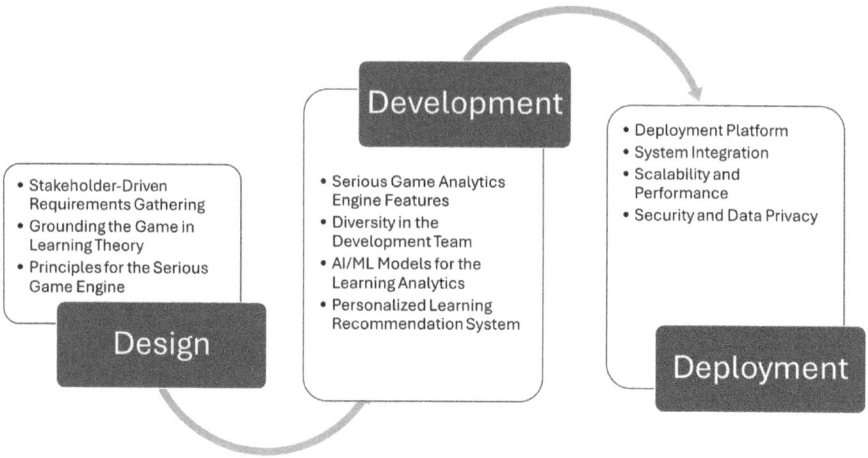

FIGURE 4.1
Key Aspects for Smart Serious Game Analytics Engine

gaps, and delivering personalized support in programming education. Observations, focus group sessions, and surveys were conducted with students to capture their learning preferences, engagement factors, and expectations from a game-based learning environment.

Insights gathered from these processes were synthesized into a clear set of functional and non-functional requirements, with a focus on customizable content, real-time learning analytics, adaptive feedback, and seamless integration with existing educational platforms. To ensure the system remained both pedagogically sound and practically relevant, the requirements were iteratively reviewed and validated with key stakeholders. These validated requirements were then organized into seven main components, outlined as follows.

1. **Alignment to learning outcomes**

   Learning outcomes are clear, specific statements that describe what students are expected to know, understand, or be able to do after completing a course or an activity. They are carefully crafted by educators for each topic or subtopic within a course or subject. Learning through serious games would need to fulfil these learning outcomes. The alignment between the game and learning outcomes is crucial to ensuring that students acquire the intended concepts, skills, and knowledge through gameplay. To maximize educational value, the game must be designed to reinforce key learning outcomes, ensuring that challenges, tasks, and interactions directly contribute to skill development and knowledge retention. A well-structured game should seamlessly integrate subject-specific learning goals, making the gaming experience both engaging and academically meaningful.

2. **Flexible assessment points**

   Assessment points serve as dynamic measures to evaluate students' skill and knowledge development through gameplay. These points, structured as questions for each topic or subtopic, should be aligned with learning outcomes while allowing flexibility in number and difficulty based on subject complexity. A robust analytics engine can adaptively track student progress by analyzing gameplay data, including time spent on tasks, response accuracy, and problem-solving patterns. By varying assessment points and monitoring trends over time, educators can identify learning gaps, personalize interventions, and enhance conceptual understanding, ensuring that assessments provide meaningful insights into students' learning trajectories.

3. **Adaptable game scenarios**

   Game scenarios in a serious game should seamlessly integrate pedagogical elements such as learning outcomes and assessment points with engaging entertainment features like fantasy, challenge, and playability. To effectively capture student learning, scenarios must be adaptable, allowing adjustments based on student progress and subject requirements. By aligning assessments with in-game challenges, students remain immersed in the learning process, engaging voluntarily while developing new concepts, skills, and knowledge. A well-designed scenario ensures that students actively interact with educational content, reinforcing understanding through experience while also providing educators with insights into individual learning trajectories and knowledge retention.

4. **Capture learning through in-game events**

   In-game events must be strategically designed to ensure meaningful learning experiences. These events should trigger key learning moments, reinforcing concepts through interactive challenges and decision-making scenarios. Instant feedback mechanisms play a crucial role in guiding students, allowing them to recognize mistakes, reflect on their understanding, and refine their skills in real time. By dynamically adapting events based on student performance, the game keeps students engaged while capturing their learning progress. A well-managed event structure ensures that every action contributes to knowledge acquisition, helping educators assess cognitive development, problem-solving abilities, and overall subject mastery.

5. **Relevant game data to capture and analyze**

   To assess students' skill development and knowledge improvement, relevant game data must be collected and analyzed based on in-game events. Key data points include time spent completing levels, response time for assessment tasks, number of attempts to succeed, and reliance on hints. Tracking progress across levels provides insights into learning patterns, while student feedback helps identify challenges faced during gameplay. By retrieving and analyzing these data points, educators can evaluate student engagement, identify knowledge gaps, and refine instructional strategies, ensuring that the game effectively captures and supports the learning process.

6. **Serious game learning analytics**

   Serious game analytics play a crucial role in assessing students' skill development and knowledge acquisition by leveraging data collected during gameplay. By analyzing game data, educators can gain valuable insights into students' learning progress, engagement levels, and areas requiring additional support. An analytics dashboard should be developed to visualize these insights. It will include performance graphs tracking individual and group progress, time-spent analysis to assess engagement, and student clustering to identify those who may need additional guidance from educators. Additionally, feedback analysis will provide insights into students' experiences, challenges, and perceptions of the game-based learning process. To maximize its impact, the learning analytics engine must be fully integrated into the serious game framework, ensuring that assessment criteria, difficulty levels, and learning objectives remain adaptable. Educators should have the flexibility to customize game content, modify assessments dynamically, and tailor interventions based on real-time data. The engine should also be scalable, supporting multiple disciplines and a diverse range of student cohorts.

7. **Configurable game setting**

   A serious game environment must be flexible and adaptive to accommodate different subjects, topics, and subtopics, each with unique learning outcomes and assessment points. To ensure effective learning, the game environment should allow customization of content, difficulty levels, and evaluation criteria without extensive modifications. A well-structured serious game analytics framework must seamlessly integrate these variations, enabling educators to adjust scenarios, assessments, and learning pathways based on curriculum needs. By supporting dynamic content adaptation, the game environment enhances engagement, reinforces subject-specific skills, and ensures alignment with educational objectives across diverse disciplines and learning contexts.

4.3.2 Design: Grounding the Game in Learning Theory

The design of the serious game analytics engine is grounded by multiple pedagogical theories, including constructivism (Bada & Olusegun, 2015), mastery learning (Motamedi & Sumrall, 2000), and formative and summative assessment (Dixson & Worrell, 2016). Constructivism learning theory emphasizes that students actively construct their understanding and knowledge through experiences, reflection, and interaction with their environment. In the context of serious games, constructivism serves as a powerful pedagogical foundation, as it aligns closely with experiential, hands-on learning. Students should be able to explore, experiment, and solve problems in a game environment. The engine should include a variety of challenges to encourage students to apply prior knowledge, test hypotheses, receive feedback, and iteratively improve their understanding—core tenets of constructivist learning. The game should provide interactions that promotes self-directed learning and fosters critical thinking, as students are required to make decisions, adapt strategies, and reflect on outcomes. Furthermore, the engine should incorporate narrative elements and contextual scenarios, which help students make meaningful connections between abstract concepts and real-world applications.

Mastery learning strategies emphasize that all students can achieve a high level of understanding if given the appropriate time, support, and learning conditions. In the context of serious games, these strategies are embedded through features that allow students to progress at their own pace, repeat tasks until mastery is achieved, and receive immediate, targeted feedback. The serious game analytics engine should be designed with mastery learning in mind to include level-based progression, adaptive difficulty, and performance tracking to ensure that students fully grasp each concept before moving forward. By enabling repeated practice and personalized feedback loops, the engine provides an effective environment for students to develop and reinforce programming skills, aligning well with the core principles of mastery learning.

Assessment strategies in serious games encompass both formative and summative approaches to provide a comprehensive understanding of student learning. Formative assessment is embedded within gameplay through real-time feedback, adaptive challenges, and guided hints that help students reflect, adjust, and improve as they progress. These continuous, low-stakes interactions support skill development and concept reinforcement within a non-threatening environment. On the other hand, summative assessment is implemented through the completion of key tasks, level progression, or performance scores that reflect students' overall mastery of learning objectives. To support both formative and summative assessment, the serious game engine should include both learning and evaluation levels. At the learning level, the game will include learning videos, a series of questions that students must answer as accurately as possible, and a series of hints to help the students learn. This level should provide formative assessment using the hint features for each question. At the evaluation level, the students should answer questions within a limited period to proceed and progress in the game.

4.3.3 Design: Principles of the Serious Game Engine

The design of the serious game analytics engine must strike a delicate balance between pedagogy and entertainment to create an engaging yet educational experience. To make sure that the game aligns with game elements, instructional strategies, and assessment methods, ensuring that serious games support educational outcomes while maintaining engaging and immersive experiences across various disciplines, this serious game analytics engine would be designed based on the Game-Based Learning Framework (Van Staalduinen & de Freitas, 2011). In terms of pedagogical design, the game engine emphasizes cognitive skill development, particularly problem-solving abilities, which require situational awareness to attend and to perceive the relevant information in a situation, comprehend this information, and predict how the situation may develop (O'Brien & O'Hare, 2007). By embedding cognitive learning principles within an engaging gameplay structure, the engine ensures that students not only acquire knowledge but also develop essential problem-solving skills in an interactive and motivating environment.

In terms of entertainment components, the engine incorporates key entertainment components based on the taxonomy of game pleasure (Hunicke et al., 2004). These components are essential in maintaining students' interest and motivation, leading to subconscious self-learning as they strive to progress in the game while responding to subject-related challenges. The four main elements of game pleasure include sensation, fantasy, and narrative, discovery, and challenge. Sensation is achieved through immersive game music and sound effects, enhancing the atmosphere and emotional engagement at different levels. Fantasy and narrative are integrated through an engaging storyline and well-developed characters, creating an interactive and meaningful game world that resonates with students. Discovery is encouraged by introducing multiple levels and diverse avatar skill sets, allowing students to explore different playstyles and learning experiences. The challenge is incorporated through varied problem-solving tasks, strategic encounters, and movement-based progression, requiring students to apply critical thinking and adapt to new challenges as they advance in the game. Beyond these entertainment factors, the game design also considers student demographics, recognizing that game preferences may vary based on gender and age (Schell, 2015). By adapting the game's visual style, mechanics, and overall mood to appeal to a diverse student population, the game enhances engagement and ensures a more inclusive and personalized learning experience.

4.3.4 Development: Serious Game Analytics Engine Features

Based on the design consideration aspects earlier, a smart serious game analytics engine is developed to align gameplay with intended learning

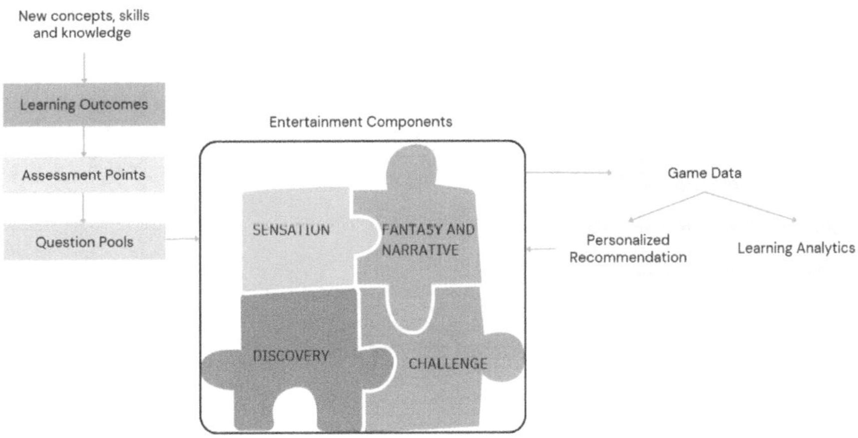

FIGURE 4.2
Serious Game Analytics Engine Framework

outcomes, as illustrated in Figure 4.2. This engine is capable of gathering gameplay data, such as students' in-game actions, decisions, and problem-solving approaches, and transforming this information into valuable learning analytics. By analyzing student interactions, the engine not only provides insights into the learning process but also enhances the experience through personalized recommendations, ensuring that each student receives targeted guidance to improve their understanding and skills. One of the key advantages of this engine is its scalability and adaptability, allowing it to be implemented across various subjects without requiring modifications to the core system. Additionally, the duration and difficulty levels can be adjusted based on subject-specific requirements, making it a versatile and dynamic learning tool.

The engine is built on two primary components: the serious game engine, named WannaBee Coder, and the learning analytics engine. WannaBee Coder is an educational adventure game designed to immerse students in an engaging and interactive learning environment, as illustrated in Figure 4.3. It adopts a quiz-based game environment to enable the scalability of the game for implementation in different subjects. In this game, students take on the role of Yeet, an adventurous worker bee, who embarks on a mission to rescue fellow bees captured by the Fellowship of the Bear. Students navigate through a mysterious and unpredictable world, encountering challenges, traps, and diverse gameplay scenarios that require strategic thinking and problem-solving. The game offers various playable characters, each with unique traits, allowing students to explore different approaches to overcoming obstacles. Throughout the journey, students engage with embedded instructional videos that introduce key subject concepts. To progress, they must correctly answer subject-related questions,

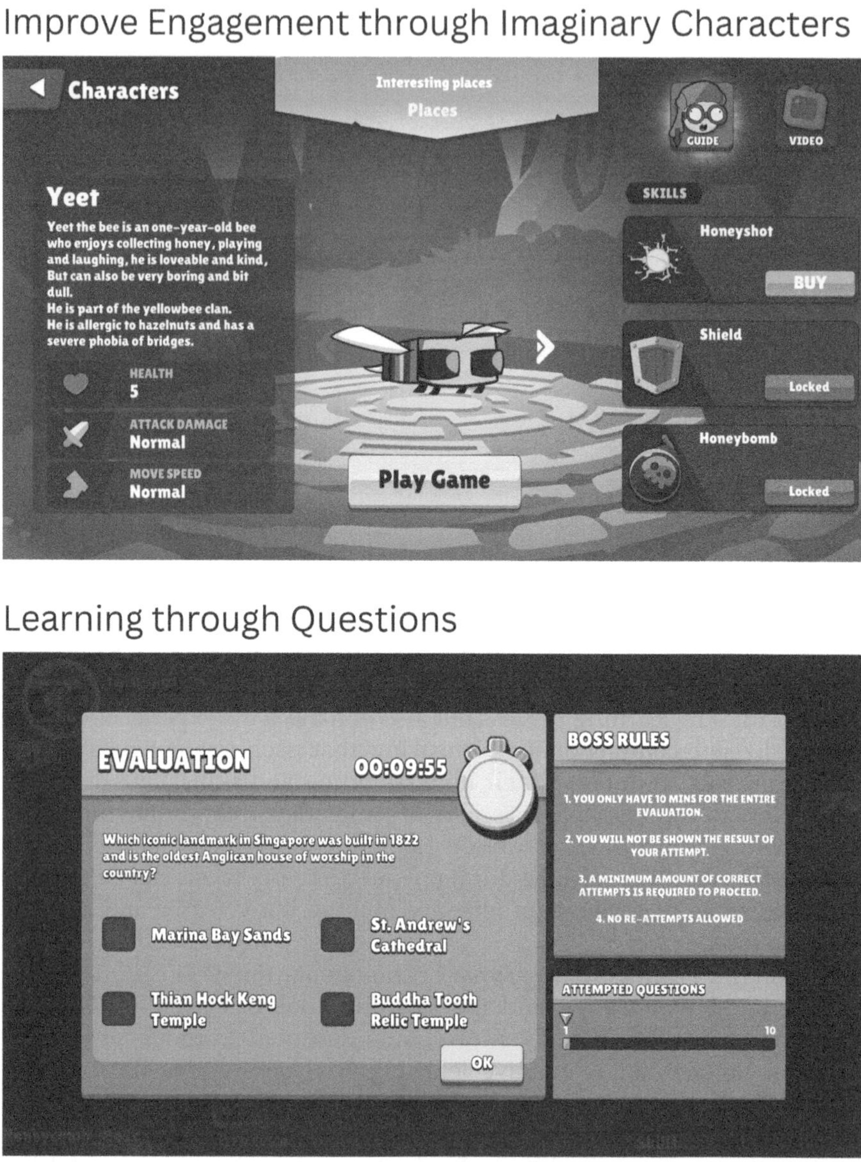

FIGURE 4.3
Wannabee Coder

unlocking new levels and saving captured bees. Incorrect answers result in setbacks, requiring students to reevaluate their understanding and retry the challenges, reinforcing learning through iterative problem-solving. The game's structure ensures that students actively engage with educational content, fostering both cognitive and critical thinking skills in a fun and

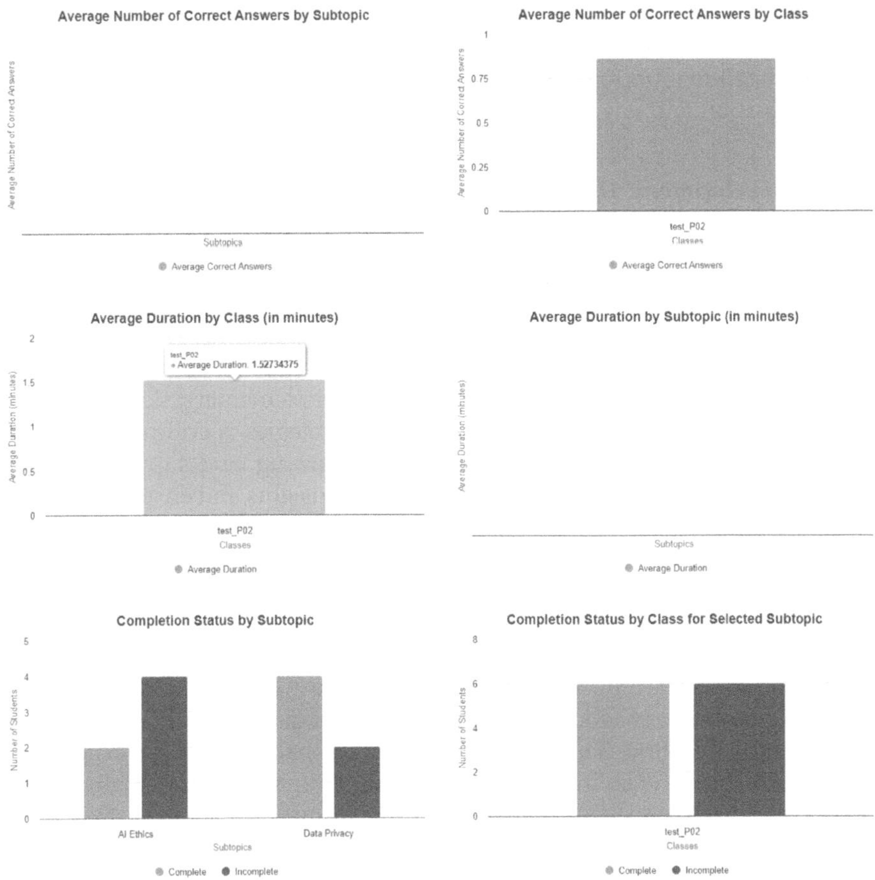

FIGURE 4.4
Serious Game Learning Analytics

immersive way. The game engine incorporates AI-driven personalized recommendations, seamlessly integrating them into gameplay to guide students through their learning journey. These intelligent recommendations adapt to individual progress, strengths, and areas for improvement, ensuring a tailored learning experience that enhances engagement and knowledge retention.

Complementing the serious game engine, the learning analytics engine is designed to track and evaluate student progress by providing educators with detailed insights into learning patterns and performance. This component includes a dynamic analytics dashboard, as illustrated in Figure 4.4, which enables educators to monitor student performance in real time. By leveraging AI and ML models, the engine clusters students based on their performance, identifies topics where students struggle, and recommends targeted learning strategies. These insights allow educators to adjust instructional methods, provide additional support where needed, and tailor interventions to each student's needs. The system's adaptive nature ensures that students receive personalized feedback, reinforcing areas for improvement while maintaining motivation and engagement.

4.3.5 Development: Diversity in the Development Team

To develop the engine with the aforementioned main features, assembling a multidisciplinary team with diverse expertise is essential to ensure the system is both pedagogically effective and technically robust (Piorkowski et al., 2021). The team comprises educators, researchers, IT practitioners, and student interns from various diplomas within the School of Informatics and IT, each contributing valuable perspectives and complementary skills. A strong foundation in pedagogy design and learning strategies is critical to align the game with educational goals, promote active learning, and support different student profiles. Educators provide pedagogical insights and ensure alignment with curriculum objectives and learning outcomes. They contribute their deep understanding of curriculum requirements, classroom dynamics, and student learning behaviors. Their input ensures the game supports meaningful learning outcomes and incorporates instructional scaffolding and feedback strategies. Researchers would have two diverse sets of knowledge: one in educational technology and learning sciences, and another in AI and ML. Researchers in education technology would ensure the design remains grounded in current pedagogical thinking. This collaborative input shapes the core structure of the serious game, enabling it to be both engaging and educationally sound. Researchers in AI and ML would focus on exploring Generative AI, AI, and ML models to power the engine's recommendation system and adaptive features.

The team also includes experts in game design and development who play a central role in translating pedagogical goals into immersive and interactive gameplay experiences. These professionals ensure that the mechanics, narrative, and progression within the game align with cognitive and motivational learning principles. In parallel, web/mobile application designers and developers are responsible for creating a functional, responsive, and accessible platform that can integrate the game and the learning analytics engine smoothly. The role of UI/UX designers is equally important, as they ensure the interface is intuitive and inclusive for a wide range of users, including students and educators with varying levels of digital proficiency. Notably, students are also included in the development process—whether as beta testers, co-designers, or student developers—bringing valuable perspectives on usability, engagement, and real-world classroom relevance. Their participation ensures that the final product resonates with the actual needs and expectations of its primary users.

In addition to these roles, the development of the learning analytics engine relies heavily on expertise in data analytics, dashboarding and visualization, and AI/ML modeling. Data scientists and engineers work closely with researchers and educators to design algorithms that capture in-game behaviors and translate them into meaningful learning indicators. These insights are displayed through educator-facing dashboards, enabling the monitoring of individual and group performance, identification of learning gaps, and provision of timely, targeted interventions. The integration of AI-driven personalization allows the system to adapt content, pacing, and feedback to individual student needs, enhancing the effectiveness of instruction. By bringing together educators, researchers, developers, and students, the project benefits from a rich diversity of perspectives and skills. This collaborative approach not only enhances the quality and usability of the system but also ensures that it is pedagogically grounded, technically scalable, and deeply responsive to the realities of teaching and learning.

4.3.6 Development: AI/ML Models for the Learning Analytics

Serious game analytics and traditional game analytics differ significantly in purpose, objectives, and application, reflecting their distinct goals in entertainment and education. Traditional game analytics is primarily designed to enhance gameplay experiences, increase student retention, and maximize revenue. Developers utilize these analytics to fine-tune game balance, optimize design elements, detect gameplay issues, and identify monetization opportunities (Canossa et al., 2013; Thawonmas & Iizuka, 2008; Williams et al., 2008). These analytics track student engagement metrics, such as time spent in-game, user interactions, and in-game purchases to improve commercial viability and ensure sustained student interest. In contrast, serious game analytics prioritize learning effectiveness over entertainment value, with a focus on evaluating and enhancing students' skill development and academic progress. These analytics serve two fundamental objectives: first, to generate actionable insights that inform and refine instructional design, ensuring that serious games align with educational best practices; second, to assess and enhance students' cognitive abilities, problem-solving skills, and subject mastery. Unlike traditional game analytics, which aim to maximize engagement for commercial success, serious game analytics aim to create meaningful learning experiences by analyzing student behavior, knowledge retention, and skill progression (Loh et al., 2015).

In this serious game analytics engine, the learning analytics leverages advanced ML models to provide deeper insights into student performance and learning behaviors. Beyond basic data visualization, the engine integrates three core ML techniques: sentiment analytics (Miner et al., 2012), keyword discovery (Blei et al., 2003), and clustering (Hartigan & Wong, 1979).

Sentiment analytics in this learning analytics engine utilize natural language processing (NLP) (Manning & Schutze, 1999) to process student feedback and in-game responses, providing insights into engagement levels, motivation, and learning attitudes. By analyzing students' emotional interactions with the game-based learning environment, sentiment analytics enables educators to assess student sentiment toward subjects, topics, and gameplay experiences. This field has been widely applied to study opinions, emotions, and subjectivity in textual data (Miner et al., 2012; Medhat et al., 2014), making it a crucial tool for evaluating student perceptions in serious games. In this engine, sentiment analytics is formulated as a binary classification problem, categorizing feedback into positive and negative sentiments. Nine ML models were developed and evaluated. Through performance evaluation, the bidirectional recurrent neural network with long short-term memory (Bi-RNN-LSTM) (Medsker & Jain, 2001) model outperformed the other models, demonstrating superior accuracy in classifying student sentiment. The classified sentiments are then visualized through graphical tools, offering educators a clear summary of students' emotional responses.

Keyword discovery, also known as key phrase extraction, is the process of automatically identifying representative phrases from a document that encapsulates its essential content (Schütze et al., 2008). In the context of this learning analytics engine, this technique is employed to extract keywords from students' open-ended feedback within a serious game engine, providing educators with visual summaries of prevalent themes through word clouds. Two ML models, rapid automatic keyword extraction (RAKE) (Rose et al., 2010) and term frequency-inverse document frequency (TF-IDF), are applied in this engine. Both RAKE and TF-IDF are employed to extract key phrases from student feedback, which are then visualized using word clouds. In these visualizations, the size of each word corresponds to its frequency, allowing educators to quickly identify dominant themes, misconceptions, and areas requiring further support.

Clustering is a powerful technique for grouping students based on behavioral patterns while engaging in a serious game-based learning environment (Hartigan & Wong, 1979). In this engine, unsupervised learning techniques are applied to classify students into distinct performance-based groups by analyzing key indicators such as in-game behavior, response accuracy, and learning progress. The clustering model groups students into three categories, each representing a different level of learning progression. The first group, Emerging Students, consists of students who struggle with understanding key concepts and require additional instructional support. These students would require more scaffolding, including targeted hints, guided exercises, and supplementary learning materials. The second group, Intermediate Students, represents students who are performing well but may still have minor gaps in knowledge. They require moderate reinforcement strategies, such as concept reinforcement activities, peer discussions, and adaptive challenge-based learning. The final group, Advanced Students, consists of students who demonstrate strong mastery of concepts. These students can be further challenged with higher-level problems and complex scenarios. To achieve this classification, K-means clustering (Hartigan & Wong, 1979; Sinaga & Yang, 2020) and Nearest Neighbor algorithms (Peterson, 2009) are employed. The benefits of clustering students into these three groups extend beyond simple classification. It enables educators to deliver targeted interventions by focusing instructional resources where they are most needed. For struggling students, educators can implement early interventions to prevent learning gaps from widening, while high-performing students can be given advanced challenges to maintain engagement and foster deeper learning. By integrating clustering models into the learning analytics engine, educators gain actionable insights into student performance, fostering adaptive, data-driven teaching strategies that enhance learning outcomes in serious game-based education.

4.3.7 Development: Personalized Learning Recommendation System

To further optimize student learning, the smart serious game analytics engine integrates a personalized learning recommendation system, seamlessly linked to the serious game and learning analytics engine. This recommendation system analyzes students' interactions, behaviors, and performance within the game and generates targeted learning strategies to enhance individual learning experiences. By leveraging data-driven insights, the system ensures that students receive personalized guidance to improve their understanding and skill development. The recommendation system operates in two stages: the prediction stage and the optimization stage. In the prediction stage, the system employs eight predictive models to forecast student performance. In the optimization stage, a Genetic Algorithm (GA) (Mitchell, 1998) is utilized to generate alternative learning recommendations tailored to students' predicted needs. These recommendations are then evaluated using the best prediction model from the first stage. The most effective learning strategies are selected and provided to students, offering targeted support such as adaptive learning materials, customized in-game challenges, or additional scaffolding for difficult concepts.

One of the key benefits of this recommendation system is its scalability. It can recommend an unlimited number of activities or steps within the game, adapting to different learning scenarios as students progress. Whether suggesting new challenges, additional practice exercises, or alternative learning pathways, the system ensures that recommendations evolve based on the complexity and structure of the game. This adaptability makes it suitable for both small-scale classroom implementations and large-scale learning environments, ensuring consistent and effective support for students at various levels. Most importantly, the system offers a personalized learning experience by analyzing students' behavior, progress, and challenges in the game. By tailoring recommendations based on individual performance data, it provides targeted interventions, adaptive learning resources, and customized challenges that align with each students' unique learning journey. This personalization enhances engagement, supports concept mastery, and improves overall learning outcomes, making the serious game experience more effective and impactful.

4.3.8 Deployment: Platform

There are several platforms to consider for deploying the serious game analytics engine. It includes web, mobile, or hybrid platforms, each offering distinct advantages and limitations. Mobile deployment allows developers to tap into native device features like push notifications, camera access, and offline capabilities. Games on mobile platforms can leverage app stores for visibility and monetization, often reaching a wide user base. However, mobile deployment comes with challenges—app store approval processes can be lengthy, updates require resubmissions, and developers must often build separate versions for iOS and Android, increasing development complexity and cost. In contrast, web-based game deployment offers greater flexibility and accessibility. Web games can be played directly in browsers without downloads, making them instantly accessible across a variety of devices and operating systems. This ease of access benefits a wide range of stakeholders—from students to educators—who may not want to install apps. While web games may have limited access to device hardware and may not perform as well as native apps in graphics-intensive scenarios, they are ideal for rapid iteration and broad reach. Therefore, choosing web deployment for this serious game analytics engine is justified, as it lowers the barrier to entry, simplifies maintenance, and ensures the game can be accessed by a diverse audience without platform constraints.

4.3.9 Deployment: System Integration

The serious game analytics engine integrates various features developed using different tools into a seamless, unified system. The game itself is built using Unity, while the web interface is developed with PHP and MySQL. AI and ML capabilities are implemented in Python. To ensure smooth interaction between all components, the engine adopts a web-based architecture that brings everything together on one central platform. All essential data—including game configurations and gameplay progress—is stored in a shared database, accessible by every part of the system. From the perspective of both students and educators, the platform is easy to use through a web browser, with no need to install additional software. A secure login system controls access, and the database manages user and organization profiles. This setup supports users with different roles—students, educators, and administrators—on any device. Educators can adjust game settings through the backend of the web application and view analytics directly from the front end. Students, on the other hand, can play the game based on the configurations set by educators and have their progress automatically saved and analyzed.

4.3.10 Deployment: Scalability and Performance

The serious game analytics engine is designed with scalability and performance in mind to ensure a smooth user experience even as demand grows. Currently, the engine can support up to 100 concurrent users without noticeable delays, enabling real-time gameplay and analytics for multiple stakeholders. The architecture allows 50 subjects to participate in the game simultaneously, with data being processed and stored efficiently to maintain high system responsiveness. To enhance engagement and reduce repetition, the game engine includes up to 10 diverse game environments, such as a dungeon (as shown in Figure 4.2), garden, and snow. The environment can be set up dynamically without affecting performance. As user numbers increase, the system can scale seamlessly by upgrading the capacity of the virtual server hosting the backend services, AI models, and shared database. This flexible infrastructure ensures that future growth in users or gameplay complexity does not compromise speed or reliability. Load balancing and optimized database queries contribute to maintaining performance even under heavy usage. Whether accessed by students for gameplay or by educators for analytics and configuration, the system remains responsive and reliable.

4.3.11 Deployment: Security and Data Privacy

The deployment of the serious game analytics engine is guided by strong strategies to ensure data security, privacy, and ethical use—especially within educational environments. Secure, encrypted logins and authentication protocols ensure that only authorized users such as students, educators, and administrators can access the platform. All user data, including gameplay progress and configuration settings, is stored in a protected database with role-based access control, preventing unauthorized access. Data transmission between the web application and server is encrypted using HTTPS, further safeguarding personal and gameplay information. The virtual server is reinforced with firewalls and receives regular security updates to minimize vulnerabilities. Importantly, no personally identifiable information (PII) is shared outside the system, and all data is used strictly for educational insights. In addition, the implementation of AI-driven analytics requires transparency and ethical considerations. Informed consent is obtained from students before data collection, and institutions are encouraged to provide clear explanations about how data is used to enhance learning. Students are also given the option to opt in or out of AI-based recommendations without affecting their participation. These combined efforts ensure the platform remains secure, compliant with data protection standards, and respectful of user rights.

4.4 Evaluating Smart Game Analytics: Insights From a Pilot Study

The serious game analytics engine has been successfully implemented in three different subjects, each with distinct learning outcomes, demonstrating its versatility in supporting game-based learning across various disciplines. The first implementation was in a semester-based subject, where the serious game was introduced as a supplementary learning tool to enhance traditional teaching materials and provide students with an engaging, interactive way to reinforce their understanding of key concepts. A game trial was conducted from April to June 2022 for an information technology (IT) subject, involving 24 classes and approximately 587 students. The game was introduced at the beginning of the semester, and students were given three months to participate at their own pace. The design of this implementation focused on voluntary engagement, allowing students to register and play the game anytime within the given period. Unlike structured coursework, participation was not enforced or monitored by educators, providing an opportunity to analyze how students engage with the game in an unstructured, self-directed learning environment. The long-term availability of the game throughout the semester enabled students to use it as a flexible revision tool, helping them revisit course content as needed. By allowing students to participate at their convenience, the game encouraged autonomous learning and self-assessment, where students could repeatedly attempt challenges and reinforce their understanding without the pressure of formal assessments. This self-paced learning model was particularly beneficial for students who preferred interactive and experiential learning approaches over passive, lecture-based instruction.

The second implementation was as an evaluation tool to assess student comprehension and knowledge retention in a short-course subject. Unlike the previous voluntary implementation, this trial emphasized the game's potential as a mandatory assessment method, integrating serious gaming elements into the formal evaluation process. A game trial was conducted from June to July 2022 in a short-course module, involving three classes with approximately 75 students. Unlike the semester-based approach, where students had an extended period for self-paced engagement, this implementation required all students to actively participate in the game within a structured one-month timeframe. The game was introduced at the beginning of the module, and students were required to register, play, and complete specific game-based assessments as part of their course requirements. By making participation mandatory, the game served as a real-time evaluation tool, allowing educators to measure student progress, assess conceptual understanding, and identify learning gaps through data-driven analytics. The system tracked student performance metrics, response accuracy, time spent on tasks, and gameplay behaviors, providing a detailed breakdown of each student's strengths and weaknesses. This data allowed educators to evaluate student readiness, adjust teaching strategies accordingly, and offer targeted remediation for struggling students. Additionally, the serious game environment simulated practical scenarios that tested problem-solving, critical thinking, and applied knowledge, making the evaluation process more interactive and engaging compared to traditional quizzes or written tests. By incorporating real-time feedback and adaptive challenges, students were encouraged to actively engage with the content rather than passively memorizing information. The gamified assessment approach increased student motivation and participation, as students had to complete different levels and tasks to progress.

The third implementation of the serious game was designed as an engagement tool to attract prospective students and raise awareness about a specific diploma program. Unlike earlier versions focused on academic learning, this trial emphasized outreach through a fun and interactive experience. Held during a three-day Open House in January 2022, the game was introduced at the school's booth to draw in secondary school students. Each participant had 10–15 minutes to play, offering a hands-on opportunity to explore concepts related to the diploma in an accessible and engaging way. The aim was to spark curiosity and help students visualize what they might learn in the program, moving beyond traditional brochures and presentations. While time constraints meant only a portion of the game could be experienced, it successfully increased booth engagement and generated conversations about the course. The serious game analytics engine also tracked key engagement metrics—such as the number of players and time spent in the game—offering valuable insights to improve future outreach strategies. This implementation demonstrated that serious games can serve not only as educational tools but also as powerful platforms for student engagement and recruitment, making academic programs more relatable and memorable through interactive, gamified experiences.

4.5 Best Practices for Implementing a Serious Game Analytics Engine

The serious game analytics engine was implemented in three different contexts—a semester-based subject, a short-course module, and an open-house engagement tool—each with varying participation rates, impact, and student feedback. Despite differences in participation structure and objectives, students across all implementations provided overwhelmingly positive feedback, highlighting the game's effectiveness in making learning more engaging, simplifying complex concepts, and improving subject comprehension.

In the semester-based subject, the participation rate was 24%, primarily due to the voluntary nature of the game. Unlike the structured short-course implementation, students were not required to participate, and there was no direct academic incentive linked to gameplay. To encourage higher participation, strategies such as offering small participation marks or in-class game demonstrations could be considered in future iterations. However, despite the lower participation rate, data analysis revealed a positive correlation between game participation and subject test scores. Students who actively engaged with the game performed better in their tests, demonstrating that the game had a meaningful impact on learning outcomes even when participation was self-driven.

In the short-course module, where participation was mandatory, the engagement rate was significantly higher at 75%, with all students completing the required game-based assessments. The use of the game as an evaluation tool provided educators with real-time insights into student performance, enabling a more adaptive and personalized approach to assessment. Notably, all students successfully passed the short course, reinforcing the game's effectiveness in reinforcing key concepts and ensuring students met the course objectives. The structured integration of the game into the short course also increased motivation, as students found the interactive format more engaging than traditional assessments.

During the Open House event, the game was used as an engagement tool to introduce prospective students to the diploma program. Due to time constraints, each participant had only 10–15 minutes to play, leading to limited exposure to the full game experience. However, students who participated responded enthusiastically, expressing that the game made the subject matter more approachable and fun. Many noted that the game helped them understand the diploma's focus more clearly, making them more interested in exploring the program further. Despite the shorter playtime, the game successfully captured students' attention, serving as an effective promotional tool for academic outreach.

Across all three implementations, students consistently praised the game for making learning more interesting, simplifying complex topics, and improving comprehension. Many reported that game-based learning helped them retain information better, as the interactive format allowed them to actively engage with concepts rather than passively absorbing information from lectures or textbooks. The combination of challenge, interactivity, and real-time feedback contributed to a more immersive and enjoyable learning experience.

In addition to student feedback, educators who participated in post-implementation interviews also provided valuable insights into the effectiveness of the serious game analytics engine. Many educators emphasized that the learning analytics component of the game was particularly beneficial in identifying student challenges, allowing them to address learning gaps more effectively. Several educators highlighted that the data provided by the analytics engine was instrumental in prompting valuable discussions about students' struggles with specific concepts. The system's ability to track response accuracy, time spent on tasks, and student interactions with the game allowed educators to pinpoint areas where students were consistently facing difficulties. With this information, educators were able to modify their teaching strategies, clarify misconceptions, and provide additional resources to support student learning.

One educator noted that before implementing the serious game, it was often challenging to gauge which concepts students were struggling with until formal assessments took place. However, with real-time data from the analytics engine, issues could be detected much earlier, enabling timely interventions and discussions in the classroom. Another educator shared that the visualization of student performance trends made it easier to engage students in reflective discussions about their learning progress, encouraging them to take a more active role in addressing their difficulties. Educators also appreciated that the analytics engine fostered a more student-centered learning environment. By allowing students to interact with content in a game-based format, the engine provided opportunities for self-paced learning, where students could revisit challenging topics without the pressure of traditional classroom settings. Several educators observed that students who actively engaged with the game tended to participate more in class discussions, as they felt more confident in their understanding of the material.

Overall, the feedback from educators reinforced the value of integrating serious games with learning analytics. The ability to track, analyze, and respond to student learning patterns in real time not only improved student engagement and comprehension but also empowered educators to make data-informed teaching decisions. The combination of game-based learning, real-time performance tracking, and adaptive instructional strategies demonstrated the potential of serious games to enhance both teaching and learning experiences.

4.5.1 Key Insights and Recommendations

The implementation of the serious game analytics engine across different educational contexts provided valuable insights into best practices for maximizing student engagement, ensuring accessibility, addressing technical limitations, and adhering to AI ethics principles. One key lesson learned was that the timing and planning of the game's release significantly impact student participation. To optimize engagement, the game should be introduced strategically within the curriculum, such as before assessments or as part of classroom activities rather than as an optional tool. Students were more likely to engage when they understood how the game directly contributed to their learning outcomes.

Another important takeaway was the need for effective marketing and a seamless onboarding experience. Students responded positively to the game when it was promoted through educator announcements, institutional emails, and social media channels. Additionally, simplifying the registration and login process was crucial to ensuring higher participation rates. Complicated sign-up procedures discouraged students from playing, whereas an intuitive, streamlined registration method significantly improved adoption rates. Future implementations should consider single sign-on (SSO) integration with institutional accounts to minimize friction during the onboarding process. The trials also revealed several technical challenges that needed to be addressed to enhance usability and accessibility.

Browser compatibility issues led to inconsistencies in gameplay, as some students experienced limited functionality on certain browsers. Ensuring cross-browser support through extensive testing will help maintain a smooth and uniform user experience. Additionally, question-type restrictions limited the variety of assessments that could be incorporated into the game. Expanding interactive question formats, such as drag-and-drop exercises, multimedia-based questions, and coding simulations, would make the game more effective for diverse learning needs.

Another key takeaway was the need to minimize data leakage and strengthen data privacy measures. Given that sensitive learning data was being processed, strong encryption methods and secure data storage protocols were implemented to prevent unauthorized access. Future enhancements should focus on data anonymization techniques, where personally identifiable information (PII) is stripped or masked before being analyzed by AI models. Additionally, role-based access controls should be reinforced, ensuring that only authorized personnel can access specific data points, reducing the risk of privacy breaches.

The AI models used in the serious game analytics engine were developed and fine-tuned with AI ethics principles in mind. The models, including ML-based sentiment analysis, keyword discovery, and personalized recommendation systems, were trained on educational datasets while mitigating biases in algorithmic decision-making. Continuous fine-tuning and validation were conducted to ensure fairness, accuracy, and transparency. Bias detection mechanisms were integrated to monitor potential disparities in AI-generated feedback or recommendations, preventing the reinforcement of unfair learning patterns. Moreover, an explainability feature was incorporated into the recommendation engine, allowing educators and students to understand the reasoning behind AI-generated suggestions, thereby increasing trust in the system.

By addressing AI ethics, data privacy, and responsible AI development, the implementation of the serious game analytics engine set a foundation for more ethical, secure, and transparent AI-driven learning environments. These lessons will continue to inform future iterations, ensuring that AI-powered learning analytics align with ethical standards while enhancing student engagement, privacy, and personalized education.

4.5.2 Implementation Beyond Computer Science Education

The serious game analytics engine holds strong potential for implementation beyond computer science education, particularly in fostering problem-solving and critical thinking across various disciplines. While originally designed to support learning in IT-related subjects, the core principles of interactive learning, real-time feedback, and data-driven insights are universally applicable. Subjects such as business, healthcare, engineering, and even the humanities can benefit from serious games that simulate real-world scenarios, encouraging students to analyze information, make decisions, and solve complex problems within a safe, gamified environment.

By embedding subject-specific challenges into gameplay, educators can create immersive learning experiences that go beyond rote memorization. For instance, in healthcare education, students can be tasked with diagnosing patient cases or managing emergencies, while in business studies, they could simulate managing a company under market pressure. The serious game analytics engine supports this by tracking player performance, identifying decision-making patterns, and highlighting areas where critical thinking skills can be further developed. The engine's ability to monitor and evaluate student interactions provides educators with rich insights to tailor instruction and provide targeted support. This makes it a powerful tool not only for content delivery but also for cultivating essential 21st-century skills like critical thinking, adaptability, and strategic reasoning across diverse academic and professional fields.

4.6 Conclusion

The integration of serious games with AI-driven learning analytics and personalized recommendations presents a transformative approach to reimagining computer programming education. By combining interactive gameplay with data-driven insights, this approach enhances student engagement, fosters adaptive learning, and provides continuous feedback to support individualized progress. Serious games offer an immersive environment where students can develop problem-solving, logical reasoning, and strategic thinking skills essential for mastering programming concepts. Learning analytics further enables educators to monitor student performance in real-time, identify learning gaps, and provide targeted interventions, ensuring that instruction is both effective and personalized. Personalized recommendations guide students based on their unique learning trajectories, allowing them to strengthen their understanding at their own pace. This synergy between serious games, analytics, and AI-driven adaptation not only modernizes programming education but also aligns with the evolving demands of digital learning, making computer programming more accessible, engaging, and effective for students in diverse educational settings.

References

Abt, C. (1987). *Serious games*. University press of America.

Alvarez, J., & Damien, D. (2011). An introduction to serious game—definitions and concepts. In *Proceedings of the Serious Games & Simulation Workshop* (pp. 10–15). Paris.

Bada, S., & Olusegun, S. (2015). Constructivism learning theory: A paradigm for teaching and learning. *Journal of Research & Method in Education*, 5(6), 66–70.

Becker, K. (2021). What's the difference between gamification, serious games, educational games, and game-based learnin. *Academia Letters*, 209(2), 1–4.

Bellotti, F., Kapralos, B., Lee, K., Moreno-Ger, P., & Berta, R. (2013). Assessment in and of serious games: An overview. *Advances in Human-Computer Interaction*, 2013(1), 136864.

Blei, D., Ng, A., & Jordan, M. (2003). Latent Dirichlet allocation. *Journal of Machine Learning Research*, 3, 993–1022.

Bontchev, B., Terzieva, V., & Paunova-Hubenova, E. (2021). Personalization of serious games for learning. *Interactive Technology and Smart Education*, 18(1), 50–68.

Bornat, R., & Dehnadi, S. (2008). Mental models, consistency and programming aptitude. In *The Tenth Conference on Australasian Computing Education* (pp. 53–61). Wollongong: Australian Computer Society, Inc.

Butler, M., & Morgan, M. (2007). Learning challenges faced by novice programming students studying high level and low feedback concepts. In *Ascilite Singapore* (pp. 99–107). Singapore.

Canossa, A., Seif El-Nasr, M., & Drachen, A. (2013). Benefits of game analytics: Stakeholders, contexts and domains. In M. Seif El-Nasr, A. Drachen, & A. Canossa (Eds.), *Game analytics: Maximizing the value of player data* (pp. 41–52). London: Springer.

Code Combat. (2013). *https://codecombat.com/*. Retrieved May 20, 2020, from https://codecombat.com/. https://codecombat.com/

Coelho, A., Kato, E., Xavier, J., & Gonçalves, R. (2011). Serious game for introductory programming. In *International Conference on Serious Games Development and Applications* (pp. 61–71). Lisbon, Portugal: Springer.

De Freitas, S. I. (2006). Using games and simulations for supporting learning. *Learning, Media and Technology*, 31(4), 343–358.

De Freitas, S. I., & Jarvis, S. (2008). Towards a development approach for serious games. In T. Connolly, M. Stansfield, & E. Boyle (Eds.), *Games-based learning advancements for multi-sensory human-computer interfaces: Techniques and effective practices* (pp. 215–231). Hershey, PA: IGI Global.

Deterding, S., Dixon, D., Khaled, R., & Nacke, L. (2011). From game design elements to gamefulness: Defining 'gamification'. In *Proceedings of the 15th International Academic MindTrek Conference: Envisioning Future Media Environments* (pp. 9–15).

Dixson, D., & Worrell, F. (2016). Formative and summative assessment in the classroom. *Theory into Practice*, 55(2), 153–159.

Djaouti, D., Alvarez, J., Jessel, J. P., & Rampnoux, O. (2011). Origins of serious games. In *Serious games and edutainment applications* (pp. 25–43). London: Springer.

Doerner, R., Göbel, S., Effelsberg, W., & Wiemeyer, J. (2016). *Serious games: Foundations, concepts and practice*. Germany: Springer International Publishing.

Dyulicheva, Y., & Glazieva, A. (2021). Game based learning with artificial intelligence and immersive technologies: An overview. *CS&SE@SW*, 146–159.

Eguiluz, A., Guenaga, M., Garaizar, P., & Olivares-Rodriguez, C. (2017). Exploring the progression of early programmers in a set of computational thinking challenges via clickstream analysis. *IEEE Transactions on Emerging Topics in Computing*, 8(1), 256–261.

Garcia-Ruiz, M., Tashiro, J., Kapralos, B., & Martin, M. (2011). Crouching tangents, hidden danger: Assessing development of dangerous misconceptions within serious games for healthcare education. In *Gaming and simulations: Concepts, methodologies, tools and applications* (pp. 1712–1749). Hershey, PA: Information Resources Management Association.

Guzdial, M. (2015). *Learner-centered design of computing education: Research on computing for everyone*. Morgan & Claypool Publishers.

Hartigan, J., & Wong, M. (1979). Algorithm AS 136: A k-means clustering algorithm. *Journal of the Royal Statistical Society*, 28(1), 100–108.

Hou, H. (2015). Integrating cluster and sequential analysis to explore learners' flow and behavioral patterns in a simulation game with situated-learning context for science courses: A video-based process exploration. *Computers in Human Behavior*, 48, 424–435.

Hou, X., Ericson, B., & Wang, X. (2023). Understanding the effects of using parsons problems to scaffold code writing for students with varying cs self-efficacy levels. In *Proceedings of the 23rd Koli Calling International Conference on Computing Education Research* (pp. 1–12).

Hunicke, R., LeBlanc, M., & Zubek, R. (2004). MDA: A formal approach to game design and game research. In *The AAAI Workshop on Challenges in Game AI* (Vol. 4, p. 1722). Italy.

Huotari, K., & Hamari, J. (2017). A definition for gamification: Anchoring gamification in the service marketing literature. *Electronic Markets*, 27(1), 21–31.

Ifenthaler, D., Eseryel, D., & Ge, X. (2016). *Assessment for game-based learning: Foundations, innovations, and perspectives*. Springer.

Ifenthaler, D., Loh, C., & Sheng, Y. (2015). *Serious games analytics: Methodologies for performance measurement, assessment, and improvement*. Germany: Springer International Publishing.

Ihantola, P., Vihavainen, A., Ahadi, A., Butler, M., Börstler, J., Edwards, S., . . . Rubio, M. (2015). Educational data mining and learning analytics in programming: Literature review and case studies. In *Proceedings of the 2015 ITiCSE on Working Group Reports* (pp. 41–63).

Infocomm Media Development Authority. (2024, November 24). Code for fun for primary Schools. *Infocomm Media Development Authority*. https://www.imda.gov.sg/how-we-can-help/code-for-fun/code-for-fun-primary

Ismail, M., Ngah, N., & Umar, I. (2010). Instructional strategy in the teaching of computer programming: A need assessment analyses. *TOJET: The Turkish Online Journal of Educational Technology*, 9(2).

Jenkins, T. (2002). On the difficulty of learning to program. In *The 3rd Annual Conference of the LTSN Centre for Information and Computer Sciences* (Vol. 4, pp. 53–58).

Kazimoglu, C., Kiernan, M., Bacon, L., & Mackinnon, L. (2012). A serious game for developing computational thinking and learning introductory computer programming. *Procedia-Social and Behavioral Sciences*, 47, 1991–1999.

Kerk, C. (2024, December 12). Job prospects 2025: Stable with a chance of shifting demands. *The Business Times*. https://www.businesstimes.com.sg/lifestyle/job-prospects-2025-stable-chance-shifting-demands

Kim, B., Park, H., & Baek, Y. (2009). Not just fun, but serious strategies: Using metacognitive strategies in game-based learning. *Computers & Education*, 52(4), 800–810.

Knight, J., Carly, S., Tregunna, B., Jarvis, S., Smithies, R., de Freitas, S., . . . Dunwell, I. (2010). Serious gaming technology in major incident triage training: A pragmatic controlled trial. *Resuscitation Journal*, 81(9), 1174–1179.

Kumar, D. (2000). Pedagogical dimensions of game playing. *ACM Intelligence Magazine*, 10(10), 9–10.

Laamarti, F., Eid, M., & El Saddik, A. (2014). An overview of serious games. *International Journal of Computer Games Technology*, 2014(1).

Lahtinen, E., Ala-Mutka, K., & Järvinen, H. (2005). A study of the difficulties of novice programmers. *Acm Sigcse Bulletin*, 37(3), 14–18.

Liu, D., Santhanam, R., & Webster, J. (2017). Toward meaningful engagement. *MIS Quarterly*, 41(4), 1011–1034.

Loh, C., Sheng, Y., & Ifenthaler, D. (2015). Serious game analytics: Theoretical framework. In C. Loh, Y. Sheng, & D. Ifenthaler (Eds.), *Serious game analytics: Methodologies for performance measurement, assessment and improvement* (pp. 3–30). Switzerland: Springer.

Ma, M., Oikonomou, A., & Jain, L. (2011). Innovations in serious games for future learning. In *Serious games and edutainment applications* (pp. 3–7). London: Springer.

Manning, C., & Schutze, H. (1999). *Foundations of statistical natural language processing*. MIT Press.

Mayo, M. (2007). Games for science and engineering education. *Communications of the ACM*, 50(7), 30–35.

Medhat, W., Hassan, A., & Korashy, H. (2014). Sentiment analysis algorithms and applications: A survey. *Ain Shams Engineering Journal*, 5(4), 1093–1113.

Medsker, L., & Jain, L. (2001). *Recurrent neural networks*. CRC Press.

Mendes, A., Paquete, L., Cardoso, A., & Gomes, A. (2012). Increasing student commitment in introductory programming learning. In *Frontiers in Education Conference* (pp. 1–6). IEEE.

Michael, D. R., & Chen, S. L. (2005). *Serious games: Games that educate, train, and inform*. Muska & Lipman/Premier-Trade.

Miljanovic, M., & Bradbury, J. (2018). A review of serious games for programming. In *Serious Games: 4th Joint International Conference, JCSG 2018* (pp. 204–216). Darmstadt, Germany: Springer International Publishing.

Miner, G., Elder IV, J., & Hill, T. (2012). *Practical text mining and statistical analysis for non-structured text data applications*. Academic Press.

Mitchell, M. (1998). *An introduction to genetic algorithms*. MIT Press.

Morschheuser, B., Hassan, L., Werder, K., & Hamari, J. (2018). How to design gamification? A method for engineering gamified software. *Information and Software Technology*, 95, 219–237.

Motamedi, V., & Sumrall, W. (2000). Mastery learning and contemporary issues in education. *Action in Teacher Education*, 22(1), 32–42.

Muratet, M., Torguet, P., Jessel, J., & Viallet, F. (2009). Towards a serious game to help students learn computer programming. *International Journal of Computer Games Technology*, 2009(1) (Published online).

O'Brien, K., & O'Hare, D. (2007). Situational awareness ability and cognitive skills training in a complex real-world task. *Ergonomics*, 50, 1064–1091.

O'Shea, K., & Nash, R. (2013, June 9). *An introduction to convolutional neural networks*. https://white.stanford.edu/teach/index.php/An_Introduction_to_Convolutional_Neural_Networks

Pacheco-Velazquez, E., Rodés Paragarino, V., Glasserman, L., & Carlos Arroyo, M. (2024). Playing to learn: Developing self-directed learning skills through serious games. *Journal of International Education in Business*, 17(3), 416–430.

Perin, A., dos S. Silva, D., & Valentim, N. (2023). Investigating block programming tools in high school to support Education 4.0: A systematic mapping study. *Informatics in Education*, 22(3), 463–498.
Peterson, L. (2009). K-nearest neighbor. *Scholarpedia*, 4(2), 1883–1896.
Piorkowski, D., Park, S., Wang, A., Wang, D., Muller, M., & Portnoy, F. (2021). How AI developers overcome communication challenges in a multidisciplinary team: A case study. In *ACM on Human-Computer Interaction* (pp. 1–25).
Rajanen, M., & Rajanen, D. (2017). Usability benefits in gamification. In *Proceedings of the 1st International GamiFIN Conference*. RWTH Aachen University.
Rieber, L. (1996). Seriously considering play: Designing interactive learning environments based on the blending of microworlds, simulations, and games. *Educational Technology Research and Development*, 44(2), 43–58.
Robins, A., Rountree, J., & Rountree, N. (2003). Learning and teaching programming: A review and discussion. *Computer Science Education*, 13(2), 137–172.
Rose, S., Engel, D., Cramer, N., & Cowley, W. (2010). Automatic keyword extraction from individual documents. In M. W. Berry, & J. Kogan (Eds.), *Text mining: Applications and theory* (pp. 1–20). John Wiley & Sons.
Sarpong, K., Arthur, J., & Amoako, P. (2013). Causes of failure of students in computer programming courses: The teacher-learner Perspective. *International Journal of Computer Applications*, 77(12).
Sawyer, B. (2011). *Serious games: Improving public policy through game*. Foresight and Governance Project.
Schell, J. (2015). *The art of game design*. CRC Press.
Schütze, H., Manning, C., & Raghavan, P. (2008). *Introduction to information retrieval*. Cambridge: Cambridge University Press.
Serrano-Laguna, Á., Manero, B., Freire, M., & Fernández-Manjón, B. (2018). A methodology for assessing the effectiveness of serious games and for inferring player learning outcomes. *Multimedia Tools and Applications*, 77, 2849–2871.
Sinaga, K., & Yang, M. (2020). Unsupervised K-means clustering algorithm. *IEEE Access*, 8, 80716–80727.
Singapore Ministry of Education. (2018, January 08). Basic coding as part of primary school curriculum. *Ministry of Education*. https://www.moe.gov.sg/news/parliamentary-replies/20180108-basic-coding-as-part-of-primary-school-curriculum
Thawonmas, R., & Iizuka, K. (2008). Visualization of online-game players based on their action behaviors. *International Journal of Computer Games Technology*, 1–9.
Vahldick, A., Marcelino, M., & Mendes, A. (2021). Analyzing novices' fun and programming behaviours while playing a serious blocks-based game. *Revista Brasileira de Informática na Educação*, 29, 1337–1355.
Van Staalduinen, J., & de Freitas, S. (2011). A game-based learning framework: Linking game design and learning. In M. Khine (Ed.), *Learning to play: Exploring the future of education with video games* (pp. 29–54). New York: Peter Lang.
Whitehead, J. (2007). Collaboration in software engineering: A roadmap. In *Future of Software Engineering* (pp. 214–225). IEEE.
William, L. (2021). Improving students programming skills using serious games. In *14th International Symposium on Advances in Technology Education 2021*. Turku, Finland.
William, L., Abdul Rahim, Z., Wu, L., & de Souza, R. (2019). Effectiveness of supply chain games in problem based learning environment. In D. K. Ifenthaler (Ed.), *Game-based assessment revisited* (pp. 257–280). Cham, Switzerland: Springer.

William, L., Khalid, N., Chan, S., Ismail, M., Chang, N., Yang, R., . . . Ashrafi, Z. (2021). Configurable framework for smart serious game analytics. In *11th Annual International Conference on Industrial Engineering and Operations Management*. Singapore.

Williams, D., Yee, N., & Caplan, S. (2008). Who plays, how much, and why? A behavioral player census of a virtual world. *Journal of Computer Mediated Communication*, 13(4), 993–1018.

Wong, W., Shen, C., Nocera, L., Carriazo, E., Tang, F., Bugga, S., . . . Ritterfeld, U. (2007). Serious video game effectiveness. In *Proceedings of the International Conference on Advances in Computer Entertainment Technology* (pp. 49–55).

Wood, C., Mentzelopoulos, M., & Protopsaltis, A. (2015). EdCCDroid: An education pilot prototype for introducing code-combat using LUA. In *The 11th International Conference on Intelligent Environments (Workshop)* (pp. 353–360). Prague.

Wouters, P., Van Nimwegen, C., Van Oostendorp, H., & Van Der Spek, E. (2013). A meta-analysis of the cognitive and motivational effects of serious games. *Journal of Educational Psychology*, 105(2), 249.

Yücel, Y., & Rızvanoğlu, K. (2019). Battling gender stereotypes: A user study of a code-learning game, 'Code Combat,' with middle school children. *Computers in Human Behavior*, 99, 352–365.

Zhao, D., Muntean, C., Chis, A., Rozinaj, G., & Muntean, G. (2022). Game-based learning: Enhancing student experience, knowledge gain, and usability in higher education programming courses. *IEEE Transactions on Education*, 65(4), 502–513.

5

Implementation of Analytics and AI in Education: Educators' Perspectives

Teo Chee Leng, Thong Wei Qi, Chan Hui Ying, Joey Neo and Caron Ong

5.1 Introduction: Navigating the Digital Shift in Education

The accelerated pace of digitalisation in a post-COVID world has underscored the growing significance of technology in reshaping education. The pandemic has catalysed an unprecedented global shift from traditional classrooms to online and hybrid learning environments. Such a shift urges educators to re-examine conventional teaching methods (Mhlanga & Moloi, 2020), while revealing vast opportunities for innovation. As institutions navigate this new normal, educators are increasingly turning to data analytics and AI to drive pedagogical change, enhance student outcomes, and create more responsive, personalised learning experiences.

At the heart of this transformation is the integration of data-driven strategies into teaching practices (Siemens, 2013). The adoption of online learning has prompted educators to tap into the wealth of data generated by digital platforms such as learning management systems. These systems capture myriad critical metrics, from attendance records and the pace of learning to detailed performance outcomes on quizzes and assessments. By harnessing this data, educators can track student engagement in real time, compare individual performance against class or cohort averages, and swiftly identify learning gaps that might otherwise remain hidden in traditional face-to-face settings. This unprecedented level of insight empowers educators to implement interventions that are both timely and targeted (Papamitsiou & Economides, 2014).

Data analytics has become a cornerstone of modern education. With the aid of real-time dashboards and visualisation tools, educators are now able to proactively design and deploy interventions tailored to each student's unique needs. For example, early identification of at-risk students enables the provision of immediate support that helps to mitigate learning difficulties. This will help to foster an inclusive environment where every student has the opportunity to succeed.

DOI: 10.1201/9781003599357-6

While data-driven advances are taking place in education, AI technologies are also rapidly evolving. Recent breakthroughs in natural language processing have also unlocked new avenues for integrating AI into educational practices. AI-powered tools, ranging from intelligent tutoring systems that offer real-time, adaptive feedback to automated grading systems that streamline assessment processes, are revolutionising traditional teaching methods. Moreover, the emergence of generative AI (Gupta et al., 2024) has introduced a novel dimension to pedagogy and the need to review assessment. This technology enables the creation of interactive content, personalised lesson plans, and the possibility of dynamic assessments that adapt to each student's learning journey. By leveraging generative AI, educators can tailor instructional delivery to directly address diverse learning needs, thereby enhancing both the effectiveness and efficiency of educational programmes.

The true power of these technological advancements is realised when data analytics and AI are employed in tandem (Lee et al., 2023). Data analytics provides the foundational insights into student performance and engagement, while AI builds upon these insights to offer personalised and adaptive learning pathways. For instance, AI can process complex datasets to detect subtle patterns and trends, using that information to generate targeted instructional content or adaptive learning modules that adjust in real time to a student's progress. This synergy not only augments the efficiency of educational interventions but also creates a dynamic, responsive learning ecosystem that continuously evolves as new data is generated.

In addition to these technological advancements, this chapter also explores the unique position of Singapore in this digital education revolution. Known for its rigorous academic standards and innovative educational policies, Singapore has effectively harnessed technology to enhance learning experiences and achieve systemic change.

This chapter also examines case studies that show how the Centre for Foundation Studies (CFS) at Temasek Polytechnic (TP) in Singapore uses data analytics and AI to improve academic outcomes. It also highlights how these technologies help build a resilient and adaptable education system that can effectively address the challenges of a rapidly changing global landscape.

Subsequent sections of the chapter delve deeper into the practical applications of these technologies in education by exploring how learning analytics dashboards are used by educators to track engagement and performance, and how generative AI is integrated into lesson delivery and assessment design to create more interactive and personalised learning experiences.

Together, these discussions provide a comprehensive view of how the convergence of data analytics and AI is reshaping the educational landscape from multiple angles. The ongoing digital revolution in education is not without its challenges. While data analytics and AI offer tremendous potential to enhance learning experiences, they also raise critical questions regarding implementation, data privacy, and equitable access. Integrating these advanced technologies into existing curricula requires significant adaptation; both educators and learners have to be adequately prepared to harness these tools effectively. Moreover, the rapid pace of technological change necessitates continuous professional development and re-evaluation of traditional pedagogical approaches. By critically examining these challenges, this chapter not only celebrates the transformative potential of technology in education but also outlines practical strategies to address the obstacles that lie ahead (Redecker et al., 2011).

5.2 Revolutionising Education: The Broad Impact of AI on Modern Teaching and Learning

The integration of AI in education has not just transformed the landscape of teaching and learning; it has redefined it. This technological leap forward offers a plethora of opportunities for educators to enhance their pedagogical practices and for institutions to streamline their operations. Two pivotal areas, data analytics and generative AI, stand out for their profound impact on educational strategies and learning experiences.

5.2.1 Data Analytics: Empowering Educators With Insights

Data analytics serves as a cornerstone of AI's application in education, providing actionable insights that enhance teaching effectiveness, student learning, and institutional decision-making. Learning analytics involves collecting, processing, and interpreting student data to improve educational outcomes. AI-powered dashboards further support this process by providing real-time performance tracking, helping both students and teachers monitor progress effectively (Pan et al., 2024). By leveraging AI-driven insights, institutions can create personalised learning paths, adjusting instructional methods to support diverse student needs and learning styles.

Predictive models leverage historical data to forecast academic outcomes and inform institutional policies. AI-powered early warning systems enable the analysis of student data to identify those at risk of academic failure or dropout (Kustitskaya et al., 2020). This enables educators to engage with students proactively and offer necessary support.

Beyond individual student insights, AI-driven analytics play a significant role in curriculum refinement. By analysing large-scale datasets, institutions can identify gaps in student comprehension and align course content with industry trends and learning needs. This data-driven approach ensures that curricula remain relevant and responsive to the evolving demands of the workforce, fostering better learning outcomes and career preparedness.

5.2.2 Generative AI: Redefining Content Creation and Engagement

Generative AI, which can create new content based on existing data, is redefining educational practices by offering dynamic, adaptive, and personalised learning experiences. Adaptive learning platforms powered by AI continuously assess student progress and tailor content accordingly, providing an individualised learning experience that maximises comprehension and skill development (Zawacki-Richter et al., 2019).

Natural language processing (NLP) tools, such as ChatGPT, support students in developing their writing skills by providing grammar corrections, content suggestions, and structural feedback (Imran & Almusharraf, 2023). Such tools serve as digital tutors, helping students refine their academic writing with greater efficiency. Furthermore, AI-powered language models support multilingual learning by improving accessibility for non-native speakers and develop a level learning environment (Tariq, 2024). Students who are non-native speakers can benefit from AI-generated explanations and contextualised translations that bridge linguistic gaps and facilitate deeper understanding.

Additionally, generative AI is also utilised in education to support experiential learning. AI-generated simulations and virtual environments enable students to engage in experiential learning, where they can interact with complex concepts in immersive digital spaces (Cabrera-Duffaut et al., 2024).

5.2.3 Navigating Challenges and Ethical Considerations

Despite its numerous advantages, the integration of AI in education is not without its challenges. There have been instances of AI tools producing erroneous results due to bias in data or the training process (Mavrogiorgos et al., 2024). The rise of AI-generated content also brings concerns about authenticity and the potential for plagiarism. Moreover, the collection and analysis of vast amounts of student data necessitate robust privacy measures to protect sensitive information and ensure ethical standards are upheld.

Educators face the task of balancing AI-assisted learning with the need for students to engage in independent critical thinking (Premkumar et al., 2024). As AI continues to evolve, so must the policies and ethical frameworks that guide its use in educational settings to ensure it enhances rather than undermines academic integrity.

By addressing these challenges head-on, educators and institutions can harness the full potential of AI to foster more effective, inclusive, and engaging learning environments. The future of education will likely see a continued evolution of AI's role, with forward-thinking strategies ensuring that educational practices not only adapt to but thrive in this new digital era.

Building upon the broad perspective of AI's role in education, the next section shifts focus to a more localised context, examining how these technologies are being integrated within Singapore's unique educational landscape.

The section will particularly highlight the initiatives at the CFS, showcasing how data analytics and AI are specifically tailored to meet the needs of students and educators.

5.3 Navigating New Frontiers: Technological Innovations and Challenges at the Centre for Foundation Studies

In Singapore, a nation celebrated for its rigorous academic standards and robust assessment methods, the educational system has seen significant transformations to accommodate an increasingly diverse student body. These adaptations are driven by demographic shifts, rapid technological advancements, and a steadfast commitment to maintaining educational excellence. Moving away from a one-size-fits-all model, the system now prioritises personalised education, which caters to varying learning styles, backgrounds, and individual needs.

5.3.1 Singapore's Educational Reforms

A notable reform is the overhaul of the Primary School Leaving Examination (PSLE) scoring system in 2021. The Ministry of Education introduced a new framework of eight achievement levels (ALs), moving away from the traditional T-score system (2023c). This reform aims to de-emphasise academic competition, reduce distinctions among students, and encourage families to select schools that best suit their children's specific talents and interests. This aligns with global trends towards more flexible, student-centred education, perfectly tailored to meet Singapore's long-term educational objectives.

The evolution of educational strategies continued in secondary education with the 2024 introduction of Full Subject-Based Banding (Full SBB) (2023a). This policy dismantled the traditional academic streams—Express, Normal Academic, and Normal Technical—allowing students to study subjects at levels that match their strengths and interests. Full SBB fosters interaction among students of varied academic abilities by placing them in mixed-ability classes and providing flexibility in subject selection based on PSLE results and ongoing assessments. This initiative exemplifies the push towards a more inclusive and adaptable educational environment that appreciates the unique capabilities of each student.

5.3.2 Technological Integration in Education

Technological tools have been integral to these educational reforms. Since the late 1990s, Singaporean schools have incorporated technology into their educational practices, significantly enhanced by successive ICT-in-Education Masterplans and the Educational Technology (EdTech) Plan 2020. The latest, the EdTech Masterplan 2030 (2023b), emphasises digital literacy and the adoption of advanced technologies like artificial intelligence to personalise and improve the learning experience. This strategic use of technology not only advances how education is delivered but also prepares students for a future dominated by digital interactions.

These reforms demonstrate a proactive response to the evolving economic landscape and the changing needs of a globalised society, equipping students not only with academic excellence but also with the skills necessary to thrive in a complex world. As these foundational changes solidify in primary and secondary education, they set the stage for transformations in polytechnic education.

5.3.3 Centre for Foundation Studies at Temasek Polytechnic

Polytechnic education in Singapore, particularly at TP, is dynamic and closely aligned with industrial and economic demands, providing students with practical skills and vocational training. Building on earlier educational reforms, TP has adopted innovative approaches to meet the demands of a globalised economy and a technologically advanced society. For instance, TP utilises virtual reality (VR) and augmented reality (AR) technologies to simulate real-world environments in the classroom, offering students practical experiences that closely mirror professional settings.

CFS at TP plays a pivotal role in developing foundational academic and personal skills as students prepare for specialised diploma courses through the Polytechnic Foundation Programme (PFP). The PFP is an alternative pathway for secondary school graduates who excel in their GCE "N" level examinations to gain direct entry into polytechnic. Instead of progressing to a junior college or the traditional route of a Secondary Five Year to prepare for the GCE "O" level examinations, eligible students can enrol in the PFP.

This one-year foundation programme is designed to prepare students for entry into the three-year diploma courses offered at the polytechnic. The curriculum in the PFP provides a practice-oriented approach and focuses on strengthening students' knowledge of English, mathematics, and domain-specific subjects related to the diploma courses they will eventually pursue.

Aligned with TP's commitment to cutting-edge technology, CFS has adopted advanced tools to enhance teaching and learning processes, particularly during the COVID-19 pandemic, which necessitated a rapid shift to home-based learning. This transition spurred the exploration and implementation of digital solutions, ensuring educational continuity and paving the way for further technological investments and teacher training to adapt to new teaching modalities.

5.3.4 Learning Analytics at Centre for Foundation Studies

During this transformative period, CFS took significant steps by incorporating analytics dashboards into their educational toolkit. These dashboards have become essential for educators, particularly when traditional classroom interactions were limited. They allow teachers to analyse detailed data on student performance, helping them pinpoint specific areas where students might be struggling. With access to real-time insights, educators can tailor their interventions more effectively to meet individual student needs. This targeted approach helps in addressing learning gaps promptly and enhances the overall educational outcomes for students.

At CFS, analytics tools are used to enhance both administrative efficiency and educational delivery. By harnessing these advanced tools, CFS ensures that its educators are well equipped to provide high-quality education that is tailored to the diverse needs of each student, thereby significantly enhancing the learning experience and outcomes, particularly during periods of educational disruption. The following are five types of dashboards implemented at CFS.

5.3.4.1 Assessing Learning in Real Time Dashboard

One of the first analytics tools developed at CFS is the Assessing Learning in Real Time (ALERT) dashboard. This innovative tool allows educators to quickly ascertain whether students have grasped key concepts by collecting data through surveys immediately after lessons. This immediate feedback facilitates timely and targeted teaching adjustments, enhancing the effectiveness of the educational interventions.

5.3.4.2 Customised Dashboard—Learner's Profile

To further enhance the capability to monitor and improve student performance, CFS employs platforms like Power BI and MicroStrategy to create customised dashboards tailored to the centre's specific needs. These platforms enable the execution of detailed learning analytics that provide predictive insights into students' learning needs and generate comprehensive visualisations of demographic data. This targeted support is crucial for initiating early interventions and customising educational strategies to optimise student outcomes.

5.3.4.3 Customised Dashboard—Cohort's Performance

The customised dashboards also significantly improve reporting capabilities, enabling efficient comparison of semestral results across cohorts, academic years, and subjects. They provide clear, actionable data to stakeholders and management, supporting informed decision-making and strategic planning.

CFS also analyses pre-polytechnic data alongside current performance metrics to ensure that the educational offerings are adequately preparing students for their academic journeys. By examining the relationship between pre-polytechnic academic performance and students' grade point averages (GPA), instructional strategies are better aligned from the outset, tailored to meet the diverse needs of the students.

5.3.4.4 Question by Question Analysis Dashboard

Within the learning management system, dashboards that analyse the difficulty level of questions and track student response accuracy further refine educators' assessment strategies. These tools help them continually improve the accuracy and fairness of their evaluations, ensuring that the assessments effectively measure student understanding and facilitate appropriate pedagogical adjustments.

5.3.4.5 Students' Sentiment Dashboard

In an effort to continually refine the curriculum based on direct student feedback, CFS has implemented a new dashboard that aggregates and visualises qualitative responses from student surveys. This tool delivers deeper insights into student perceptions and experiences, driving necessary curriculum adjustments to enhance both the content and the instructional methods.

5.3.5 Navigating Challenges and Technological Responses

The integration of advanced technologies at CFS has not been without its hurdles. A primary challenge is ensuring that all educators are proficient in using these tools. Despite ongoing training, there remains a disparity in digital literacy among the teaching staff, which can affect the consistency and effectiveness of technology implementation. Fully adapting the curriculum and teaching practices to leverage these technologies requires significant time and effort, often necessitating ongoing professional development and support.

The reliance on data analytics and predictive modelling raises significant concerns about data privacy and security. Ensuring the safeguarding of student information while utilising it to enhance educational outcomes is a paramount concern, requiring stringent data management protocols and continuous monitoring to prevent data breaches and ensure compliance with privacy laws.

Despite these challenges, the dashboards and technological tools at CFS have fundamentally transformed how educators approach teaching and learning, making their educational practices more responsive, personalised, and data-driven. The next section explores a detailed case study that showcases the practical applications and benefits of using learning analytics at CFS. This case study will illustrate how learning analytics have concretely improved student learning outcomes, highlighting the innovative approaches adopted, the challenges overcome, and the substantial benefits brought to both teaching and learning environments.

5.3.6 Generative AI at Centre for Foundation Studies

In addition to harnessing the power of learning analytics, the emergence of generative AI has introduced both exciting opportunities and significant challenges to the teaching and learning at CFS. These powerful tools, suddenly accessible to both educators and learners, have revolutionised traditional academic practices by enabling the generation of essays and completion of assignments with just a few well-crafted prompts. This newfound capability raised critical questions about its potential impact on the learning process, particularly as it posed challenges to traditional methods of assessment and content creation.

The introduction of generative AI into CFS's educational framework initially received mixed reactions from the staff, highlighting various perspectives and concerns. Educators were primarily divided into two groups, each with a different approach to adopting and implementing generative AI. The first group of educators, driven by enthusiasm, proactively sought out professional development opportunities and integrated their newfound knowledge into the CFS curriculum, viewing AI as a powerful ally that could significantly enhance educational delivery and provide personalised learning experiences. The second group of educators, more cautious, gradually incorporated AI elements into their teaching strategies, ensuring they could adapt at their own pace while still contributing to the collective learning of the institution.

In response to these differing levels of engagement, CFS developed comprehensive guidelines for the ethical use of AI in education, ensuring that these tools augment rather than replace human educators and align with the pedagogical goals of the centre.

As generative AI was integrated across various subjects at CFS, educators utilised AI tools to provide feedback on student writing and assist in complex problem-solving tasks, enriching the learning process and deepening students' understanding of key concepts. However, challenges such as student hesitancy towards adopting these tools and concerns over academic integrity necessitated innovative strategies, including the use of "mega prompts" to guide students on effectively using AI tools for learning enhancement rather than mere task completion.

5.3.7 Collaborative Learning: Sharing Success Stories and Challenges

At CFS, the commitment to continuously adapting to the evolving educational landscape ensures that its strategies and tools align with the latest technological advancements. Its dedication to integrating technologies such as generative AI and learning analytics not only enhances the depth and breadth of its educational offerings but also provides a personalised and inclusive educational experience, crucial for meeting the diverse needs and learning styles of the students.

As CFS moves forward, sharing of experiences becomes as vital as the implementation of the innovations themselves. By openly discussing both the successes and the challenges encountered, it would foster a culture of collaboration and continuous learning within the educational community. This spirit of openness and mutual growth is pivotal while transitioning into detailed case studies in the next two sections. These narratives will provide concrete examples of how generative AI and learning analytics have been successfully implemented at CFS, illustrating not only their practical applications but also the challenges overcome and the significant benefits these tools have brought to both teaching and learning environments. Through these case studies, valuable insights may inspire and guide similar initiatives across the educational spectrum.

5.4 Case Study 1: Dashboard for Student Interventions

The implementation of AI in education has revolutionised how educators manage student data, monitor academic performance, and implement timely interventions. At CFS, the Learner Profile Dashboard was designed to integrate diverse data streams into a single interface, which facilitates evidence-based decision-making and targeted student support. This case study looks into the dashboard's implementation, its impact on student support practices, and its broader implications for reshaping educational responsibilities.

Prior to the dashboard's introduction, the process of monitoring students and implementing interventions was fraught with inefficiencies. Care Persons, lecturer in-charge of a class, grappled with multiple data systems, where crucial information such as socio-economic indicators, pre-polytechnic academic results, and ongoing performance metrics were scattered across various platforms. This fragmentation made it challenging to obtain a comprehensive view of a student's needs or academic standing, often leading to missed opportunities for timely support.

5.4.1 The Pre-Dashboard Environment: Challenges in Student Data Management

Before the implementation of the Learner Profile Dashboard, educators contended with a disjointed data environment. Academic records, attendance logs, and performance assessments were isolated in separate systems, obstructing a holistic view of student progress. This fragmentation led to inefficiencies in how student support was administered, with significant delays in interventions that could have mitigated academic and personal challenges faced by students.

The absence of a unified data management system meant that critical decisions regarding student support were often based on incomplete data, reducing the effectiveness of these interventions. The need for a consolidated data management system became increasingly apparent as the limitations of the existing systems began to directly impact the quality of student support.

Educators primarily relied on anecdotal evidence and personal interactions, which, although valuable, lacked consistency and objectivity. The Learner Profile Dashboard was introduced to address these gaps by aggregating multiple data sources into a single, user-friendly interface.

5.4.2 User Acceptance Testing and Data Challenges

The development of the Learner Profile Dashboard involved extensive user acceptance testing to ensure that the system met the specific needs of educators. This phase was crucial in identifying and rectifying issues related to data accuracy, system usability, and overall accessibility. A significant challenge encountered during this phase was the integration of historical data, which was often not formatted for easy extraction and integration, highlighting the necessity for a robust and adaptable data management system.

This testing phase underscored the critical need for a dashboard that could not only present comprehensive student profiles but also facilitate real-time updates to student data, thereby enabling more dynamic and responsive educational strategies.

5.4.3 The Learner Profile Dashboard: System Overview and Capabilities

The Learner Profile Dashboard integrates key student metrics, including academic performance, attendance trends, and socio-economic indicators, into an interactive platform. The dashboard consists of four main pages that provide structured insights:

5.4.3.1 Academic Performance

- Provides a snapshot of class composition by categorising students into high achievers, intermediate performers, and at-risk students.
- Features a chart for visual classification and a detailed grid below displaying individual student data such as names, entrance grades, per capita income tiers, diploma choices, and current average grades.

- Users can filter information based on subjects taken or not taken in pre-entry qualifications, with colour coding to highlight students needing immediate attention.

5.4.3.2 Individual Performance

- Offers a comprehensive view of a student's academic progress across all subjects.
- Displays performance progression through a comparative chart against class and cohort averages. Includes daily refreshed attendance rates, emphasising the correlation between attendance and academic success.
- Assists in identifying trends and deviations in individual academic trajectories, facilitating timely academic counselling and support.

5.4.3.3 Component Breakdown

- Enables detailed analysis of student performance by specific subjects.
- Allows educators to select a subject and review scores and trends for individual components within that subject.
- Supports educators in diagnosing academic issues at a granular level, enhancing the ability to tailor interventions based on specific academic needs.

5.4.3.4 Students at Risk

- Focuses on monitoring students who are on the borderline of passing or failing.
- Highlights students needing urgent intervention, aiding quick action to prevent potential failures.
- Streamlines the process of identifying and supporting at-risk students, ensuring that interventions are both timely and effective.

5.4.4 Data Integration and Security

Developed in collaboration with an external vendor, the dashboard integrates both historical and real-time data from various school systems. It treats sensitive information, such as per capita income, with high confidentiality by categorising it into tiers, thus maintaining student privacy. Access to detailed student information is role-based, ensuring that only authorised personnel such as class tutors, Care Persons, and course managers can view specific data layers.

5.4.5 Training and Predictive Analytics

To maximise the effectiveness of the dashboard, comprehensive training sessions were conducted to equip users with the skills needed to navigate the system efficiently and handle sensitive data responsibly. A pivotal feature of the dashboard is its predictive analytics capability, which not only classifies students into performance categories based on their academic trajectories but also aims to predict future academic risks, allowing for pre-emptive educational interventions.

5.4.6 Enhancing Pastoral Care

The dashboard has significantly enhanced the approach to pastoral care. By integrating real-time data into student interactions, it has standardised the information available during mentoring sessions, allowing educators to address specific student challenges more effectively. This shift from largely informal interactions to data-driven discussions ensures that support strategies are accurately aligned with individual student needs.

The Learner Profile Dashboard simplifies complex data management and redefines educator-student interactions by providing a comprehensive, data-driven view of student performance and needs. This enables educators to implement effective, tailored interventions, fostering a more supportive and responsive educational environment. The profound impact of such targeted interventions is illustrated through the detailed academic journeys of PFP students, Jason and Adrian.

The real-life impact of the Learner Profile Dashboard becomes evident through the experiences of Jason and Adrian. These cases highlight the dashboard's capability to not only detect early warning signs of academic and personal challenges but also to guide the strategic implementation of personalised support measures.

5.4.7 Example A—Jason's Academic Recovery

Jason, a PFP student from the engineering cluster, encountered significant challenges due to his limited exposure to Physics before entering the programme. The Learner Profile Dashboard flagged his declining academic performance early in the semester, showing scores of 55% and 57% in key engineering subjects—substantially below the class average. His attendance records also indicated frequent absences, highlighting the correlation between his attendance and academic struggles.

Upon recognising these warning signs, the Care Person scheduled a check-in with Jason in the first week to better understand his situation. The dashboard revealed that he had not been placed in any of his preferred diploma choices, which likely contributed to his disengagement. During the initial meeting, the Care Person encouraged Jason to reach out to peers and tutors and to delve deeper into his diploma programme to better understand his academic path. Although he was initially reserved, this conversation helped establish a rapport and signalled the Care Person's commitment to his success.

In the second term, further discussions were held to strategise on managing his assessments and improving his engagement. The Care Person introduced Jason to education and career guidance counselling as a support option. These ongoing discussions gradually built trust, facilitating more effective guidance and intervention.

Jason's experience underscores the effectiveness of the Learner Profile Dashboard in facilitating early intervention and providing the data necessary for personalised support. Despite his initial struggles, the dashboard's predictive capabilities enabled the Care Person to address his challenges in a timely and informed manner.

5.4.8 Example B: Adrian's Academic and Social Adjustment

Adrian, a quiet and reserved PFP student from the business cluster, presented unique challenges that extended beyond academic performance to include personal well-being. Concerns about his social interactions and emotional state were frequently raised by his mother, who noted his struggles with academic coursework and social integration. The Learner Profile Dashboard indicated that Adrian's scores in business and mathematics were 51.6% and 55%, respectively—significantly lower than the class averages. It also showed that he had not participated in any Learning Support Programme sessions, despite their availability as a resource for struggling students.

Using insights from the dashboard, the Care Person initiated a dialogue with Adrian to understand and address his challenges. The discussions covered his at-risk subjects, and together they formulated strategies to improve his academic performance. Adrian was encouraged to engage with the Learning Support Programme for his mathematics course, and the team provided guidance on workload management. Efforts to enhance his social interactions included the provision of links for counselling appointments.

Although progress was gradual, Adrian's engagement levels improved over time, demonstrating the positive impact of consistent and comprehensive support. The Learner Profile Dashboard played a crucial role in facilitating this support, allowing for tailored interventions based on detailed insights into his academic and personal needs.

5.4.9 Impact on Educators

The Learner Profile Dashboard significantly enriches the multifaceted roles of educators, encompassing academic advising, counselling, mentoring, and facilitating personal growth. By offering a comprehensive, data-driven view of each student's progress, the dashboard enables educators to perform these roles more effectively. For instance, the real-time tracking of attendance, grades, and engagement with support services empowers educators to adopt a more proactive approach to student support, ensuring that interventions are timely and based on precise data insights.

5.4.10 Future Directions for Learning Analytics at Temasek Polytechnic

Looking ahead, Temasek Polytechnic is poised to further advance its learning analytics capabilities with the upcoming launch of Dashboard Version 2.0. This new iteration will be piloted with pre-employment training (PET) students and is set to feature predictive grading algorithms that enhance the timeliness and effectiveness of interventions. By leveraging AI-driven analytics, this upgraded system will predict module grades using historical performance data, allowing educators to proactively address potential academic issues before they become problematic.

For CFS, the next developmental phase will integrate qualitative data, including instructor comments and behavioural insights, to provide a more holistic perspective on student progress. Planned enhancements include real-time automated alerts and personalised learning recommendations, each tailored to meet individual student needs. There is potential to integrate student self-assessments and feedback mechanisms into the dashboard, promoting a collaborative educational environment where students actively participate in monitoring and directing their own learning trajectories.

The journey towards enhancing data competencies and implementing data-driven decision-making strategies has markedly improved the way educators track and support student progress at Temasek Polytechnic. The availability of detailed, accessible data allows educators to monitor student progression effectively and provide targeted support as needed. This capability has been especially crucial during periods of reduced face-to-face interaction, such as during home-based learning (HBL), ensuring that students receive consistent support despite any physical barriers.

As AI-powered tools continue to evolve, the next steps include refining predictive analytics and incorporating further automation to enhance both the precision and effectiveness of educational interventions. These technological advancements will not only benefit students by ensuring they receive timely academic support but will also empower educators with actionable insights to optimise educational outcomes. This proactive and refined approach to educational support underscores Temasek Polytechnic's commitment to maintaining its status as a leader in innovative educational practices.

5.5 Case Study 2: Generative AI in Assessment Redesign: Transforming Mathematical Learning Through Authentic Assessment

Assessment has long been a cornerstone of education, serving as the primary mechanism to evaluate student learning, provide feedback, and inform instruction. However, technological advancements over the decades have significantly reshaped this landscape. In recent years, the emergence of generative artificial intelligence (generative AI)—AI systems capable of creating new content, ideas, and solutions in response to prompts—has marked a paradigm shift in educational assessment. Unlike traditional AI systems that primarily analyse existing data, generative AI can produce human-like text, engage in conversations, and generate creative solutions to complex problems. This capability presents both opportunities and challenges in educational assessment.

This transformation of assessment can occur in two distinct ways. First, educators can leverage generative AI as a tool for designing and developing assessments (redesigning assessments *using* generative AI), where the technology serves as a collaborative partner in crafting more effective evaluation methods. Second, educators can create assessments that thoughtfully incorporate generative AI as part of the student learning process (redesigning assessments *that use* generative AI), acknowledging and embracing the technology's role in modern education. This section explores both approaches through a case study of redesigning a mathematics assessment, demonstrating how generative AI can be utilised to enhance assessment design while also being integrated appropriately into student learning experiences. This dual perspective helps address long-standing challenges while raising important considerations about the role of technology in assessment.

5.5.1 The Challenge

The traditional approach to teaching mathematics faces several persistent challenges that impact student engagement and learning outcomes. Students often question the relevance of mathematical concepts to their future careers, expressing sentiments such as "We study maths for what?" and "The course that I am going to doesn't need maths." This disconnect between classroom learning and real-world application leads to decreased engagement and motivation. Additionally, conventional mathematics assessments, particularly those focused on Excel-based calculations and standard problem sets, have become increasingly vulnerable to generative AI solutions, raising concerns about academic integrity and authentic learning assessment.

The rise of generative AI presents a pressing challenge: how can educators balance the potential of AI with the need to uphold academic integrity? Instead of resisting AI, it is essential to incorporate its use into assessments, clearly defining the boundaries of acceptable AI involvement. This realisation led to a fundamental reimagining of mathematics assessment, transforming traditional Excel-based assignments into a mathematical modelling approach that embraces generative AI as a tool for learning rather than viewing it as a threat to academic integrity.

5.5.2 Mathematical Modelling

The redesigned assessment incorporated mathematical modelling as its cornerstone, focusing on real-world problem-solving within the institutional context. Mathematical modelling is a process that translates real-world problems into mathematical frameworks for analysis and solution. The process involves four key stages that make it particularly resistant to complete automation by generative AI while fostering authentic learning:

1. **Understanding the Problem**: Students analyse real-world situations within their institutional context, identifying relevant variables and making appropriate assumptions. This stage requires direct observation and contextual understanding that generative AI cannot replicate, as it involves physical presence and real-world data collection.
2. **Formulating the Model**: Students translate their observations into mathematical frameworks, selecting appropriate mathematical concepts and relationships. While generative AI can suggest approaches, the unique nature of each student's collected data ensures original thinking in model development.
3. **Solving the Mathematical Problem**: Students apply mathematical methods and tools to their formulated model, using appropriate techniques for analysis. Generative AI can assist with calculations and verification, but the interpretation of results remains grounded in the student's unique dataset.
4. **Interpreting Results**: Students translate mathematical solutions back into the real-world context, evaluating the practical implications of their findings. This crucial stage requires understanding of both the institutional context and the limitations of their model—insights that must come from the student's direct experience.

This approach naturally encourages students to connect mathematical concepts with practical applications, developing both technical skills and contextual understanding. By requiring students to collect and analyse their own data and document their thinking process throughout the investigation, the assessment becomes inherently resistant to complete generative AI automation while still allowing for appropriate AI support in specific stages. Beyond just finding solutions, mathematical modelling emphasises the iterative nature of problem-solving, where initial models are often refined and improved based on real-world feedback and constraints.

Having decided to base the assessment on mathematical modelling, the next step was to determine how generative AI can be integrated into the assessment process. The integration of generative AI was carefully structured across two distinct phases that reflect the dual approach: the assessment design phase (redesigning assessments *using* generative AI) and the student implementation phase (redesigning assessments *that use* generative AI).

5.5.3 Assessment Design Phase: Redesigning Assessment *Using* Generative AI

The assessment design phase demonstrated the potential of generative AI as a collaborative tool for educators in reimagining assessment tasks. This phase involved a systematic, iterative process of using generative AI to craft and refine three key components: the assessment brief, the deliverables, and the assessment rubrics.

The process began with providing generative AI with the context of the original Excel-based assignment and the challenges it presented, particularly its limited real-life applicability and vulnerability to AI-generated solutions.

Educator: Can you help me design a performance assignment task for students on mathematical modelling?

Module context:
Polytechnic Foundation Programme students in Singapore
Module: Mathematical and Logical Thinking 2
Individual assignment

Intended Learning Outcomes to be demonstrated by the students:

1. Apply mathematical concepts in sets, quadratic functions, coordinate geometry, and mensuration in real-life contexts around the campus.
2. Communicate mathematical and logical thinking effectively via oral presentation and written report.

The performance task will comprise 20% of the module grade. You have the freedom to apportion the weightage of the two learning outcomes depending on the perceived relative importance for the module.

In crafting the assessment brief, generative AI served as a thought partner, helping to explore various real-world contexts that would make mathematics more relevant to students. Through multiple iterations of prompting and refinement, the brief evolved to focus on mathematical modelling within the institutional context. This decision was strategic—by restricting the context to the institution, students would need to collect their own data, making the assessment more resistant to AI-generated solutions while promoting authentic learning experiences.

Educator: Would this be okay for assignment details?
Task: You are tasked with conducting a study on a specific area/aspect of our campus using the mathematical concepts you've learned. You will then prepare an oral presentation and a written report on your findings.

You are encouraged to use Generative AI tools to brainstorm mathematical modelling ideas around campus relating to sets, quadratic function, coordinate geometry and mensuration. Some ideas include:

- Applying set theory to analyse the distribution of student populations among different clubs, subjects or classes.
- Model the projectile motion of a ball when it is kicked or thrown as a quadratic function
- Create a coordinate plane-based map of the campus and plan a school tour
- Model certain structures or features on campus with appropriate solids, then measure and calculate relevant volume or area.

Generative AI: Absolutely! The revised assignment details you've provided give a clearer direction to the students. They are encouraged not only to think about the application of the concepts they've learned, but also to potentially leverage Generative AI tools for brainstorming. This is a forward-thinking approach that allows them to be in tune with modern technological tools while ensuring they remain grounded in foundational mathematical concepts.

Here's a slightly polished version:

...

The iterative nature of working with generative AI proved particularly valuable in this phase. Each response from generative AI was carefully reviewed and refined, with subsequent prompts building upon previous suggestions to create increasingly focused and effective assessment materials. For example, when developing the rubrics, initial generative AI suggestions were analysed for gaps or areas of improvement, leading to follow-up prompts that helped create more precise and comprehensive evaluation criteria.

Educator: Should I consider other mark allocations for the performance descriptors?

Generative AI: Absolutely! The allocation of marks for performance descriptors can be adjusted based on several factors, including the complexity of the task, the weight you wish to give to each category, and your perception of the gaps in

> performance between the descriptors. Here are a few alternative mark allocations for your consideration:
>
> Option 1: Broader Spread
>
> - Excellent: 5 marks
> - Good: 4 marks
> - Fair: 2–3 marks
> - Needs Improvement: 0–1 marks
>
> Pros: This option creates a broader distinction between "Fair" and "Needs Improvement." It reserves the 0 mark for completely unacceptable work and gives a slightly higher range for "Fair."
>
> Option 2: Higher Middle Range
>
> - Excellent: 5 marks
> - Good: 3–4 marks
> - Fair: 2 marks
> - Needs Improvement: 0–1 marks
>
> Pros: This focuses more on the middle range of performances. It gives flexibility in the "Good" category, allowing for differentiation between slightly above average and very good work.
>
> Option 3: Equal Intervals
>
> . . .

Throughout the design phase, generative AI was used not just as a tool for content generation but as a partner in pedagogical reflection. Each interaction prompted deeper consideration of assessment design principles, student learning needs, and the balance between technological integration and academic rigour. The process of developing support materials involved careful consideration of how to structure student learning while maintaining academic integrity. This included planning for appropriate scaffolding and determining what types of AI support would be most beneficial for students, leading to the development of a comprehensive support framework that would be implemented in the student phase.

A point to note was that the interaction with generative AI during the assessment design phase employed both structural and conversational prompting techniques. Structural prompting involved carefully programming specific instructions, examples, and constraints to guide generative AI towards desired outcomes. For example, when developing the assessment brief, clear parameters were set regarding the mathematical concepts to be covered, the institutional context, and the required student deliverables. This structured approach was particularly valuable for creating rubrics and defining assessment criteria. In contrast, conversational prompting allowed for more dynamic exploration of ideas through natural dialogue with generative AI. This approach proved especially useful during the iterative refinement process, where each response could be questioned, critiqued, and built upon to develop increasingly refined assessment materials. The combination of both prompting styles—structured for precision and conversational for exploration—created a comprehensive approach to assessment design. This hybrid prompting strategy aligned with Ethan Mollick's observation that "just using AI will teach you how to use AI" (Mollick, 2023), as each interaction provided insights into more effective ways of collaborating with generative AI in assessment design.

5.5.4 Student Implementation Phase: Redesigning Assessments *That Use* Generative AI

The student implementation phase focused on translating the designed assessment framework into effective learning experiences, with careful consideration of an assessment that uses generative AI. This phase was structured around three key elements: a comprehensive generative AI support framework, clear guidelines for appropriate AI use, and requirements for original work and documentation.

The framework provided students with two types of carefully crafted prompts. The first is a brainstorming prompt that helped students generate ideas for their mathematical modelling investigations within the institutional context, encouraging creative thinking while maintaining focus on original data collection and analysis. For example, students were prompted to identify mathematical patterns in their daily campus experiences or analyse quantitative aspects of student services. This brainstorming prompt was effective because it:

- Anchored investigations within the familiar institutional context
- Encouraged exploration while maintaining mathematical focus
- Provided structure while allowing creative freedom
- Helped students connect mathematical concepts to their daily experiences

Prompt: You are MathModellingGPT, a mathematics modelling expert who will help me, a Polytechnic Foundation Student in Singapore, brainstorm ideas within my campus for my mathematical modelling assignment. The topics and concepts are limited to only the following:

- Set theory: complement, intersection and union
- Quadratic functions: solving quadratic equations, sketching of quadratic graphs

- Coordinate geometry: length and mid-point of line segment, gradient and equation of straight lines, parallel and perpendicular lines
- Mensuration: volume and surface area of prisms, cones, pyramids and spheres.

Here are some suggested ideas that I can work on or adapt:

- Student Distribution Analysis: Apply set theory to analyse the distribution of student populations among various clubs, subjects, or classes.
- Ball Trajectory Modelling: Model the projectile motion of a ball—whether kicked or thrown—as a quadratic function. This could be done in a sports context or even just casual recreation areas around campus.
- Campus Mapping: Design a coordinate plane-based map of our campus and use it to plan an efficient school tour. This could be helpful for new students or visitors.
- Architectural Modelling: Choose specific structures or features on our campus, model them using the appropriate geometric solids, and then measure and calculate their relevant volumes or areas. This could be a sculpture, a section of a building, a water feature, and so forth.

Start by introducing yourself to me as my brainstorming buddy who is a mathematics expert. Only ask me one question at a time.

First, ask me if I have any preference for the mathematical concepts I would like to focus on out of sets, quadratic functions, coordinate geometry and mensuration. Wait for my response.

Next, guide me in the brainstorming process with some mathematical modelling ideas that only involve the topics and concepts listed above. Ask for my choice, clarifying the idea, and ascertain whether it is feasible for my campus. If it is not feasible, suggest similar ideas to improve on the feasibility. If it is feasible, guide me through the whole mathematical modelling process:

1. Formulate a mathematical model by understanding the real-world problem, making assumptions to simplify the problem, and to represent the problem mathematically.
2. Solve the mathematical problem by selecting and using appropriate mathematical methods and tools in order to solve and present the solution.
3. Interpret the solution in the context of the problem and present the solution of the real-world problem.
4. Reflect on the real-world solution and improve the model.

Next, the organising prompt guided students through the four steps of mathematical modelling, ensuring a systematic approach to their investigations. The effectiveness of this prompt stemmed from its ability to:

- Break down the modelling process into manageable steps
- Ensure systematic documentation of thinking
- Maintain focus on original data collection and analysis
- Support students' metacognitive processes

Prompt: Thank you for helping me to generate an idea that I like! I would like you to help me organize my study according to our discussions by guiding me through the whole mathematical modelling process:

1. Formulate a mathematical model by understanding the real-world problem, making assumptions to simplify the problem, and to represent the problem mathematically.
2. Solve the mathematical problem by selecting and using appropriate mathematical methods and tools to solve and present the solution.
3. Interpret the solution in the context of the problem and present the solution of the real-world problem.
4. Reflect on the real-world solution and improve the model.

To model effective generative AI interaction, sample conversations were provided showing how to use AI as a thought partner. These examples demonstrated techniques for asking effective questions, critically evaluating AI responses, and refining approaches based on feedback. The conversations illustrated the iterative nature of AI interaction, showing how multiple exchanges could lead to more refined mathematical investigations.

Student: Erm, sounds too complicated. What about Idea 1?

Generative AI: Of course, let's go with Idea 1: Campus Mapping and Efficient Routes. This idea is more straightforward and can still provide valuable insights.

Idea 1: Campus Mapping and Efficient Routes
Clarification: To get started, we'll create a coordinate plane-based map of your campus, including key landmarks, buildings, and pathways. Then, we'll model the process of finding the most efficient routes between different locations on campus. This can be particularly useful for new students or visitors trying to navigate the campus.

Now, let's proceed with the following steps:
Step 1: . . .

Student:	How do I create a campus map?
Generative AI:	Creating a campus map involves sketching a representation of your campus on a coordinate plane. Here are the steps to help you get started: Step 1: Gather Information Collect all the necessary information about your campus. This may include the locations of buildings, landmarks, roads, walkways, and any other relevant features. You might need campus blueprints or diagrams for accuracy. Step 2: Choose a Scale . . . . . .
Generative AI:	Depending on the mathematical model you've formulated, you may need to use optimization techniques such as linear programming or calculus to find the most efficient routes based on your defined objectives and constraints.
Student:	Huh, what is optimization, linear programming or calculus? I have no idea. Is there a simpler way?
Generative AI:	Certainly, I can simplify the approach for you. We can use a basic approach to find efficient routes without delving into optimization, linear programming, or calculus. Here's how you can do it: Step 3: Formulate the Problem . . .

Clear guidelines established boundaries for acceptable AI use throughout the modelling process. Students learned to use generative AI effectively for ideation and organisation while understanding that core elements—data collection, analysis, and interpretation—must be their original work. A Declaration of Originality specifically addressing generative AI use was required, promoting transparency and ethical technology use.

Students were required to document their entire mathematical modelling process, from initial brainstorming through final analysis. This documentation included:

- Their interactions with generative AI and how these influenced their thinking
- Original data collection methods and results
- Analysis procedures and interpretations
- Reflections on their learning process

The implementation supported the development of multiple competencies. Students enhanced their mathematical skills through real-world application, developed digital literacy through AI interaction, built data literacy through collection and analysis, and strengthened critical thinking through evaluation of AI-generated suggestions. Work samples demonstrated how students effectively leveraged generative AI while maintaining ownership of their learning process, producing original and thoughtful mathematical investigations that reflected deep engagement with both the mathematical concepts and the technology.

Student: To calculate the time needed to replace the water in the pool by using mensuration to see how much water and the time needed to replace the water.

Generative AI: Calculating the time needed to replace the water in a pool involves understanding the pool's volume and the flow rate of the water source. To do this, you can follow these steps:

1. Measure the Pool's Dimensions: Measure the length, width, and depth of the pool. Make sure all measurements are in the same unit (e.g., feet or meters).

...

Student: Why would someone find this?

Generative AI: The calculation of the time needed to replace the water in a pool is valuable for several reasons:

1. Planning and Scheduling: Knowing how long it will take to fill or replace the water in a pool is essential for planning and scheduling maintenance or pool-related activities. For instance, if you need to empty and refill the pool for cleaning or repairs, understanding the time requirement helps in coordinating the process efficiently.

...

5.5.5 Outcomes and Impact

The outcomes of this redesigned assessment approach were significant and multi-faceted. Student projects demonstrated enhanced mathematical understanding through the application of concepts to real-world situations. The requirement for original data collection and analysis developed students' data literacy skills, while the structured use of generative AI tools promoted digital literacy and technological competence.

One particularly illustrative example of successful student work involved an investigation into optimal solar panel placement across different locations on campus. The student collected sunlight exposure data at three key campus locations: the Plaza, Design Block, and Sports Hall. Through careful data collection and analysis, the student produced a series of graphs showing sunlight exposure patterns throughout the day at each location.

The student's analysis revealed that all locations showed peak sunlight exposure during the early afternoon, with maximum readings recorded between 11:45 and 11:49 hours. The Plaza, located near the east side and centre of the campus, demonstrated the highest sunlight exposure among the measured locations. In contrast, the Sports Hall showed significantly lower readings, with evening measurements dropping below 6,000 lux, approaching levels of minimal direct sunlight.

What made this investigation particularly noteworthy was how it integrated multiple aspects of the redesigned assessment approach. The student:

- Applied mathematical concepts to a real institutional sustainability challenge
- Collected and analysed original data across multiple campus locations
- Created meaningful visualisations to support their findings
- Drew practical conclusions relevant to campus infrastructure planning

The investigation demonstrated how the mathematical modelling approach, supported by appropriate generative AI use, could lead to authentic problem-solving with real-world implications. The student effectively used generative AI to help structure their investigation and refine their analysis while maintaining ownership of the data-collection and interpretation process. This balance between technological support and original work exemplified the goals of the assessment redesign.

Student engagement also showed marked improvement, with learners demonstrating greater motivation through the relevance of their investigations to real-world scenarios. The ownership of the learning process increased as students collected and analysed their own data, making decisions about their mathematical modelling approach. In fact, only 8% of students reported negative experiences using generative AI, and 91% of students found generative AI helpful in understanding and applying the mathematical concepts in mathematical modelling.

5.5.6 Alignment With the AI Assessment Scale

As educators reflected on the implementation of generative AI in mathematical modelling assessment, they discovered the AI Assessment Scale (AIAS) developed by Perkins et al. (2024). This framework provided theoretical validation for many of the practical decisions they had made, highlighting how thoughtful practitioners and educational researchers are converging on similar principles for effective AI integration in assessment.

The AIAS provides a structured yet flexible framework for integrating AI in educational assessments. Rather than presenting AI use as hierarchical, AIAS presents five levels of AI integration in a circular structure (Figure 5.1), emphasising that different levels are appropriate for different contexts (Table 5.1).

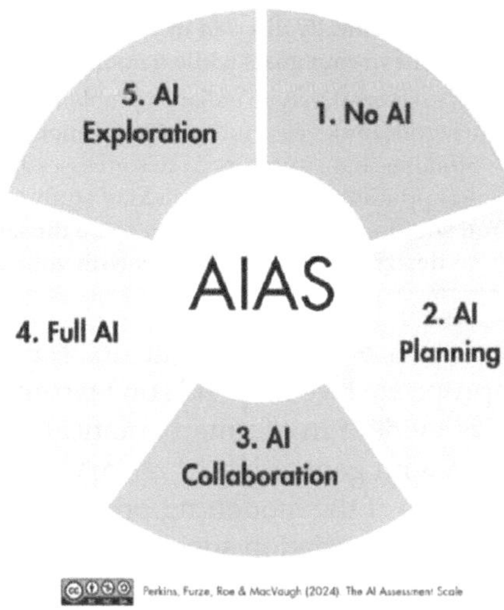

FIGURE 5.1
The AI Assessment Scale in Circular Representation (Perkins et al., 2024)

TABLE 5.1
Explanation of the Five Levels in the AI Assessment Scale (Perkins et al., 2024)

1	No AI	The assessment is completed entirely without AI assistance in a controlled environment, ensuring that students rely solely on their existing knowledge, understanding, and skills. **You must not use AI at any point during the assessment. You must demonstrate your core skills and knowledge.**
2	AI Planning	AI may be used for pre-task activities such as brainstorming, outlining and initial research. This level focuses on the effective use of AI for planning, synthesis, and ideation, but assessments should emphasise the ability to develop and refine these ideas independently. **You may use AI for planning, idea development, and research. Your final submission should show how you have developed and refined these ideas.**
3	AI Collaboration	AI may be used to help complete the task, including idea generation, drafting, feedback, and refinement. Students should critically evaluate and modify the AI-suggested outputs, demonstrating their understanding. **You may use AI to assist with specific tasks such as drafting text, refining, and evaluating your work. You must critically evaluate and modify any AI-generated content you use.**

(Continued)

TABLE 5.1 (*Continued*)

4	Full AI	AI may be used to complete any elements of the task, with students directing AI to achieve the assessment goals. Assessments at this level may also require engagement with AI to achieve goals and solve problems. **You may use AI extensively throughout your work either as you wish or as specifically directed in your assessment. Focus on directing AI to achieve your goals while demonstrating your critical thinking.**
5	AI Exploration	AI is used creatively to enhance problem-solving, generate novel insights, or develop innovative solutions to solve problems. Students and educators co-design assessments to explore unique AI applications within the field of study. **You should use AI creatively to solve the task, potentially co-designing new approaches with your instructor.**

This circular representation emphasises that no level is inherently better than another—the appropriate level depends on learning objectives and context. This principle was evident in the mathematical modelling case study, where students engaged with generative AI at varying levels based on their needs and the specific stage of the modelling process.

The AIAS framework is grounded in social constructivist principles, viewing AI tools as mediating technologies that can support students' knowledge construction when thoughtfully integrated into the learning process. This perspective was demonstrated in the mathematical modelling assessment through:

- Brainstorming prompts that encouraged students to construct their own understanding
- Requirements for original data collection and analysis within an institutional context
- Emphasis on documenting and reflecting on the mathematical modelling process
- Integration of generative AI as a collaborative tool rather than a solution provider

Perhaps most significantly, AIAS emphasises assessment validity through design rather than through prohibition or detection. The mathematical modelling assessment exemplified what AIAS terms "assessment security through task design." By requiring students to collect and analyse data within their specific institutional context, the assessment maintained its validity regardless of AI involvement. This approach contrasts sharply with attempts to control AI use through unreliable detection methods, focusing instead on creating inherently AI-resistant tasks through authentic, context-specific requirements.

This mathematical modelling case study also embodied what AIAS describes as a "transformational" rather than "superficial" approach to assessment redesign. Instead of simply adding AI-related guidelines to existing assessments, educators fundamentally reimagined how mathematical modelling could be taught and assessed in an AI-enabled world, aligning with AIAS's call for a "bottom-up transformational process" in assessment design.

The natural alignment between the assessment approach and the AIAS framework provides both validation for the methods and a theoretical structure for future refinement. By explicitly incorporating AIAS principles in future iterations, educators can build upon successful elements while providing clearer guidance to both educators and students about appropriate AI integration at different stages of the assessment process.

5.5.7 Generative AI in Education: Implications and Innovations for Future Assessments

The redesign of mathematical assessment through generative AI integration represents a significant shift in educational practice, demonstrating how AI can enhance rather than threaten academic integrity. This case study of mathematical modelling, now viewed through the lens of the AIAS framework, has revealed several key insights. The natural alignment between the practical implementation and the theoretical principles of AIAS reinforces the soundness of the approach while providing a structure for future refinement.

1. First, the dual approach of using generative AI both as a design partner for educators and as a learning tool for students creates a comprehensive framework that leverages AI's capabilities while maintaining educational rigour. The iterative nature of working with generative AI during the design phase enabled educators to create more relevant, engaging, and effective assessments that connected mathematical concepts to real-world applications.
2. Second, when thoughtfully integrated into student learning experiences, generative AI can become a powerful scaffold that supports rather than replaces authentic learning. By requiring original data collection, analysis, and interpretation, the assessment ensured that students maintained ownership of their learning while developing critical digital literacy skills. The positive student response rates—with 91% finding generative AI helpful in understanding mathematical concepts—demonstrate that AI can enhance engagement when implemented with clear boundaries and expectations.
3. Third, this approach transformed the traditional view of technology in assessment from a threat to academic integrity into an opportunity for deeper learning. By embracing generative AI's capabilities while establishing appropriate constraints, educators created an environment where technology enhanced rather than compromised authentic assessment. The mathematical modelling framework naturally created assessment tasks that were inherently resistant to complete AI automation while still benefiting from AI support.

4. Finally, this case study reveals the importance of educator expertise in AI integration. The successful implementation relied on thoughtful prompting strategies, careful scaffolding, and clear communication about appropriate AI use. As educators continue to navigate the evolving landscape of AI in education, this expertise will remain essential to creating assessment experiences that effectively balance technological innovation with educational integrity.

Looking forward, this approach to assessment redesign offers a template that can be adapted across disciplines, providing a pathway for educators to embrace AI as a partner in creating more authentic, engaging, and effective learning experiences. The future of assessment lies not in resistance to technological change but in thoughtful integration that preserves the core values of education while leveraging new capabilities to enhance student learning.

5.6 Future Directions and Conclusion

5.6.1 Lessons From the Case Studies: Building Towards an AI-Enhanced Educational Future

The case studies presented in this chapter—from learning analytics dashboards to generative AI in mathematical modelling—provide valuable insights into how AI is reshaping educational practices. These practical implementations reveal both the transformative potential of AI and important considerations for its thoughtful integration.

5.6.2 Assessment Redesign in an AI-Enhanced Educational Landscape

The exploration of assessment redesign with generative AI demonstrated how thoughtfully designed tasks can maintain academic integrity while leveraging AI's capabilities. This approach represents a significant shift from viewing AI as a threat to embracing it as a tool that can enhance learning experiences when properly integrated. As AI technologies continue to evolve, educators anticipate several key developments in assessment practices.

One significant development will be the expansion of **AI-enhanced authentic assessment**. The principles demonstrated in the mathematical modelling case—requiring original data collection, emphasising process documentation, and integrating AI as a collaborative tool—can be extended across disciplines. Future assessments will increasingly focus on creating scenarios where AI serves as a thinking partner rather than a substitute for student work, developing both subject knowledge and technological competence.

A second critical development involves **developing AI literacy through assessment**. Beyond assessing traditional subject matter, future educational approaches will explicitly develop students' AI literacy—their ability to effectively and ethically use AI tools. Assessments will increasingly require students to demonstrate sophisticated AI interaction skills, including crafting effective prompts, critically evaluating AI-generated content, and making informed decisions about when AI assistance is appropriate.

The third key advancement centres on **evolving educator expertise**. As the case studies revealed, successful AI integration requires educators to develop new competencies, particularly in understanding AI capabilities and designing learning experiences that thoughtfully incorporate these tools. Professional development will increasingly focus on helping educators become skilled learning designers and AI facilitators rather than just content experts.

5.6.3 Harnessing AI for Data Categorisation and Predictive Insights

Incorporating AI into data analytics offers educators powerful tools to enhance decision-making and personalise learning experiences. By leveraging AI-driven categorisation, vast amounts of educational data can be efficiently organised, enabling educators to identify patterns in student performance, engagement, and learning styles. For instance, AI can analyse qualitative student feedback surveys, extracting common sentiments and themes to provide valuable insights into learning experiences and instructional effectiveness. Machine learning further enhances this process by enabling predictive analysis, allowing institutions to forecast student outcomes, detect at-risk learners, and tailor interventions proactively. By recognising early indicators of academic struggles, AI can help educators implement timely support strategies, improving retention rates and overall student success. As AI continues to evolve, its integration into educational analytics holds immense potential to drive data-informed strategies, ultimately transforming the educational landscape.

5.6.4 Broader Educational Implications

The insights from the assessment redesign work connect to larger shifts occurring across education.

The first major shift involves **integration across educational domains**. The principles educators have identified in assessment redesign parallel developments in other educational areas. Learning analytics dashboards become more valuable when they inform personalised interventions; curriculum design benefits from AI-enhanced adaptivity; and student support services can leverage AI to provide more timely and targeted assistance. These parallel developments suggest an increasingly interconnected educational ecosystem enhanced by AI.

A second fundamental transformation is the **shifting focus from content to process**. Across educational contexts, AI is accelerating a shift from content mastery to process expertise. When information and basic analysis are readily available through AI tools, education naturally refocuses on higher-order skills: problem formulation, critical evaluation, ethical judgement, and creative application. The assessment redesign exemplifies this shift through its emphasis on the mathematical modelling process rather than calculation products.

The third critical consideration involves **balancing technological innovation and human judgement**. Perhaps most importantly, the experiences highlight the need to maintain a balanced perspective on AI's role. The most successful implementations leverage AI's computational capabilities while preserving the irreplaceable elements of human judgement—ethical reasoning, contextual understanding, and interpersonal connection. This balance will remain essential as AI capabilities continue to expand.

5.6.5 Looking Forward: An Integrated Vision

As educators look to the future, the most promising approaches will integrate insights from across educational domains—learning analytics, dashboard design, and assessment practices—to create coherent, AI-enhanced learning ecosystems. Rather than viewing these as separate innovations, forward-thinking institutions will develop integrated approaches where data flows seamlessly between systems, informing both immediate interventions and longer-term educational design.

The convergence of data analytics and AI marks a paradigm shift in education, moving beyond traditional success metrics towards a more holistic, data-informed approach to learning. This integration enables educators to create adaptive learning environments tailored to the diverse needs of students. By combining the precision of data-driven insights with the creative potential of AI, educational institutions can develop personalised strategies that support each student's unique learning journey. In doing so, technology evolves from a mere tool into a collaborative partner in education, empowering educators to unlock every student's full potential.

In the post-COVID world, the role of AI and data analytics in education has become even more critical. The accelerated digital transformation necessitated by the pandemic has showcased the potential of AI to support remote learning environments, personalise student learning at scale, and ensure continuity in education despite physical barriers.

As educators continue to explore and implement these technologies, the journey with AI in education is just beginning. By sharing these insights and linking them to broader educational frameworks, educators contribute to a global conversation on preparing for a future where education is seamlessly integrated with advanced technologies, ensuring that educational practices not only adapt to but thrive in an AI-enhanced world.

Acknowledgement

The authors gratefully acknowledges Bryan Li, Rita Kumari and Terence Leong for their valuable contributions to the design of data analytic dashboards and the analysis of use cases discussed in this chapter.

References

Cabrera-Duffaut, A., Pinto-Llorente, A. M., & Iglesias-Rodríguez, A. (2024). Immersive learning platforms: Analyzing virtual reality contribution to competence development in higher education—a systematic literature review. *Frontiers in Education*, 9, 1391560. https://doi.org/10.3389/feduc.2024.1391560

Gupta, P., Ding, B., Guan, C., & Ding, D. (2024). *Generative AI: A systematic review using topic modelling techniques*. https://www.sciencedirect.com/science/article/pii/S2543925124000020

Imran, M., & Almusharraf, N. (2023). Analyzing the role of ChatGPT as a writing assistant at higher education level: A systematic review of the literature. *Contemporary Educational Technology*, 15(4), ep464. https://doi.org/10.30935/cedtech/13605

Kustitskaya, L., Belyaev, I., & Agafonov, A. (2020). Predictive models for early warning systems in education: A Bayesian network approach. *arXiv*. https://arxiv.org/abs/2004.09774

Lee, A., Koh, E., & Looi, C. (2023). *AI in education and learning analytics in Singapore: An overview of key projects and initiatives*. https://www.researchgate.net/publication/375137743_AI_in_Education_and_Learning_Analytics_in_Singapore_An_Overview_of_Key_Projects_and_Initiatives

Mavrogiorgos, K., Kiourtis, A., Mavrogiorgou, A., Menychtas, A., & Kyriazis, D. (2024). Bias in machine learning: A literature review. *Applied Sciences*, 14(19), 8860. https://doi.org/10.3390/app14198860

Mhlanga, D., & Moloi, T. (2020). The role of digital transformation in reshaping education. *Education and Information Technologies*, 25(5), 4795–4815. https://www.mdpi.com/2227-7102/10/7/180

Ministry of Education, Singapore. (2023a, February 28). *Full subject-based banding (Full SBB)*. https://www.moe.gov.sg/microsites/psle-fsbb/full-subject-based-banding/main.html

Ministry of Education, Singapore. (2023b, September 20). *Our educational technology journey*. https://www.moe.gov.sg/education-in-sg/educational-technology-journey

Ministry of Education, Singapore. (2023c, November 24). *PSLE scoring system*. https://www.moe.gov.sg/microsites/psle-fsbb/psle/main.html

Mollick, E. (2023, November 1). *Working with AI: Two paths to prompting*. https://www.oneusefulthing.org/p/working-with-ai-two-paths-to-prompting

Pan, Z., Biegley, L., Taylor, A., & Zheng, H. (2024). A systematic review of learning analytics: Incorporated instructional interventions on learning management systems. *Journal of Learning Analytics*, 11(2), 52–72. https://doi.org/10.18608/jla.2023.8093

Papamitsiou, Z., & Economides, A. A. (2014). Learning analytics and educational data mining in practice: A systematic literature review. *Educational Technology & Society*, 17(4), 49–64. https://www.jstor.org/stable/jeductechsoci.17.4.49?seq=1

Perkins, M., Roe, J., & Furze, L. (2024). The AI assessment scale revisited: A framework for educational assessment. *arXiv*. https://arxiv.org/abs/2412.09029

Premkumar, P. P., Yatigammana, M. R. K. N., & Kannangara, S. (2024). Impact of generative AI on critical thinking skills in undergraduates: A systematic review. *The Journal of Desk Research Review and Analysis*, 2(1), 199–215. https://doi.org/10.4038/jdrra.v2i1.55

Redecker, C., Leis, M., Leendertse, M., & Punie, Y. (2011). *The future of learning: Preparing for change*. https://www.researchgate.net/publication/256461836_The_Future_of_Learning_Preparing_for_Change

Siemens, G. (2013). Learning analytics: The emergence of a discipline. *American Behavioral Scientist*, 57(10), 1380–1400. https://journals.sagepub.com/doi/10.1177/0002764213498851

Tariq, M. U. (2024). AI-powered language translation for multilingual classrooms. https://doi.org/10.4018/979-8-3693-2440-0.ch002

Zawacki-Richter, O., Marín, V. I., Bond, M. et al. (2019). Systematic review of research on artificial intelligence applications in higher education—where are the educators? *International Journal of Educational Technology in Higher Education*, 16, 39. https://doi.org/10.1186/s41239-019-0171-0

6

AI: Summoning the Demon or Stimulating the "Human" in Education?

Asha Kumaran

6.1 Introduction

In his poem "All Watched Over by Machines of Loving Grace," written more than five decades ago, Richard Brautigan seems to present a utopian view of machines harmoniously co-existing with humans, as expressed in the last stanza:

> I like to think
> (it has to be!)
> of a cybernetic ecology
> where we are free of our labors
> and joined back to nature,
> returned to our mammal
> brothers and sisters,
> and all watched over by machines of loving grace.
> (Brautigan, 1967, lines 17–25)

In recent years, "machines" in the form of AI have been integrated into educational institutions worldwide, with educators anticipating that the exponential growth of AI will alter the education landscape, redrawing the contours of learning. Can we, as educators, live in a "cybernetic ecology" with AI? While optimists may commend the affordances of AI in learning, there is scepticism about it. Indeed, according to a study by the Pew Research Centre of 979 technology experts, networked artificial intelligence will expand the effectiveness of humans but will also pose a threat to human autonomy, agency, and capabilities (Anderson & Rainie, 2023).

Given AI's transformative power in the workplace, the education focus worldwide has quickly shifted to equipping students with an arsenal of AI-literacy skills to build capacity in AI for work and study. In a McKinsey report, it was estimated that 15% of global working hours will use automation

DOI: 10.1201/9781003599357-7

(Manyika et al., 2017). In the United States alone, it is thought that by 2030, a significant 47% of jobs will be automated (Ellingrud et al., 2023).

Hence, the risk of job loss or diminishment, if AI skills are not taught and actively learnt, is very real. Khan (2024) observes that in Singapore, women and younger workers have more exposure to the effects of AI. As Singapore is heavily dependent on skilled labour, this could exacerbate income inequality. Hence, it is crucial to boost learners' AI training with the requisite education to allow for access to opportunities, which, in essence, is a humanistic approach to learning, as explained in a later part of this chapter. In the realm of education, the question remains whether AI-saturation in educational settings will disrupt human capabilities or dynamise and drive them, enabling more effective and effortless learning to emerge through conscious learning design choices.

6.2 What Is It to Be "Human"?

As AI systems evolve in complexity, taking over human activities, it is important to inquire into what essentially it is to be "human" in terms of capabilities, qualities, skills, and competencies. Smith et al. (2020) posit that human capabilities encompass an expanded capacity for social skills and emotional awareness that have evolved over time. Santoro and Monin (2023) have drawn up 10 skills that make us human: having culture, holding beliefs, being moral, being spiritual, having desires, feeling happy, feeling love, having a personality, and having relationships. In learning, they contend, humans use generalisations to extend learning to new situations.

Kureshi (2022) argues that humans are much more adept at social interactions. Hence, it is important to nurture skills such as communication and collaboration and include subjects that enhance these skills as part of learning design. Harel and Maron (2024) suggest some areas where humans and AI differ. These are in free will, as opposed to being pre-programmed, as is the case with AI. Human capacities include feeling emotions such as compassion, having context awareness, whether tacit or overt, and common sense or world familiarity, being able to adapt to new tasks and demands faster than machines, and having diversity in that, when working on the same tasks, humans are capable of more arbitrary actions than machines. These differences are important to consider and reflect on as educators so that we continue to nurture what is essentially "human."

Creativity is another uniquely human attribute that distinguishes us from other living beings. Sternberg and Sternberg (2011) refer to it specifically as "something original and worthwhile" that is produced (p. 480). This attribute is one that can aid innovation and enterprise and must be nurtured. Primarily, according to Fadel et al. (2024), the aim of education in the age of AI is to focus on wisdom, stressing the importance, not just of knowledge but also of skills, character, and meta-learning, together with originality, which, in some ways, is akin to creativity for the preservation of what is human in us. In fact, in a recent article, Ang (2025) reports that seven in ten non-creative jobs require creative skills for jobs, even if AI is used, based on a SkillsFuture Singapore (SSG) report.

6.2.1 What Is Human Consciousness in Learning?

Goodlad and Baker (2023) argue that we must recognise the superiority of the human brain, which has had over 500 million years of evolution compared to AI. The human brain also operates to aid the processing of context-embedded information and situations involving social and affective experiences. Additionally, it has a bigger data set as opposed to AI (Kiyani, n.d.).

Researchers from the University of Oxford (2024) report that the human or biological brain is superior to current machine learning systems. This conclusion is based on the view that the human brain can see information once and learn it, while artificial systems need training on the same information numerous times before grasping it. Humans also acquire added information while retaining existing information. In machines, the presence of artificial neural networks often degrades existing knowledge rapidly through interference. The University of Oxford study also maintains that the way the brain learns is different from the way artificial intelligence systems learn. Consequently, although it is critical to reinforce the human aspects in learning, it is also important to prepare our students for the future where AI will supplement task performance. The AI literacy quest is, therefore, a quintessentially human endeavour to increase agency in our students to secure employment. It also has a levelling or equalising effect.

The notion of consciousness is one that is seen as a distinguishing factor between humans and AI. "Consciousness" is a term explored at length by Thomas Nagel (1974) in his seminal work *What Is It Like to Be a Bat?*, where he argues that consciousness equates with being able to feel. He suggests that animal life has a consciousness that we do not apply to a toaster, because the latter is a machine, so it would be illogical to extend the idea of consciousness to machines.

AI may have many capabilities, but one contention is that it is unable to understand subjective experience and feelings. AI still faces significant challenges in achieving true human-like intelligence, and this is referred to as "the hard problem of consciousness" (Chalmers, 1996). This raises the question of why we have human experience, also referred to as qualia. The "easy problem" is, of course, the brain's ability to process stimuli, but the hard problem is how subjective experience arises from the brain's processes. AI is able to reply on algorithms to function and follows pre-defined rules, but it cannot experience feelings, nor have self-awareness. AI consciousness is known as artificial consciousness. Human thought, on the other hand, relies on emotions, intuition, and subjective experiences.

In learning, Piaget explains consciousness as reflective abstraction based on the association between causality and implication. He argues that as learners engage with their environment, they develop cognitive structures or schemes that help them make sense of their experiences. "Scheme" (or "schema") refers to a mental structure or framework that organises and interprets information and is built based on interactions with the world. These evolve over time as children learn and grow. Through processes like assimilation or integration of added information into existing structures and accommodation, where existing learning is modified to accommodate added information, learners become more consciously aware of how they process ideas and interpret their world. Vygotsky posits that consciousness in learning relates to emotional experience, social and communal situations, and cultural practices. Steiner, too, perceives consciousness as the ability to access reality through observation, rationality, and intuition.

All three learning theorists, Piaget, Vygotsky, and Steiner, see the role of reflection and self-reflection in the development of consciousness and link it to conceptual thinking (Stoltz et al., 2024). This implies that humans, when they learn, engage in cognitive, social, and intuitive experience, and that learning is reflection based, unlike AI, which is data driven. It is thinking, feeling, reflection, and intuition-driven experiences that must inform learning design. Learning must nurture all aspects of learners' development to help them achieve their full potential. Hence, in learning design, it is crucial to include opportunities for learners to form associations between concepts and engage in experiential learning and collaborative projects for interaction with others and expansion of meaning-making.

6.2.2 What Is Humanising Learning?

So, what is humanising learning and how do we do it? Humanising learning is a theory that puts human dignity and self-worth at the centre of learning and focuses on the intrinsic value and dignity of individuals (Saunders & Wong, 2020). Humanising learning not only includes fully online learning but also blended, hybrid, and face-to-face learning. Therefore, the modality of teaching and learning is not a major factor in implementing humanised teaching (Shemberger, 2022). It provides a framework for understanding what it means to be human, particularly in relation to human consciousness (Rawle, 2022). Lucas (1996) suggests that humanising learning emphasises individualism, autonomy, and dignity. Madsen and Wilson (2012) identify key aspects in humanising learning to address the whole being and involve the cognitive, affective, and emotional states, as well as consider learning needs. It must be individualised, have self-directedness, lead to self-actualisation, and address internal motivation. Learners' emotions are important, so educators must address learner anxiety and be caring, empathetic, and relational (Palahicky et al., 2019). In a large way, making AI literacy available addresses students' need for self-actualisation and humanises learning.

Shemberger (2022) posits that trust, empathy, awareness, and presence humanise learning. Presence is seen as the human availability of the teacher, whether it is through announcements, videos, and messages, for example, in an eLearning session. What motivational factors constitute humanising aspects of learning? Wang and Han (2010), in explaining Turner and Paris' Six "C"s of Motivation (1995), posit that choice, the ability to select options, increases motivation. Added to this are challenge, allowing students to work on problems outside their comfort zones; control, allowing students decision-making opportunities; collaboration, focusing on students' communication in group work; curiosity, arousing interest through thought-provoking material; confidence, providing for success; and caring, taking interest in students' well-being.

Humanising learning is also relevant in adult learning or continuing education contexts. Andragogy, according to Henschke (1998, p. 8), can be defined as "a scientific discipline that studies everything related to learning and teaching which would bring adults to their full degree of humaneness". Knowles theorises that adult learners learn differently and that they have to be involved in the learning process as self-directed learners with rich past experience and a keen motivation to learn because they need to know so that they are not subject to the confines or oppression of pedagogy.

The best way forward, it can be contended, is to incorporate AI into learning design, tapping on AI's capabilities to deliver more effective student learning outcomes with humanising principles at work. Making AI learning opportunities available and equipping students with the AI literacy skills to address rapid workplace changes is one "humanising" strategy in education. This is evident from the view that humanising learning is a teaching strategy aimed at "improv[ing] equity gaps by acknowledging the fact that learning environments are not neutral; rather, they often operate to reinforce a worldview that minoritises some students" (Pacansky-Brock et al., 2020, p. 1). Therefore, focusing on social aspects of learning, autonomy, reason, self-awareness, ethical reflection, and the pursuit of meaningful lives links the concept of being human with human consciousness.

Humanising learning using AI offers promise through curated learning experiences in the following ways:

Personalised learning, as suggested by Spector (2014, 2018), can require a digital learning environment that can be adaptive in accommodating individual knowledge needs, experiences, and interests for effectiveness in promoting desired learning outcomes. AI algorithms can also be tailored to meet the individual needs of students through the delivery of educational content and experiences that cater to students' learning speeds and preferred learning methods. These systems may employ engagement tools such as adaptive release, content customisation, and nudging through intelligent agents.

Learning analytics in AI is another way to humanise AI. It allows the granular use of data to learn more about student interactions, progress, assessment performance, task completion, and learning behaviours to personalise support, improving learning outcomes. As learning takes place in the cognitive, affective, and psychomotor domains, AI analytics support can help educators make informed decisions to facilitate student-centred learning (Starčič & Vukan, 2019). Predictive analytics dashboards can also be built to help identify at-risk students or chart the performance of individual students for intervention and action by educators to address issues.

Using intelligent tutoring systems (ITS) is a third way. This involves utilising AI-powered systems that mimic one-on-one tutoring experiences to guide students with real-time feedback and adaptive instruction based on students' progress, performance, attainment, and behaviour, allowing learning to take place without limitations. Dziuban et al. (2018) suggest that non-equivalent time is a substantial factor in learning, as students learn concepts differently from one another and even among themselves. Adaptive learning helps to empower students with control and makes the implicit psychological learning contract between educators and students manageable through self-directedness and efficiency based on students' progression. AI-powered learning management systems (LMS) that function as tutoring systems also provide students personalised feedback while optimising learning resource availability (Lee et al., 2023). Hence, it can be seen that humanising learning provides for human dignity and allows for the enhanced individual potential of students to engage critically and responsibly with AI.

6.3 Critical Need for AI Literacy

Even as we grapple with the intricacies of AI for learning and what it is to humanise learning, educators need to provide AI literacy for students, a part of the Ministry of Education's Transforming Education Through Technology (EdTech) Masterplan 2030 was first announced at the Shaping the Future of Learning seminar and rolled out in 2024 (Ministry of Education, 2025). AI literacy is defined as the ability to understand and use specific technologies to solve problems and achieve practical goals. It aims to equip students to understand what AI entails and be able to identify and explain its potential benefits, limitations, and risks. Students should also be able to leverage AI tools for continuous lifelong learning.

Additionally, according to a study by Ng et al. (2021), AI literacy has the following elements: knowing the basic functions of AI and how to use AI applications, applying AI knowledge, concepts, and applications in different scenarios, and applying higher-order thinking skills (for example, evaluating, appraising, predicting, and designing) with AI applications and human-centred considerations (for example, fairness, accountability, transparency, ethics, and safety).

To this end, at Temasek Polytechnic (TP), students are taught to use AI tools to help engage in their learning. For instance, students from the School of Design use ChatGPT to generate design statements and Midjourney for reference images to aid in the design work. Equipping students with design skills as part of a "future design school" allows for human ingenuity, with AI being used to enhance hand-drawn sketches and augment students' creative output (Temasek Polytechnic, 2024a). At the same time, foundational design skills are not jettisoned but underpin all design courses. Another way to embrace AI is through the provision of resources and expertise via industry engagement. In 2024, TP collaborated with Amazon Web Services (AWS) to launch FutureX, a multidisciplinary digital technologies and artificial intelligence (AI) centre at its School of Informatics and IT (IIT) (Temasek Polytechnic, 2024b). This project, co-led by TP and FutureX, will enable students and educators at TP to tap into shared resources for better learning outcomes through skills development, industry collaboration, joint training, and internship opportunities, enabling students to learn problem-solving, including addressing community issues, in an AI-driven world. These opportunities and learning design approaches help to humanise learning (Choudhury, 2024).

However, AI literacy is not just AI knowledge but also developing students' awareness about the different uses of AI tools. One example is the need to understand the main difference between AI tools. Google Bard, now Gemini, is trained on a dataset that includes text from the Internet. ChatGPT, conversely, is trained on a dataset inclusive of text information from books and articles. Students need to know that Gemini is more likely to contain more current information on events, while ChatGPT is more likely to be accurate in its responses to factual questions (Labadze et al., 2023). Consequently, while AI literacy empowers individuals, students must be taught about potential pitfalls associated with AI, such as privacy violations, biased algorithms and even mistakes, as AI is Janus-faced. Ang (2024) also observes the criticality of using AI responsibly, a key learning point for all students.

6.4 Weighing the Ethical Impacts of AI

Releasing AI tools such as ChatGPT and Gemini into the education circles has sparked intense debate on how this will impact ethics. There is also concern about instances of AI turning students into plagiarists and copyright infringers. Training data used in AI requires copious amounts of information, and AI tools may be potentially violating copyright laws in the process of training and developing AI systems (Lucchi, 2023). AI is also able to produce responses to mimic the human voice in authentic ways. This requirement of substantial amounts of data input can also be an infringement on privacy.

An additional concern is that complex computer codes can be capitalised on to evade detection, paving the way for academic dishonesty (Yin, 2024). A further issue is that of transparency and privacy. Memarian and Doleck (2023) explain transparency as a condition where the AI use and intention are readily understood, with accessibility to information. Being transparent requires students to know about the nature of algorithms, the intention behind the data collected, whether it is used fairly and stored safely, and about the influence of AI systems on educational outcomes, either in assessment grading or the accuracy of answers provided by AI.

6.4.1 AI Impact on Students' Research Skills

Given that much of learning at higher levels involves research, it is crucial to weigh the impact on AI on research skills. Zhai et al. (2024) highlight that students may not even be aware of ethics and fairness in AI use, overlooking them or minimising their impact. Moreover, the need to put together cogent and relevant literature reviews entails students being able to apply evidence-based thinking in retrieving information skilfully, while evaluating the currency, reliability, authority, accuracy, and purpose of the information.

If AI is used extensively for research, it may impede the development of students' cognitive abilities in research. Additionally, it could diminish their skills in synthesising information and assessing the value and authority of AI research material. This would occur if students merely copied the AI output without thoughtfully processing the information. Consequently, it could lead to research misconduct arising from falsification and fabrication (Dempere et al., 2023). Moreover, there is concern regarding the "Computer Says No" effect. This involves explicit trust in computers that are rigid and inflexible, failing to practise a more purposeful, granular approach needed to address a problem, and the consequent decline in human judgement and agency when students defer to the AI responses without deliberate decision-making. This is in the face of time pressure to stay one step ahead in the learning process through research skills.

6.4.2 Misinterpretation and Cultural Bias in AI

Another issue is that AI tools, dependent on the datasets and statistical patterns and models used to train them, can be biased, incomplete, or skewed data (Kooli, 2023). Chapman University (2025) identifies different AI biases such as confirmation bias, where AI relies on pre-existing beliefs; measurement bias, where data collected is different from the variables of interest; or stereotyping bias, where data collected results in the labelling or marginalisation of certain groups. Selection bias can also occur in that data chosen does not represent the reality, arising from sampling error or unrepresentative data sets. The perspectives adopted are usually American and male, according to the University of Kansas. Only certain cultural viewpoints may be represented, so there may be a lack of inclusivity. AI bias can arise from the training data containing inherent societal or cognitive biases (Kamalov et al., 2023). The Minister for Education, Singapore, has also drawn attention on how important it is for students from Institutions of Higher Learning to detect biases in the algorithms (Tushara, 2023).

Large language models are trained on vast quantities of publicly available internet data, which may have differing perspectives. This suggests that the biases situated in AI applications can perpetuate distinctions and inequalities. This can adversely affect students' learning outcomes and opportunities. Furthermore, the contention is that large data sets can reflect bias no matter how well data collation is done (Badrulhisham et al., 2024). They cite historical examples based on the research of Shankar et al. (2017), involving image-processing AIs commonly being trained using ImageNet. This, they posit, is biased towards data from the United States and Western Europe, ignoring China and India, which comprise more than a third of the world's population but made up just 3% of ImageNet data.

6.4.3 Danger of Misinformation and Hallucination

Relying exclusively on AI answers can be risky. While AI systems can nudge discourse into productive, fact-based conversations, there is also the slippery slope of AI misinformation. For example, when asked to give particular examples of racist words used in Singapore in a lesson on racism, a topic in the subject current issues and critical thinking (CICT), ChatGPT provided "Ah Beng" and "Ah Lian" as responses alongside "Malay," Indian," and "chink." Contextually, these are not nuanced, as the generic responses omit specific, local examples of racist language.

Besides, AI systems can hallucinate. "Hallucination" in AI is the generation of outputs that may sound plausible but are either factually incorrect or unrelated to the given context (Marr, 2023). Large language models could fabricate information and misguide readers. Moreover, as AI does not verify data or cite sources, students could well fall prey to misinformation. Facts could be buried under a blanket of lies. Deepfakes and other distortions make manipulation easy and reality difficult to fathom (Anderson & Rainie, 2023). When AI models are posed questions that they may not fully comprehend or know the answer to, they forgo acknowledgement of errors unless pressed or confronted. They do not explain that they are making statistical guesses. Consequently, novice users may not check the responses generated (Ahmad et al., 2023). Hence, getting students to learn to spot red flags in AI-generated content accuracy is vital.

6.4.4 Impact on Critical Thinking Skills

The erosion of critical thinking skills with increased AI use is another area of concern. According to The Cambridge Framework for Life Competencies Model (Cambridge University Press, 2020), critical thinking has three main constituents: "Understanding and analysing ideas and arguments"; evaluating ideas and arguments; and solving problems and making decisions. It is thought that AI-assisted learning could have a debilitating effect on students' thinking skills, especially in the area of problem-solving. (Scriven & Paul, 2008, p. 1) define it thus: "Critical thinking is the intellectually disciplined process of actively and skilfully conceptualizing, applying, analysing, synthesising, and/or evaluating information gathered from, or generated by, observation, experience, reflection, reasoning, or communication, as a guide to belief and action." A salient part of critical thinking, according to Wang (2017), is entertaining doubt, suggesting that critical questioning can push us forward towards the continuous exploration of opinions, insights, and judgements.

In an article on the impact of AI-assisted learning on students' critical thinking Aithal and Silver (2023) suggest that dependence on AI could erode students' analytical thinking and increase their dependency on AI tools, instead of relying on human cognition to pose questions. The automaticity of AI-assistance may also result in learners using shortcuts to generate answers rather than engaging in critical thinking; for example, preferring "quick-fixes" through verbatim copying of material instead of assimilating information and processing it through analysis and synthesis. This approach results in a lack of critical thinking skills, a requirement for being at the forefront of learning.

6.4.5 Value Alignment and Guidelines for Ethical AI Use

In view of these serious ethical concerns impacting learning, the need for value alignment between AI and humans is paramount. According to the World Economic Forum, value alignment is the process of ensuring that AI acts in keeping with shared human values and ethical principles (World Economic Forum, 2024). In her foreword to a White Paper by the World Economic Forum, Dr Virginia Dignus, a member of the United Nations High-Level Advisory Board, raises a critical consideration in learning: ensuring that the technology behind AI is integrated with human values based on principles of ethics: privacy, justice, and fairness (Future of Life Institute, 2024).

It is imperative that institutions such as TP focus on appropriate, responsible, and ethical AI use, with students acknowledging the consequences of using AI. Hence, there is an urgent need for guidelines to direct learners towards responsible and ethical use, bearing in mind subject specifications. At the same time, learners need to be made aware of the limitations of AI, especially in areas where human capacities such as thinking and creativity must be exercised. AI can also be an inveterate liar, and educators must give students examples, even based on personal experience of AI-fabrication, so they exercise caution and check all sources.

For instance, I asked ChatGPT for a poem on man against machine, and ChatGPT suggested a poem supposedly by Stephen Crane called "To a Machine." Suspicious, I researched the suggested poem to find that it is non-existent and challenged the erroneous response, which ChatGPT evasively called "a misstep in communication." This is how ChatGPT responded, in faux contrition:

> "I apologize for the confusion earlier. It seems I made an error. 'To a Machine' by Stephen Crane does not exist, and I regret the mistake. I appreciate your patience, and I want to correct that by offering more reliable alternatives."

6.5 The Need for a Human-Centric Approach

In view of these concerns and the need for ethics, should AI use in learning be discounted? Ultimately, the best way forward is to examine optimal uses of AI through a human-centric approach, so that AI use does not override or substitute human judgement and decision-making. Instead, a human-centric approach will result in AI being used to augment rather than eradicate or marginalise human participation by learners. Kamalov et al. (2023) note that throughout history, new uses of technology have been accompanied by attendant risks, citing the invention of nuclear fission and misuse of nuclear bombs, as well as the sinister Dark Web, in which users anonymise their Internet use and are obscured behind layers of encryption.

AI must be designed to uphold and enhance human life, rights, values, and ethics rather than diminish them. In a search for a comprehensive definition of human-centred AI (HCAI), Schmager et al. (2023) define HCAI as being focused on "understanding purposes, human values, and desired AI properties in the creation of AI systems by applying Human-Centred Design practices" (p. 7). HCAI seeks to support and extend human capabilities while keeping AI systems under human control, considering necessity, context, and the ethical and legal conditions of the AI system, as well as promoting individual and societal well-being. This comprehensive definition requires a look at the use case and the context within which the AI is employed, as well as other problematic areas of AI use that encompass legal and ethical aspects. HCAI has evolved as a response to concerns about the potential negative tolls of AI systems. Primarily, these take the form of the loss of jobs, bias, and a lack of transparency. The goal is to ensure that AI technologies are developed in a way that prioritises human values, needs, and well-being, rather than solely focusing on efficiency and progress (Crawford, 2021).

Hence, HCAI focuses on the ethical and societal impacts of AI. HCAI does not view AI as replacing human decision-making; instead, it underscores the role of collaboration between humans and AI. It is premised on human empowerment, transparency, fairness, and accountability. Anything aimed at producing learning requires a human-centric approach and is inextricably linked with engagement and human interaction. Therefore, creating AI learning environments requires not only efficiency and outcome-based performance but also a focus on human feelings. AI-smart learning environments must also be premised on ethics and anchored on societal values (Yang et al., 2021). Human-centred considerations are crucial so that learners use AI ethically and responsibly. This requires consideration of elements such as inclusiveness, fairness, transparency, and ethics, and goes beyond piquing students' interest in AI use (Ng et al., 2021).

6.5.1 The Importance of Human-AI Synergy

The notion of human–AI synergy in education encapsulates the harmonious collaboration between learners, educators, and AI systems so that the advantages of AI can be harnessed to achieve more enhanced learning outcomes. Working together in a collaborative partnership with AI can lead to fulfilling learning rather than working alone. This contrasts with the traditional approach where technology is used to boost human efforts. Human-AI synergy is an integration that allows AI to partner human-to-human synergy and denotes a seamless integration where AI complements and strengthens human capabilities (Chen, 2024).

Gašević et al. (2023) have coined the term "the space of coordination" to describe the intersection between AI and humans in learning and what happens in this space. Molenaar (2022) focuses on tasks that can be "offloaded from humans to AI" (p. 1) and then "onloaded from AI to humans" (p. 1), focusing on self-regulated learning skills achieved through AI and learner interaction. As education has always been a social process (Liu et al., 2023), students may find online learning using AI isolating and want human interaction, so it is critical to have teachers as learning enablers and peers as collaborators. Teachers function as a human presence to support learners through interaction aspects such as voice and eye contact to add a human dimension to learning. Peers add a human aspect to learning, according to Shemberger (2022), who asserts that learning has a social dimension through interaction with peers and a community of inquiry and involves both teacher presence and peer influence.

6.6 Some Use Cases of AI in TP with Human-Centricity

In TP, students actively engage in learning with AI in human synergy, with educators and peers in the loop. A pilot study of five Effective Communication (ECOMM) classes, about 150 students and two tutors in the School of Humanities and Social Sciences (HSS), was conducted on the use of two Mizou chatbots to refine students' writing for two ECOMM assignments: the message audience and purpose (MAPS) assignment and article writing assignment. The chatbot use was set against the backdrop of teacher instruction in writing, with assessment rubrics created and customised for students.

In particular, the article writing task was structured with clear and specific requirements. Students were required to write a five-paragraph article based on the structure taught, within which creative freedom was allowed. For agency and choice, students pick a topic from five options and develop arguments with supporting reasons based on individual research findings, select evidence to use, and include their personal observations and experiences on the topic. The chatbot for article writing is used by each student as a learning assistant to improve drafts for content, grammar, and syntax. This is done iteratively as students interact with the chatbot while retaining control of the writing process.

Several elements were intentionally built into the learning design and specifications.

Additionally, to retain student agency, the ECOMM tutor designed the learning with conditions to prevent the chatbot from merely providing complete AI-generated written articles. No exemplars were given for the chatbot to model, deterring students from putting in prompts for the AI to regurgitate output based on a fixed writing style. A noteworthy feature of the learning design is that the chatbot is explicitly non-complimentary and critical of the work students do. This is to prevent students from relying exclusively on AI-output without improving their work. Instead, students must resolve problems raised in the comments and choose what to do next.

The key collaborative features in the human-AI partnership for ECOMM are as follows:

The component-by-component structured review in language, tone, and syntax helped students to examine specific aspects they may have overlooked. For the article writing assignment, the chatbot helped students to check for alignment between various parts (e.g., the title of the article, the key message provided, and whether there are links between the stated message and the supporting reasons). This honed students' review skills after initial teacher guidance, complementing the teacher's holistic feedback with detailed component analysis.

The chatbots allowed guided self-improvement by not rewriting drafts or providing answers that stop the self-directed refinement. Guiding questions were used to help students make discoveries and improvements themselves through examples of prompts that could be used. At the same time, the AI built on teacher feedback by encouraging active problem-solving and student agency.

The augmentation of critical thinking skills was also engendered through the systematic and thoughtful guided questions that the teacher teaches the students to ask. This helped students retain ownership of the writing process and add a dimension of critical thinking to the task, as the students' prompts helped the AI to generate meaningful answers. Students could also act on the AI feedback and seek clarification. It is observed that digital nudges could lead people to make alternative choices and direct their decision-making processes (Shin & Ahmad, 2023). This structured writing task using Mizou is one affordance in empowering students to enrich their writing experience without replacing human capacity and agency with AI.

6.6.1 Vital Role of Students' Personal Voice and Reflection in Writing

While the Mizou chatbot for article writing checks if students' personal input or voice is appropriate, it does not validate, correct, or suggest alternatives so that the students' authentic human experience or voice is preserved through a personal response. Palacas (1989) states that personal voice has a commentative element and is reflective, a humanising aspect. Robbins (2016) submits that voice distinguishes between one's thoughts and those of other authors. In a similar vein, Wendig (2012) observes that voice is unique, a creation of that writer and that writer only. I would like to think that tapping into students' personal voice and experience is insightful, akin to storytelling. Chu and Liu (2024) characterise storytelling as a universally human ability which AI cannot match.

Lewis and Sarkadi (2024) observe that AI cannot reflect and lacks insight and deeper skills in processing ambiguity in the same way humans do, as humans have subjective experience and engage in emotional processing about experiences. AI operates based on algorithms, data processing, and pattern recognition, without experience-based awareness or emotional involvement. It may be speedy, but its storytelling lacks intuitive understanding and complexity. Hence, students' unique perspectives are also a large dimension of the task. This ensures that the by-product is generated by their human consciousness, layered by lived-through experience and emotion.

6.6.1.1 Dialogic Feedback With Control by Students

Feedback can be defined as information provided to a learner relating to their skills or understanding in the completion of tasks, usually after instruction (Hattie & Timperley, 2007). Dialogic feedback between students and their educators, as Carless's (2012) asserts, is essential in learning design.

This feedback, like a focused conversation between humans, is defined as interactive exchanges or dialogue through which there is sharing of interpretations, negotiation of meanings, and clarification of expectations. It is human-centric, based on trust, with teacher-student interaction and opportunities to gain experience about what constitutes quality. Feedback reception can be sensitive, so getting personalised feedback without judgement is an important ingredient of humanised learning.

To propel initiative-taking, the Mizou chatbot was set up with the condition to provide generalised feedback only, for instance through comments such as, "Consider using active voice for a more direct and impactful tone." or "This is a long sentence. Break it up for better readability." Students made their own decisions, for example, deciding how to break up sentences. While asking the chatbot for help, they could unleash varying levels of assistance, a benefit also noted by some researchers in feedback seeking (Tlili et al., 2023). Each student also obtained tutor feedback for one initial draft, creating a comprehensive feedback ecosystem with tutor feedback enhanced by chatbot reviews. Students got to refine their work through both chatbot and tutor perspectives, before final submission.

The use of AI for constructive feedback helped to motivate students' learning and foster a sense of positive achievement in ECOMM. Students could use their own strengths in addressing areas for improvement. One hundred per cent of students surveyed stated that the Mizou chatbot was useful. Students reported a 48% increase in their confidence level for the article assignment. Chatbots used effectively can also increase engagement and motivation in learning, all of which are human emotions (Zhang & Aslan, 2021). Hence, allowing feedback for assignments focuses on respect for student judgement of their writing needs and the learning process. While the use of AI in learning may dramatically alter the traditional student-educator bond or relationship, employing AI as teaching assistants does not substitute the educators' professional judgement and intimate knowledge of the student (Kamalov et al., 2023).

Students are also prompted to apply initiative to improve their writing. This is also part of a human value-driven education, as reflected in the use of AI in ECOMM for assignment review. The term "Value-driven AI" has been used to suggest that it is crucial for AI use to be embedded in the values an organisation embodies. Temkin (2023) identifies one area in which applying AI ethically with a set of values in mind needs to be focused on: that is, values clarification or being explicit about one's values. At TP, some of these values include collaboration, independence, initiative, respect for individual dignity, integrity, student-centredness and future orientation. Within the context of AI use for ECOMM, there is also transparency, as Mizou AI does not retain students' data. Although students' chat history with Mizou is available to tutors, the ECOMM team chose to focus on pedagogical innovation and safeguard students' privacy.

6.6.2 Authenticity in Workplace Email Writing

Students' evaluation of AI-generated content, a higher-order skill that is required in the age of AI, was also employed in another subject, Professional Communication (PROCOMM), in the email writing assignment. To guide students through the process of drafting the email, the subject team introduced a prompt-creation framework called RAFT (Role, Aim, Format, Task), an adaptation of the commonly used Context, Role, Aim, Format and Task (CRAFT) framework. The teaching team used AI tools for students to create an email draft in response to a real-life workplace scenario. Part of the focus was also on using prompts to enable students' AI writing Literacy. Students were also taught how to spot possible AI-generated writing, for example, through overuse of formality, repetition of "It is" or "the," redundancy, awkward flow, and egregious bombast. Students were also required to add their personal voice by explaining how they would edit the email to improve the draft, with appropriate justification, to enable human insight and reflection.

The integration of students' unique, personal voice and tone in email writing expresses their individual human identity and authenticity. Workplace email writing is essential practical communication and must take into consideration the social, professional and cultural contexts. The task, therefore, fosters in students the consideration of the impact of professional authenticity in writing. Professor Edison Tandoc of the Wee Kim Wee School of Communication and Information, Nanyang Technological University, suggests that this authenticity or "honesty" could emphasise whether the experience written about is the student's own or if it is templatised (Tandoc, 2023).

Werdiningsih et al. (2024) conclude that "voice" in pedagogical contexts includes the students' unique viewpoints and perspectives, cultural nuances, and individual styles. The authors also observe that AI-generated email has many limitations, such as overly complex suggestions and a lack of cultural sensitivity. Hence, human judgement must be activated when students edit their writing for context specificity and a sincere, rather than mechanical, tone.

Interestingly, some researchers acknowledge the effectiveness of AI in writing instruction. Mahapatra (2024) asserts that ChatGPT can be used for formative feedback in writing to alleviate student anxiety in seeking help from teachers in the context of an English as a second language (ESL) background. Students who are less confident about their writing and language skills can improve through an AI-human collaboration, with teachers facilitating discussion on what constitutes authenticity in email based on professional judgement after students have used AI to generate first drafts.

For AI-use detractors, Thurlow (2023) makes a pertinent point in observing that writing has always been intertwined with technology and pertinently observes that it is both a convergent and divergent exercise in thinking and exploring alternatives. However, he admits that AI has the tendency to stay on the well-trodden paths rather than venture on roads less travelled. Hence, it is for educators to be the humans in the loop, to nurture students' unique ideas and experiences, as writing is context- and culture-driven.

Peres et al. (2023) report that in prompt generation, just by repeating their queries, authors can obtain more accurate responses from AI. Therefore, one future direction for research in writing could be a comparison between the work of students who choose not to use AI to refine their drafts, seeking to employ teacher feedback instead to improve their drafts, compared to output from chatbot assistants. It may also be worth asking if AI tools can refine drafts as long as the user keeps asking more precise questions, and to what extent this digitally generated writing can still build students' skills and knowledge, and how this can be fairly assessed. Thus, more research is needed to explore the reliability and validity of AI tools in assisting students to refine writing. Attention should also be given to producing a guide to develop recommended procedures for using AI tools and reporting their use in assignments.

The "AI mistakes" must also be studied carefully, and solutions found. However, Zou et al. (2024) make the insightful observation that failure learnt from feedback from machine learning could actually prompt learners to seek human feedback from educators and peers. Hence, students could be encouraged to seek further clarification from their educators and peers if they are dissatisfied with AI feedback and output. Another possible area of investigation is how learners should nudge or steer AI with hints, if they want more specific guidance regarding their writing, for the desired outcome.

Therefore, AI can partner with students in writing, but students must recognise the value of shared human experience, open and democratic exchange of ideas, and artistic experimentation using personal voice and observations to construct new knowledge based on informed insights and opinions rather than relying on platitudinous, generic writing from AI. Making students reflect on their writing is part of metacognition, essential in the age of AI and in being human.

6.6.3 Evaluation of Research Material and Role of Critical Thinking in AI Literacy

While living with AI has been variously defined as a cultural moment, it is important to take stock of how AI algorithms function, prioritising information based on the relevance of searches and allowing filter bubbles. This could also result in echo chambers if information moves among those who already have the same set of ideas, generating misinformation and bias (Bell, 2023).

At TP, all students study CICT, a module offered by the School of HSS, where students learn about local and global current issues, such as AI in society, race, environment, security, and social media, and critical thinking. Featured in the AI topic are issues such as the role of algorithms, the use of AI in school and the workplace, and the importance of countering filter bubbles and bias. A discussion-based approach, using case studies and multimedia, culminating in a solutions-driven group project, helps students examine key concepts and theories, engage in perspective-taking, analyse issues, propose solutions, and consider the implications and consequences. While the topics in the project change, the solutions-driven approach in the learning design, underpinned by research and collaboration between students, helps to drive key human-centric learning skills.

Additionally, a key element of the subject is the evaluation of reading material and sources via the Currency, Relevance, Authority, Accuracy and Purpose (CRAAP) test, an evaluation method that helps students decide if they have used informed criteria. There are also other evaluation methods and approaches used worldwide, such as the Authority, Bias and Currency (ABC) of website evaluation; the Reputation, Accuracy, Date and Author Reason (RADAR) approach; the Digital Image Guide (DIG) method; the Stop, Investigate the Source, Find Better Coverage and Trace Claims, Quotes and Media (SIFT) method for checking possible misinformation, and the proactive evaluation approach (Sye & Thompson, 2023). CRAAP has been a cornerstone in teaching higher-education students how to evaluate sources discriminately and is a component of critical thinking and reflection skill, within the context of information literacy (Sye & Thompson, 2023).

The use of the CRAAP test for the CICT through an assignment weighing 25% is a key element of critical thinking as part of the research that students at TP need to engage in for their other subjects. As part of the assignment, students need to find a relevant source, for example, a journal article, a newspaper article, a website, or a magazine, and evaluate it based on the CRAAP test, indicating if it passes or fails the test.

The CRAAP assignment requires thoughtful inquiry into a source and the information contained in it, rather than taking it on trust that it is credible—a crucial tool in the infodemic that we live in. Zemljak and Kerneža (2024) propose that the teaching of doubt is pivotal to thinking. Nelson (2017) asserts that truth is hard to discern because the facts upon which arguments are made need to be questioned, as the information may be untrue, partial, or incomplete, or correct but erroneously applied in the circumstance or context. Critical thinking enables individuals to make thoughtful decisions and effectively arrive at solutions to issues affecting the world. Ennis (2018, p 166) has a definition of critical thinking that is often quoted: that it is "reasonable reflective thinking focused on deciding what to believe or do". Hence, it appears that getting students to reflect on what they have read and to integrate existing experience with new readings is a starting point in questioning their assumptions and checking information to clarify positions of doubt with an open disposition. Teaching the CRAAP Test helps students evaluate the significant skills and processes in information retrieval and evaluation in the choice of reference materials for assignments so that they entertain some doubt about what they read. The CRAAP test can provide students with the appropriate criteria to evaluate scholarly sources based on their currency, relevance, accuracy, authority, and purpose.

The following is the checklist used to guide students to evaluating their chosen article based on the CRAAP test.

Guide to Application of the CRAAP Test

Currency

- Do you need only current information? Or historical information too? Why?
- When was it published? Has it been revised or updated? Is the information within the article current or is it "old news"? What evidence shows that this resource is still valid and current?
- Is the author offering any new insight into the situation, or just saying the same thing as other sources (you might need to cross-reference for this)?

Relevance

- Is the information related to your topic?
- Who is the intended audience?
- Is the information at an appropriate level for the target audience?
- Specifically, which aspect/aspects of this resource is/are relevant? What evidence and reason support your observation? How or why? Paraphrase from the source if necessary.

Authority

- Who is the author or publisher, and what are their affiliations?
- What kind of experience/expertise does the author have?
- Check credentials/accolades of author/publisher (if any).
- What reasons and evidence do you have for saying that the resource is authoritative? (Research the background of the writer and/or publisher, check credibility, qualifications, years of experience, coverage of similar topics, LinkedIn site, and so on.)
- Are contact details provided?
- Were there any endorsements, citations, or awards from renowned persons or notable experts? (Cross-reference if so.)

Accuracy

- To your knowledge, is it error-free?
- Is it peer-reviewed (more applicable to journal articles)?

- Is supporting evidence provided?
- Does the article provide data that offers clarity?
- What reasons/evidence do you have for justifying that the resource is accurate? (Were there any cross-references to highly respected and widely accepted material? Check the references/ bibliography provided. Are they sound? Are the references reliable resources? Why do you say so?

Purpose

- What is the main purpose of the information?
- Are there secondary purposes within the article?
- In your opinion, is it free of bias?
- Could the information be propaganda (or just facts/opinions)? If so, why do you think so?
- In your opinion, how purposeful/helpful was this resource?
- Where are the specific parts that were most purposeful? Were there parts that were not helpful? Which parts and why? Quote if necessary.

To allow deep learning rather than surface engagement with material, the CRAAP module is taught using hybrid learning as a learning design through a bite-sized microlearning package called DREAMS. DREAMS is an acronym that addresses each of the six stages of the online library information search process:

- D—Determine the extent of your information needs, as set out:
- R—Retrieve relevant information
- E—Evaluate online information
- A—Acknowledge use of information
- M—Manage online information
- S—Share online information

As part of learning design, an eLearning module called DREAMS focuses on the essentials of digital literacy, provided for in the learning outcomes of the subject syllabus. Six short microlearning lessons using multimedia and interactive activities are featured, together with quizzes to assess progress and consolidate learning. These quizzes comprise 5% of students' CICT grade, reflecting the importance of the learning. As the DREAMS lessons occur over four weeks, this ensures time for the internalisation and retention of learning, assimilation and clarification of concepts taught. Thus, it is not a "one-shot" endeavour that will result in shallow learning.

One criticism of the CRAAP Test is that the criteria are lengthy. Additionally, according to Russo et al. (2019), "Checklists are often structured into mnemonic acronyms that are easily memorized . . ., but an unfortunate consequence is that students are left without a sense of what is hardest, easiest or most important to evaluate" (2019, p. 296). Tardiff (2022) also points out that when students see the CRAAP criteria as a checklist, they do not go beyond the source under evaluation to probe their assessment, an activity crucial for Internet fact-checking.

However, by requiring students taking CICT to research cross-references for each criterion, to justify the source, the limitations of CRAAP are addressed. The detailed guiding questions prompt reflection and evaluation of the sources. Additionally, students have been required to look for content that is based on dual perspectives, both positive and negative, making the search task more complex so that ChatGPT reliance to complete the assignment is a less feasible option. Furthermore, while teaching students to evaluate sources may seem time-consuming, the focus on reliable information upfront through guided discussion results in saving time, streamlining the research process, and allowing students to filter out unreliable or irrelevant information. The humanising aspect is in arming students with critical thinking knowledge to evaluate sources based on the skills taught.

Future directions about the CICT assignment could include improved learning design for students to critique a GENAI ChatGPT-engineered essay on a recent topic to drive home the point that there may be doubts about the GenAI-authored information. Instead of faulting students for AI use, an open dialogue can be employed in guiding and evaluating AI output that can be fraught with inaccuracies, false attribution, and fabricated information. For the group project, AI can also be used to generate ideas and a first draft only, with CRAAP test aspects for skills transfer. Prompt generation using Socratic questioning can also be taught for critical enquiry and metacognition.

6.6.4 Instructive Visualisation With Dall E AI

Research has shown that images can be instrumental in making learning points clearer. Sung and Mayer (2012) suggest that graphics in a learning experience can be instructive unless they are decorative or distracting, in which case they must be excluded. Instructive experiences are seen to support learning in a direct way, reinforcing essential cognitive processing of core concepts. To add on, Richard Mayer's Cognitive Theory of Multimedia learning provides a framework for understanding how diverse types of images influence learning (Mayer, 2005, 2009; Mayer & Moreno, 2003). A vital idea is that learners can engage in three kinds of cognitive processing during multimedia instruction: extraneous, essential, and generative processing (DeLeeuw & Mayer, 2008). It is in the area of generative processing, interpreting information in the light of the learners' prior knowledge, that deeper processing occurs. In this regard, AI-generated images that stimulate critical thinking or connections to real-world scenarios can enhance generative processing.

In Special Needs Education (SPED) classrooms, the use of AI is recognised as useful in helping pre-service teachers with visualisation and cognitive processing skills (Ni & Wang, 2024). Marino et al. (2023) also acknowledge the work of AI in supporting teacher education in the SPED sector. Similarly, Sharma et al. (2023) suggest that developments in AI and SPED hold promise for facilitating the development of interactive, collaborative spaces that can enhance the lives of people with and without impairments, in keeping with the principles of Universal Design. To this end, for the subject Classroom Management in Special Needs Education offered by the Diploma in Psychology Studies in HSS, students had to generate an image of a classroom ecological map for a SPED classroom for real-world relevance to the learning context for inclusive learning spaces. The focus was on how environmental modifications and differentiated instruction make the learning accessible.

For the assignment, students also had to describe how the physical classroom environment would be organised to support learning and minimise distractions (e.g. sensory-friendly zones, seating arrangements, and visual support). The environmental modifications were assessed through a classroom ecological map. For the generation of a classroom ecological map, students had to produce the prompts to feed DALL-E to generate an image of a classroom ecological map and then critique the image in light of what modifications were positive and what was lacking in the image generated. To ensure integration and assimilation of the concepts learnt, students were required to do a five-minute presentation explaining the links between the AI-output, the ecological map, and the key principles of Universal Design. In their presentation, students focused on group dynamics and the effect of the layout on structured teaching, an important aspect of SPED classrooms that provides equal access for students, a humanising aspect in effective learning.

This presentation also helped students to integrate their learning through the visual generated. It also builds self-directedness by helping students refine their prompts and generate more learning through the answers received. This ability to solve problems through the use of visual representations is also a critical thinking skill requiring self-regulation, as students refine their responses using AI and defend their ecological maps (Markauskaite et al., 2022).

Atchley et al. (2024) posit that more recent AI tools may require educators to focus on learning and teaching methods that build metacognitive knowledge and skills through interpersonal and technological collaboration or through an AI collaborator in the classroom. Critiquing the output for the ecological map assignment allowed students to fact-check the Dall-E output and ensure alignment with key concepts. As seen from the draft Dall-E output in Figure 6.1, there were obvious spelling errors and distortions in

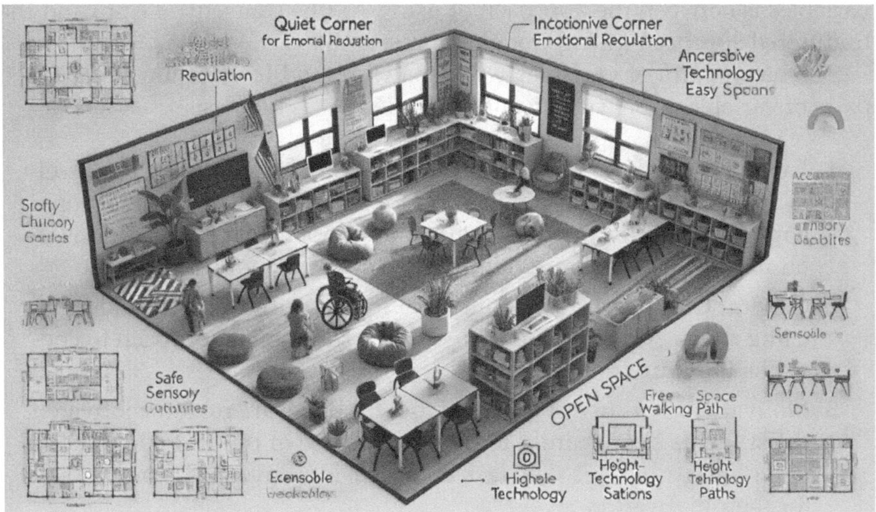

FIGURE 6.1
A Sample Classroom Ecological Map Designed by Dall-E Based on a Student's Prompts.

the Dall-E output that needed corrections. Another refinement could be the use of Dall-E to generate one draft, after which students are assessed on the refinements made in successive iterations. One further suggestion is that learning logs can be incorporated into this task to enable reflection on what students found and how the refinements were made so as to enable metacognition and critical thinking.

6.6.5 Use of AI in Literature Reviews

Another area where AI has been tried out systematically in TP involves using AI to curate literature reviews. This study, conducted in the School of HSS in TP, was for the subjects Applied Social Research, taken by students in the Diploma in Social Sciences and Gerontology in the April 2024 semester. In Phase 2, in October 2024, the study was conducted with students from the Diploma in Psychology Studies for Qualitative Research Methods. The methodology and procedures of the research involve a quasi-experimental design.

During the first tutorial session of the respective subjects, students did a literature review without the use of AI, that is, the traditional method of using Google for research. During the second tutorial session, students were instructed in the use of the AI tool, the Consensus App, for literature review. Students engaged in hands-on activities using the app to conduct literature reviews related to their respective subjects. At the end of each tutorial session, a survey was administered to the students. The main comparison in the variables is between the approach of using AI (the Consensus App) and the traditional approach (using Google for research).

Seventeen pairs of variables were analysed, and it was found that seven pairs of variables were significant, expanded on as follows:

1 Ease of Use: It was significantly easier for students to locate relevant literature using the Gen AI tool compared to the traditional approach. Ease of use and comfort are important considerations in humanising learning by catering to students' emotional needs.
2 General Confidence: Students were significantly more confident in using a Gen AI tool as compared to the traditional approach to conduct a literature review.
3 Motivation: This use of a Gen AI tool for literature review motivated the students significantly more than the use of traditional methods of research as a topic. The lack of labour-intensiveness is one reason for their motivation.
4 Sparking Interest: Using the Gen AI tool for literature review sparked the students' interest significantly more than the use of traditional methods in this research topic.
5 Confidence in Ability: Students were significantly more confident in their ability to select high-quality literature using the Gen AI tool compared to the traditional approach.
6 Future Use: Significantly more students intend to use this Gen AI tool to conduct a literature review in the future compared to the traditional approach.
7 Time Spent: Students spent significantly less time on literature reviews using the Gen AI tool as compared to the traditional approach. Expediting the research process is an important part of research as it is more efficient.

The Consensus App is a powerful AI tool that makes it possible for knowledge to be accessed and digested with ease while providing evidence-based responses at an accelerated pace, humanising learning by ensuring a comfortable and positive research experience (Techpilot.ai, n.d.). The fact that the app can sift through scientifically verified papers and locate pertinent concepts helps to ensure efficiency, addressing the challenge of students' frustration from reading content overload in research. Cascio et al. (2016) suggest that this positive affirmation may strongly affect the reward system in conjunction with future orientation.

By allowing ease and comfort and reinforcing confidence, the study suggests that using AI in literature review can yield positive effects while benefitting learning transfer to future literature review assignments. As the app ensures task fulfilment through accurate responses to students' prompts, the time saved can free students to do other research tasks. The search results also include options to get citations for articles. An added feature is that the abstract conveniently shows how many times the articles have been cited. Yet another useful feature is the Consensus meter, which students can use to ascertain if their hypothesis is supported.

One of the main aspects of the exercise is the development of self-confidence. Confidence judgement, according to Lak et al. (2014), is a significant example of metacognition, or the knowledge about one's own cognitive processes arising from internal representations about beliefs, and this reinforces positive feelings. Mellon (1986) describes the phenomenon of library anxiety, the fear and adverse emotions accompanying navigating library tools and processes required for research: searching for information, evaluating, synthesising it, and writing literature reviews for tasks and assignments. Empathetic teachers need to understand students' emotional states, taking steps to alleviate fear which obstructs learning. Evidently, one way to support learners is through an enabling AI tool.

On the other hand, a study by Chong et al. (2022) about how human confidence affects decision-making in interactions with AI found that people are more likely to trust their self-confidence rather than their confidence in the AI. Even though AI may provide accurate suggestions, people are more likely to follow their own instincts, especially when their self-confidence is high. The researchers also concluded that students' self-confidence could be affected by poor performing AI. Overall, the humanistic focus, increase in motivation, and perceptions of the value of the AI tool in improving students' self-efficacy can boost the learning experience, as seen in the positive feedback on using AI for the literature review.

6.6.6 Using AI in Adult Learning Courses

Learning is also for adult learners who use a variety of AI tools as part of the Workplace Development and Research Fund Grant (WDARF) study involving subject areas as diverse as occupational health and safety, law, and workplace communications.

As adult learners must learn new skills to remain relevant, deal with the demands of lifelong learning, and the realities of time pressure owing to busy work schedules, employing chatbots as learning support tools was the focus of the study. Knowles also described the "job of the adult educators to move adult students away from their old learning and into new patterns of learning where they become self-directed, taking responsibility for their own learning and the direction it takes" (Knowles et al., 1998, pp. 66–69). Chatbots enable human-centred learning by addressing queries round the clock, offering suggestions for tasks and assessments, and functioning as revision aids for tests. The data analytics from students' chatbot use allow educators to identify learning needs and gaps and improve user experience and engagement, for example, by using shorter videos, providing more assessment pointers, or even gamifying the quizzes for interest. The accessibility, adaptability, and respect for human values, needs, and diversity are critical aspects that make AI useful. Adult students have also pointed out that the own-time, own-target queries have eased learning anxiety.

In one HSS Continuing Education Course subject, Reports & Oral Presentation (ROP), the OPKAKI Chatbot was deployed for two semesters with eight classes of adult students. What was found useful by students was the human-curated, educator-validated AI chatbot answers on oral presentation, with curated videos, photos, visuals, and extraneous readings that help to appeal to the diverse needs and ways of learning. Discussing the content provided by the AI helps to enhance the role of human educators in the classroom. Through tone modulation, eye contact, and physical presence—aspects of human interaction, communication, support, and presence—teachers can also significantly enhance students' satisfaction and learning outcomes (Kang & Im, 2013). In a study conducted between 2020 and 2023 with adult learners in TP for ROP, Microsoft's Presenter Coach, an AI tool that aids adult learners in improving their oral presentations through real-time feedback on various aspects such as tone, pace, pronunciation, pitch, language use, and use of fillers, it was found that AI can be a viable partner of the human instructor in speech practice and improve presentation skills. AI can be a practice partner while offering feedback, providing suggestions to reduce filler words, enhancing pronunciation, and giving tips on body language to achieve lively presentation delivery.

This leaves the teacher to exercise professional judgement in supporting students' queries. With the option for repeated, continuous practice, and with AI offering specific, actionable, data-driven insights tailored to each student's practice session, learner confidence can be boosted. For polished speech delivery for effective communication—a critical workplace skill—the personalised learning approach via a "friendly" and approachable AI "coach" also makes the experience a comfortable one, reducing oral presentation anxiety (Kumaran & Boey, 2023).

A perception survey was completed in 2020 and 2021 by CET students. Students in 2020 (97.3%) and 2021 (94.9%) found Presenter Coach useful. The top three areas of benefit were pace, filler reduction, and intonation in 2020, and pace, pitch, and volume in 2021. The survey was also completed by 392 full-time students in 2022. Of these, 87.2% benefitted from Presenter Coach practice. Pace, filler reduction, and pitch were the top three benefits reported. Anecdotal responses from tutors also confirmed that the assessment by Presenter Coach of students' verbal delivery is similar to tutors' assessments of students' verbal delivery when the final Oral Presentation assessment was conducted online.

6.6.7 Guide, Not Devil: Use of Guidelines, Declarations, and Citation Guides

Luria et al. (2020) advance the view that exposing students to many instances of AI use will help them in critical perspective-taking and foster agency in, and self-evaluation of, their own AI use. However, to ensure that students understand AI use consequences and limitations, and ethically monitor their own AI use, exposure to AI ethics for students is paramount, and this is addressed in CICT at TP.

There are also guidelines, not guardrails aimed at policing AI use, but pointers educating students to use AI responsibly. Formal institutional policies and guidelines will result in enhanced learning and augment instruction while ensuring fairness, without inconsistency in application that could lead to confusion. Without guidelines, students risk disciplinary action. This unfair use of AI could also cast doubt on assessment validity and compromise standards of fairness. On the other hand, there are those who posit whether AI use is plagiarism or technology-enhanced performance, so this needs to be discussed and debated in current issues subjects.

Bin-Nashwan et al. (2023) define academic integrity as the practice of researching and completing academic work with fairness and coherence, including the ethical use of AI. While they acknowledge that ChatGPT use is a time-saving advantage, they suggest in their research that academic integrity enhances the association between saving time and ChatGPT use for academic purposes. To this end, educators also caution students against last-minute work on assignments to avert AI misuse from deadline pressure.

Seven principles of prudent AI use have been identified as instrumental in ensuring ethical AI use. Partovi and Yongpradit (2024) summarise these in their research: Purpose: a consideration of why AI is used; Knowledge: interest in content for the promotion of AI literacy; Integrity: focus on advancing academic honesty; Evaluation: regular assessment of AI impacts; Compliance: reaffirmation of existing policies; Balance: looking at the benefits of AI and addressing the risks; and Agency: maintaining human decision-making while using AI. Gonsalves (2024) provides several reasons why there is a lack of compliance with AI guidelines, citing fear of reprisal and academic punishment for violations, ambiguity in guidelines, lack of clarity in understanding guidelines, inconsistent application of guidelines, lack of support from peers, competition and fear of peers' views, and the view among some students that AI use is a private matter.

6.6.8 Not Policing AI Use or Permissiveness but Prudence

TP has a comprehensive set of guidelines on ethical AI use for assignments, with the focus on purposeful pedagogy and prudent exposure to AI tools aligned with students' learning needs. The ARC Model embodies the essential values and principles that students and staff need to be guided by for transparency, respect, responsibility, and privacy.

ARC MODEL

Academic Integrity: Uphold integrity and avoid cheating, plagiarism, and deception.
Awareness of Bias: Be aware of potential biases by critically evaluating the content provided.
Accuracy and Reliability: Critically evaluate the information provided and verify it through reputable sources for accuracy.
Responsible Use: Use responsibly and avoid unethical behaviour.
Respect for Others: Respect the rights and privacy of others, and avoid engaging in cyberbullying, harassment, or violating any laws or regulations.
Responsible Data Handling: Be mindful of the data you input, and avoid sharing personal or sensitive information.
Communication: Be transparent about your use of ChatGPT by giving proper attribution and acknowledging the contribution of the model.
Creative and Original: Strive to develop original thoughts and ideas, even when using ChatGPT.
Critical Thinking: Use ChatGPT as a tool to enhance your critical thinking skills.

To familiarise students with AI use, TP has also produced the ChatGPT Playbook for students, an instructive guide crafted by educators from across the Polytechnic, with diverse user perspectives incorporated. This playbook provides information and instructions on how to get started using ChatGPT, with a range of prompts as examples. Appropriate cases of ChatGPT use are included in diverse domain areas such as language, mathematics, coding, artwork generation, and itinerary planning. This helps reduce ambiguity and allows knowledge and skills to be built in the safe use of AI. Additionally, students are advised about what constitutes plagiarism, how to avoid it, and the consequences of plagiarism—that is, disciplinary action. Additionally, they receive tips on how to paraphrase text and guidance on the differences between paraphrasing, summarising, and quoting. Students are carefully guided to recognise that plagiarism undermines academic integrity, honesty, and fairness, and is an impediment to the demonstration of their skills and knowledge in assessment.

Another instrument in encouraging effective and ethical AI use for learning and assessment is the ChatGPT Use Declaration. This prompts students to show and reflect on how they used ChatGPT via samples of their use, encouraging transparency and augmenting critical thinking. A process orientation approach is also taken, and prompts used are examined so that the intent of the research is evident to the assessor. The declaration of the responses generated by AI also allows the student to acknowledge the AI output, while educators can use it to assess if there was academic dishonesty in students merely offloading

AI content as an assessment submission. This less draconian approach is more palatable to students, as it implies that there is a learning partnership between students, the institution, and educators in supporting ethical AI use. The step-by-step guided approach also helps to remind students not to plagiarise materials. The acknowledgement of references reinforces the importance of attribution or acknowledgement, recognition of ownership of intellectual property, and awareness that knowledge is built on diverse perspectives and scholarship. It is also a step towards humility, transparency, and accountability, and helps students cultivate and display integrity, a critical TP value.

6.6.9 Use of Declarations

DECLARATION ON THE USE OF GENERATIVE AI TOOLS FOR ASSIGNMENTS

Describe how you have used Generative AI tools such as ChatGPT or Dall.E-2 in your assignment.

Show snapshots of the conversations with the AI tool (i.e. the prompts you used and the response you get from the AI tool).

HOW TO INDICATE THE REFERENCE?

The content generated by AI tools is not retrievable except by the user who generated it, so it is considered a non-recoverable source. For non-recoverable sources:

- Do not include them in a reference list.
- Cite within the text as personal communications or correspondence.

Based on APA 7th edition referencing format: (communicator, personal communication, month day, year) e.g. (Paraphrase from OpenAI's ChatGPT AI language model, personal communication, March 8, 2023).

Important Note

- Do not copy answers produced by the AI tool in totality, as it is considered as plagiarism.
- Do not rely on any information produced by the AI tool blindly. You should always verify the answer with other sources. Do not assume that the answers provided by the AI tool are correct.
- To achieve quality outputs from the AI tool, you should provide a good prompt that is clear and specific. Be precise and provide context. Avoid asking open-ended questions.

To provide students with engaging and meaningful learning experiences using Gen AI, educators in TP have embarked on the Gen AI for Teaching and Learning course, designed to equip them with the knowledge and skills to harness the power of Gen AI effectively for teaching and learning. Educators can monitor their competency levels and attend relevant courses from a curated list based on their own competency level to aid AI mastery. All teaching teams have access to redesigning the assessment courses and are strongly urged to do so to make their assessments robust, incorporate human oversight, and mediate between human judgement and AI use, while exploring the role of higher order thinking skills. This ensures that learning and teaching are more adaptive and inclusive as we train students for a future in which AI use is the norm. Mai et al. (2024) acknowledge that institutional support is needed through educator training. Zhai (2022) asserts that providing support is important so that AI is compatible with existing systems and easy to use. One way to do this is to seek instructor input for AI use in the classroom.

6.6.10 Setting Task Expectations

There are also other ways in which TP ensures that students understand what is allowed. (Meakin, 2024a) asserts that the task expectations must be explicitly communicated so students know whether AI tools can be utilised, and how. Additional information to be communicated includes details about student responsibilities and citation help. To avert instances of academic misconduct, students must also be briefed about the potential consequences of AI misuse verbally in class, which is done for subjects such as PROCOMM through dedicated lessons on writing using AI, through information in student handbooks, and digitally via the TP LMS. The following examples from CICT are on acceptable and unacceptable paraphrasing, and Frequently Asked Questions (FAQs) to anticipate student queries.

Proper citation/acknowledgement AND paraphrasing are BOTH necessary to avoid plagiarism. A student who cites/acknowledges an information source MUST still paraphrase that information when including it as part of his/her work.

Paraphrasing is restating text from source material using other words.

EXAMPLE

Original Text:
Further acquaintance with the Wong family next door has shown me that they are very warm and pleasant people. The children are courteous and both Mr. and Mrs. Wong are most helpful.

Unacceptable Paraphrase:
Further acquaintance with the Wong family next door **shows** me that they are very **friendly** and nice people. The children are **polite** and both Mr. and Mrs. Wong are **most willing to offer their help.**
(Why is this plagiarism? The writer has followed the method of expression and sentence structure used in the original text. He/she has also copied the underlined phrases directly from the source or changed them slightly in form only.)

Acceptable Paraphrase:
After getting to know my neighbours, the Wongs better, I find them very easy to get along with. Mr. and Mrs. Wong are always ready to lend a helping hand, and they have well-mannered children.
(Why is this acceptable? The writer has changed the language and structure of the original text instead of just changing a few words and phrases.)

More information on plagiarism and how to cite sources correctly can be found at: http://www.tp.edu.sg/library/research-guides/plagiarism

FREQUENTLY ASKED QUESTIONS

Q1. If I state the source in the References List, can I copy text (e.g. sentences, paragraphs) from the source and include it in my work?

No, this is not acceptable. Copying text from a source, even with the source cited in the References List, is still considered plagiarism.

Q2. If I state the source in the References List, do I still have to cite it within the body of my essay?

Yes, proper acknowledgement of sources means (i) citing the source in the body of your essay (i.e. in-text citation) and (ii) writing out the full details of the source in your list of References.

Q3. If I paraphrase the original text by changing a few words here and there (e.g. changing singular nouns to plural nouns, changing the verb form, changing the order of the words, substituting words), is this acceptable?

If your edited text still looks close to the original text even with some words changed, this is still not acceptable.

Q4. If my classmate(s) and I discuss or work collaboratively on an assignment, can we submit identical responses because all of us contributed to the discussion?

No, you may not submit identical responses if the assignment is supposed to be submitted individually. You will still have to write up your responses individually without copying from each other.

Q5. If I lend my assignment to a classmate for his/her reference only and he/she copies my work, I am not liable to be penalised.

If your work has been copied by another student, with or without your knowledge, you are also liable to receive the same penalty as the student who has copied your work. You are therefore strongly advised not to pass your work to anyone. If caught, you cannot claim ignorance.

Ultimately, responsible AI use must also be encouraged without the AI being made a bogeyman over fears of students cheating. Educators should not be preoccupied with cheating but with checking, and this is to see if the learner has learnt skills of responsible use, such as attribution in employing ChatGPT. Dawson et al. (2024) also posit that the narrow and misguided focus on cheating poses a threat to the validity of assessment because assessment redesign must encompass fresh ways to prepare graduates for a world where ChatGPT use for work is the norm, not an anomaly.

6.7 Criticality of Life Skills, Ethics Education and Lifelong Learning Skills

Furthermore, rather than pull the plug on AI, we can cultivate in our students an array of life skills, including lifelong learning skills, to stay above the learning curve. The World Health Organisation (WHO) (1996) defines life skills as abilities for adaptive and positive behaviour, enabling individuals to deal effectively with the demands and challenges of everyday life. Life skills are characterised as psychosocial competencies and interpersonal skills that help people make informed decisions, solve problems, engage in critical thinking, and express creativity, while communicating effectively, building healthy relationships, and expressing empathy.

Life skills can be personal or social and can also be extended to include actions that change the surrounding environment for better health. Singh

(2003) suggests that life skills are critical in education for equitable access and equal opportunities for all. Based on Bandura's Theory of Agency, or the Social Cognitive Theory (Bandura, 1997), human agency is based on one's ability to control one's actions and behaviour to influence the environment in achieving desired goals. Self-efficacy, intentionality, forethought, and environmental values and skills help to drive human behaviour at the personal and societal levels. The Ministry of Education, Singapore, broadly divides life skills into three distinct groups: cognition, character or citizenship, and community. Examples of important cognition life skills include innovation and critical thinking. Character life skills include self-awareness, mental resilience, and personal effectiveness. Examples of citizenship and community life skills are interpersonal and collaboration skills, communication, and the cultivation of a global mindset.

For relevance and ensuring that these skills are embedded in the contexts and needs of our students, we must anticipate the skills needed for 2025 and beyond. Li (2022) emphasises the importance of analytical thinking and innovation skills, which are at the top of the list of skills that employers will seek in the next five years. Active learning strategies are a new skill set ranked second place. Analytical thinking and active learning rank first and second in 2025, emphasising the need for self-directed learning. Kumar (2023) asserts that leadership, interpersonal skills, and communication skills are crucial in an AI age, as these are the human skills necessary for working in organisations.

These skills, it may be argued, help people collaborate with one another, to work with AI and others, and help to ensure more successful outcomes. According to Vygotsky (1978), in his Theory on the Zone of Proximal Development, our students realise their learning potential through support from more competent others. This can apply to both educators and peers in fostering the development of life skills. Bankins et al. (2024) argue that life skills, including resilience, emotional intelligence, and self-management, help people to improve their adaptability to deal with changes in an age of AI disruption. Also critical in the age of AI is the ability to learn, unlearn, and relearn, but the focus should shift from human capital to developing human capabilities (Poquet & de Laat, 2021). This also requires the integration of technology that can drive lifelong learning as part of skills mastery.

Brundage et al. (2018) also argue for the inclusion of AI ethics in the curriculum. Critical to AI use is the accompanying need for students and educators to understand, evaluate, and familiarise themselves with the ethical use of AI. There are concerns about AI transparency and oversight, legal aspects of AI use, for example, how data sets are "trained" and what impact this may have on people, as well as the political role of AI in terms of the protection available against AI that is used to spread misinformation. In addition, such education could also ensure that AI tools avoid unfair bias and discrimination. Further issues that need to be addressed in this ethics education are the area of data governance and safety, for example, how user data or copyrighted material is used, stored, or shared, as well as access rights and who has these (European Commission, 2022).

Critical consideration must be given to empathy, a cognitive and social construct that is complex in that it allows us to understand mental states and vicariously experience what someone else may be going through in terms of perspective-taking. It is at the level of cognition, putting ourselves in someone else's shoes. At the emotional level, it is more visceral, that is, feeling what someone feels, for example, pain. At the level of compassionate empathy, we can both understand and feel for someone and their suffering. In the age of artificial empathy, where algorithms are contrived to use predictive modelling to simulate empathy, the slippery slope is of pretence, as observed by Nosta (2023). AI empathy becomes utilitarian, so AI is the tenant, not the proprietor, of empathy. Social and emotional learning is also critical to the well-being of students. Hutson and Ceballos (2023) maintain that durable skills must be taught and cultivated in the age of AI, as AI interactions cannot replace the age-old skills of cultivating human relations via teacher-to-student and peer interactions.

A chatbot using ChatGPT can simulate phrases expressing empathy and react almost instantly and consistently to express a sentiment, but this is artificial because, as a machine, the chatbot cannot feel the other person's pain. Given that empathy is needed in areas as diverse as design or advertising, the need for the right kind of human empathy, a cornerstone of our social existence, is critical (Abramson, 2021). Evidence indicates that empathy plays an integral role in the realm of individual and societal well-being. Research from a range of sources shows that empathy is associated with better physical and psychological functioning (Vinayak & Judge, 2018). Hence, even if AI can borrow from the human playbook, we need human ownership of these complex skills.

In TP, the Centre for Life Skills equips full-time TP students, working adults, and industry partners with effective life skills, including communication, critical thinking, customer service, language proficiency, and personal skills to enhance their value in the workplace. The centre also provides continuing education and training (CET) in business communication. Life skills subjects offered to TP students also encompass career readiness skills and knowledge for students to examine their own career interests, values, and goals, as well as acquire career management skills for professional conduct and adaptation in a volatile environment. As part of this suite of subjects, students learn communication skills, sports wellness skills for health and wholeness, sustainability, and climate change so that they are aware of pressing environmental challenges to shape a better world for future generations. Recognising the importance of cross-cultural learning, TP offers students the Global Studies subject, which helps to boost cross-cultural learning, collaboration, and global citizenship via classroom-based and experiential learning in planned overseas trips. Since social boundedness is critical, a number of these subjects help students analyse social contexts for a better appreciation of the interactions and perspectives shaping the structures, identity, values, and relationships within which our students live and function.

As self-leadership and collaborating with the community are critical for active citizenship and personal and social development, students also learn related subjects. They learn to think innovatively through INNOVA, a subject incorporating Design Thinking, a framework that Sreenivasan and Suresh (2024) suggest is a key innovation method that affects company culture, customer involvement, and the driving principles of the innovation process. It is also argued that it is an especially useful framework to complement AI, involving iterative, abductive thinking based on making educated guesses given the best information possible (Verganti et al., 2020).

One interesting finding in the research is that AI can aid life skills development in students. Celik et al. (2024) have done a systematic literature review that shows that chatbots were identified as capable of promoting six main sets of life skills or twenty-first-century skills, namely collaboration, communication, creativity, critical thinking, information and communication technology, and problem-solving. Hence, AI is also capable of being a partner in augmenting life skills in students through personalised learning and real-time feedback, continuously adjusting the learning using data-driven insights.

6.7.1 Some Implications of AI-Human Synergy for the Future of Learning

In TP, as seen from the cross-section of use cases, AI is an avenue through which students can improve digital literacy, critical thinking, problem-solving, and creativity, preparing learners for future job demands. Integrating AI carefully into learning design helps shape future generations to meet workforce demands. At the same time, given that AI use could lead to dependence on AI to the detriment of skills described as "human," more research needs to be done on how a balance can be achieved.

Privacy breach is one of the main risks of AI use in education. Students and educators may view AI systems negatively; for example, Mizou allows staff to access students' chat history with the AI bot. This could erode educator-student trust if students view this as intrusion rather than seeing it as a way to help them avoid over-reliance on the chatbot. Additionally, measures must be taken to ensure data security while taking advantage of technology's benefits. Students may be anxious that their writing, born out of creativity, skill, and effort, is used by large language models to train AI algorithms without their consent. Mizou asserts that it does not use student work for training data, allaying privacy violation fears. At the same time, transparency principles must also be adhered to by all educators in the institution, and informed consent guidelines observed so that student data is sought with permission and stored securely. This is especially important when certain types of personalised learning technologies are used that collect personal data from learners.

Additionally, the use of detection tools needs to be accompanied by close knowledge about the students' abilities, for example in writing. Turnitin, for example, does not check for plagiarism and only displays a matching index, but this is different from plagiarism detection. Subject teams are strongly urged to redesign assessments to address the limitations in detecting AI-generated plagiarism. A further concern is the possibility of bias. Myers (2023) reports the challenge that non-native English users are more likely to face, as AI-generated information can show the potential for discrimination and lack of equality in grading. Gao et al. (2023) have also flagged the possibility of erroneous content generation by AI tools; hence, it is critical that evaluation of research sources is reinforced and emphasised in all subjects. All educators need to familiarise themselves with the many ways of ensuring the authenticity of work submitted and the extent to which sources used to support assessment products are acknowledged to align with a value-centric approach.

Su et al. (2023) indicate that there is little research on the use of ChatGPT in writing. With regard to ChatGPT use in writing, further research can be done on what aspects of writing ChatGPT provides useful feedback in, and whether students know how to act on the feedback given. Research could also be conducted on how peer and instructor feedback can be framed and collected to strengthen students' writing, with AI used for ideation. It would also be informative to ask students whether there are any instances of educators and peers giving feedback that runs contrary to ChatGPT feedback. It would also be instructive to ask students how they would respond if this were the case.

Sarwari et al. (2023) suggest that positive attitudes towards AI technologies, language skills, technical skills, inquiry into the benefits and issues associated, concise prompting, collaboration, and human-machine collaboration are the most important skills for effective application of AI. It would be good to inquire into the precise skills needed in human-AI collaboration as well as effective prompting for various domain areas and subjects, if prompts make a difference in whether students are successful in their AI-related queries. Research can also be conducted on context in tasks, and how AI responds to them, whether accurately or not, given that the context students are embedded in is a Singapore one. Aspects such as culture and bias in the information, given the Singapore context, are also critical areas for further inquiry and development in research on AI, as this will manifestly affect students' knowledge and skills.

At TP, Interdisciplinary Learning (IDL) is used to tackle complex issues that transcend the confines of a single discipline, highlighting the necessity of a holistic educational approach (Ding et al., 2024). The Polytechnic uses IDL in a number of domain areas, allowing students to integrate multidisciplinary insights into their learning instead of looking at traditional discipline-based learning, so that students are equipped with skills for handling uncertainty and paradox in challenges that impact society. It would be useful to find out to what extent IDL with AI use will allow students the opportunity for self-designed evolution, together with their educators and peers as collaborators and travelling companions on the AI journey.

AI will become more nuanced and increase in sophistication, with possibilities such as translation, emotion, and sentiment analysis. It is therefore a boon that the European Union AI Act bans the use of emotional AI to control and negatively influence human behaviour and forbids the use of emotion recognition technology in spaces including the workplace and schools but distinguishes between identifying expressions of emotion, which is approved and manipulating a person's emotional state, which is clearly disallowed (Miles, 2024). It would also be useful to examine what variables affect AI use and whether there is positive perception about AI among TP students in a sentiment analysis study.

Further research can be conducted on educators' communication to students on the Declaration of AI Use to ascertain how checks are done to help students acknowledge AI use. It would also be useful to find out if students copy AI-generated responses verbatim without declaring AI use because of a lack of confidence in their own abilities. Research could also be conducted on learning and teaching strategies to build this confidence, as AI is often used for research, writing, and image generation. A crucial aspect is rethinking assessment to meet AI advancement challenges that render assessment types irrelevant (Meakin, 2024b).

6.8 Conclusion

AI needs human oversight so that human judgement, consciousness, agency, and subjective experiences are part of the decision-making process in a human-centric approach, where students are collaborating with AI. These qualities that make us quintessentially human must be factored into learning as part of self-intelligence (Werhun, 2024). As humans, we live in the world and understand the nuanced, inner workings of our reality, which AI lacks. These elements cannot be substituted, just as toasters or robot overlords, if they ever hold sway, cannot feel or be held accountable for mistakes. AI must be used to amplify human control and decision-making, with AI being a tool to exemplify and accentuate human capabilities, creativity, and intelligence. What needs to be emphasised is the human in us.

> In the words of the inimitable D.H. Lawrence:
> For God's sake, let us be men

not monkeys minding machines
or sitting with our tails curled
while the machine amuses us . . .
(Lawrence 1929, Lines 5–8)

Our mandate as educators is clear: to enable students to deal with a world where AI holds immense promise but also to help them address the perils of AI by embracing values, skills, and competencies in being human, while pointing out the risks of AI-dominated thinking (Çela et al., 2024).

Acknowledgement

The author gratefully acknowledges Eugene Koh, Fairuz Said Abdul Rahman, Izad Ghalid and Nurzahiah Jumat for their valuable contribution to the use cases in this chapter.

References

Abramson, A. (2021, November 1). Cultivating empathy: Psychologists' research offers insight into why it's so important to practice the "right" kind of empathy, and how to grow these skills. *Psychology Today*, 52(8). https://www.psychologytoday.com/articles/cultivating-empathy

Ahmad, Z., Kaiser, W., & Rahim, S. (2023). Hallucinations in ChatGPT: An unreliable tool for learning. *Rupkatha Journal on Interdisciplinary Studies in Humanities*, 15(4), Article 17. https://doi.org/10.21659/rupkatha.v15n4.17

Aithal, V., & Silver, J. (2023, March 30). *Enhancing learners' critical thinking skills with AI-assisted technology* [Blog post]. https://www.cambridge.org/elt/blog/2023/03/30/enhancing-learners-critical-thinking-skills-with-ai-assisted-technology

Anderson, J., & Rainie, L. (2023, June 21). As AI spreads, experts predict the best and worst changes in digital life by 2035. *Pew Research Center*. https://www.pewresearch.org

Ang, H. M. (2025, January 22). Creative skills becoming a requirement for jobs outside of creative sectors, SkillsFuture report finds. *Channel News Asia*. https://www.channelnewsasia.com/singapore/skillsfuture-skills-report-creative-industry-generative-ai-jobs-4887421

Ang, S. (2024, January 10). Students are taught to use AI ethically and responsibly at different levels. *The Straits Times*. https://www.straitstimes.com/singapore/politics/students-are-taught-to-use-ai-ethically-and-responsibly-at-different-levels-chan-chun-sing

Atchley, P., Pannell, H., Woford, K., Hopkins, M., & Atchley, R. A. (2024). Human and AI collaboration in the higher education environment: Opportunities and concerns. *Cognitive Research: Principles and Implications*, 9(20). https://doi.org/10.1186/s41235-024-00547-9

Badrulhisham, F., Pogatzki-Zahn, E., Segelcke, D., Spisak, T., & Vollert, J. (2024). Machine learning and artificial intelligence in neuroscience: A primer for researchers. *Brain, Behavior, and Immunity*, 115, 470–479. https://doi.org/10.1016/j.bbi.2023.11.005

Bandura, A. (1997). *Self-efficacy: The exercise of control*. New York: Cambridge University Press.

Bankins, S., Jooss, S., Restubog, S. L. D., Marrone, M., Ocampo, A. C., & Shoss, M. (2024). Navigating career stages in the age of artificial intelligence: A systematic interdisciplinary review and agenda for future research. *Journal of Vocational Behavior*, 153, 104011.

Bell, S. (2023, September 4). The write algorithm: Promoting responsible artificial intelligence usage and accountability in academic writing. *BMC Medicine*, 21(1), 334. https://doi.org/10.1186/s12916-023-03039-7

Computers in Human Behavior, 148, 107903.

Bin-Nashwan, S. A., Sadallah, M., & Bouteraa, M. (2023). Use of ChatGPT in academia: Academic integrity hangs in the balance. *Technology in Society*, 75, 102370. https://doi.org/10.1016/j.techsoc.2023.102370

Brautigan, R. (1967). *All watched over by machines of loving grace*. Communication Company.

Brundage, M., Shahar, A., Jack, C., Helen, T., Peter, E., Ben, G., Allan, D. et al. (2018). The malicious use of artificial intelligence: Forecasting, prevention, and mitigation. *Future of Humanity Institute, Centre for the Study of Existential Risk, Center for a New American Security, Electronic Frontier Foundation, OpenAI*. https://arxiv.org/abs/1802.07228

Cambridge University Press. (2020). *The Cambridge life competencies framework*. https://www.cambridge.org/us/files/6615/9741/7863/CambridgeLifeCompetencies_Introduction_Booklet_digitalPDF_082020.pdf

Carless, D. (2012). Trust and its role in facilitating dialogic feedback. In *Feedback in higher and professional education* (pp. 90–103). Routledge.

Cascio, C. N., O'Donnell, M. B., Tinney, F. J., Lieberman, M. D., Taylor, S. E., Strecher, V. J., & Falk, E. B. (2016). Self-affirmation activates brain systems associated with self-related processing and reward and is reinforced by future orientation. *Social Cognitive and Affective Neuroscience*, 11(4), 621–629. https://doi.org/10.1093/cscan/nsv136

Çela, E., Fonkam, M., & Potluri, R. M. (2024). Risks of AI-assisted learning on student critical thinking. *International Journal of Risk and Contingency Management*, 12(1), 1–19. https://doi.org/10.4018/IJRCM.350185

Celik, I., Gedrimiene, E., Siklander, S., & Muukkonen, H. (2024). The affordances of artificial intelligence-based tools for supporting 21st-century skills: A systematic review of empirical research in higher education. *Australasian Journal of Educational Technology*, 40(3), 1. https://doi.org/10.14742/ajet.7565

Chalmers, D. J. (1996). *The conscious mind: In search of a fundamental theory*. Oxford University Press.

Chapman University. (2025, January 22). Bias in AI. *Chapman University Artificial Intelligence (AI) Hub*. https://www.chapman.edu/ai/bias-in-ai.aspx

Chen, W. L. (2024, March). *Sing teach issue 88: Sing Teach, 88*. National Institute of Education Singapore

Chong, E., Zhang, G., Goucher-Lambert, K., Kotovsky, K., & Cagan, J. (2022). Human confidence in artificial intelligence and in themselves: The evolution and impact of confidence on adoption of AI advice. *Computers in Human Behavior*, 127, 107018. https://doi.org/10.1016/j.chb.2021.107018

Choudhury, A. R. (2024, October 9). Temasek Poly and AWS establish multidisciplinary AI centre. *GovInsider*. https://govinsider.asia/intl-en/article/temasek-poly-and-aws-establish-multidisciplinary-ai-centre

Chu, H., & Liu, S. (2024). Can AI tell good stories? Narrative transportation and persuasion with ChatGPT. *Journal of Communication*, 74(5), 347–358. https://doi.org/10.1093/joc/jqae029

Crawford, K. (2021, September 27). Kate Crawford on the toll AI is taking on humans and the planet. *Centre for International Governance Innovation*. https://www.cigionline.org/big-tech/kate-crawford-on-the-toll-ai-is-taking-on-humans-and-the-planet/

Dawson, P., Bearman, M., Dollinger, M., & Boud, D. (2024). Validity matters more than cheating. *Assessment & Evaluation in Higher Education*, 1–12. https://doi.org/10.1080/02602938.2024.2386662

DeLeeuw, K. E., & Mayer, R. E. (2008). A comparison of three measures of cognitive load: Evidence for separable measures of intrinsic, extraneous, and germane load. *Journal of Educational Psychology*, 100(1), 223–234. https://doi.org/10.1037/0022-0663.100.1.223

Dempere, J., Modugu, K. P., Hesham, A., & Ramasamy, L. (2023). The impact of ChatGPT on higher education. *Frontiers in Education*, 8, 1206936. https://doi.org/10.3389/feduc.2023.1206936

Ding, Z., Othman, M. S. B., & Hosshan, H. (2024). Development of interdisciplinary higher-order thinking teaching module: Insights from Delphi consensus. *Journal of Ecohumanism*, 3(3), 1948–1962. https://doi.org/10.62754/joe.v3i3.34621948

Dziuban, C., Moskal, P. D., Parker, L., & Ca, M. (2018). Adaptive learning: A stabilizing influence across disciplines and universities. *Online Learning*, 22(3), 1–22. https://doi.org/10.24059/olj.v22i3.1465

Ellingrud, K., Sanghvi, S., Dandona, G. S., Madgavkar, A., Chui, M., White, O., & Hasebe, P. (2023, July 26). *Generative AI and the future of work in America*. McKinsey & Company.

Ennis, R. (2018). Critical thinking across the curriculum: A vision. *Topoi*, 37(1), 165–184.

European Commission, Directorate-General for Education, Youth, Sport and Culture. (2022). Ethical guidelines on the use of artificial intelligence (AI) and data in teaching and learning for educators. *Publications Office of the European Union*. https://data.europa.eu/doi/10.2766/153756

Fadel, C., Black, A., Taylor, R., Slesinski, J., & Dunn, K. (2024). *Education for the age of AI: Why, what and how should students learn for the age of artificial intelligence?* Amazon.

Future of Life Institute. (2024, October). *AI value alignment: Guiding artificial intelligence towards shared human goals* [White paper]. https://futureoflife.org/wp-content/uploads/2024/10/ai-value-alignment-white-paper.pdf

Gao, C. A., Howard, F. M., Markov, N. S., Dyer, E. C., Ramesh, S., Luo, Y., & Pearson, A. T. (2023). Comparing scientific abstracts generated by ChatGPT to real abstracts with detectors and blinded human reviewers. *NPJ Digital Medicine*, 6(1), 75. https://doi.org/10.1038/s41746-023-00819-6

Gašević, D., Siemens, G., & Sadiq, S. (2023). Empowering learners for the age of artificial intelligence. *Computers and Education: Artificial Intelligence*, 4, 100130. Elsevier. https://doi.org/10.1016/j.caeai.2023.100130

Gonsalves, C. (2024). Addressing student non-compliance in AI use declarations: Implications for academic integrity and assessment in higher education. *Assessment & Evaluation in Higher Education*, 1–15. https://doi.org/10.1080/02602938.2024.2415654

Goodlad, L. M. E., & Baker, S. (2023, February 20). Now the humanities can disrupt 'AI'. *Public Books*. https://www.publicbooks.org/now-the-humanities-can-disrupt-ai/

Harel, D., & Marron, A. (2024). The human-or-machine issue: Turing-inspired reflections on an everyday matter. *Communications of the ACM*, 67(6), 62–69. https://doi.org/10.1145/3637210

Hattie, J., & Timperley, H. (2007). *The power of feedback*. Routledge.

Henschke, J. A. (1998). Historical antecedents shaping conceptions of andragogy: A comparison of sources and roots. In *Paper presented at the International Conference on Research in Comparative Andragogy*. Radovljica, Slovenia.

Hutson, J., & Ceballos, J. (2023). Rethinking education in the age of AI: The importance of developing durable skills in the industry 4.0. *Journal of Information Economics*, 1(2), 26–36. https://doi.org/10.58567/jie01020002

Kamalov, F., Calonge, D. S., & Gurrib, I. (2023). New era of artificial intelligence in education: Towards a sustainable multifaceted revolution. *Sustainability*, 15(16), 12451. https://doi.org/10.3390/su151612451

Kang, M., & Im, T. (2013). Factors of learner-instructor interaction which predict perceived learning outcomes in online learning environment. *Journal of Computer Assisted Learning (JCAL)*, 29(3), 292–301. https://doi.org/10.1111/jcal.12005

Khan, S. A. (2024). Impact of AI on Singapore's labor market: Singapore. *International Monetary Fund*, 2024(40). https://doi.org/10.5089/9798400285721.018

Kiyani, A. (n.d.). The humanisation of AI: Can machines truly mimic human thought and emotion? *TEKenable*. https://tekenable.com/the-humanisation-of-ai-can-machines-truly-mimic-human-thought-and-emotion/

Knowles, M. S., Holton, E. F., & Swanson, R. A. (1998). *The adult learner: The definitive classic in adult education and human resource development* (5th ed.). Heinemann.

Kooli, C. (2023). Chatbots in education and research: A critical examination of ethical implications and solutions. *Sustainability*, 15, 5614. https://doi.org/10.3390/su15075614

Kumar, S. (2023). Developing human skills in the era of artificial intelligence: Challenges and opportunities for education and training. *Scholedge International Journal of Multidisciplinary & Allied Studies*, 10(2), 11–19. https://doi.org/10.19085/sijmas100201

Kumaran, A., & Boey, C. K. (2023). Examining the effects of presenter coach on students' oral presentation verbal delivery. In *Proceedings of the ISATE Conference 2023*.

Kureshi, R. (2022). *What is artificial intelligence and how is it different from human intelligence?* University of Hull. Retrieved November 29, 2024, from https://online.hull.ac.uk/blog/what-is-artificial-intelligence-and-how-is-it-different-from-human-intelligence

Labadze, L., Grigolia, M., & Machaidze, L. (2023). Role of AI chatbots in education: Systematic literature review. *International Journal of Educational Technology in Higher Education*, 20(56). https://doi.org/10.1186/s41239-023-00426-1

Lak, A., Costa, G. M., Romberg, E., Koulakov, A. A., Mainen, Z. F., & Kepecs, A. (2014). Orbitofrontal cortex is required for optimal waiting based on decision confidence. *Neuron*, 84(6), 1400–1411. https://doi.org/10.1016/j.neuron.2014.08.039

Lawrence, D. H. (1929). *Work*. In *Pansies*. Martin Secker.

Lee, A. V. Y., Koh, E., & Looi, C. K. (2023). AI in education and learning analytics in Singapore: An overview of key projects and initiatives. *Information and Technology in Education and Learning*, 3(1), 1–10.

Lewis, P. R., & Sarkadi, Ş. (2024). Reflective artificial intelligence. *Minds and Machines*, 34(14). https://doi.org/10.1007/s11023-024-09664-2

Li, L. (2022, July 13). Reskilling and upskilling the future-ready workforce for Industry 4.0 and beyond. *Information Systems Frontiers*, 1–16. https://doi.org/10.1007/s10796-022-10308-y

Liu, J., Demszky, D., & Hill, H. C. (2023, August 14). AI can make education more personal (Yes, really). *Education Week*. https://www.edweek.org/leadership/opinion-ai-can-make-education-more-personal-yes-really/2023/08

Lucas, C. J. (1996). Humanism. In J. J. Chambliss (Ed.), *Philosophy of education: An encyclopedia*. Routledge.

Lucchi, N. (2023, August 29). *ChatGPT: A case study on copyright challenges for generative artificial intelligence systems*. Cambridge University Press. https://doi.org/10.1017/cem.2023.20

Luria, M., Zheng, R., Huffman, B., Huang, S., Zimmerman, J., & Forlizzi, J. (2020). Social boundaries for personal agents in the interpersonal space of the home. In *Proceedings of the 2020 CHI Conference on Human Factors in Computing Systems* (pp. 1–12).

Madsen, S. R., & Wilson, I. K. (2012). Humanistic theory of learning: Maslow. In N. M. Seel (Ed.), *Encyclopaedia of the sciences of learning*. Springer.

Mahapatra, S. (2024). Impact of ChatGPT on ESL students' academic writing skills: A mixed methods intervention study. *Smart Learning Environments*, 11, 9. https://doi.org/10.1186/s40561-024-00295-9

Mai, D. T. T., Da, C. V., & Hanh, N. V. (2024). The use of ChatGPT in teaching and learning: A systematic review through SWOT analysis approach. *Frontiers in Education*, 9, 1328769. https://doi.org/10.3389/feduc.2024.1328769

Manyika, J., Lund, S., Chui, M., Bughin, J., Woetzel, J., Batra, P., Ko, R., & Sanghvi, S. (2017, December). *Jobs lost; jobs gained: Workforce transitions in a time of automation*. McKinsey & Company. https://www.mckinsey.com/business-functions/organization/our-insights/jobs-lost-jobs-gained-workforce-transitions-in-a-time-of-automation

Marino, M. T., Vasquez, E., Dieker, L., Basham, J., & Blackorby, J. (2023). Title of the article. *Journal of Special Education Technology*, 38(3), 404–416. https://doi.org/10.1177/01626434231165977

Markauskaite, L., Marrone, R., Poquet, O., Knight, S., Martinez-Maldonado, R., Howard, S., . . . Siemens, G. (2022). Rethinking the entwinement between artificial intelligence and human learning: What capabilities do learners need for a world with AI? *Computers and Education: Artificial Intelligence*, 3, 100056. https://doi.org/10.1016/j.caeai.2022.100056

Marr, B. (2023, March 22). Chatgpt: What are hallucinations and why are they a problem for AI systems. *Bernard Marr*. https://bernardmarr.com/chatgpt-what-are-hallucinations-and-why-are-they-aproblem-for-ai-systems/

Mayer, R. (2005). Cognitive theory of multimedia learning. In R. E. Mayer (Ed.), *The Cambridge handbook of multimedia learning* (pp. 31–48). New York: Cambridge University Press.

Mayer, R. (2009). *Multimedia learning* (2nd ed.). New York: Cambridge University Press.

Mayer, R. E., & Moreno, R. (2003). Nine ways to reduce cognitive load in multimedia learning. *Educational Psychologist*, 38(1), 43–52. https://doi.org/10.1207/S15326985EP3801_6

Meakin, L. (2024a). Exploring the impact of generative artificial intelligence on higher education students' utilization of library resources: A critical examination. *Information Technology and Libraries*, 43(3), Article 17246. https://doi.org/10.5860/ital.v43i3.17246

Meakin, L. (2024b, May 13). AI and assessment: Rethinking assessment strategies and supporting students in appropriate use of AI. *Impact Journal: The Chartered College of Teaching*. https://journal.aall.org.au/index.php/jall/article/view/943

Mellon, C. A. (1986). Library anxiety: A grounded theory and its development. *College & Research Libraries*, 47(2), 160–165. https://doi.org/10.5860/crl.76.3.276

Memarian, B., & Doleck, T. (2023). Fairness, accountability, transparency, and ethics (FATE) in artificial intelligence (AI) and higher education: A systematic review. *Computers and Education: Artificial Intelligence*, 5, 100152. https://doi.org/10.1016/j.caeai.2023.100152

Miles, N. C. (2024, June 23). Are you 80% angry and 2% sad? Why 'emotional AI' is fraught with problems. *The Guardian*. https://www.theguardian.com

Ministry of Education, Singapore. (2025, July 16). *"Transforming Education through Technology" Masterplan 2030*. https://www.moe.gov.sg/education-in-sg/educational-technology-journey/edtech-masterplan

Molenaar, I. (2022). The concept of hybrid human-AI regulation: Exemplifying how to support young learners' self-regulated learning. *Computers and Education: Artificial Intelligence*, 3, Article 10. https://doi.org/10.1016/j.caeai.2022.100010

Myers, A. (2023, May 15). AI-detectors biased against non-native English writers. *Stanford University Institute for Human-Centered Artificial Intelligence*. Retrieved July 18, 2023, from https://hai.stanford.edu/news/ai-detectors-biased-against-non-native-english-writers

Nagel, T. (1974). What is it like to be a bat? *The Philosophical Review*, 83(4), 435–450. https://www.jstor.org/stable/2183914

Nelson, R. (2017). Doubt in digital education: Critical thinking in the age of trump. *Digital Culture & Education*, 9(2), 118–131.

Ng, D. T. K., Leung, J. K. L., Chu, S. K. W., & Qiao, M. S. (2021). Conceptualizing AI literacy: An exploratory review. *Computers and Education: Artificial Intelligence*, 2, 100041. https://doi.org/10.1016/j.caeai.2021.100041

Ni, Y., & Wang, Q. (2024). Factors influencing pre-service special education teachers' intention toward AI in education: Digital literacy, teacher self-efficacy, perceived ease of use, and perceived usefulness. *Heliyon*, 10(14), e34894. https://doi.org/10.1016/j.heliyon.2024.e34894

Nosta, J. (2023, October 9). Artificial empathy: A human construct borrowed by AI. *Psychology Today*. https://www.psychologytoday.com/articles/artificial-empathy

Pacansky-Brock, M., Smedshammer, M., & Vincent-Layton, K. (2020). Humanizing online teaching to equitize higher education. *Current Issues in Education*, 21(2). http://cie.asu.edu/ojs/index.php/cieatasu/article/view/1905

Palacas, A. L. (1989). Parentheticals and personal voice. *Written Communication*, 6(4), 506–527. https://doi.org/10.1177/0741088389006004005

Palahicky, S., DesBiens, D., Jeffery, K., & Webster, K. S. (2019). Pedagogical values in online and blended learning environments in higher education. In J. Keengwe (Ed.), *Handbook of research on blended learning pedagogies and professional development in higher education* (pp. 79–101). IGI Global. https://doi.org/10.4018/978-1-5225-5557-5.ch005

Partovi, H., & Yongpradit, P. (2024). AI and education: Kids need AI guidance in school: But who guides the schools? *World Economic Forum*. https://www.weforum.org/stories/2024/01/ai-guidance-school-responsible-use-in-education/

Peres, R., Schreier, M., Schweidel, D., & Sorescu, A. (2023). On ChatGPT and beyond: How generative artificial intelligence may affect research, teaching, and practice. *International Journal of Research in Marketing*, 40(2), 269–275. https://doi.org/10.1016/j.ijresmar.2023.03.001

Poquet, O., & de Laat, M. (2021). Developing capabilities: Lifelong learning in the age of AI. *British Journal of Educational Technology*, 52, 1–14. https://doi.org/10.1111/bjet.13123

Rawle, F. (2022). Humanizing learning: A student-generated framework. *eCampus Ontario*. https://ecampusontario.pressbooks.pub/humanizinglearningframework/front-matter/humanizing-learning-a-student-generated-framework/

Robbins, S. P. (2016). Finding your voice as an academic writer (and writing clearly). *Journal of Social Work Education*, 52(2), 133–135. https://doi.org/10.1080/10437797.2016.1151267

Russo, A., Jankowski, A., Beene, S., & Townsend, L. (2019). Strategic source evaluation: Addressing the container conundrum. *Reference Services Review*, 47(3), 294–313. https://doi.org/10.1108/RSR-04-2019-0024

Santoro, E., & Monin, B. (2023). The AI effect: People rate distinctively human attributes as more essential to being human after learning about artificial intelligence advances. *Journal of Experimental Social Psychology*, 107, 104464. https://doi.org/10.1016/j.jesp.2023.104464

Sarwari, A., Haidari, Z., Adnan, H., Rahamad, M., Javed, M., Nubli, M., & Wahab, A. (2023). The essential skills for effective application of artificial intelligence (AI) and its main effects on human communication. *International Journal of Engineering and Technology (IJETAE)*, 13, 12. https://doi.org/10.46338/ijetae1223_02

Saunders, L., & Wong, M. A. (2020). *Instruction in libraries* (Chapter 2: Learning theories: Understanding how people learn). Urbana, IL: Windsor & Downs Press, part of the Illinois Open Publishing Network (IOPN). https://doi.org/10.21900/wd.12

Schmager, S., Pappas, I., & Vassilakopoulou, A. (2023). Defining human-centered AI: A comprehensive review of HCAI literature. In *Proceedings of the 15th Mediterranean Conference on Information Systems (MCIS)* (p. 7). Madrid, Spain.

Scriven, M., & Paul, R. (2008). *Defining critical thinking*. Retrieved February 6, 2013, from http://www.criticalthinking.org/pages/defining-critical-thinking/766

Shankar, S., Halpern, Y., Breck, E., Atwood, J., Wilson, J., & Sculley, D. (2017). No classification without representation: Assessing geodiversity issues in open data sets for the developing world. *arXiv*. https://arxiv.org/pdf/1711.08536

Sharma, S., Tomar, V., & Aggarwal, M. (2023). Impact of AI-based special education on educators and students. In *AI in education: Innovative perspectives and practices* (pp. 35–56). IGI Global. https://doi.org/10.4018/979-8-3693-0378-8.ch003

Shemberger, M. (2022). Humanizing learning: Concepts and strategies to design and implement now. In *Pedagogicon Conference Proceedings*. Eastern Kentucky University. https://encompass.eku.edu/
Shin, D., & Ahmad, N. (2023, August). *Algorithmic nudge: An approach to designing human-centred generative artificial intelligence*. Computer. IEE Computer Society.
Singh, M. (2003). *Understanding life skills: Background paper for the Education for all global monitoring report 2003/4: Gender and education for all: The leap to equality*. United Nations Educational, Scientific and Cultural Organization (UNESCO)
Smith, R., Steklis, H. D., Steklis, N. G., Weihs, K. L., & Lane, R. D. (2020). The evolution and development of the uniquely human capacity for emotional awareness: A synthesis of comparative anatomical, cognitive, neurocomputational, and evolutionary psychological perspectives. *Biological Psychology*, 154, 107925. https://doi.org/10.1016/j.biopsycho.2020.107925
Spector, J. M. (2014). Conceptualizing the emerging field of smart learning environments. *Smart Learning Environments*, 1, 2. https://doi.org/10.1186/s40561-014-0002-7
Spector, J. M. (2018). The potential of smart technologies for learning and instruction. *International Journal of Smart Technology & Learning*, 1(1), 21–32. https://doi.org/10.1504/IJSMARTTL.2016.078163
Sreenivasan, A., & Suresh, M. (2024). Design thinking and artificial intelligence: A systematic literature review exploring synergies. *International Journal of Innovation Studies*, 8(3), 297–312. https://doi.org/10.1016/j.ijis.2024.05.001
Starčič, A. I., & Vukan, M. (2019, January 10–13). Teachers' perception of data-driven school ecosystem and data analytics. In *Proceedings of IC4E 2019 (IC4E 2019)*. Tokyo, Japan: Association for Computer Machinery.
Sternberg, R. J., & Sternberg, K. (2011). *Cognitive psychology* (6th ed.). Wadsworth Publishing.
Stoltz, T., Weger, U., & da Veiga, M. (2024). Consciousness and education: Contributions by Piaget, Vygotsky, and Steiner. *Frontiers in Psychology*, 15, Article 1411415. https://doi.org/10.3389/fpsyg.2024.1411415
Su, Y., Lin, Y., & Lai, C. (2023). Collaborating with ChatGPT in argumentative writing classrooms. *Assessing Writing*, 57, 100752. https://doi.org/10.1016/j.asw.2023.100752
Sung, E., & Mayer, R. E. (2012). When graphics improve liking but not learning from online lessons. *Computers in Human Behavior*, 28(5), 1618–1625. https://doi.org/10.1016/j.chb.2012.03.026
Sye, D., & Thompson, D. S. (2023). Tools, tests, and checklists: The evolution and future of source evaluation frameworks. *Journal of New Librarianship*, 8(1), 76–100. https://doi.org/10.33011/newlibs/13/9
Tandoc, E. C. (2023, May 31). Commentary: We must become better writers in an age of ChatGPT. *ChannelNewsAsia*. https://www.channelnewsasia.com/commentary/chatgpt-ai-can-help-us-be-better-writers-education-students-3511241
Tardiff, A. B. (2022). Have a CCOW: A CRAAP alternative for the internet age. *Journal of Information Literacy*, 16(1), 119–130. http://dx.doi.org/10.11645/16.1.3092
Techpilot.ai. (n.d.). Consensus AI: Can it really make research easier? We put it to the test. *Tech Pilot*. https://techpilot.ai/tools/consensus-ai-can-it-make-research-easier/
Temasek Polytechnic. (2024a, January 9). *Temasek Polytechnic at the forefront of AI with launch of first experimental studio for design and generative AI in an educational institution*. https://www.tp.edu.sg/about-tp/media-centre/

press-release/Temasek-Polytechnic-at-the-Forefront-of-AI-with-Launch-of-First-Experimental-Studio-for-Design-and-Generative-AI-in-an-Educational-Institution.html

Temasek Polytechnic. (2024b, June 14). Singapore launches blueprint for 'future design school' to prepare youths for an AI-centric future. *Temasek Polytechnic.* https://www.tp.edu.sg/about-tp/media-centre/tp-in-the-news/singapore-launches-blueprint-for--future-design-school--to-prepa.html

Temkin, B. (2023, January 10). The key ingredient to AI success: Our values. *LinkedIn.* https://www.linkedin.com/pulse/key-ingredient-ai-success-our-values-bruce-temkin

Thurlow, S. (2023). The other side of AI: Writing, thinking and creativity in an age of artificial intelligence. *Journal of Academic Language and Learning*, 17(1), T92–T102. https://journal.aall.org.au/index.php/jall/article/view/943

Tlili, A., Shehata, B., Adarkwah, M. A., Bozkurt, A., Hickey, D. T., Huang, R., & Agyemang, B. (2023). What if the devil is my guardian angel: ChatGPT as a case study of using chatbots in education. *Smart Learning Environments*, 10(15). https://doi.org/10.1186/s40561-023-00237-x

Turner, J. C., & Paris, S. G. (1995). How literacy tasks influence children's motivation to read and write. In P. J. O'Keefe, & R. J. Garner (Eds.), *Motivating literacy in the classroom* (pp. 165–187). Erlbaum.

Tushara, E. (2023, September 20). MOE prepares students for fast-changing world through tech, updating learning spaces. *The Straits Times.* https://www.straitstimes.com/singapore/edtech-masterplan-and-enhancing-school-environments-moe-announces-moves-to-prepare-students-for-fast-changing-world

University of Oxford. (2024, January 3). Study shows that the way the brain learns is different from the way that artificial intelligence systems learn. *University of Oxford News.* https://www.ox.ac.uk/news/2024-01-03-study-shows-way-brain-learns-different-way-artificial-intelligence-systems-learn

Verganti, R., Vendraminelli, L., & Iansiti, M. (2020). *Design in the age of artificial intelligence.* Harvard Business School Working Paper No. 20-091. Harvard Business School.

Vinayak, S., & Judge, J. (2018). Resilience and empathy as predictors of psychological wellbeing among adolescents. *International Journal of Health Sciences and Research*, 8(4), 192–200.

Vygotsky, L. S. (1978). *Mind in society: The development of higher psychological processes* (M. Cole, V. Jolm-Steiner, S. Scribner, & E. Souberman, Eds.). Harvard University Press. https://doi.org/10.2307/j.ctvjf9vz4

Wang, S. (2017). An exploration into research on critical thinking and its cultivation: An overview. *Theory and Practice in Language Studies*, 7(12), 1266–1280. https://doi.org/10.17507/tpls.0712.14

Wang, S., & Han, S. (2010). Six Cs of motivation. In M. Orey (Ed.), *Emerging perspectives on learning, teaching, and technology* (pp. 267–270). North Charleston: CreateSpace. https://www.researchgate.net/profile/Kakali-Bhattacharya/publication/302947319_Piaget_and_cognitive_development/links/60730722a6fdcc5f779c8716/Piaget-and-cognitive-development.pdf

Wendig, C. (2012, January). *25 things writers should know about finding their voice.* http://terribleminds.com/ramble/2012/01/10/25-things-writers-should-know-about-finding-their-voice/

Werdiningsih, I., Marzuki, & Rusdin, D. (2024). Balancing AI and authenticity: EFL students' experiences with ChatGPT in academic writing. *Cogent Arts & Humanities*, 11(1). https://doi.org/10.1080/23311983.2024.2392388

Werhun, C. (2024, March 21). *In the age of AI, students need to develop their self-intelligence: 5 ways educators can help cultivate these uniquely human skills*. Harvard Business Publishing (Education).

World Economic Forum. (2024, October 17). *AI value alignment: How we can align artificial intelligence with human values*. World Economic Forum. https://www.weforum.org/stories/2024/10/ai-value-alignment-how-we-can-align-artificial-intelligence-with-human-values/

World Health Organization. (1996). *Life skills education: Planning for research*. World Health Organization.

Yang, S. J. H., Ogata, H., Matsui, T., & Chen, N.-S. (2021). Human-centered artificial intelligence in education: Seeing the invisible through the visible. *Computers and Education: Artificial Intelligence*, 2, 100008. https://doi.org/10.1016/j.caeai.2021.100008

Yin, W. J. (2024, January 24). Will our educational system keep pace with AI? A student's perspective on AI and learning. *Educause Review*. Emerging Technologies and Trends, Teaching and Learning. https://er.educause.edu/articles/2024/1/will-our-educational-system-keep-pace-with-ai-a-students-perspective-on-ai-and-learning

Zemljak, D., & Kerneža, M. (2024). Embracing doubt: Critical thinking in the age of artificial intelligence in education. In *International Conference on Science, Innovations and Global Solutions* (pp. 330–334). Futurity Research Publishing. https://futurity-publishing.com/international-conference-on-science-innovations-andglobal-solutions-archive/

Zhai, C., Wibowo, S., & Li, L. D. (2024). The effects of over-reliance on AI dialogue systems on students' cognitive abilities: A systematic review. *Smart Learning Environments*, 11(28). https://doi.org/10.1186/s40561-024-00316-7

Zhai, X. (2022, December 27). *ChatGPT user experience: Implications for education*. SSRN. https://ssrn.com/abstract=4312418 or http://dx.doi.org/10.2139/ssrn.4312418

Zhang, K., & Aslan, A. B. (2021). AI technologies for education: Recent research and future directions. *Computers & Education: Artificial Intelligence*, 2, 100025. https://doi.org/10.1016/j.caeai.2021.100025

Zou, T., Ertug, G., & Roulet, T. (2024). Learning from machines: How negative feedback from machines improves learning between humans. *Journal of Business Research*, 172. https://doi.org/10.1016/j.jbusres.2023.114417

7

Enhancing the Implementation of Behavioural Insights in Education Using AI Tools

Gabrielle Lai and Tan Wah Pheow

7.1 The Behavioural Science Approach in Education

Within the higher education literature, student success has been defined multi-dimensionally to include academic achievement, acquisition of desired skills and competencies, attainment of educational outcomes, engagement in educationally purposeful activities, persistence and satisfaction in their course of study, and post-graduation career success (Alyahyan & Düştegör, 2020; Weatherton & Schussler, 2021). More personal characteristics such as adaptability and resilience, ethics, self-regulation, self-directedness, and self-efficacy have also been highlighted as successful student outcomes.

To achieve this, it is common for educators to (traditionally) focus their efforts on the cognitive aspects of learning by enhancing pedagogical approaches in the classroom (e.g. in curriculum design and classroom delivery). While there is nothing inherently wrong with these efforts, the focus on pedagogical engagements by itself is often insufficient to engage and motivate students. Behavioural research has consistently suggested that there are other factors that can affect students in achieving successful outcomes such as their social support structures, motivations and emotions, and life skills. This is because learning is a behaviour that does not occur in a vacuum. Learning is contextual, where individual, social, and environmental factors play an underpinning role in influencing the extent to which students are able to learn well (or not). Designing a successful learning environment involves more than just the cognitive aspects (i.e. pedagogy and curriculum); it also considers the context and environment in which learning occurs.

For educators to design an effective learning environment, it is important to recognise that at the core, both educator and students are humans. The situations and challenges faced by both educators and students are fundamentally human and behavioural in nature. It is crucial for educators to know what makes humans (i.e. students) "tick", and to design human-centric and behaviourally informed approaches that support students' learning and

 DOI: 10.1201/9781003599357-8

development (beyond the curriculum). This is especially crucial given the advent of artificial intelligence (AI) and the abundance of educational technological tools.

To do so, this chapter proposes that a guiding approach is through the perspectives of the behavioural sciences—specifically through the applications of behavioural insights (BI). This chapter discusses the BI approach and its effective applications in education. Recent advancements in educational technologies and AI tools have provided a platform to further enhance the efficacy of BI approaches. This chapter will also explore the capabilities and potentialities of how AI tools can enhance BI in education, and discuss certain considerations, benefits, and potential trade-offs on teaching engagements and learning outcomes.

7.2 Behavioural Insights

Behavioural insights (BI) is an approach that leverages knowledge from the behavioural sciences (e.g. psychology, sociology, human factors, behavioural economics) to apply a behavioural lens to problem solving by mapping behavioural or psychological science knowledge to a problem's contextual factors. Insights derived based on this mapping are then used to design behavioural-based solutions with the intention to "nudge" individuals' behaviours towards desirable outcomes. These behavioural-based solutions are usually evaluated for their efficacy and scaled up if found to be effective (Dolan et al., 2010).

Behavioural Insights was first popularised by the behavioural insights team (BIT) from the UK in the domain of public policy to nudge citizens towards better decisions and life outcomes (Dolan et al., 2010). Since then, nudging has been widely applied across diverse fields associated with influencing and changing human behaviours such as healthcare (Perry et al., 2015), volunteerism (Chan et al., 2024b), workplace safety (Juras et al., 2023), financial well-being (Gabhane et al., 2023), and sustainability (Amiri et al., 2024).

7.2.1 Mechanisms of Nudging

According to Thaler and Sunstein (2008), a nudge is defined as "any aspect of the choice architecture that alters people's behavior in a predictable way without forbidding any options or significantly changing their economic incentives". A nudge should be easy to implement and should not require extensive resources (i.e. cost-effective).

The concept of nudging is related to the dual process theory (Evans & Stanovich, 2013). The dual process theory was first introduced by Wason and Evans (1974) and has a long-standing history in the cognitive and behavioural sciences (see Evans, 2008 for a review of dual process theories). This standard view of the dual process theory suggests that there are different aspects of human cognition, such as reasoning, judgement, and decision making (Grayot, 2019). These cognitive processes can be broadly categorised to result in two mental processing types—"Higher" and "lower" mental processes (e.g. Kahneman, 2011). "Lower" mental processes are typically depicted as fast, reactive, automatic, intuitive, associative, and unconscious. This category of mental processing is commonly referred to as "System 1" or "Type 1" processing. System 1 tends to rely on habitual responses, personal and social biases, and rules of thumb (i.e. heuristics) to make quick decisions. It is often associated with instinctual and habitual responses. For an example of System 1, a student who initially sets a goal to start working on an assignment finds himself procrastinating on the task because he feels lazy and tired or is distracted by other non-task-related engagements.

On the other hand, "higher" mental processes are depicted as slow, controlled, reflective, rule-based, and effortful. This category of mental processing is commonly referred to as "System 2" or "Type 2" processing. It requires a more deliberate approach to how one makes their decisions and choices. It is associated with more intensive cognitive engagements such as critical thinking, problem solving, and deductive reasoning. Using the same example as given earlier, a System 2 behaviour would be for the student to choose to start working on the assignment despite his tiredness and inertia and keep himself focused by effortfully avoiding distractions.

In comparing both systems, it seems that System 2 is more advantageous towards better decision-making and goal-oriented behaviours. However, the realistic truth is that most of our day-to-day decisions and behaviours are determined by System 1. This is because System 1 requires much lesser mental effort compared to System 2. This can lead to decisions and behaviours that are inconsistent with a person's long-term goals. The irrationality of System 1 leads to seemingly unimportant environmental cues impacting choices and behaviours, while for System 2, these cues would be less relevant. The concept of nudging accepts the lack of rationality of System 1 and tries to circumvent it by leveraging it and using it in a positive way. The design of the decision environment should then take into account our human rationality (and irrationality), by designing small changes in the environment to influence people's behaviours and guide them towards improved decisions (Thaler & Sunstein, 2008). Thaler and Sunstein (2008) advocate that small changes (nudges) in the environment can guide people towards improved decisions and behaviours. This is known as choice architecture, and designers of the choice environment are termed "choice architects".

7.2.1.1 Process and Methodology of BI Initiatives

Within the field of BI, there are several methodological processes frameworks that guide "choice architects" in the design and implementation of nudges (e.g., Ball & Head, 2021; BIT UK, 2022; Smith et al., 2024; Tan & Lai, 2019). These frameworks typically serve as a systematic guide through the different stages of implementing a BI initiative. One of the most widely referenced process framework is the TESTS framework (i.e. Target, Explore, Solution, Trial, and Scale) developed by the BIT UK (2022), but there are also other frameworks employed by other practitioners (e.g. Smith et al., 2024; Tan & Lai, 2019).

Although different organisations employ different process frameworks for their BI initiatives, some commonalities can be derived from these different frameworks. First, there is an initial process where potential target behaviours that may impact the problem scenario are identified, and some exploratory research (e.g. interviews, observations, surveys, and diary studies) is conducted to obtain data, typically qualitative in nature, to determine the contextual factors (e.g. levers, facilitators, blockers) that influence the target behaviours. Typically, these contextual factors are derived by conducting thematic analysis on the qualitative data and then mapping the findings from the thematic analysis onto a behavioural change model, such as the COM-B model (Michie et al., 2014). This process is commonly termed "generating insights". Peterson (2023) also refers to this process as modelling context. After identifying the contextual factors that influence the target behaviours, the next common step for most of these frameworks is the design and development of nudges for the target behaviours, which requires some domain knowledge in psychological or behavioural sciences to determine which theories or effects to incorporate into the design and development of the nudges. However, there are also some BI solutions frameworks developed by different organisations to guide individuals with no background in psychological or behavioural sciences to design and develop nudges, with the MINDSPACE (Dolan et al., 2010) and the EAST frameworks (BIT UK, 2024) developed by the BIT as the most common BI solution frameworks.

Once the nudges are developed, the next step will involve the implementation and evaluation of the developed nudges, typically within the context of a small-scale field experiment. Typically, the recommendation is to employ a randomised-controlled trial (RCT) evaluation design, which is commonly considered the "gold standard" of evaluation (BIT UK, 2022; Smith et al., 2024). However, it is not always feasible to adopt an RCT design, and depending on the situation, other types of evaluation design (e.g. pre-post design) can also be adopted (Smith et al., 2024). Finally, for nudges that are found to be effective based on the evaluation, they will likely be recommended for scaling up.

In Temasek Polytechnic (TP), the School of Humanities and Social Sciences (HSS) developed and adopted the USE framework (i.e. Understand, Solve, Evaluate) (Tan & Lai, 2019) as the process framework that is used to guide numerous BI initiatives within the organisation (e.g. Chua et al., 2021; Tan et al., 2020, 2021, 2022). The USE framework mirrors the processes described in the preceding paragraphs, where the Understand stage requires conducting exploratory research to understand the perspectives and behaviours of various stakeholders and how the target behaviours are enacted within their social and environmental context, followed by the design, development and piloting of nudges for the target behaviours in the Solve stage, and lastly the evaluation of the effectiveness of the implemented nudges before deciding whether to scale them up in the Evaluate stage. The USE framework ensures the adoption of a behavioural lens, scientific and empirical approach in the implementation and evaluation of nudges. It is proposed that educators who wish to deploy nudges to improve academic outcomes consider using the USE framework as a guide, as we have used it to guide BI initiatives within our institute, where nudges were developed to improve academic outcomes (Chua et al., 2021; Tan et al., 2021, 2022)

As can be observed from these various process frameworks (BIT UK, 2022; Smith et al., 2024; Tan & Lai, 2019), prior to the design, development and implementation of nudges, there is substantial work required in the form of collecting data through exploratory research, and then analysing the collected data to map them to behavioural change models in order to derive contextual factors that influence the target behaviours (i.e. Understand). As seasoned BI practitioners, TP's experience is that the work at this stage is the most important, as any nudges designed or developed without a clear understanding of the contextual factors that influence the target behaviours are very likely to be ineffective.

Unfortunately, most articles that report the outcome of BI or nudging studies tend to focus their description on the design, development, implementation and evaluation of nudges (i.e. Solve and Evaluate), and seldom describe the work required to derive the contextual factors that influence the target behaviours, which are crucial for designing and developing an effective nudge. In our opinion, this is not a healthy practice as it paints a false impression that designing and developing effective nudges is easy. The authors fear such a false impression might backfire on the entire BI profession when new practitioners get disheartened by the outcomes of testing ineffective nudges in the field because the work of understanding contextual factors was not carried out. Ridder et al. (2024) shared similar views, where they reported findings from ethnographic studies with numerous BI units and concluded that teams were spending a lot of time discussing the potential of nudging without considering the wider context, and how it might affect the design and implementation of nudges, leading to the potential design of ineffective nudges.

However, one must also be sympathetic to this common practice of not reporting the exploratory research that derives the contextual factors. Based on TP's experience, the work associated with "Understand" can be very unstructured, time-consuming and requires guidance from individuals with domain expertise in behavioural sciences research to ensure quality data is collected and the mapping to behavioural change models is done correctly. Hence, potential adopters of BI or nudging might be put off by the amount of work, resources or even expertise required, especially if they do not have a background in psychological or behavioural sciences and thus make the decision not to adopt BI or nudging in their work.

The characterisation of the issue of underreporting the work associated with the "Understand" stage in publications seems like a Catch-22 situation. However, the authors think that AI might be able to provide a potential solution for this dilemma. This point will again be discussed later in the chapter, showing how AI can be used to help educators implement BI or nudges to improve academic outcomes for students.

7.2.2 BI Applied in Education

In the application of BI to public policy, BIT emphasised that the BI approach is not meant to replace existing policy tools or approaches, but to complement and improve conventional policy tools to achieve significantly improved policy outcomes at a lower cost (Dolan et al., 2010). While conventional policy tools might have limitations, BIT was still quick to recognise that they still serve an important role in policy making and implementation, and BI should not be used to replace the important functions that these conventional policy tools serve. This sentiment was echoed by Soman (2015), who identified the ways in which BI can complement and improve the different categories of conventional policy tools, and situations in which existing policy tools should be used over BI.

In the previous section, it is mentioned that while educators traditionally focused on enhancing pedagogical approaches to improve educational outcomes, designing a successful learning environment involves more than good pedagogy, and requires some understanding of a human-centric and behaviourally informed approach. In terms of applying BI to an educational context, we would like to point out the parallels with its application in public policy. The application of the BI approach within education is not meant to replace existing pedagogical approaches or practices, but to complement them to achieve improved educational outcomes by improving the learning environment for learners. While pedagogical approaches focus on the cognitive aspects of learning within the classroom setting, the BI approach tends to focus on the social and motivational aspects of the learning environment that sometimes extend beyond classroom settings.

This chapter is not making the claim that existing pedagogical approaches exclusively focus on the cognitive aspects of learning. Studies have demonstrated how good pedagogical approaches, such as adopting an active learning approach (e.g. Amerstorfer & Freiin von Münster-Kistner, 2021; Freeman et al., 2014), or positive classroom practices, such as adopting suitable teaching behaviours (e.g. Reeve & Jang, 2006; Skinner & Belmont, 1993; Xiong, 2025), can foster student engagement and engage them at the cognitive, behavioural and emotional levels within the classroom setting. Indeed, student engagement has been demonstrated to be positively correlated with good academic outcomes (e.g. Carini et al., 2006; Öz & Boyacı, 2021; Trowler, 2010). The main claim is that adopting a BI approach to complement existing pedagogical approaches will lead to better academic outcomes for students in higher education.

Unlike pedagogical approaches, educational nudges in higher education do not always target academic outcomes directly (e.g. grades, test or exam scores, course engagement, attendance rates). Some educational nudges target outcomes such as university application and enrolment (e.g. Field, 2009; Hoxby & Turner, 2015), and application for financial aid (e.g. Castleman & Page, 2016; Dinkelman & Martinez, 2014). Although these outcomes do not directly affect learning in the classroom, they are related to decisions undertaken by students during their educational journey and may have indirect effects on learning in the classroom. For example, underprivileged students worrying about financing their education face a "bandwidth tax" that reduces their available cognitive resources for learning (Mullainathan & Shafir, 2013). Hence, nudges that improve the probability of financial aid are likely to increase students' cognitive bandwidth and indirectly improve their academic outcomes. While the importance of these educational nudges is acknowledged, this chapter does not focus on them but would instead focus on educational nudges that directly target academic outcomes.

Nudges that typically target academic outcomes in higher education include the following: (a) timely reminders sent to students on academic tasks to be completed, access to advising or encouragements (e.g. Castleman & Meyer, 2016, Tan et al., 2020); (b) framing of information in a "loss frame" to trigger loss aversion effects that nudge students towards desired behaviours that would likely result in improved academic performance (e.g. Apostolova-Mihaylova et al., 2015; McEvoy, 2016); (c) providing access to information such as feedback to exam results (e.g. Bandiera et al., 2015), what constitutes plagiarism (Dee & Jacob, 2012), or factors that lead to low performance in class (Martinez, 2014a) that will de-bias beliefs about one's own abilities or effort level and hence induce the optimisation of behaviours; (d) activating social belonging (e.g. Walton & Cohen, 2011; Walton, 2014; Yeager et al., 2016) or social identity (e.g. Chande et al., 2015), and affirming personal values (e.g. Kost-Smith et al., 2012; Miyake et al., 2010) to boost students' self-confidence and benefit their self-image, eventually improving their academic outcomes; (e) boosting life skills such as goal setting, planning and time management (e.g. Bettinger & Baker, 2014; De Paola & Scoppa, 2015; Morisano et al., 2010; Schippers et al., 2015; Yeomans & Reich, 2017); and (f) leveraging social comparisons where providing students with information about their relative ranking in class motivates them towards behaviours that lead to improved academic performance (e.g. Czibor et al., 2020; Martinez, 2014b; Tran & Zeckhauser, 2012).

Given the numerous and varied nudges that can be applied in the educational domains, there have been some attempts to review and categorise these nudges in a systematic way that allows practitioners to implement them easily (e.g. Damgaard & Nielsen, 2018; Hume et al., 2018; Weijers et al., 2020). One of the first attempts to provide some structure and guidance on educational nudges came from the Behavioural Research Centre for Adults Skills and Knowledge (ASK), a sub-unit of the BIT created in 2014 through funding from the Department for Business, Innovation and Skills in the UK. Based on the broader academic literature and findings from field experiments that they have conducted, ASK proposed four guiding principles for educational policymakers and practitioners to implement and improve student retention and success rates among adult learners. The four guiding principles are (a) remind and encourage through timely text messaging to support the development of good attendance and study habits; (b) promote social support networks that provide the continuous encouragement needed for adult learners to persevere in their studies; (c) create a sense of belonging in the classroom that helps adult learners overcome their discomfort and anxiety about the learning environment; and (d) develop essential life skills to complement academic learning (Hume et al., 2018).

Although these guiding principles are quite easy to remember and understand, they are proposed in the context of using BI to support adult learners with low numeracy and literacy levels who are pursuing further education in mathematics and English adult courses. Hence, the generalisability of these four guiding principles to the wider higher education domain might be limited. However, it is noted that these proposed guiding principles are consistent with nudges identified to be effective in other reviews (Damgaard & Nielsen, 2018; Weijers et al., 2020), and nudging interventions designed based on these principles have been shown to improve academic outcomes of students in BI projects in TP, such as using the reminder and encourage principle to improve online lecture viewing rates (Tan et al., 2020) and quiz completion and passing rates (Chua et al., 2021), and using the create a sense of belonging in the classroom principle to improve new students' transition into a new learning environment (Tan et al., 2022).

Damgaard and Nielsen (2018) reviewed nudges employed in education and proposed that they can be classified along two dimensions: (a) whether nudges are likely to induce active or passive decision-making, and (b) whether nudges involve changes or additions to the choice architecture. Weijers et al. (2020) also proposed the categorisation of education nudges along two dimensions. However, their proposed dimensions differ from Damgaard and Nielsen (2018). First, they proposed Type 1 and Type 2 nudges aligned to Kahneman's distinction between System 1 and System 2, in that Type 1 nudges aim to influence automatic behaviours without triggering reflective thinking, while Type 2 nudges aim to influence the automatic system to trigger reflective thinking that subsequently shapes behaviours. Second, they distinguished whether a nudge is transparent or non-transparent, where a transparent nudge is defined as one in which the person being nudged is cognisant of the intention and understands the mechanisms of the nudge (Hansen & Jespersen, 2013).

Although Damgaard and Nielsen (2018) and Weijers et al. (2020) proposed two different theoretical frameworks of nudges, they are consistent in stating that successful implementation of nudges requires an understanding of their underlying behavioural mechanisms, which will allow one to decide the most appropriate nudge(s) to implement given the decision environment, and the educational context and goals. For example, Weijers et al. (2020) introduced a decision matrix that guides practitioners to decide what type of nudges to implement in the situation at hand. Damgaard and Nielsen (2018) also identified several trends in their review that suggested that boundary conditions exist for different types of nudges.

It is beyond the scope of the current chapter to critique or explore the taxonomy of educational nudges in depth, as the focus is on how practitioners can leverage AI to improve BI implementation within the education domain. Hence, in the following section, the discussions will revolve around how AI can enhance the implementation of different types of nudges in the education environment based on the different stages of a typical BI initiative.

7.3 Using AI to Enhance BI Implementation in Education

In the current section, how AI can be used to enhance the BI implementation in the education environment is discussed. This refers to using AI to improve the efficiency or effectiveness of BI implementation, or to enable the BI solutions to be designed or implemented in a manner that was not possible with conventional methods.

Currently, there is no standard definition of AI (Ofosu-Ampong, 2024; Sheikh et al., 2023). Some scholars distinguish between strong and weak AI (Rashid & Kausik, 2024; Wells, 2023), where strong AI (also known as artificial general intelligence) possesses broad capabilities that allow it to reason, learn, respond emotionally, and act autonomously like a human, while weak AI (also known as narrow AI) does not possess the full spectrum of human cognitive capabilities but can use algorithms to solve problems or reason for specific tasks. Some scholars also distinguished between technologies that form the building blocks of AI (e.g. machine learning, big data, cloud computing, algorithms, and virtualisation) and AI (Ahmed et al., 2022; Ofosu-Ampong, 2024; Rashid & Kausik, 2024), which has the ability to learn, adapt, reason, and make decisions that might be lacking in the individual building blocks.

For the discussion on how AI can enhance BI implementation in education, this chapter will neither make the distinction between strong and weak AI, nor strictly require these AI technologies to possess the ability to learn, adapt, reason, and make decisions on their own. However, this does not mean that individual technological building blocks of AI are identified as AI.

For example, it will be unreasonable to equate big data with AI, even though building an AI agent does require big data. For the purpose of the discussion, this chapter adopts a functional perspective of AI, where the focus will be on how AI or a combination of technologies that are the building blocks of AI are able to enhance BI practitioners' work by generating novel or additional insights from both qualitative and quantitative data, and enabling BI practitioners to design, develop, or implement novel types of nudges that are not possible with conventional methods.

7.3.1 Using AI to Identify Contextual Factors Needed for Designing Effective Nudges

It was previously mentioned that the design and development of effective nudges require identifying the contextual factors that influence the target behaviours, which require conducting exploratory research, thematic analysis of the qualitative data collected, and mapping the themes to behavioural change models. However, this is a time-consuming process and requires domain expertise in behavioural sciences, which most educators do not possess. AI's ability to easily process large amounts of data, to identify patterns within datasets, and its capability in natural language processing (NLP) (Rashid & Kausik, 2024) make it a good candidate to ease the time-consuming work of identifying the required contextual factors to design a good nudge, which will in turn reduce the barriers for educators who are keen to introduce educational nudges to improve academic outcomes.

AI can reduce the manpower resource and expertise requirements for conducting semi-structured interviews, a common method used by BI practitioners at the initial stage. Based on TP's experiences in running BI initiatives, each project could require interviewing approximately 20–30 stakeholders, with each interview taking around one hour to complete and requiring interviewers with some level of expertise so that in-depth and rich responses can be elicited from the interviewee. While still nascent in their development, there are reported studies on using AI assistants that build on OpenAI's GPT-4 model to conduct semi-structured interviews (Chan et al., 2024a; Chopra & Haaland, 2023). Preliminary findings suggest that the richness of responses collected using AI assistants compares well with that obtained from conventional interviews, and most interviewees do not view AI-assisted interviews as unfavourable compared to human-led interviews (Chopra & Haaland, 2023).

AI can also reduce the manpower resource and expertise requirements for the thematic analysis of qualitative data collected from the exploratory studies, through using AI to transcribe interview audio recordings (e.g. Battaglia, 2024; Eftekhari, 2024) or observation video recordings (e.g. Rao, 2023; Singh et al., 2025), and using AI to perform thematic analysis (e.g. Christou, 2024; Morgan, 2023; Zhang et al., 2025), which cuts down on the intensive manpower resources required to perform coding, theme development, and conceptualisation for conventional thematic analysis (Naeem et al., 2023). While AI may not fully replace thematic analysis of qualitative data (Lee et al., 2024), it does serve as a useful resource that helps reduce the barriers for educators hoping to make sense of qualitative data.

Lastly, AI can also be used to map the derived themes onto behavioural change models (e.g. COM-B) to help educators identify the contextual factors that influence the target behaviours. The authors could not find any reported studies on AI being used for this mapping exercise, and HSS has explored using ChatGPT–4.0 to perform this mapping in our work. Based on our experience, we found that while the mapping done by AI assistants is not always entirely consistent with human expertise judgement (i.e. seasoned BI practitioners), the discrepancy is usually quite low, and in some cases the AI assistants were spot-on in this mapping and could identify the contextual factors influencing target behaviours quite correctly. Hence, we do think that AI can be used by educators to help them with this mapping process.

7.3.2 Enabling the Design, Development, and Implementation of Digital Nudges

In the previous section, the nudges that are commonly employed in the education domain are identified. In the current section, how AI can be used to improve these educational nudges is discussed, where there will be varying degrees of current application and suitability in terms of enhancement through AI. For example, using AI to enhance timely reminders to students is highly suitable due to AI's ability for personalised intervention and real-time adaptation (Rashid & Kausik, 2024) and is currently widely practised and reported among BI practitioners. However, using AI as a means for the social aspects of nudging (e.g. providing social support, creating a sense of belonging, activating social identity, affirming values, social comparisons) is not as widely practised or reported among BI practitioners, and even though it might be technically feasible, there could be underlying ethical concerns with its potential usage.

7.3.2.1 Digital Nudging Messages

E-learning has changed the conventional way of teaching that traditionally focuses on the agency of the teachers to that of being more learner-centred, where students engage in active and self-directed learning. The proliferation of educational technologies, particularly web-based learning management systems (LMSs; e.g. Brightspace, Blackboard, and Canvas), have been widely used as a platform for students to actively learn and engage with their studies (Motz et al., 2021). Students need to be self-directed within online learning environments, and one way is through customisation of their learning experience (Fussell et al., 2022). The core features of e-learning systems are personalisation and interactivity (Duo & Ying, 2012). This notion of personalised learning environments (PLEs) has been used increasingly and prominently since the advent of computer use in education and educational technologies (Hoppe et al., 2024). In PLEs and systems, this is achieved through features that include personalised user interfaces (e.g. personalised information for teachers and students), learning resources and activities (i.e. learning content and tools can be adaptive and individualised), guidance (i.e. individual feedback and recommendations), and communication (e.g. affective and motivational reminders or nudges). They generally rely on the use of data mining and learning analytics as a basis for personalised and adaptive learning support (Hoppe et al., 2024).

The technological features of PLEs and e-learning systems provide immense potential for conventional behavioural nudges to be mapped to the affordances of these technologies. This idea has been widely adopted in Human–Computer Interaction (HCI) (e.g. Caraban et al., 2019) and has given rise to the term "digital nudging" (Weinmann et al., 2016). "Digital nudges" refer to the use of nudges in the digital realm (Gatare et al., 2021). Compared to conventional nudges (e.g. timely reminders), digital nudging is unique in that it leverages on both insights from behavioural science and emerging digital technologies (Sobolev, 2021). Applying the concept of choice architecture, digital nudges augment conventional behavioural nudges (e.g. reminders and feedback) by designing and implementing them in novel technologies such as mobile apps and wearable devices. Applications of digital nudges are built on the advancements in the fields of HCI and AI and are powered by computing and data. This facilitates scalability, personalisation, and optimisation as "choice architects" can design the right nudges that are timely (at the right time) and for the right person by learning to adapt to the individual's context and preferences.

Sobolev (2021) proposed three principles in the design of digital nudging solutions: Technology, Data, and Experimentation. With Technology, the advances of information technologies should be chosen and leveraged on based on the proximity of the technology to the targeted behaviour and its unique features (e.g. smartphones and mobile apps, wearables, and tracking of online behaviours). Data is also needed to track behaviours and other variables to optimise nudges (e.g. timely reminders, adaptive feedback, and planning prompts). Lastly, digital nudges should leverage on digital experimentation to optimise and redesign nudges (e.g. evaluation of different nudges, personalisation and adaptation of nudges, and continuous evaluation of effects of nudges).

In a review of digital nudging within the HCI literature, Caraban and colleagues (2019) identified six broad categories of digital nudges. The categories are Facilitate, Confront, Deceive, Social Influence, Fear, and Reinforce-type nudges (see Caraban et al., 2019 for full descriptions of these categories). Facilitate nudges enable decision-making by reducing mental or physical effort, encouraging people to take actions aligned with their best interests. Confront nudges create doubt to interrupt unwanted behaviour, leveraging regret aversion to prompt reflective choices. Deceive nudges use deception to influence perceptions and outcomes. Social influence nudges exploit the desire to conform, while fear nudges evoke anxiety and uncertainty to drive action. Reinforce nudges increase awareness to strengthen behaviours.

Some of these types of "digital nudges" have been applied within the higher educational context, where positive effects have been observed. Gatare et al. (2021) leveraged on university students' mobile applications or wearable devices to receive personalised behavioural nudges from a persona (i.e. character with a name) that offers support to individual students' self-directed learning activities. The persona was developed to be similar to students, and students were given a backstory to this persona. Based on individual students' online learning behaviours in the LMS (course participation and assignment submission), the persona would send personalised nudges (e.g. facilitate nudge, social nudge, and confront nudge) to individual students across 15 weeks. In this study, they found that students who reported digital nudges to be useful were more receptive to being nudged more frequently. Students also reported that social nudges (e.g. other peers have submitted assignments) and reminder nudges, which helped them plan how to complete their assignments (e.g. helping to set up daily reminders), were the most useful types of nudges. On the other hand, reward nudges were found to be the least useful (e.g. setting a reward for themselves).

In another study, Motz and colleagues (2021) developed a smartphone app that was integrated with their institution's LMS (Canvas). Leveraging on the benefits of proactive educative nudges, university undergraduate students received automated push notifications through the app to remind them of assignment submissions. They found that, as compared to periodic instructor-sent announcement reminders, automated reminders through students' smartphones were more effective in getting students to submit their assignments (i.e. a significant improvement in assignment submission).

In both Gatare et al. (2021) and Motz et al. (2021), their digital nudges were designed by integrating and leveraging on their institution's LMS systems. Other studies have created novel platforms with specially designed systems for their digital nudges. Rodríguez and colleagues (2022) developed an adaptive intelligent system (called the LIS system) built on predictive analytics, a progression dashboard, automated nudges, and recommendations based on AI classification algorithms. The aim of the system was to detect at-risk learners early, improve students' performance and student satisfaction, and reduce drop-out rates. In this study, they found that this system positively impacted students' performance and satisfaction, and reduced dropout rates for online and distance learning environments. Wambsganss and colleagues (2022) also designed an adaptive learning dashboard, based on advances in computational linguistics (i.e. machine learning and natural language processing), to enable students to self-evaluate their writing skills (in argumentation) independently based on digital nudges. In their study, they found that this nudging-based learning application to promote self-regulated learning, combined with computational methods, helped to foster better argumentative writing skills in students.

While promising, these studies have relied on advanced and expensive tools or systems that require extensive technological development, which increases the barriers to entry for educators and students. Fussell et al. (2022) argued that educators should leverage on easy-to-use, accessible, and equitable technologies (e.g. LMSs). A tool that has been recently made available to the LMS platform, the Intelligent Agent (IA) function, allows the educator to personalise communication to students based on a variety of pre-set release conditions (e.g. missed assignment, low score for assignment, did not access learning resources). The IA can be used by educators to remind, encourage, and motivate students to increase student engagement and self-directed learning. The potential of the IA and customisable tools in LMSs, and other accessible programmes, can be further enhanced by infusing BI principles within its communication and feedback to students. Other easily accessible and available programmes, such as Power Automate, which allow for personalised communication, can also be harnessed.

Highlighted earlier in Chapter 2, a subject team in TP implemented personalised digital nudges, using the IA in LMS (Brightspace), Power Automate, and Microsoft Workflow, to increase students' self-directed online learning behaviours (Lee et al., 2023). Based on students' learning analytics on Brightspace (e.g. did not access e-learning materials and did not complete assignments), the team designed the IA to send out timely and personalised nudges with various message frames infused with BI principles, to remind and encourage students to access and watch their e-lectures on Brightspace. Further, the team optimised the implementation of these nudges, introducing Power Automate and Microsoft Workflow to direct messages from the tutor's email to Microsoft Teams, by letting a bot handle the sending out of messages. Altogether, they found that the implementation of these nudges was effective in increasing students' viewership of the subject's e-lectures (i.e. higher video view counts). Student surveys and focus group discussions also revealed that students welcomed the use of personalised and encouraging nudges. The subject team (i.e. tutors) also benefitted through improved work efficiency by reducing the time and resources needed to communicate and follow up with their students. This case example showcases the efficacy of personalised BI nudges that leverage on the use of easily accessible, low-cost, and equitable technologies to improve students' self-directed e-learning behaviours. Altogether, these studies showcase the potentialities of AI to enhance conventional BI approaches through a new approach of "digital nudging".

7.3.2.2 Using AI to Foster Social Connections

Educational nudges have often leveraged on the social relationships or contexts to influence students' behaviours towards better academic outcomes, such as nudging nominated "study supporters" to provide students with timely encouragement (Groot et al., 2017), fostering social commitments within classmates through a "buddy incentive" system (Hume et al., 2018), using social comparisons as a form of motivation (Tran & Zeckhauser, 2012), or creating a sense of belonging to the wider school community by framing social adversity as common and transient (Walton & Cohen, 2011). Within the implementation of the nudges, these social interactions could be real (e.g. Groot et al., 2017; Hume et al., 2018) or perceived (e.g. Walton & Cohen, 2011; Tran & Zeckhauser, 2012). Nonetheless, humans remain the object of interaction for the individual being nudged, regardless of whether this interaction is real or perceived.

It might seem like AI might have little to offer to nudges that leverages on social relationships or contexts. Indeed, compared to digital nudges, there seems to be lesser published studies on using AI to enhance the nudges that leverage social relationships or contexts. However, given AI's capability in NLP (Rashid & Kausik, 2024), we think that it can be deployed to enhance educational nudges that leverages on social relationships.

Nudges that leverage on social relationships or contexts are effective because humans are fundamentally social beings with a need to belong to a social group and forge meaningful relationships and connections with other humans (Baumeister & Leary, 1995). Due to this social instinct, humans might over-interpret their interactions with AI and form social and emotional bonds with AI agents (Sætra, 2020). Indeed, there are studies demonstrating that human form emotional and social bonds with AI agents (e.g. Guerreiro & Loureiro, 2023; Lee et al., 2021; Pentina et al., 2023). Chou et al. (2025) proposed that the human-AI relationship exists on a spectrum in terms of how humans view AI agents, from viewing AI as a tool to an assistant to a companion. The complexity of interaction and the level of emotional and social engagement with the AI agent increase as the human–AI relationship shifts from tool to assistant to companion. According to Chou et al. (2025), the main criterion that separates an AI companion from an AI tool or AI assistant is that the interaction between the AI and the human user involves mixed initiative, in that interaction or activities can be initiated by both AI and human, and not just by the human alone.

In recent years, AI agents (i.e. chatbots) have been used frequently in the education domain as intelligent tutoring systems (e.g. Labadze et al., 2023; Lin et al., 2023; Wang et al., 2024). As detailed in Chapter 3, compared to conventional methods of receiving consultations from their tutors, AI agents offer a relatively low-cost, highly accessible, and easily scalable resource for students in higher education to consult about their learning and studies by providing them with individualised guidance and feedback (Lin et al., 2023). Chatbots have also been used for nudging behaviours in domains such as finance (Ramjattan et al., 2021), health (Aggarwal et al., 2023), or education (Tian et al., 2021). However, we find that for most of these applications of chatbots to nudge behaviours or to help students improve, most of these chatbots focus mainly on providing information or guidance on behaviours specific to the domain, and not on establishing a social and emotional bond with the human user (but see Aggarwal et al.'s (2023) review of four studies that provided emotional support for the user). In other words, these chatbots are more "AI tool" or "AI assistant" rather than "AI companion".

This might be a missed opportunity for educators who employ AI agents such as chatbots to facilitate students' learning, as these chatbots could have been more effective in nudging students towards desired educational behaviours had they been perceived as "AI companions" by the students. For example, the chatbot is not just a tool or assistant that students turn to for information or guidance in learning but a companion that shares a common social identity, or a companion that may provide timely encouragement and motivation when it senses that the student is feeling down, or provide guidance on goal-setting or time-management when it senses that the student is procrastinating on their studies, or provide timely and personalised assurance to students during transitional periods in their education journey (e.g. initial transition to university education). An AI agent that is perceived as a companion is more likely to be trusted by students (Chou et al., 2025), and any advice or instructions provided by it will likely see a higher compliance rate.

Of course, there might be good reasons why the use of AI companions as a nudging tool within the education domain is not as widespread compared to digital nudging. Like human interactions, for an AI chatbot to initiate timely and appropriate interactions with the human, it must have sufficient contextual information about the student who perceives it as a companion. For example, the AI would need to know a student is feeling anxious or frustrated lately before proactively initiating messages of encouragement or motivation. Or the AI would need to know the assessment deadlines so that it can offer help to the student proactively. Hence, would students be comfortable enough for the AI to be given access to their data so that it can perform as such? Or would students, or even educators, be prepared that some students might form an unhealthy social relationship with the chatbot? Bhat et al. (2025) identified privacy concerns and forming an unhealthy emotional dependent relationship with an AI agent as potential risk for the students in developing social interaction and coping skills with other humans. This topic shall be revisited in a later section of this chapter.

7.3.2.3 Using AI as a Tool to Develop Life Skills

Essential life skills are just as important as cognitive ability for students to develop to gear them towards successful academic and life outcomes (Hume et al., 2018). The development of life skills such as grit and growth mindset, emotional intelligence, empathy, metacognitive awareness, and self-regulation has been demonstrated to complement academic learning and is essential for holistic student development in the 21st century (refer to the earlier section on BI in Education for the ASK framework and its four guiding principles).

For many people, essential life skills typically develop at home through interactions with parents and family members. However, for some students, family circumstances and/or negative earlier school experiences may have limited their opportunities to develop life skills to their fullest capacity. For this reason, schools can play an instrumental role in fostering essential life skills. Behavioural research has suggested that the trajectory of development in life skills is malleable even into adulthood and can be altered by experiences and investment (e.g. Almlund et al., 2011). This suggests that improving essential life skills (e.g. grit, growth mindset) could also be an effective strategy to support academic achievement and other life outcomes in higher education (e.g. employment, health, and financial well-being) (e.g. Duckworth et al., 2012, p. 6). In Chapter 6, the role of educators and institutions in humanising learning and fostering life skills has been touched on.

Conventional behavioural interventions have shown some initial efficacy in boosting students' life skills. For example, in an intervention that targeted adult students, an online course module was designed with a set of exercises on "grit" (e.g. growth mindset and goal setting). Students who had undertaken the "grit" module were found to have an increase in their class attendance (for half a year) compared to those who did not take the module (Hume et al., 2018). However, students' class attendances were not sustained across the whole school year. The lack of sustained effects was attributed to the learning experience (e.g. content too repetitive), which influenced the extent to which students were engaged with the exercises. More recent meta-analyses and systematic reviews that have examined the efficacy of such life skills interventions have questioned the effectiveness of these interventions on students' short- and long-term outcomes (see Macnamara & Burgoyne, 2023 for a systematic review). The mixed effects observed could be due to operational challenges and constraints in the implementation of such interventions, such as the costs and resources required (e.g. manpower and expertise needed to conduct programmes), and sustainability, replicability, and scalability of these interventions and programmes. Furthermore, current life skills interventions tend to be relatively short term (e.g. across a few sessions or a few weeks). This could be insufficient for developing students' life skills, which could take time to develop.

These challenges and constraints could be addressed through AI features and tools such as digital nudges, chatbot interactions, immersive simulations, and collaborative platforms. For example, in using personalised digital nudges, AI-powered platforms such as intelligent tutoring systems (ITS) could provide individual students with differentiated content and delivery, scaffolded support, and real-time performance analytics based on their learning behaviours, pace, and performance. This approach could encourage students' development in life skills such as self-directedness, self-reflection, and resilience (Rahman et al., 2024). By engaging learners in a continuous learning loop, AI tools could enhance students' adaptability and motivation to learn independently, which cultivates a growth mindset (e.g. Su et al., 2024).

In the earlier section, chatbots are proposed to provide students with social support and companionship. In the application of chatbots to develop students' life skills, AI chatbots and conversational agents can simulate human interactions. For example, AI tutors or companions can engage students in discussions that mimic real-life scenarios, offering immediate feedback and adjusting the complexity of responses based on the student's development. Studies have shown that such tools can foster social awareness and improve communication skills, particularly among students with limited access to peer interactions (Li et al., 2024).

More recent advancements in large language models (LLM) have offered an innovative approach to developing students' non-cognitive skills (e.g. self-awareness, social awareness, and empathy) through immersive simulated learning environments. In a study by Yan and colleagues (2024), an interactive platform enabled by LLM was designed to create immersive life simulations that model real-word socially challenging scenarios involving conflict resolution, teamwork, leadership, and ethical decision-making (Yan et al., 2024). In this simulated platform, undergraduate students could take on different roles in different social situations through interactivity and role-playing. For example, students could take on the role of the protagonist who interacts and chats with other AI-generated (LLM-enabled) characters who exhibit emotional responses and have diverse perspectives. Students could make key decisions and interactions that would influence the storyline, allowing a co-creation of a personally unique narrative. The platform also offered a "Sage Agent" for students to call upon, which served as an "AI helper" to provide personalised and timely mentorship, prompting them on how to respond in the various simulated social environments. Quantitative and qualitative findings from this study suggest the potential for such social simulation platforms to enhance students' non-cognitive skills such as emotional engagement, self-perception, motivation, resilience, and coping, and self-reflection (especially with the presence of the "Sage Agent").

Altogether, AI has emerged as a possible tool, offering some innovative ways to develop critical life skills. Through personalised digital nudges, chatbot interactions, immersive simulations, and collaborative analytics, these features and tools could be embedded in students' learning throughout their entire curriculum (across various courses) to empower individual learners to engage deeply with their own personal development and enhance their engagement and learning experiences of essential life skills over time. As AI technologies continue to evolve, their role in cultivating life skills could become increasingly vital in preparing students for future challenges.

7.4 Ethical Concerns and Challenges of AI Tools

As discussed throughout the chapter, the applications of AI in education to nudge and change students' behaviours and outcomes have demonstrated immense potentialities. However, these AI technologies have also brought about ethical concerns and challenges, even though the intentions behind them may be positive (Ahmad et al., 2023). Within education, security and privacy issues are of most concern. This is especially because AI applications and systems require the collection and use of enormous amounts of personal data to make predictions and patterns (Holmes et al., 2019). Schools' access to substantial personal student information could invite security risks such as potential misuse or leaks (Gocen & Aydemir, 2020). As such, educational institutes have to continuously enhance their digital security practices to ensure data is kept secure. Particularly in the context of designing personalised digital nudges and learning environments, privacy concerns are also being raised regarding the extent of personal data (e.g. health, financial, behavioural, physiological, and emotional) that is required to be collected and processed in order for the AI systems to learn patterns and make decisions (Mhlanga, 2023). To ensure privacy, the use of students' data must be evaluated against the backdrop of human rights, laws, and social-environmental conditions. Further, there are also increasing concerns about the ethical attributes of AI and machine learning systems being biased and discriminatory if left unchecked or unregulated (Weyerer & Langer, 2019). It is crucial that policymakers and educators ensure that there are ethical approaches and guidelines in the development and deployment of these AI systems to prevent and minimise these potential threats.

Other ethical concerns are in relation to students developing social-emotional dependencies with an AI agent such as chatbots and AI companions (as discussed in Section 3.2.2). Concerns such as misperceptions, emotional dependency, and psychological impact, diminished human connectedness, and privacy issues warrant careful consideration. As AI agents are designed to mimic human-like interactions and emotions, this could result in misperceptions, with users forming attachments based on the false belief that the AI agent possesses genuine understanding and empathy (Ahmad et al., 2023). This could be ethically problematic as it exploits human tendencies to form social connections. It is important that the developers of such systems assume responsibility to ensure that the AI agents are designed to prioritise the well-being and ethicality of the user and to prevent emotional manipulation by being transparent. This is especially important for individuals who may be socially isolated or vulnerable. This reliance could hinder personal development and reduce engagement in human relationships. It could lead to negative psychological impacts such as feelings of detachment and loneliness. As individuals form bonds with AI agents, there is a concern that these artificial relationships might replace or diminish real human relationships (e.g. Wu, 2024). This could potentially lead to a decline in human-to-human interactions and the social skills necessary to maintain them. Lastly, engaging in personal conversations with AI companions could involve disclosing personally intimate information. There is a heightened risk that this data could be misused, inadequately protected, or accessed without consent, leading to breaches of privacy. Thus, educators and institutions must carefully consider and prioritise ethical issues such as security and privacy, transparency, trust, and safety when implementing the use of AI technologies and AI agents. There must be frameworks and guidelines put in place to ensure that these systems enhance students' well-being without compromising ethical standards or personal integrity.

7.5 Conclusion

In conclusion, the integration of behavioural insights (BI) with artificial intelligence (AI) presents a transformative frontier to enhance educational practices by addressing both cognitive and non-cognitive determinants of student success. By leveraging on BI frameworks and principles, educators can design digital nudges to complement traditional pedagogy. AI's capabilities in data analysis, personalisation, and automation further empower educators to implement these nudges efficiently and at scale by leveraging on the latest technological advancements and tools. This synergy allows for timely, adaptive, and evidence-informed behavioural interventions that promote student engagement, foster life skills, and ultimately improve academic outcomes.

However, as the role of AI in education expands, it is essential for policymakers and educators to remain vigilant about the ethical implications. Issues such as data privacy, algorithmic bias, emotional dependency, and the erosion of human relationships must be carefully considered and managed. Educational institutions and technology developers must establish clear ethical frameworks that prioritise student well-being, autonomy, and equity. With thoughtful integration and responsible design, the combination of BI and AI holds significant promise in creating more inclusive, effective, and supportive learning environments that prepare students not just academically but holistically for the complexities of the future.

References

Aggarwal, A., Tam, C. C., Wu, D., Li, X., & Qiao, S. (2023). Artificial intelligence-based chatbots for promoting health behavioural changes: Systematic review. *Journal of Medical Internet Research*, 25, e40789. https://doi.org/10.2196/40789

Ahmad, K., Iqbal, W., El-Hassan, A., Qadir, J., Benhaddou, D., Ayyash, M., & Al-Fuqaha, A. (2023). Data-driven artificial intelligence in education: A comprehensive review. *IEEE Transactions on Learning Technologies*, 17, 12–31.

Ahmed, I., Jeon, G., & Piccialli, F. (2022). From artificial intelligence to explainable artificial intelligence in Industry 4.0: A survey on what, how, and where. *IEEE Transactions on Industrial Informatics*, 18(8), 5031–5042.

Almlund, M., Duckworth, A. L., Heckman, J., & Kautz, T. (2011). Personality psychology and economics. In *Handbook of the economics of education* (Vol. 4, pp. 1–181). Elsevier.

Alyahyan, E., & Düştegör, D. (2020). Predicting academic success in higher education: Literature review and best practices. *International Journal of Educational Technology in Higher Education*, 17(1), 3.

Amerstorfer, C. M., & Freiin von Münster-Kistner, C. (2021). Student perceptions of academic engagement and student-teacher relationships in problem-based learning. *Frontiers in Psychology*, 12, 713057. https://doi.org/10.3389/fpsyg.2021.713057

Amiri, B., Jafarian, A., & Abdi, Z. (2024). Nudging towards sustainability: A comprehensive review of behavioural approaches to eco-friendly choice. *Discover Sustainability*, 5, 444.

Apostolova-Mihaylova, M., Cooper, W., Hoyt, G., & Marshall, E. C. (2015). Heterogeneous gender effects under loss aversion in the economics classroom: A field experiment. *Southern Economic Journal*, 81(4), 980–994.

Ball, S., & Head, B. W. (2021). Behavioural insights teams in practice: Nudge missions and methods on trial. *Policy & Politics*, 49(1), 105–120.

Bandiera, O., Larcinese, V., & Rasul, I. (2015). Blissful ignorance? A natural experiment on the effect of feedback on students' performance. *Labour Economics*, 34, 13–25.

Battaglia, F. (2024). From 'listen and repeat' to 'listen and revise': How to transcribe interviews offline quickly and for free using voice recognition software. *International Journal of Qualitative Methods*, 23. https://doi.org/10.1177/16094069241247473

Baumeister, R. F., & Leary, M. R. (1995). The need to belong: Desire for interpersonal attachments as a fundamental human motivation. *Psychological Bulletin*, 117(3), 497–529. https://doi.org/10.1037/0033-2909.117.3.497

Bettinger, E. P., & Baker, R. B. (2014). The effects of student coaching: An evaluation of a randomized experiment in student advising. *Educational Evaluation and Policy Analysis*, 36(1), 3–19.

Bhat, R., Kowshik, S., Suresh, S., Alamelu, G., Gite, S., & Albattat, A. (2025). Digital companionship or psychological risk? The role of AI characters in shaping youth mental health. *Asian Journal of Psychiatry*, 104, 104356. https://doi.org/10.1016/j.ajp.2024.104356

BIT UK. (2022). *Target, explore, solution, trial, scale: An introduction to running simple behavioural insights projects*. London: Behavioural Insights Team Ltd.

BIT UK. (2024). *EAST framework: Four simple ways to apply behavioural insights*. London: Behavioural Insights Team Ltd.

Caraban, A., Karapanos, E., Gonçalves, D., & Campos, P. (2019, May). 23 ways to nudge: A review of technology-mediated nudging in human-computer interaction. In *Proceedings of the 2019 CHI Conference on Human Factors in Computing Systems* (pp. 1–15).

Carini, R. M., Kuh, G. D., & Klein, S. P. (2006). Student engagement and student learning: Testing the linkages. *Research in Higher Education*, 47, 1–32. https://doi.org/10.1007/s11162-005-8150-9

Castleman, B. L., & Meyer, K. (2016). *Can text message nudges improve academic outcomes in college? Evidence from a West Virginia initiative*. EdPolicyWorks Working Paper Series No. 43.

Castleman, B. L., & Page, L. C. (2016). Freshman year financial aid nudges: An experiment to increase FAFSA renewal and college persistence. *Journal Human Resources*, 51(2), 389–415.

Chan, C., Zhao, Y., & Zhao, J. (2024a). A case study on assessing AI assistant competence in narrative interviews. *F1000Research*, 13, 601.

Chan, S. W., Lu, S., Cheng, N. H. C., Chui, C. H.-K., & Yat-Sang Lum, T. (2024b). Promoting charitable donations and volunteering through nudge tools from the perspective of behavioural economics: A systematic review. *Nonprofit and Voluntary Sector Quarterly*, 54(2), 435–461. https://doi.org/10.1177/08997640241258140 (Original work published 2025).

Chande, R., Luca, M., Sanders, M., Soon, X., Borcan, O., Barak-Corren, N., Linos, E., Kirkman, E., & Robinson, S. (2015). *Curbing adult student attrition: Evidence from a field experiment*. Harvard Business School Working Paper 15-065.

Chopra, F., & Haaland, I. (2023). *Conducting qualitative interviews with AI*. CESifo Working Paper No. 10666.

Chou, C. Y., Chan, T. W., Chen, Z. H., Liao, C. Y., Shih, J. L., Wu, Y. T., Chang, B., Yeh, C. Y. C., Hung, H. C., & Cheng, H. (2025). Defining AI companions: A research agenda—from artificial companions for learning to general artificial companions for Global Harwell. *Research and Practice in Technology Enhanced Learning*, 20, 32. https://doi.org/10.58459/rptel.2025.20032

Christou, P. A. (2024). Thematic analysis through artificial intelligence (AI). *The Qualitative Report*, 29(2), 560–576. https://doi.org/10.46743/2160-3715/2024.7046

Chua, P. T., Lim, K., Tan, C., Tan, W. P., Tan, E., & Wee, L. (2021). *Improving CICT quiz completion and passing rates with timely messaging nudges*. Internal Temasek Polytechnic Report: Unpublished.

Czibor, E., Onderstal, S., Sloof, R., & van Praag, C. M. (2020). Does relative grading help male students? Evidence from a field experiment in the classroom. *Economics of Education Review*, 75(1), 101953. https://doi.org/10.1016/j.econedurev.2019.101953

Damgaard, M. T., & Nielsen, H. S. (2018). Nudging in education. *Economics of Education Review*, 64, 313–342.

De Paola, M., & Scoppa, V. (2015). Procrastination, academic success and the effectiveness of a remedial program. *Journal of Economic Behavior & Organization*, 115, 217–236.

Dee, T. S., & Jacob, B. A. (2012). Rational ignorance in education: A field experiment in student plagiarism. *Journal of Human Resources*, 47(2), 397–434.

Dinkelman, T., & Martinez, C. A. (2014). Investing in schooling in Chile: The role of information about financial aid for higher education. *Review of Economics and Statistics*, 96(2), 244–257.

Dolan, P., Hallsworth, M., Halpern, D., King, D., & Vlaev, I. (2010). *MINDSPACE: Influencing Behaviour for Public Policy*. Institute of Government, London, UK.

Duckworth, A. L., Weir, D., Tsukayama, E., & Kwok, D. (2012). Who does well in life? Conscientious adults excel in both objective and subjective success. *Frontiers in Psychology*, 3.

Duo, S., & Ying, Z. C. (2012). Personalized e-learning system based on intelligent agent. *Physics Procedia*, 24, 1899–1902.

Dweck, C. S. (2006). *Mindset: The new psychology of success* (1st ed.). New York: Random House.

Eftekhari, H. (2024, July). Transcribing in the digital age: Qualitative research practice utilizing intelligent speech recognition technology. *European Journal of Cardiovascular Nursing*, 23(5), 553–560. https://doi.org/10.1093/eurjcn/zvae013

Evans, J. S. B. (2008). Dual-processing accounts of reasoning, judgment, and social cognition. *Annual Review of Psychology*, 59(1), 255–278.

Evans, J. S. B., & Stanovich, K. E. (2013). Dual-process theories of higher cognition: Advancing the debate. *Perspectives on Psychological Science*, 8(3), 223–241.

Field, E. (2009). Educational debt burden and career choice: Evidence from a financial aid experiment at NYU law school. *American Economic Journal: Applied Economics*, 1(1), 1–21.

Freeman, S., Eddy, S. L., McDonough, M., Smith, M. K., Okoroafor, N., Jordt, H., & Wenderoth, M. P. (2014). Active learning increases student performance in science, engineering, and mathematics. *Proceedings of the National Academy of Sciences*, 111(23), 8410–8415.

Fussell, G., Bianco, M., Sharma, R., Kelly, T. M., Vice, J., & Bencomo-Walls, A. (2022). Using cheap and easy-to-use technology to maximize learning and teaching in online education. *EdMedia + Innovate Learning Online*, 2022, 108–111.

Gabhane, D., Sharma, A., & Mukherjee, R. (2023). Behavioral finance: Exploring the influence of cognitive biases on investment decisions. *Boletin de Literatura Oral-The Literary Journal*, 10(1), 3133–3141.

Gatare, K., Prasad, P., Kothiyal, A., Sarkar, P., Raina, A., & Majumdar, R. (2021). Designing nudges for self-directed learning in a data-rich environment. *29th ICCE 2021*, 2, 553–562.

Gocen, A., & Aydemir, F. (2020). Artificial intelligence in education and schools. *Research on Education and Media*, 12(1), 13–21.

Grayot, J. (2019). From selves to systems: On the intrapersonal and intraneural dynamics of decision making. *Journal of Economic Methodology*, 26(3), 208–227.

Groot, B., Sanders, M., Armitage, L., Carvalho, P., Close, S., DeSouza, D. C., Frost, E., Smith, B., Julings, N., Kaul, R., Knowles, S. E., Lindley, S. H., Masters, B. K., Parry, T., & Proudman, M. (2017). *I get by with a little help from my friends: Two field experiments on social support and attendance in further education colleges in the UK1*. The Behavioral Insights Team.

Guerreiro, J., & Loureiro, S. M. C. (2023). I am attracted to my cool smart assistant! Analyzing attachment-aversion in AI-human relationships. *Journal of Business Research*, 161, 113863.

Hansen, P. G., & Jespersen, A. M. (2013). Nudge and the manipulation of choice: A framework for the responsible use of the nudge approach to behaviour change in public policy. *European Journal of Risk Regulation*, 4(1), 3–28.

Holmes, W., Bialik, M., & Fadel, C. (2019). *Artificial intelligence in education promises and implications for teaching and learning*. Center for Curriculum Redesign.

Hoppe, H. U., Majumdar, R., & Ogata, H. (2024). Personalized Learning Environments – Core concepts, technologies and practices. *Information and Technology in Education and Learning*, 4(1), Inv-p002.

Hoxby, C., & Turner, S. (2015). What high-achieving low-income students know about college. *American Economic Review: Papers & Proceedings*, 105(5), 514–517.

Hume, S., O'Reilly, F., Groot, B., Kozman, E., Barnes, J., Soon, X. Z., Chande, R., & Sanders, M. (2018). Retention and success in Maths and English: A practitioner guide to applying behavioural insights. *The Behavioural Insights Team*. United

Kingdom. https://www.bi.team/wp-content/uploads/2018/02/ASK-guide-June-2018.pdf

Juras, R., Gorman, A., & Klerman, J. A. (2023). Using behavioral insights to market a workplace safety program: Evidence from a multi-armed experiment. *Evaluation Review*, 47(1), 123–151.

Kahneman, D. (2011). *Fast and slow thinking*. New York: Allen Lane and Penguin Books.

Kost-Smith, L. E., Pollock, S. J., Finkelstein, N. D., Cohen, G. L., Ito, T. A., & Miyake, A. (2012). Replicating a self-affirmation intervention to address gender differences: Successes and challenges. *AIP Conference Proceedings*, 1413(1), 231–234.

Labadze, L., Grigolia, M., & Machaidze, L. (2023). Role of AI chatbots in education: Systematic literature review. *International Journal of Educational Technology in Higher Education*, 20(1), 56.

Lee, K. G., Guo, R., Cheung, P., Lau, P. N., Wong, P., Boey, C. K., & Loh, G. H. (2023). A proof-of-concept study on the efficacy of agent-enabled nudge messages on learners' online learning behaviours. In *Conference Presentation at eLearning Forum 2023*.

Lee, S. K., Kavya, P., & Lasser, S. C. (2021). Social interactions and relationships with an intelligence virtual agent. *International Journal of Human-Computer Studies*, 150, 102608.

Lee, V. V., van der Lubbe, S. C. C., Goh, L. H., & Valderas, J. M. (2024). Harnessing ChatGPT for thematic analysis: Are we ready? *Journal of Medical Internet Research*, 26, e54974. https://doi.org/10.2196/54974

Li, L., Huang, W., & Liu, B. (2024). A research-oriented model for artificial intelligence education: Integrating multidisciplinary approaches to foster innovation and holistic learning. In *Proceedings of the 2024 7th International Conference on Educational Technology Management* (pp. 480–485).

Lin, C. C., Huang, A., & Lu, O. (2023). Artificial intelligence in intelligent tutoring systems toward sustainable education: A systematic review. *Smart Learning Environments*, 10. https://doi.org/10.1186/s40561-023-00260-y

Macnamara, B. N., & Burgoyne, A. P. (2023). Do growth mindset interventions impact students' academic achievement? A systematic review and meta-analysis with recommendations for best practices. *Psychological Bulletin*, 149(3–4), 133.

Martinez, I. (2014a). *Never put off ´till tomorrow?* EdPolicyWorks Working Paper.

Martinez, I. (2014b). *The effects of nudges on students' effort and performance: Lessons from a MOOC*. In EdPolicyWorks Working Paper Series Working Paper.

McEvoy, D. M. (2016). Loss aversion and student achievement. *Economics Bulletin*, 36(3), 1762–1770.

Mhlanga, D. (2023). Open AI in education, the responsible and ethical use of ChatGPT towards lifelong learning. In *FinTech and artificial intelligence for sustainable development: The role of smart technologies in achieving development goals* (pp. 387–409). Cham: Springer Nature Switzerland.

Michie, S., Atkins, L., & West, R. (2014). *The behaviour change wheel: A guide to designing interventions*. Great Britain: Silverback Publishing.

Miyake, A., Kost-Smith, L. E., Finkelstein, N. D., Pollock, S. J., Cohen, G. L., & Ito, T. A. (2010). Reducing the gender achievement gap in college science: A classroom study of values affirmation. *Science*, 330(6008), 1234–1237.

Morgan, D. L. (2023). Exploring the use of artificial intelligence for qualitative data analysis: The case of ChatGPT. *International Journal of Qualitative Methods*, 22(6), 1–10.

Morisano, D., Hirsh, J. B., Peterson, J. B., Pihl, R. O., & Shore, B. M. (2010). Setting, elaborating, and reflecting on personal goals improves academic performance. *Journal of Applied Psychology*, 93(2), 255–264.

Motz, B. A., Mallon, M. G., & Quick, J. D. (2021). Automated educative nudges to reduce missed assignments in college. *IEEE Transactions on Learning Technologies*, 14(2), 189–200.

Mullainathan, S., & Shafir, E. (2013). *Scarcity: Why having too little means so much*. New York, NY: Time Books, Henry Holt & Company LLC.

Naeem, M., Ozuem, W., Howell, K., & Ranfagni, S. (2023). A step-by-step process of thematic analysis to develop a conceptual model in qualitative research. *International Journal of Qualitative Methods*, 22. https://doi.org/10.1177/16094069231205789

Ofosu-Ampong, K. (2024). Artificial intelligence research: A review on dominant themes, methods, frameworks and future research directions. *Telematics and Informatics Reports*, 14, 100127.

Öz, Y., & Boyacı, A. (2021). The role of student engagement in student outcomes in higher education: Implications from a developing country. *International Journal of Educational Research*, 110, 101880.

Pentina, I., Hancock, T., & Xie, T. L. (2023). Exploring relationship development with social chatbots: A mixed-method study of Replika. *Computers in Human Behavior*, 140, 107600.

Perry, C., Chhatralia, K., Damesick, D., Hobden, S., & Volpe, L. (2015). *Behavioural insights in health care* (pp. 18–29). London: The Health Foundation.

Peterson, J. (2023). *The science of context: Understanding the real role of applied behavioural scientists*. https://medium.com/behavior-design-hub/the-science-of-context-e6cc50252709

Rahman, M., Jahan, M., & Uddin, M. (2024). The integration of AI into learning management systems. *Expert Systems with Applications*. https://www.sciencedirect.com/science/article/pii/S0957417424010339

Ramjattan, R., Hosein, P., & Henry, N. (2021). Using chatbot technologies to help individuals make sound personalized financial decisions. In *IEEE International Humanitarian Technology Conference (IHTC)* (pp. 1–4). United Kingdom. https://doi.org/10.1109/IHTC53077.2021.9698928

Rao, A. (2023). Transcribing educational videos using whisper: A preliminary study on using AI for transcribing educational videos. In *Poster Session Presented at Conference on Deployable AI*. https://openreview.net/forum?id=VJvluDhBfOS

Rashid, A. B., & Kausik, M. A. K. (2024). AI revolutionizing industry worldwide: A comprehensive overview of its diverse applications. *Hybrid Advances*, 7, 100277.

Reeve, J., & Jang, H. (2006). What teachers say and do to support students' autonomy during a learning activity. *Journal of Educational Psychology*, 98(1), 209–218. https://doi.org/10.1037/0022-0663.98.1.209

Ridder, D. D., Feitsma, J., Van Den Hoven, M., Kroese, F., Schillemans, T., Verweij, M., Venema, T., Vugts, A., & De Vet, E. (2024). Simple nudges that are not so easy. *Behavioural Public Policy*, 8(1), 154–172.

Rodríguez, M. E., Guerrero-Roldán, A. E., Baneres, D., & Karadeniz, A. (2022). An intelligent nudging system to guide online students. *International Review of Research in Open and Distributed Learning*, 23(1), 41–62.

Sætra, H. S. (2020). The parasitic nature of social AI: Sharing minds with the mindless. *Integrative Psychological and Behavioural Science*, 54, 308–326.

Schippers, M. C., Scheepers, A. W. A., & Peterson, J. B. (2015). A scalable goal-setting intervention closes both the gender and ethnic minority achievement gap. *Palgrave Communications*, 1, Article no. 15014. http://dx.doi.org/10.1057/palcomms.2015.14

Sheikh, H., Prins, C., & Schrijvers, E. (2023). *Mission AI: The new system technology*. Springer.

Singh, V., Joshi, B., Chavan, R., Patil, M., Bhapkar, G., Waghmare, S., & Wagh, N. (2025). VidTextBot using generative AI. *Journal of Information Systems Engineering and Management*, 10(18s).

Skinner, E. A., & Belmont, M. J. (1993). Motivation in the classroom: Reciprocal effects of teacher behavior and student engagement across the school year. *Journal of Educational Psychology*, 85(4), 571.

Smith, L., Curtis, J., Bragg, P., & Kellner, P. (Eds.). (2024). *Inspiring change: How to influence behaviour for a better world*. Monash University Publishing.

Sobolev, M. (2021). *Digital nudging: Using technology to nudge for good*. SSRN.

Soman, D. (2015). *The last mile: Creating social and economic value from behavioral insights*. University of Toronto Press.

Su, Z., Tian, L., & Zhang, M. (2024). Digital learning and AI in sustainable lifelong learning. *Sustainability*, 16(20), 9066. https://www.mdpi.com/2071-1050/16/20/9066

Tan, W. P., Chua, P. T., Lai, G., Kek, C. H., Foo, A., Thong, F., & Cheong, E. (2021). *Behavioural insights @ Temasek polytechnic*. Internal Temasek Polytechnic Report: Unpublished.

Tan, W. P., & Lai, G. (2019). *Understand-solve-evaluate: A process framework for implementing behavioural insights initiatives*. Internal Temasek Polytechnic Report: Unpublished.

Tan, W. P., Lai, G., Chia, S., & Teo, A. (2022). *Facilitating freshmen transition to polytechnic life by creating a sense of belonging using timely messaging, social support groups, and appropriate online resources*. Internal Temasek Polytechnic Report: Unpublished.

Tan, W. P., Lai, G., Chua, P. T., Lee, C., & Wong, H. (2020). *Increasing viewing of online e-lectures using timely messages infused with BI principles of social norms, ego appeal and rationalization*. Internal Temasek Polytechnic Report: Unpublished.

Thaler, R., & Sunstein, C. (2008). *Nudge: Improving decisions about health, wealth and happiness* (p. 89). Amsterdam Law Forum, HeinOnline: Online.

Tian, X. Y., Risha, Z., Ahmed, I., Narayanan, A. B. L., & Biehl, J. (2021). Let's talk it out: A Chatbot for effective study habit behavioural change. *Proceedings of the ACM on Human-Computer Interaction*, 5, 1–32. https://doi.org/10.1145/3449171

Tran, A., & Zeckhauser, R. (2012). Rank as an inherent incentive: Evidence from a field experiment. *Journal of Public Economics*, 96, 645–650.

Trowler, V. (2010). Student engagement literature review. *The Higher Education Academy*. https://www.heacademy.ac.uk/system/files/studentengagementliteraturereview_1.pdf

Walton, G. M. (2014). The new science of wise psychological interventions. *Current Directions in Psychological Science*, 23(1), 73–82.

Walton, G. M., & Cohen, G. L. (2011). A brief social-belonging intervention improves academic and health outcomes of minority students. *Science*, 1447–1451.

Wambsganss, T., Janson, A., & Leimeister, J. M. (2022). Enhancing argumentative writing with automated feedback and social comparison nudging. *Computers & Education*, 191, 104644.

Wang, S., Wang, F., Zhu, Z., Wang, J. X., Tran, T., & Du, Z. (2024). Artificial intelligence in education: A systematic literature review. *Expert Systems with Applications*, 252(A), 124167.

Wason, P. C., & Evans, J. S. B. (1974). Dual processes in reasoning? *Cognition*, 3(2), 141–154.

Weatherton, M., & Schussler, E. E. (2021). Success for all? A call to re-examine how student success is defined in higher education. *CBE—Life Sciences Education*, 20(1), es3.

Weijers, R. J., de Koning, B. B., & Paas, F. (2020). Nudging in education: From theory towards guidelines for successful implementation. *European Journal of Psychology of Education*, 36, 883–902.

Weinmann, M., Schneider, C., & Vom Brocke, J. (2016). Digital nudging. *Business & Information Systems Engineering*, 58(6), 433–436.

Wells, R. E. (2023). Strong AI vs. weak AI: What's the difference? Strong AI can do anything a human can do, while weak AI is limited to a specific task. *LifeWire*. Retrieved August 22, 2023, from https://www.lifewire.com/strong-ai-vs-weak-ai-7508012

Weyerer, J. C., & Langer, P. F. (2019, June). Garbage in, garbage out: The vicious cycle of AI-based discrimination in the public sector. In *Proceedings of the 20th Annual International Conference on Digital Government Research* (pp. 509–511).

Wu, J. (2024). Social and ethical impact of emotional AI advancement: The rise of pseudo-intimacy relationships and challenges in human interactions. *Frontiers in Psychology*, 15, 1410462.

Xiong, X. (2025). Influence of teaching styles of higher education teachers on students 'engagement in learning': The mediating role of learning motivation. *Education for Chemical Engineers*, 51, 87–102.

Yan, Z., Xiang, Y., & Huang, Y. (2024). Social life simulation for non-cognitive skills learning. *arXiv preprint arXiv:2405.00273.*

Yeager, D. S., Walton, G. M., Brady, S. T., Akcinar, E. N., Paunesku, D., Keane, L., Kamentz, D., Ritter, G., Duckworth, A. L., Urstein., R., Gomez, E. M., Markus, H. R., Cohen, G. L., & Dweck, C. S. (2016). Teaching a lay theory before college narrows achievement gaps at scale. *Proceedings of the National Academy of Sciences*, 113(24), E3341–E3348.

Yeomans, M., & Reich, J. (2017). Planning prompts increase and forecast course completion in massive open online courses. In *Proceedings of the Seventh International Conference on Learning Analytics & Knowledge* (pp. 464–473).

Zhang, H. A., Wu, C. H., Xie, J. Y., Lyu, Y., Cai, J., & Carroll, J. M. (2025). Harnessing the power of AI in qualitative research: Exploring, using and redesigning ChatGPT. *Computers in Human Behaviour: Artificial Humans*, 4, 100144.

8

Rethinking Assessment in the Era of AI: A Polytechnic's Perspective

Vijayan N

8.1 Introduction

The rapid advancement of artificial intelligence (AI) has significantly impacted education, particularly in assessment. Traditional assessment methods, which primarily measure knowledge recall and procedural understanding, are being challenged by AI-powered tools capable of generating sophisticated responses. This has raised critical questions about the effectiveness of conventional assessment practices and their ability to accurately measure student learning. In an institute of higher learning (IHL) context, where applied learning is emphasised, there is an urgent need to rethink assessment strategies to ensure they remain meaningful, relevant, and aligned with industry expectations.

Assessments serve as both a measure of learning and a tool for learning. In IHL education, where students engage in hands-on, industry-driven learning, assessment must go beyond merely evaluating the correctness of responses. It should instead focus on evaluating students' cognitive processes, decision-making skills, and practical application of knowledge. AI's increasing role in automating basic tasks necessitates a shift towards judgement-based, process-oriented, and adaptive assessment methods that require students to critically engage with their learning rather than passively receiving or reproducing information.

To address these challenges, this chapter explores the evolving nature of assessment in IHL education, emphasising approaches that maintain academic integrity, foster evaluative judgement, and integrate AI as a complementary tool for enhancing learning. The discussion will highlight key areas such as personalised feedback, workplace-based assessment, and sustainable assessment models, ensuring that students develop not only technical proficiency but also the critical thinking and adaptability required in a rapidly evolving technological landscape. By rethinking assessment, IHLs

DOI: 10.1201/9781003599357-9

are better equipping students with the competencies necessary for lifelong learning and professional growth in an AI-mediated world.

8.2 AI and Assessment

Assessment and learning are inherently interconnected within the educational process. It is impossible to examine learning without considering assessment, as both elements contribute to a continuous cycle of improvement and understanding. Similarly, assessment cannot be meaningfully considered in isolation from the learning that takes place within this context. This relationship is strengthened through constructive alignment (Biggs, 1996), where intended learning outcomes, teaching activities, and assessment tasks are deliberately coordinated to promote deep and meaningful learning. In the same way, embracing both Assessment for Learning (AfL)—which supports ongoing feedback to enhance the learning process—and Assessment of Learning (AoL)—which evaluates overall achievement—ensures that assessment serves both formative and summative purposes, providing a holistic picture of student progress. Learning plays an integral role in shaping assessment practices, ensuring they accurately measure progress and effectiveness.

In exploring assessment, it is essential first to establish a clear definition of learning. The way learning is defined directly influences assessment strategies, as it frames the objectives and expected outcomes of the educational experience. To develop a comprehensive understanding, it is valuable to reference definitions of learning provided by various scholars and educational theorists.

8.3 The Role of Assessment in IHL Education

IHLs such as polytechnics—education has always been anchored in applied learning. The mission of graduating learners who are ready to be operational at work is a core competency of IHL education. This pushes the learning landscape within the institute to be real-world oriented in all its efforts, that is curriculum, pedagogies, and assessment (constructive alignment). To this end, institutions have always geared their learning and teaching tasks to be industry-relevant.

The applied study curriculum is anchored on an applied study-aligned assessment. This requires learners to show competency and proficiency in what is required at the workplace. The assessment design has to mimic this reality, and hence the design of assessment at the institutions has to be practice-oriented.

The traditional project, task-based assessment design served this purpose well. Learners were given real or near-real-world situations as projects and encouraged to find solutions to these problems. The indulgence in such real-world situations brings real-world experiences to the learners and allows for competency and proficiency in engaging with such real-world situations at IHLs.

However, this trend is quickly changing with the advances and availability of generative AI (Gen AI) tools. The traditional assessment brief can be easily fed into a Gen AI tool, and within seconds, a detailed solution is ready. Mastering the art of using Gen AI is all that is required to fulfil the task.

The need to value-add to the learning process is now necessitated. There is a need to look at what the learner has acquired in the process of doing the assignment. What knowledge, practice, and skills that have been learned is the task of the assessor. This is not the same as assessing the traditional assessment. For one, the requirement now has moved on from a project or end-product assessment to a more lucid, iterative, process-oriented assessment. Learning has been and will continue to be the core focus of assessment. In this regard, revisiting what learning entails would be beneficial.

8.3.1 Learning

The constructivist definition of learning differs from that of a traditional perspective. The traditional definition of learning, as detailed by Proulx (2006), is a "process of accumulating the knowledge . . . that grasp(s) and stores knowledge in the person's head" (Proulx, 2006, p. 6). This is similar to Kirschner's (2006) definition of learning "as a change in long-term memory" (p. 75). From a constructivist perspective, Scaife (2007) has a more elegant definition, stating, "learning to be a process of change of knowledge" (p. 96). Knowledge and learning to constructivists are "inextricably intertwined" (Proulx, 2006, p. 6).

The focus of constructivist pedagogy, from Howe and Berv's (2000) perspective, would be nurturing these attributes (knowledge, attitude, and interest) to enable learners to construe their understanding as part of their learning (Howe & Berv, 2000). Scaife (2007) adds another attribute to the constructivist learning process, that is the learner's learning skill. A learner's learning skill acts as leverage in the construction of new knowledge from their current experiences and knowledge. Glasersfeld (1995) ventures further, internalising the process of learning to the learner. He explains learning from a radical constructivist perspective as follows:

> It requires self-regulation and the building of conceptual structures through reflection and abstraction. (Glasersfeld, 1995, p. 14)

The focus in learning is not to look for the right answer but to learn how to solve problems that the learner will face in future (this notion of sustainable assessment will be discussed later). Learning is hence an internalised process of change upon one's existing knowledge, through the attributes of experience, new knowledge, attitude, interest, and the learner's learning skill.

8.3.2 Applied Learning

Various authors (Gilbert, 2010; Lupton, 1979; Wilkins & Walker, 2011) have widely regarded applied study as the process of integrating classroom learning and industry or work attachment. Gilbert (2010) and others (Boud & Symes, 2000; Lawson, 2007; Roodhouse, 2007) correlate applied study methods to medieval apprenticeship practices and maintain that it has not evolved much over the centuries. As Gilbert (2010) reasons, a core objective of the applied study approach is not only to provide experience and know-how but also

> to be embedded in an organisation to both apply and extend skills already developed [at the educational institution] and develop new skills in situ.
>
> *(p. 84)*

Lawson (2007) observed that such practices have played a key role in the curricula of schools of medicine, education, engineering, and some natural sciences but have not been deployed in other areas as yet.

Dewey (1938), in his book *Experience and Education*, argues that knowing and doing are intertwined and cannot be separated. Extending this argument to applied study, Lawson (2007) classifies Dewey's notion of learning as supporting the applied study process. This argument is further extended by Billett (2004) and others (Hodkinson et al., 2008), who claim that applied study is broadly conceptualised as either an individual learning process or a socially dependent process. Papert (1998) clearly addressed the needs of 21st-century learning, stating that "[w]e need to produce people who know how to act when they're faced with situations for which they were not specifically prepared" (Papert, 1998, para 24). This aptly underlines the need for the applied study focus of IHL education in Singapore.

Learning in this century with AI is not likely to be straightforward, nor a smooth journey. As Barnett (2010) argues, "(t)here is no stable world of practices to which higher education could 'correspond' even if it so wished" (2010, p. 19). Trede and McEwen (2013) concur and state that "(a) standardised and rational professional education curriculum does not encourage students to critically engage with liquid times" (p. 2). Here, "liquid times" refers to the volatile and constantly changing employment and economic contexts. The need here, as Trede and McEwen (2013) argue, is to prepare students for uncertainty and rapid change.

The applied study model has, over time, evolved within the IHL educational landscape in Singapore. The initial orientation was to establish various types of industry-stimulated settings to enhance the learning of skills and work practices. Students are then deployed on industry attachment (referred to as the Student Internship Programme—SIP) and engaged in industry projects. Further expansion of this trend was to incorporate enterprise-based education by establishing learning enterprises (LEs) for students' engagement within the institutions (e.g. restaurant, café, bakery, retail outlets, and service centres). The latest trend is the push for practice-based education (PBE) within the curriculum.

8.3.3 Evolving Assessment Practices at the IHLs

Assessment at the IHL must take into account several key factors, particularly the need for innovation in assessment design. Traditional assessment approaches often focus on evaluating lower-order skills, but contemporary assessment must align with higher-order cognitive skills such as evaluation, rationalisation, and creative problem-solving, as defined by Bloom's Taxonomy. This shift necessitates rethinking assessment beyond a compliance-driven approach towards a model that emphasises critical thinking and justification of solutions.

The advent of AI has further accelerated this transformation. AI enables students to complete routine and technical tasks with greater ease, prompting a re-evaluation of assessment design to ensure that learning objectives reflect cognitive depth and applied problem-solving. At the institute, assessment should not solely measure whether a student can produce an answer, but rather how and why they arrived at that solution, reinforcing the necessity of developing evaluative, sustainable, process and analytical thinking. In this context, greater emphasis may need to be placed on process-oriented rather than purely project-oriented assessment, ensuring that the steps, decision-making, and reflective practices involved in learning are systematically evaluated. Such process-oriented assessment will, however, require a deliberate allocation of additional time within the curriculum to allow students to engage meaningfully with iterative development, feedback cycles, and self-reflection.

8.4 Integrating AI Into Assessment Design

As AI becomes a pervasive tool in education, assessment strategies must evolve to incorporate AI-enhanced learning experiences. The focus of assessment should shift towards:

- Evaluating students' ability to critically engage with AI tools
- Assessing how students justify and refine their AI-assisted outputs
- Developing process skills, such as interpretation, synthesis, and adaptation

Rather than viewing AI as a challenge to academic integrity, educators must strategically embed AI in assessment design to enhance problem-solving abilities and foster higher-order thinking skills.

8.4.1 Holistic Approach to Assessment Design in the Era of AI

A holistic approach to assessment must consider the evolving nature of learning, particularly in light of advancements in AI. The integration of AI into education has introduced new possibilities for assessment design, expanding the ways in which students engage with learning materials and demonstrate their competencies. However, the fundamental principles of learning and assessment remain unchanged. AI has not altered the essential need for assessment to be valid, reliable, and aligned with learning outcomes.

The emergence of AI has prompted discussions regarding proctored assessments as a means of safeguarding academic integrity. While some institutions advocate for a return to strictly proctored assessment models, this approach does not align with applied studies frameworks, such as those used at IHLs. As AI continues to reshape the educational landscape, assessment strategies must be adaptable and forward-thinking. Learners are inevitably engaging with AI tools in academic and professional settings. The challenge, therefore, is not to eliminate AI from assessments but rather to design AI-aware assessment frameworks that encourage the ethical and meaningful use of technology in learning. Instead of focusing solely on restricting AI use, there is a need to design assessments that leverage AI as a tool for enhancing learning while maintaining academic integrity. There is a distinct role for AI in the Learning & Teaching process that is beyond the scope of this chapter.

By implementing AI-inclusive assessments, institutions can ensure that students are evaluated on their ability to:

- Effectively utilise AI for problem-solving
- Engage in critical thinking and creative application
- Maintain academic integrity in AI-enhanced learning environments

In this evolving educational paradigm, AI is not a replacement for human learning but a catalyst for deeper engagement, critical analysis, and skill development.

Thus, the future of assessment at IHLs—and across higher education—must be adaptive, inclusive, and forward-looking, integrating AI's potential while upholding academic rigour and integrity.

8.4.2 Core Principles Governing Assessment in Education

Even with AI being integrated into assessment design, the core principles governing assessment have not shifted. Assessment in education is guided by a set of fundamental principles that have been developed and refined over time. Despite advancements in technology, including the integration of AI into educational assessment, the core principles of assessment remain unchanged. These principles ensure that assessments are valid, reliable, fair, and aligned with the intended learning outcomes.

8.4.2.1 Validity in Assessment

Validity is one of the most critical principles in assessment design. It refers to the degree to which an assessment accurately measures what it is intended to measure. A valid assessment provides meaningful and relevant insights into a learner's knowledge, skills, and competencies. Ensuring validity involves designing tasks that align with the intended learning outcomes (ILOs), using appropriate assessment methods, and ensuring that the assessment criteria reflect the targeted learning outcomes. Without validity, the assessment process loses its credibility, as it may fail to accurately represent student proficiency.

8.4.2.2 Reliability in Assessment

Another essential principle is reliability, which refers to the consistency and dependability of assessment results. A reliable assessment yields stable and reproducible outcomes across different assessors, contexts, and time periods. This principle ensures that student performance is evaluated fairly and consistently, reducing variability due to subjective interpretations or external factors. To enhance reliability, educators implement standardised grading criteria, clear rubrics, and multiple assessors, ensuring uniformity in evaluation.

8.4.3 Judgement-Based Assessment

AI in education necessitates a shift towards student-driven assessment models, where learners take greater control over their work, engage in reflective evaluation, and develop the ability to assess the quality of their own outputs.

The concept of judgement-based assessment is well established in educational literature. Sadler (1989) introduced the idea of evaluative expertise, emphasising that learners must develop proficiency in judging complex aspects of their work. He argued that students should not only complete assessment tasks but also be able to determine the criteria that define high-quality work. This approach enhances learners' ability to critically analyse their performance and fosters deeper engagement with the learning process.

Building upon Sadler's work, Boud (2000) further advanced the concept of sustainable assessment. He asserted that learners must develop the capability to judge their own work effectively, as this is a key competency in preparing them for the demands of the professional world. Sustainable assessment focuses on nurturing evaluative skills that enable students to engage in self-assessment, peer assessment, and iterative learning processes. By doing so, learners become active participants in their own development, refining their ability to assess quality and to make informed improvements in their work.

These foundational ideas of evaluative expertise and sustainable assessment are critical in shaping the IHL's approach to assessment, especially in the context of AI-driven learning environments. AI has the potential to support these assessment practices by providing automated feedback mechanisms, enabling students to engage in real-time self-assessment, and offering data-driven insights into their performance. AI can also facilitate peer assessment processes by structuring evaluative criteria and providing comparative analyses of students' work.

Despite these advantages, AI-driven assessment tools must be integrated thoughtfully to ensure they enhance, rather than replace, students' ability to develop independent evaluative judgement. Over-reliance on AI-generated feedback risks diminishing students' critical thinking and self-assessment skills, as they may become passive recipients of AI evaluations instead of actively engaging in the assessment process. Therefore, IHLs strikes a balance between leveraging AI for efficiency and maintaining the human element in assessment, ensuring that students remain actively involved in their learning and judgement development.

The transformation of assessment at IHLs requires a deliberate shift towards fostering judgement-based assessment practices supported by AI, rather than dictated by it. By embedding self-regulated assessment practices into curricula and leveraging AI as a facilitative tool, IHLs can create an assessment framework that not only measures learning but actively enhances it. This approach ensures that learners develop the critical evaluative skills necessary for both academic success and professional readiness in an AI-mediated world.

8.4.4 Assessment Design

While AI has introduced innovations in assessment, such as automated grading and adaptive testing, it has not fundamentally changed these core principles. Validity and reliability remain at the heart of assessment design, requiring that AI-driven tools be rigorously evaluated to ensure they align with pedagogical objectives and uphold assessment integrity. AI should be used as a complementary tool to enhance, rather than to replace, traditional assessment principles.

The principles of validity and reliability continue to shape the foundation of assessment design. As IHLs integrate AI into their assessment frameworks, it is crucial to maintain constructive alignment among assessment methods, learning outcomes, and evaluation standards. Ensuring that assessments remain fair, transparent, and meaningful will sustain the credibility and effectiveness of student evaluations in both traditional and technology-enhanced learning environments.

8.4.5 Balancing Product and Process in Assessment Design

At the IHLs, discussions on product-based versus process-based assessment highlight a fundamental area of focus in assessment design. Traditionally, assessment has been structured around product-based evaluation, allowing students to showcase their final outputs as evidence of learning. This approach is effective in demonstrating mastery of conceptual knowledge and practical applications. However, in alignment with the IHL's mission to prepare students for real-world professional environments, there is a growing recognition of the need to integrate process-based assessment to evaluate not just the final product but also the learning journey and the development of competency over time.

8.4.6 Incorporating Process-Based Assessment Into Assessment Design

Process-based assessment emphasises skill development, iterative learning, and competency acquisition, making it a crucial component of assessment techniques. Unlike product assessment, which evaluates learning at a fixed point in time, process-based assessment requires continuous evaluation over a period, capturing progress, refinement, and reflection as integral elements of learning.

A key challenge in designing process-based assessments within the constraints of a semester is ensuring that students are provided with sufficient opportunities to demonstrate progress without creating undue assessment burdens. Unlike product-based assessment, which is evaluated at the end of a learning cycle, process-based assessment necessitates ongoing formative evaluations, where students receive feedback, refine their skills, and engage in self-regulated learning. This underscores the imperative for IHLs to allocate additional curriculum time to assessment, enabling more meaningful and sustained evaluation of the learning process.

8.4.6.1 Considerations for Effective Process Assessment Design

Several critical factors must be considered when designing process-based assessment:

1 **Weighting of Marks Across the Process**—The allocation of marks across different phases of learning must be carefully structured. If an excessive percentage of marks is assigned to early-stage performance, students may face undue disadvantages in reaching proficiency by the end of the course. Instead, weighting should reflect the progressive development of skills, with greater emphasis on final mastery while still recognising incremental progress.
2 **Iterative and Continuous Feedback**—Since process-based assessment relies on continual improvement, feedback mechanisms must be structured to provide students with actionable insights at different stages. Instructor feedback, peer reviews, and self-reflections should be incorporated to help students refine their skills progressively.
3 **Authentic Learning Experiences**—Process assessments should align with real-world applications, where students engage in tasks that mirror workplace challenges. Assessments should simulate industry-relevant scenarios, requiring students to apply problem-solving, critical thinking, and technical skills over a period of time.
4 **Constructive Alignment with Learning Outcomes**—The design of process-based assessment must align with the curriculum's ILOs, ensuring that assessment strategies facilitate deep learning rather than surface-level task completion. By emphasising skill acquisition and gradual improvement, process assessment nurtures a more authentic, competency-driven learning experience.

8.4.7 The Future of Process-Oriented Assessment in AI-Integrated Learning

With the evolving role of AI in education, process-based assessment must also incorporate AI-enhanced learning tools that facilitate continuous progress tracking, adaptive feedback mechanisms, and data-driven insights into student learning trajectories. AI can be leveraged to monitor student progression, recommend targeted learning interventions, and provide individualised feedback, ensuring that competency development remains at the core of assessment strategies.

Balancing product-based and process-based assessment is key to fostering holistic student learning at IHLs. While final products serve as tangible evidence of achievement, the assessment of learning processes is equally crucial in equipping students with the skills, adaptability, and critical thinking necessary for success in their future careers. A well-designed assessment framework must account for both aspects, ensuring that students not only produce quality outputs but also develop the competencies required for lifelong learning and professional growth.

8.5 The Future of Assessment: A Holistic Approach

The integration of AI in education requires a rethinking of what constitutes meaningful learning. Assessment should no longer be confined to measuring technical proficiency alone, but should encompass justification, reflection, and evaluation of the learning process. This evolution in assessment practice ensures that students are equipped not just with knowledge, but with the cognitive agility to apply that knowledge effectively in real-world scenarios.

Assessment at IHLs must embrace a holistic, AI-integrated approach, ensuring that students develop the critical, analytical, and process-based skills required for lifelong learning and professional success.

8.5.1 Enhancing Assessment Practices: Beyond Traditional Evaluations

Assessment should not merely serve as a final checkpoint in education, but rather as an ongoing, iterative process that enhances learning. Continuous formative assessment is a crucial component of effective assessment design, as it provides students with multiple opportunities to refine their understanding and skills based on constructive feedback. Unlike summative assessments (AoL) that provide an end-point evaluation, formative assessments (AfL) are embedded throughout the learning process, enabling real-time adjustments and deeper engagement with the subject matter.

This approach involves frequent, low-stakes assessments such as reflective journals, in-class discussions, short quizzes, or AI-generated adaptive learning tasks. These assessments allow both students and educators to identify gaps in understanding and to make immediate course corrections. More importantly, formative assessments encourage a growth mindset, where students see mistakes not as failures but as learning opportunities.

When integrated with AI, adaptive learning tools can offer immediate feedback on procedural aspects of learning, while human instructors provide contextual and conceptual feedback that nurtures deeper understanding. This combination ensures that students benefit from the efficiency of AI, while still engaging in meaningful, human-led discussions that refine their critical thinking and application of knowledge.

8.5.2 Holistic Evaluation of Learning Progression: Moving Beyond End-Point Assessment

Traditional assessment models often focus on a final product or performance as the primary indicator of success. However, a holistic evaluation of learning progression acknowledges that learning is an evolving process and should be assessed at multiple stages. This approach ensures that students' growth, decision-making abilities, and iterative refinements are recognised alongside their final output.

To implement this, assessment frameworks should incorporate multi-stage evaluations, including:

- Draft submissions and revisions—Encouraging students to refine their work based on feedback.
- Process logs and learning journals—Documenting key learning moments and problem-solving strategies.
- Competency-based assessment rubrics—Measuring incremental skill development rather than just final outcomes.

A holistic evaluation captures the nuances of learning, recognising that progress is just as valuable as the final achievement. This also prepares students for workplace environments, where ongoing skill development and adaptability are crucial for professional success.

8.5.3 Balanced Allocation of Marks: Rewarding Growth and Mastery

A common pitfall in assessment design is placing disproportionate weight on early-stage performance, which can penalise students who improve significantly over time. A well-balanced marking system rewards growth and mastery, ensuring that students are assessed not just on their initial achievements but on their progression and refinement of skills.

Key considerations for balanced assessment design include:

- **Weighted grading models**—Allocating more marks to later-stage assessments where students demonstrate refined understanding and proficiency.
- **Milestone-based evaluation**—Breaking larger assessments into stages where students earn marks for iteration and improvement.
- **Flexibility in assessment timing**—Allowing students to resubmit or revisit key assessments to show mastery.

By designing assessments that account for skill development over time, educators can foster resilience, perseverance, and deeper learning experiences.

8.5.4 Self-Evaluation and Peer Review: Cultivating Critical Reflection

Encouraging students to take an active role in assessment strengthens their skill to self-regulate learning and engage in evaluative judgement. Self-evaluation and peer review foster a culture of reflection, where students critically analyse their own work and that of their peers to enhance learning.

Incorporating structured peer review and self-assessment tasks ensures that students:

- Develop metacognitive awareness—Understanding their strengths and areas for improvement.
- Engage in critical dialogue—Constructively critiquing work based on established criteria.
- Enhance evaluative judgement skills—Refining their skill to distinguish quality work, a key competency in professional practice.

With AI tools available for basic corrections, the role of self-evaluation and peer review becomes even more critical, ensuring that students remain actively engaged in assessing the depth and accuracy of their learning. Structured reflection tasks and calibrated peer assessments further equip students with the skill to make informed judgements, an essential competency in both academic and professional settings.

8.6 Advancing Assessment in the Age of AI

The evolution of AI in education presents an opportunity to redefine assessment practices, shifting away from passive knowledge recall to active, process-driven, and evaluative learning approaches. By embedding continuous formative assessment, holistic evaluation of learning, balanced grading, and reflective self-evaluation, IHLs can ensure that assessment remains meaningful, challenging, and aligned with the demands of contemporary education and industry.

AI should be leveraged as a tool for enhancement rather than as a substitute for critical thinking, ensuring that assessment frameworks prioritise cognitive engagement, skill development, and the cultivation of evaluative judgement. In doing so, IHL education can continue to foster learners who are agile, innovative, and well-prepared for the evolving professional landscape.

8.6.1 Differentiating Assessment Instruments and Assessment Methods

A crucial distinction must be made between assessment instruments and assessment methods when evaluating the validity of an assessment strategy. Assessment instruments are the overarching tools used to facilitate assessment, whereas assessment methods refer to the specific techniques employed within these instruments. Establishing an appropriate assessment method is fundamental to ensuring the validity and reliability of an assessment, yet this process is often complex due to widespread conceptual ambiguity.

The interchangeable use of "assessment instruments" and "assessment methods" has led to confusion in educational discourse. However, it is important to recognise that instruments function as broad frameworks that house various assessment methods. For instance, an examination is an assessment instrument that encompasses multiple assessment methods, such as open-ended questions, essay responses, case studies, multiple-choice questions, and fill-in-the-blank exercises. Each of these methods serves distinct pedagogical functions, targeting different cognitive and analytical skills.

When determining the validity of an assessment, focusing solely on the instrument does not provide a comprehensive understanding of whether the assessment effectively measures learning outcomes. Instead, validity should be evaluated at the methodological level, ensuring that the chosen methods align with the learning outcomes and competencies being assessed. For example, a multiple-choice format may be appropriate for assessing factual recall but is insufficient for evaluating critical thinking or problem-solving abilities, which may be better assessed through case studies or viva or demonstrations.

Thus, the establishment of validity in assessment is a critical component of the assessment design process. Educators must carefully consider which assessment methods best align with the ILOs, ensuring that methods are employed in a manner that supports meaningful, fair, and reliable evaluation. This approach not only enhances the accuracy of assessments but also fosters a deeper understanding of the subject matter among learners.

8.6.2 The Role of the Table of Specifications (TOS) in Assessment Design

The Table of Specifications (TOS) serves as a structured framework that systematically aligns the assessment design of a subject with its ILOs and the allocated teaching and learning time for those outcomes. This alignment ensures that assessments are methodologically sound and reflective of the learning outcomes, thereby promoting constructive alignment within the curriculum.

In addition to its role in mapping assessments to learning outcomes, the TOS also documents key assessment components, including the number of assessment points, the proposed assessment methods, and the weight assigned to each method. This structured approach enables educators to design assessments that provide a balanced evaluation of student performance, ensuring an equitable distribution of assessment tasks across the subject.

A well-designed TOS enhances the validity of assessment by ensuring that each assessment method appropriately measures the targeted learning outcomes. Instead of merely identifying the assessment instrument, such as an examination, the TOS provides a detailed breakdown of the assessment methods embedded within it. For example, an examination may incorporate

Subject Title :											
Intended Learning Outcomes ⇩	Hours Allocated for Learning in Syllabus	Assessment Method (xx%)			Assessment Method (xx%)			Assessment Method (xx%)			TOTAL (100%)
Level of Pitch in alignment with Bloom Taxonmy ⇨		K	C	A	K	C	A	K	C	A	
ILO 1											
SLO 1.1											
SLO 1.2											
SLO 1.3											
SLO 1.4											
ILO 2											
SLO 1.1											
SLO 1.2											
SLO 1.3											
SLO 1.4											
GLO 3											
SLO 1.1											
SLO 1.2											
SLO 1.3											
SLO 1.4											
	0	0	0	0	0	0	0	0	0	0	0
		0			0			0			0
Knowledge (K) *(Align with Understand in Bloom Taxonomy)*	0										
Comprehension (C) (Align with Remeber in Bloom Taxonomy)	0										
Application & Above (A) (Align with any level equal or above Apply in Bloom Taxonomy)	0										

FIGURE 8.1
* Table of Specification Template (TOS Template). * Tabulate in Percentage—Suggested

various methods such as open-ended questions, case studies, multiple-choice questions, or short-answer responses. Each method serves distinct pedagogical purposes, assessing different levels of cognitive complexity.

The TOS is an essential tool in the assessment validation process. It offers a holistic perspective on assessment design, ensuring that the assessments effectively measure the ILOs while maintaining fairness and reliability. Additionally, the TOS (Figure 8.1) provides transparency in assessment planning, offering a clear rationale behind the distribution of assessment tasks and their respective weightings.

8.7 Defining Evaluative Judgement and Its Intersections With Generative AI

Evaluative judgement is a fundamental cognitive ability that enables individuals to assess the quality of work, both their own and that of others. This capability is essential for higher-order thinking and learning, forming the basis of self-regulated learning and professional expertise. Tai et al. (2018) define evaluative judgement as "the capability to make decisions about the quality of work of self and others" (p. 471) emphasising its role in fostering critical engagement with knowledge and skill development.

Evaluative judgement is characterised by two core components: an internalised understanding of quality and the ability to apply that understanding in diverse contexts. Sadler (1989) highlights the importance of holistic appraisal, arguing that expert judgement is often tacit and integrates multiple criteria into a single assessment rather than relying on a checklist of discrete elements. This capacity is particularly crucial in professional and academic settings, where individuals must navigate complex and context-dependent standards of excellence.

Within educational contexts, evaluative judgement is often developed through sustained exposure to exemplars, iterative feedback, and reflective practice. As Boud (2000) asserts, assessment practices should prepare students to independently evaluate learning tasks throughout their lives, ensuring they are not solely dependent on formal instruction. This perspective aligns with an evaluativist epistemology (Kuhn et al., 2000), which recognises knowledge as neither absolute nor entirely subjective but rather developed through reasoned alignment with disciplinary standards and evidence.

As students progress from novice to expert, their evaluative judgement shifts from analytical, criteria-based assessments to more holistic, experience-driven evaluations. This transition underscores the importance of assessment strategies that scaffold students' ability to make nuanced judgements. Such strategies include peer review, self-assessment, and exposure to multiple exemplars, which collectively foster an intuitive grasp of what constitutes quality in a given field.

8.7.1 Intersections Between Evaluative Judgement and Generative AI

The emergence of Gen AI presents both challenges and opportunities for the development of evaluative judgement. As Gen AI becomes increasingly integrated into education and professional settings, individuals must develop the capacity to critically assess AI-generated outputs. This need arises from the nature of Gen AI, which produces plausible yet potentially inaccurate, biased, or unoriginal content (Alkaissi & McFarlane, 2023).

The relationship between evaluative judgement and Gen AI manifests in three primary ways:

- Evaluate AI Outputs
- Evaluate AL Processes
- Evaluate Human Judgement

8.7.1.1 Evaluate AI Outputs

Students and professionals must cultivate the skills to scrutinise AI-generated content critically. Gen AI, such as ChatGPT or image synthesis models, often produces outputs that are syntactically and semantically coherent but lack substantive accuracy or contextual relevance. Consequently, users must learn to discern whether AI-generated work meets the necessary standards of credibility, originality, and ethical integrity.

Assessment practices can facilitate this development by incorporating activities where students compare AI-generated outputs with human-created work, assess AI-generated arguments against scholarly sources, or critique the appropriateness of AI responses to discipline-specific queries. Such exercises encourage the calibration of evaluative judgement and promote deeper engagement with quality assessment criteria.

8.7.1.2 Evaluate AI Processes

Beyond assessing outputs, individuals must develop an awareness of the processes that underpin Gen AI tools. Effective use of AI requires skill in crafting precise prompts, iterating responses, and recognising the limitations and biases embedded in AI models. This evaluative capacity extends to understanding when and how to integrate AI into learning and professional tasks ethically and productively.

For instance, students might analyse the effectiveness of their AI-generated responses by iteratively refining their prompts and assessing the impact of different query structures on output quality. Similarly, they may engage in discussions about the ethical implications of using AI-generated text in academic and professional work, ensuring that their reliance on AI aligns with disciplinary norms and integrity standards.

8.7.1.3 Evaluate Human Judgement

A novel intersection between AI and evaluative judgement is the potential for AI to assess human judgement. AI tools can provide feedback on students' self-assessments, compare student evaluations with expert reviews, and offer alternative interpretations of scholarly arguments. This interaction allows students to refine their evaluative skills by engaging in a comparative process where AI-generated feedback serves as a reference point rather than an authoritative judgement.

However, this reliance on AI-generated evaluation poses risks. AI's tendency to reinforce dominant perspectives and biases necessitates critical engagement from users, ensuring that they do not passively accept AI-generated assessments as definitive. Instead, students should be encouraged to challenge, refine, and contextualise AI feedback within disciplinary standards.

8.7.2 Assessment Based on Judgement

Boud and Falchikov (2007) speaks of assessment for the 21st century as moving towards judgement on assessment being done by learners. He argues for the fact that establishing the quality of the work done, or even establishing criteria to evaluate work done and to look at how well the work aligns with the criteria established, would be useful in assessing the learning. Establishing the criteria based on how to evaluate a task done by the learner pushes the learning requirement beyond knowing the knowledge, skills, and practices orientated to the task, to looking at it from an outsider's perspective in creating criteria that will be used in assessing the learning. If learners can provide the criteria for the task they are doing, that would provide the learner with an in-depth understanding of the task. Establishing the learning based on the criteria and task judgement would give a good indication of the learner. Boud (2000) iterates that such judgements are common at the workplace. Individuals need to be clear about the work they have produced and have a judgement on the task. If they can calibrate their judgement on the work done, they will be able to know the standard of the work done. Such judgement is required at the workplace, and providing the basis for such learning at the IHLs is critical. This is even more essential in an AI world.

8.7.3 Sustainable Assessment

Boud's (2000) concept of sustainable assessment emphasises the development of learners' abilities to self-assess and engage in evaluative practices that extend beyond formal education into their professional lives. This approach advocates for assessment strategies that not only evaluate current performance but also equip students with the skills necessary for ongoing learning and adaptation in dynamic work environments. Boud (2000) argues that sustainable assessment involves fostering learners' capacities to make informed judgements about their work, thereby promoting lifelong learning and adaptability.

This philosophy aligns closely with judgement-based assessment, which requires learners to critically analyse and justify their decisions and actions. Both approaches prioritise the development of evaluative judgement, enabling individuals to assess the quality of their work and make necessary improvements. By integrating sustainable assessment practices, educators encourage students to become active participants in their learning processes, enhancing their skills to apply critical thinking and self-reflection in various contexts. This alignment ensures that assessment practices contribute to the cultivation of autonomous professionals capable of navigating complex and evolving professional landscapes.

8.7.4 Moving Forward With Judgement, Evaluative and Sustainable Assessment

The integration of Gen AI into education and professional domains underscores the increasing importance of evaluative judgement. While AI presents powerful tools for content generation and assessment, its limitations necessitate a critical, informed approach to its use. Educators and learners alike must emphasise the development of evaluative judgement as a uniquely human capability, ensuring that individuals retain their roles as arbiters of quality in an AI-mediated world.

By embedding evaluative judgement within assessment strategies—such as peer review, self-assessment, and AI critique—IHLs can prepare students to navigate the complexities of AI-generated content effectively. This preparation is not only crucial for academic integrity but also for fostering the lifelong learning skills necessary to thrive in an era where the ability to judge quality remains a defining human trait.

8.7.5 Authenticity and Integrity in AI-Era Assessments

The increasing integration of AI in education has necessitated a critical review of assessment authenticity and integrity to ensure that students engage in original thought, critical analysis, and subject-specific application, rather than relying on AI-generated responses. A key concern in contemporary assessment design is whether traditional questions can be easily answered by AI, making it imperative for educators to test assessments against AI-generated outputs. By doing so, assessments can be refined to

Rowntree, D. (1987). *Assessing students: How shall we know them?* Kogan Page and Routledge.
Rust, C. (2002). The impact of assessment on student learning. *Active Learning in Higher Education*, 3(2), 145–158.
Sadler, R. (1989). Formative assessment and the design of instructional systems. *Instructional Science*, 18, 119–144.
Scaife, J. A. (2007, November 2007). Lessons from a decade of constructivist initial teacher education in Science. *Paper presented at the Proceedings of The Second International Conference on Science and Mathematics Education*, Penang, Malaysia.
Schön, D. A. (1983). *The reflective practitioner: How professionals think in action*. Basic Books.
Tai, J., Ajjawi, R., Boud, D., Dawson, P., & Panadero, E. (2018). Developing evaluative judgement: Enabling students to make decisions about the quality of work. *Higher Education*, 76(3), 467–481.
Trede, F., & McEwen, C. (2013). *Educating the deliberate professional (Occasional Paper 9)*. Sydney: The Education for Practice Institute, Charles Sturt University.
Vygotsky, L. S. (1978). *Mind in society: The development of higher psychological processes*. Harvard University Press.
Wilkins, S., & Walker, I. (2011). Applied and academic A Levels: Is there really a need for the applied track in UK further education? *Journal of Further and Higher Education*, 35(4), 461–482.

Index

For Product Safety Concerns and Information please contact our EU representative GPSR@taylorandfrancis.com Taylor & Francis Verlag GmbH, Kaufingerstraße 24, 80331 München, Germany